SYMBOLIC AND STRUCTURAL ARCHAEOLOGY

SYMBOLIC AND STRUCTURAL ARCHAEOLOGY

EDITED BY IAN HODDER
Lecturer in Archaeology, University of Cambridge

FOR THE CAMBRIDGE SEMINAR ON
SYMBOLIC AND STRUCTURAL ARCHAEOLOGY

CAMBRIDGE UNIVERSITY PRESS
CAMBRIDGE
LONDON   NEW YORK   NEW ROCHELLE
MELBOURNE   SYDNEY

Published by the Press Syndicate of the University of Cambridge
The Pitt Building, Trumpington Street, Cambridge CB2 1RP
32 East 57th Street, New York, NY 10022, USA
296 Beaconsfield Parade, Middle Park, Melbourne 3206, Australia

First published 1982

Printed in Great Britain at the University Press, Cambridge

Library of Congress catalogue card number: 81–17992

British Library Cataloguing in Publication Data

Cambridge Seminar on Symbolic and Structural
Archaeology (1980)
Symbolic and structural archaeology. –
(New directions in archaeology)
1. Archaeology – Congresses
I. Title II. Hodder, Ian III. Series
930'.01   CC51
ISBN 0 521 24406 4

CONTENTS

List of contributors   *vi*   *Preface*   *vii*

Part one

The development of theory   **1**

1 Theoretical archaeology: a reactionary view
  Ian Hodder   *1*

2 Artefacts as products of human categorisation
  processes
  D. Miller   *17*

3 Social formation, social structures and social change
  Christopher Tilley   *26*

4 Epistemological issues raised by a structuralist
  archaeology
  M. Alison Wylie   *39*

Part two

The search for models   **47**

5 Matters material and ideal
  Susan Kus   *47*

6 House power: Swahili space and symbolic markers
  Linda Wiley Donley   *63*

7 The interpretation of spatial patterning in settlement
  residues
  H.L. Moore   *74*

8 Decoration as ritual symbol: a theoretical proposal
  and an ethnographic study in southern Sudan
  Mary Braithwaite   *80*

9 Structures and strategies: an aspect of the relationship
between social hierarchy and cultural change
D. Miller   89

10 Mortuary practices, society and ideology: an ethnoarchaeological study
Michael Parker Pearson   99

Part three
Application: the analysis of archaeological
materials   115

11 Boundedness in art and society
Margaret W. Conkey   115

12 Ideology, symbolic power and ritual communication:
a reinterpretation of Neolithic mortuary practices
Michael Shanks and Christopher Tilley   129

13 Ideology, change and the European Early Bronze Age
Stephen Shennan   155

14 Sequences of structural change in the Dutch Neolithic
Ian Hodder   162

Part four
Commentary   179
Childe's offspring
Mark Leone   179
Index   185

CONTRIBUTORS

Mary Braithwaite, Department of Archaeology, University of
    Cambridge.
Margaret Conkey, Department of Anthropology, State University of
    New York, Binghamton.
Linda Donley, King's College, Cambridge.
Ian Hodder, Department of Archaeology, University of Cambridge.
Susan Kus, Detroit, Michigan.
Mark Leone, Department of Anthropology, University of Maryland.
Danny Miller, Department of Anthropology, University College,
    London.
Henrietta Moore, Department of Archaeology, University of
    Cambridge.
Michael Parker Pearson, Department of Archaeology, University of
    Cambridge.
Michael Shanks, Department of Archaeology, University of
    Cambridge.
Stephen Shennan, Department of Archaeology, University of
    Southampton.
Chris Tilley, Department of Archaeology, University of Cambridge.
Alison Wylie, Department of Anthropology, State University of New
    York, Binghamton.

CAMBRIDGE SEMINAR ON
SYMBOLIC AND STRUCTURAL ARCHAEOLOGY

Mary Braithwaite
Steve Cogbill
Sheena Crawford
Linda Donley
Ian Hodder
Paul Lane
Danny Miller
Henrietta Moore
Ellen Pader
Mike Parker Pearson
Alison Sheridan
Chris Tilley
Alice Welbourn

PREFACE

The idea for this volume grew out of a series of graduate seminars in Cambridge in the academic year 1979–80. Preliminary drafts of a majority of the papers were presented at a conference entitled *Symbolism and Structuralism in Archaeology* in Cambridge in April 1980, organised by members of the seminar group. There has been considerable discussion within the group concerning the papers in this volume, which should be regarded as a joint editorial venture although, as will be noted in chapter 1, a wide range of often contrasting views is represented.

During the early period of exploration and development of ideas, premature conference presentations and individual seminars were given by various members of the Cambridge group in other archaeology departments in England and abroad. Individual scholars who were invited to talk to us in Cambridge in that period often felt, understandably, obliged to maintain a distinct opposition. While it is certainly the case that these presentations had occurred before our views had even begun to settle down, and that they were excessively aggressive, they played an important role in the process of enquiry and reformulation. In particular, the contrasts which were set up by us and by outside scholars allowed the views of the seminar group, and the differences of viewpoint within the group, to be clarified. The opposition highlighted our own opinions but also threw the spotlight on the blind alleys down which there was a

danger of straying. Our aggression resulted from the conviction that we were doing something new. This, too, was important. In the initial period there was a clear idea of what was wrong with existing approaches and there was a faith that something else could be done. But there may have been no clear idea of how the vague hopes could be converted into rigorous analyses. There was a phase in which there was more faith than evidence that the approach would succeed. Advances in the human sciences must often go through similar phases and I find it difficult to see how progress can be made in archaeology at the moment without the willingness of individuals to make a 'jump' and be criticised for it. It is the sense and excitement of newness which provide the energy to continue through this early stage.

Similar phases can be identified in other self-styled advances in recent archaeology, such as the Palaeoeconomy school or the New Archaeology generally. But the radical novelty of these and of our approach soon fades. It is now clear that the enquiry suggested in this volume is simply an asking of additional questions, extending both traditional and recent developments in prehistoric archaeology. It would be wrong to suggest that many answers have as yet been provided, or that all the problems have been clarified and understood. In particular, the archaeological applications in Part three of this book remain tentative and exploratory and I hope that the papers throughout this volume can be received in the spirit of enquiry and doubt with which they were conceived.

A central problem concerns verification. It is suggested here that archaeology is a cultural science, and that all social strategies and adaptation must be understood as part of cultural, symbolically meaningful contexts. For example, burial, refuse deposition and ceramic variation are not simply behavioural reflections of adaptive strategies, functioning to allow information and energy flows. They are culturally and symbolically formed as part of, respectively, concepts of death, dirt and food preparation and consumption. Equally, observation, analysis and interpretation are themselves relative. Culture, the sociology of knowledge, and meaning are central problems and must not be swept aside in attempts to achieve an apparent rigour and the veneer of a natural science. If the cultural relativity of social actions and of observation of those actions is accepted, how can adequate verification of hypotheses be achieved? This question, occurring in the wake of the reaction against the absolute rigidity and assumed scientific objectivity of logical positivism, has not yet been answered in archaeology. The contribution is in bringing it to the forefront.

The early exploratory phase is not over. The debate which has been started, or revived, is introduced in the conflicting viewpoints in the papers in this volume. Several members of the seminar group reject functionalism, but they also reject structuralism. In reaction to Leone's commentary at the end of the book, the approach of the Cambridge seminar is neither materialist nor idealist. But there are unsolved problems in relation to both verification and meaning and symbolism. The degree of determinacy in sequences of social and cultural change is unclear. The nature of culture remains to be described adequately. These questions will be discussed further in future publications.

The conference on Symbolism and Structuralism in Archaeology was funded by grants from the British Council, Cambridge University Press, and the Department of Archaeology, University of Cambridge. Mark Leone contributed to the conference and kindly agreed to wade through and comment on the papers. My warm personal gratitude is extended to members of the seminar group and to participants in the conference for their patience, criticism and faith in the directions that we have taken.

April, 1981   Ian Hodder

PART ONE

The development of theory

Chapter 1

Theoretical archaeology:
a reactionary view
Ian Hodder

Functionalism is defined as the use of an organic analogy in the explanation of societies, with particular reference to system, equilibrium and adaptation. The New Archaeology is found to be functionalist and a critique of functionalism is put forward, centring on the dichotomies between culture and function, individual and society, statics and dynamics, and on the links to positivism. Criticisms of an alternative approach, structuralism, include the lack of a theory of practice, the dichotomies between individual and society, statics and dynamics, and the paucity of rigour in the methods employed. A contextual or cultural archaeology is described which is based on the notion of 'structuration', and which attempts to resolve many of the difficulties associated with functionalism and 'high' structuralism. The main concern is with the role of material culture in the reflexive relationship between the structure of ideas and social strategies. Similarities are identified with the historical and humanistic aims of an older generation of British prehistorians such as Daniel, Piggott, Clark and Childe. Today, however, the earlier aims can be followed more successfully because of developments in social theory and ethnographic studies.

Functionalism and the New Archaeology
In defining functionalism, a simplified version of Radcliffe-Brown's (1952) account will be used since his approach can be shown to be close to that followed by many New Archaeologists (those who in the 1960s and 1970s were concerned with explanations and approaches of the types outlined by Binford and his associates). Functionalism introduces an analogy between social and organic life. Emile Durkheim (*Règles de la Methode Sociologique* 1895) defined

the 'function' of a social institution as the correspondence between it and the needs of the social organism. In the same way that the stomach provides a function for the body as a whole and allows it to survive, so any aspect of a past society can be assessed in terms of its contribution to the working of the whole society. A society is made up of interrelated parts and we can explain one component by showing how it works in relation to other components. But these are all very general statements, and there is room for a great variety of views within these general propositions. Indeed, Radcliffe-Brown (1952, p. 188) stated bluntly that the 'Functional School does not really exist; it is a myth'. Functionalism often appears to be little more than a 'dirty word' used by the opponents of anthropologists such as Malinowski, Boas and Radcliffe-Brown himself, and it may convey little meaning. So if it is to be used of the New Archaeology, a more specific definition needs to be provided.

The concept of function is closely linked to the notion of system. In the middle of the eighteenth century Montesquieu used a conception of society in which all aspects of social life could be linked into a coherent whole. What Comte called 'the first law of social statics' held that there are relations of interconnection and interdependence, or relations of solidarity, between the various aspects of society. It is possible analytically to isolate certain groups of particularly close interrelationships as systems.

According to the functionalist viewpoint as stated in systems theory, societies reach a healthy organic equilibrium, called homeostasis. Plato, in the Fourth Book of his *Republic*, saw the health of a society as resulting from the harmonious working together of its parts. The Greeks distinguished good order, social health (*eunomia*), from disorder, social illness (*dysnomia*), while the notion of malfunction and social pathology was a central concern of Durkheim. (In recent systems archaeology, pathologies have been listed and their effects examined by Flannery (1972).)

Pathologies occur during periods when the organic unity and equilibrium are upset as a result of maladaptation. A society can only continue to exist if it is well-adjusted internally and externally. Three types of adaptation can be distinguished. The first concerns the adjustment to the physical environment, the ecological adaptation. The second is the internal arrangement and adjustment of components of the society in relation to each other. Finally, there is the process by which an individual finds a place within the society in which he lives. It is through these three types of adaptation that societies survive and evolve. Many anthropologists and archaeologists, however, have discussed change largely in terms of ecological adaptation, the meeting of external constraints. It is an ecological functionalism which prevails today in archaeology.

In this chapter the term functionalism refers to the use of an organic analogy and to the viewpoint that an adequate explanation of a past society involves reference to system, equilibrium and adaptation as outlined above. Although

functionalism, and specifically ecological functionalism, were mainstays of the theoretical framework of an earlier generation of archaeologists such as Gordon Childe and Grahame Clark, they have become more widely important as a result of the New Archaeology of the 1960s and 1970s. Indeed, processual and systems archaeology is almost by definition a functionalist archaeology. As Leach (1973a, pp. 761–2) pointed out, 'Binford's remark that "behaviour is the by-product of the interaction of a cultural repertoire with the environment" may be proto-typical of the "new" archaeology, but to a social anthropologist it reads like a quotation from Malinowski writing at the time when naive functionalism was at its peak – that is to say about 1935.' This view is too extreme, but Renfrew (1972, p. 24) also states that to examine connections between subsystems as in systems theory 'is, of course, simply a statement of anthropological functionalism, that different aspects of a culture are all interrelated'.

The degree to which archaeology has adopted a functionalist conception of society and culture is apparent in the writings of the major figures of the 'new' discipline. Although the archaeological contributions of these writers differ, the notions of organic wholes, interrelated systems, equilibrium and adaptation can all be identified most clearly. For example, in Flannery's (1972) systems model for the growth of complex societies, the job of self-regulation within the sociocultural system 'is to keep all the variables in the subsystem within appropriate goal ranges – ranges which maintain homeostasis and do not threaten the survival of the system' (ibid., p. 409). According to Binford (1972, p. 107) 'we can . . . expect variability in and among components of a system to result from the action of homeostatic regulators within the cultural system serving to maintain equilibrium relationships between the system and its environment'. Similarly, for Clarke (1968, p. 88), 'the whole cultural system is in external dynamic equilibrium with its local environment'. 'Equilibrium is defined as that state in which dislocation amongst the component variety is minimised . . . Dislocation most frequently arises . . . when different networks independently transmit mutually contradictory information – presenting an anomaly at nodes in the structure of the system. Sociocultural systems are continuously changing in such a way as to minimise the maximum amount of immediate system dislocation' (ibid., p. 129). According to Hill (1971, p. 407), a set of variables is only a system if their 'articulation . . . be regulated (maintained in steady-state) by homeostatic processes'.

The importance of maintaining equilibrium with the 'environment' has also been emphasised by Renfrew (1972). Indeed, man's relationship with the environment is seen by him as one of the main aspects of systems theory. 'The whole purpose of utilising the systems approach is to emphasise man–environment interrelations, while at the same time admitting that many fundamental changes in man's environment are produced by man himself' (ibid., pp. 19–20).

'Culture . . . is essentially a homeostatic device, a conservative influence ensuring that change in the system will be minimised. It is a flexible adaptive mechanism which allows the survival of society despite fluctuations in the natural environment' (ibid., p. 486).

Thus it is thought that human sociocultural systems can be described as if they were adapting to the total social and environmental milieu. Renfrew (1972, pp. 24—5) talks of the 'essential coherence and conservatism of all cultures . . . the society's "adjustment" or "adaptation" to its natural environment is maintained: difficulties and hardships are overcome'. A similar view is expressed by Binford (1972, p. 20). 'Change in the total cultural system must be viewed in an adaptive context both social and environmental.' Indeed Binford's (1972, p. 22) definition of culture 'as the extra-somatic means of adaptation for the human organism' is one of the main tenets of systems archaeologists. 'Culture, from a systemic perspective, is defined . . . as interacting behavioural systems. One asks questions concerning these systems, their interrelation, their adaptive significance' (Plog 1975, p. 208). 'Culture is all those means whose forms are not under direct genetic control . . . which serve to adjust individuals and groups within their ecological communities . . . Adaptation is always a local problem, and selective pressures favouring new cultural forms result from nonequilibrium conditions in the local ecosystem' (Binford 1972, p. 431).

The functionalist and processual emphasis in archaeology aimed objectively to identify relationships between variables in cultural systems. There was a natural link to an empirical and positivist concept of science. 'The meaning which explanation has within a scientific frame of reference is simply the demonstration of a constant articulation of variables within a system and the measurement of the concomitant variability among the variables within the system. Processual change in one variable can thus be shown to relate in a predictable and quantifiable way to changes in other variables, the latter changing in turn relative to changes in the structure of the system as a whole' (Binford 1972, p. 21). This statement demonstrates the link between functionalism and a conception of explanation as the prediction of relationships between variables. It is thought that the relationships can be observed empirically and quantification can be used to assess the significance of associations. The way is thus open for recovering cross-cultural generalisations, and 'the laws of cultural process' (ibid., p. 199). Although Binford (1977, p. 5) appears more recently to have doubted the explanatory value of cross-cultural statistics, the above attitudes to explanation have at times been developed into a rigid hypothetico-deductive method based on a reading of Hempel (e.g. Watson, Leblanc & Redman 1971; Fritz & Plog 1970).

Critique of functionalism

I do not intend to examine the problems of applying systems theory in archaeology (Doran 1970), nor whether systems theory has really aided archaeologists in their functionalist aims (Salmon 1978). Rather, I want to consider the criticisms of functionalism itself. Martins (1974, p. 246) describes the critique of functionalism as an initiation *rite de passage* into sociological adulthood, and I have suggested elsewhere (1981) the need for a wider debate in archaeology concerning the various critiques of and alternatives to ecological functionalism.

Many of the problems and limitations of the organic analogy as applied to social systems have long been recognised. Radcliffe-Brown (1952, p. 181) noted that while an animal organism does not, in the course of its life, change its form, a society can, in the course of its history, undergo major organisational change. Other problems are not inherent to the approach but result from the particular emphasis that is given by archaeologists, perhaps as a result of the limitations of their data. For example, a systems approach which assumes that homeostatic equilibrium is the natural state of things results in the notion that all change ultimately has to derive from outside the system. Negative feedback occurs in reaction to outside stimuli, and positive feedback and deviation amplifying processes need initial external kicks. According to Hill (1977, p. 76) 'no system can change itself; change can only be instigated by outside sources. If a system is in equilibrium, it will remain so unless inputs (or lack of outputs) from outside the system disturb the equilibrium.' The result of this view has been to place great emphasis on the impact of supposed 'independent' variables from outside the sociocultural system under study. The favourite external variables have been environmental factors (e.g. Carneiro 1968), long-distance trade (Renfrew 1969), and population increase (Hill 1977, p. 92), although it is not often clear why the latter is assumed to be an independent variable. Little advance has been made in the study of factors within societies that affect the nature of change (see, however, Friedman & Rowlands 1977). But Flannery (1972) has shown how the systems approach can be extended to include internal forces of change and those forms of internal adaptation within the organic whole which have been described above.

A more fundamental limitation of the functionalist viewpoint centres on the inadequacy of function and utility in explaining social and cultural systems, and on the separation made between functional utility and culture. All aspects of culture have utilitarian purposes in terms of which they can be explained. All activities, whether dropping refuse, developing social hierarchies, or performing rituals, are the results of adaptive expedience. But explanation is sought only in terms of adaptation and function. The problem with such a viewpoint is not so much the emphasis on function since it is important to know how material items, institutions, symbols and ritual operate, and the contribution of the New Archaeology to such studies is impressive. It is rather the dichotomy which was set up between culture and adaptive utility which restricted the development of the approach.

In archaeology the split between culture and function took the form of an attack on what was termed the 'normative' approach. In Binford's (1965) rebuttal of the 'normative school', he referred to American archaeologists such as Taylor, Willey and Phillips, Ford, Rouse and Gifford who were concerned with identifying cultural 'wholes' in which there was an ideational basis for the varying ways of human life within each cultural unit. Such archaeologists aimed at identifying the normative concepts in the minds of men now dead. Binford more specifically criticised the normative studies which tried to describe the diffusion and transmission of cultural traits. It is not my concern here to identify whether the normative paradigm, as characterised by Binford, ever existed. Certainly, as will be shown below, European archaeologists such as Childe were already able to integrate a concern with cultural norms and a notion of behavioural adaptability. But in Binford's view, the normative approach emphasising homogeneous cultural wholes contrasted with the study of functional variability within and between cultural units. The normative school was seen as historical and descriptive, not allowing explanation in terms of functional process. So he moved to an opposite extreme where culture, norms, form and design had only functional value in, for example, integrating and articulating individuals and social units into broader corporate entities. In fact Binford suggested that the different components of culture may function independently of each other. Functional relationships could thus be studied without reference to cultural context, and regular, stable and predictable relationships could be sought between variables within social systems. As a result, an absolute gulf was driven between normative and processual studies. 'An approach is offered in which culture is not reduced to normative ideas about the proper ways of doing things but is viewed as the system of the total extrasomatic means of adaptation' (Binford 1972, p. 205). More recently (1978a) Binford has still more clearly separated the study of norms from the study of process. He has attacked the historical and contextual emphasis of Kroeber and Kluckhohn (ibid., p. 2). On the one hand (ibid., p. 3), artefacts are the reflections of the mental templates of the makers and these ideas in the minds of men cannot adapt intelligently to new situations. On the other hand, cultural variability is simply the result of adaptive expedience. He could ask (1978a, p. 11), 'do people conduct their ongoing activities in terms of invariant mental templates as to the appropriate strategies regardless of the setting in which they find themselves?' Indeed, his Nunamiut ethnoarchaeology is introduced as an attempt to identify whether faunal remains could be studied as being 'culture-free'. Cultural bias can only be identified (1978a, p. 38) when an anomoly occurs; when the adaptively expedient expectations are not found.

The dichotomy set up between culture and function limits the development of archaeological theory because

'functional value is always relative to the given cultural scheme' (Sahlins 1976, p. 206). All actions take place within cultural frameworks and their functional value is assessed in terms of the concepts and orientations which surround them. That an item or institution is 'good for' achieving some end is partly a cultural choice, as is the end itself. At the beginning of this chapter Durkheim's definition of the function of a social institution as the correspondence between it and the needs of the social organism was described. But the needs of the society are preferred choices within a cultural matrix. It follows that function and adaptation are not absolute measures. All daily activities, from eating to the removal of refuse, are not the results of some absolute adaptive expedience. These various functions take place within a cultural framework, a set of ideas or norms, and we cannot adequately understand the various activities by denying any role to culture. An identical point is made by Deetz (1977) in his comparison of cultural traditions in two historical periods in North America.

The above discussion is particularly relevant to the functionalist view of material items. As already noted, Binford assumes that culture is man's extrasomatic means of adaptation. According to David Clarke (1968, p. 85) 'culture is an information system, wherein the messages are accumulated survival information'. In this way material culture is seen as simply functioning at the interface between the human organism and the social and physical environment in order to allow adaptation. It has a utilitarian function (Sahlins 1976). The result of this view is that cultural remains are seen as *reflecting*, in a fairly straightforward way, what people *do*. Even work on deposition and post-depositional processes (Schiffer 1976), while adding complexity to the situation, still assumes that material culture is simply a direct, indirect or distorted reflection of man's activities. This is a continuation of earlier views of material culture as 'fossilised action'. As Fletcher (1977b, pp. 51–2) has pointed out, material culture is seen simply as a passive object of functional use; a mere epiphenomenon of 'real' life. But there is more to culture than functions and activities. Behind functioning and doing there is a structure and content which has partly to be understood in its own terms, with its own logic and coherence. This applies as much to refuse distributions and 'the economy' as it does to burial, pot decoration and art.

Linked to the separation of function and culture has been the decreased emphasis on archaeology as an historical discipline. If material items and social institutions can be explained in terms of their adaptive efficiency, there is little concern to situate them within an historical framework. The evolutionary perspective has emphasised adaptive relationships at different levels of complexity, but it has not encouraged an examination of the particular historical context. However, it is suggested here that the cultural framework within which we act, and which we reproduce in our actions, is historically derived and that each culture is a particular historical product. The uniqueness of cultures and historical sequences must be recognised. Within the New Archaeology there has been a great concern with identifying variability. But in embracing a cross-cultural approach, variability has, in the above sense, been reduced to sameness. Diachronic sequences are split into phases in which the functioning of systems can be understood in synchronic terms as instances of some general relationship. The dichotomy between diachrony and synchrony is linked to the split between culture and history on the one hand and function and adaptation on the other. The resolution of the culture/function dichotomy which is sought in this book will also reintroduce historical explanation as a legitimate topic of concern in archaeology.

Another limitation of the functionalist perspective of the New Archaeology is the relationship between the individual and society. The functional view gives little emphasis to individual creativity and intentionality. Individual human beings become little more than the means to achieve the needs of society. The social system is organised into subsystems and roles which people fill. The roles and social categories function in relation to each other to allow the efficient equilibrium of the whole system. In fact, however, individuals are not simply instruments in some orchestrated game and it is difficult to see how subsystems and roles can have 'goals' of their own. Adequate explanations of social systems and social change must involve the individual's assessments and aims. This is not a question of identifying individuals (Hill & Gunn 1977) but of introducing the individual into social theory. Some New Archaeologists have recognised the importance of this. 'While the behaviour of the group, of many individual units, may often effectively be described in statistical terms without reference to the single unit, it cannot so easily be *explained* in this way. This is a problem which prehistoric archaeology has yet to resolve' (Renfrew 1972, p. 496). The lack of resolution is inherent in the functionalist emphasis in archaeology.

Further criticism of functionalist archaeology concerns the emphasis on cross-cultural generalisations. After an initial phase in which ethnoarchaeology was used largely to provide cautionary tales and 'spoilers' (Yellen 1977), the concern has been to provide cross-cultural statements of high predictive value. Because of the preferred hypothetico-deductive nature of explanation, it became important to identify rules of behaviour and artefact deposition which were used regardless of cultural context. As already noted, such an approach was feasible because the particular historical and cultural dimensions of activity were denied. Different subsystems were identified, such as subsistence, exchange, settlement, refuse disposal and burial, and cross-cultural regularities were sought. Since the role of cultural and historical factors was not examined, it was necessarily the case that the resulting generalisations either were limited to mechanical or physical aspects of life or were simplistic and with little content. Some aspects of human activity are constrained by deter-

ministic variables. For example, it is difficult for humans to walk bare-footed on spreads of freshly knapped flint, or to work or sit in or near the smoke of fires (Gould 1980; Binford 1978*b*). Certain types of bone do hold more or less meat or marrow, and they fracture in different ways (Binford 1978*a*; Gifford 1978). The seeds sorted by wind during winnowing depend partly on wind velocity and seed density (Jones, pers. comm.). Smaller artefacts are more difficult for humans to hold and find than large artefacts and so the patterns of loss may differ (Schiffer 1976). Cross-cultural predictive laws or generalisations can be developed for these mechanical constraints on human behaviour, and ethno-archaeology has been most successful in these spheres, but attempts to extend this approach to social and cultural behaviour have been severely criticised as is shown by the debate over the hypothesis put forward by Longacre (1970), Deetz (1968), and Hill (1970) (e.g. Stanislawski 1973; Allen & Richardson 1971), and the result has been the frustration implied by Flannery's (1973) characterisation of Mickey Mouse laws. As soon as any human choice is involved, behavioural and functional laws appear simplistic and inadequate because human behaviour is rarely entirely mechanistic. The role of ethnoarchaeology must also be to define the relevant cultural context for social and ecological behaviour.

Linked to the emphasis on cross-cultural functional laws is the idea of 'predicting the past' (Thomas 1974). The percentages of modern societies in which women make pots (Phillips 1971) or in which size of settlement is related to post-marital residence (Ember 1973) are difficult to use as measures of probability for the interpretation of the past because modern societies are not independent nor do they comprise a random or representative sample of social forms. More important, however, is the lack of identity between prediction and understanding. It is possible to predict many aspects of human behaviour with some accuracy but without any understanding of the causal relationships involved. Equally, a good understanding of a social event may not lead to an ability to predict the outcome of a similar set of circumstances. Levels of probability and statistical evidence of correlation are no substitute for an understanding of causal links and of the relevant context for human action. The use of mathematical and statistical formulae which provide good fits to archaeological data leads to little understanding of the past. My own involvement in spatial archaeology, a sphere in which statistical prediction has been most successful, has shown most clearly that prediction has little to do with explanation.

The embrace of the hypothetico-deductive method and prediction in relation to interpretation of the past has allowed the definition of independent levels of theory. A distinct 'middle range theory' has been identified because it has been assumed that objective yardsticks or instruments of measurement can be obtained for the study of past systems and their archaeological residues (Binford 1978*a*, p. 45). We have general theories of social development and lower level theories concerning the formation of the archaeological record. Similarly, Clarke (1973) suggested that pre-depositional, depositional, post-depositional, analytical and interpretive theories could be distinguished despite the existence of overall controlling models. This separation of levels or types of theory is partly possible because of a model of man which separates different functional activities and sets up predictive relationships between them. Thus, depositional theory can be separated from interpretive theory because artefact deposition is adaptively expedient and can be predicted without reference to wider social theories. The hypotheses concerning social institutions and social change are thought to be different in nature from the hypotheses concerning the relationship between society and material culture. But both material items and their deposition are actively involved in social relations and we cannot separate independent levels of theory. Frameworks of cultural meaning structure all aspects of archaeological information. Leone (1978) has shown most clearly how data, analyses and interpretations are inextricably linked. The different theoretical levels should be congruent, and beyond natural processes there can be no instruments of absolute measurement.

The aim of the New Archaeology was to show the rationality of institutions with respect to their environments. The main criticisms of this general approach as described above are as follows. (1) The dichotomy set up between cultural form and objective functional expedience is misleading, and material items are more than tools holding survival information. (2) The functionalist viewpoint is unable to explain cultural variety and uniqueness adequately. (3) Social systems become reified to such an extent that the individual contributes little. (4) The cross-cultural generalisations which have resulted from functionalist studies by archaeologists have been unable to identify valid statements about social and cultural behaviour because the relevant context is insufficiently explored. (5) Different levels or types of hypothesis have been identified, but in fact all hypotheses are and should be integrated within a coherent social and cultural theory. This volume seeks to respond to these criticisms by developing alternative approaches. I wish to begin by considering various definitions of 'structure'.

Structure as system, pattern and style

In the preceding discussion of functionalism, reference has been made to the adaptive utility of material items and institutions within social and cultural systems. Subsystems (pottery, settlement, social, economic etc.) can be identified and discussed in cross-cultural perspective. Within each socio-cultural system a particular set of systemic relationships is produced in order to meet local needs at particular moments in time. In the analysis of such systems, the words 'system' and 'structure' are interchangeable. The system (or structure) is the particular set of relationships between the various components; it is the *way* the interrelationships are organ-

ised. Within New Archaeology, then, structure is the system of observable relations. Structure is the way things are done and it, like individual items and institutions, is explained as the result of adaptive expedience.

The functionalist view of structure is apparent in discussions of social organisation, social relations or social systems, none of which are distinguished from social structure. The term social structure is used by New Archaeologists to refer to bands, tribes, chiefdoms, states, as well as to reciprocal, redistributive and prestige transactions. Social structure is observed directly in burial and settlement patterns where the visible differentiation in associations and forms is seen as reflecting roles and activities organised in relation to each other. The structure of social relations as a whole is organised so as to allow adaptation to such factors as the distribution of environmental resources (uniform or localised), the availability of prestige items or valued commodities, and the relationships with neighbouring social groups.

In such systemic studies the close relationship between the terms 'structure' and 'pattern' is apparent. In identifying social and economic structures various patterns are analysed. These patterns include the distributions of settlements of different sizes and functions across the landscape, the distributions of artefacts and buildings in settlements, the distributions of resources, the distributions of artefacts among graves in cemeteries, the regional distributions of exchanged items and the regional distributions of artefacts in interaction or information exchange spheres or 'cultures'. These various patterns are 'objective' and are immediately susceptible to statistical manipulation, quantification and computerisation. The concern with pattern allows the legitimate use of a wide range of scientific software, including numerical taxonomy and spatial analysis.

The identification of pattern and the implementation of 'analytical archaeology' is extended to studies of arrangements of attributes on individual artefacts, where 'pattern' is often equivalent to 'style'. The analysis of pottery and metal decoration, and of the form of artefacts, leads to the definition of 'types' based on the association of attributes. Artefact styles are interpreted as having utilitarian or non-utilitarian functions; they are technomic, sociotechnic or ideotechnic (Binford 1972). Style is involved in the support of group solidarity (Hodder 1979) and the passing on of information (Wobst 1977).

In functionalist archaeology, structure is examined as system, organisation, distribution, pattern, or style. It is produced by people attempting to adapt to their environments. Like any artefact, structure is a tool for coping. If culture is a tool acting between people and the environment, and if the term 'culture' describes the particular adaptive organisation produced in each environmental context, then structure is also similar to culture. A culture is seen as the way material bits and pieces are assembled and associated in a geographical area in order to allow human adaptation.

Structure as code

In this chapter I wish to distinguish between system and structure (Giddens 1979), by defining structure not as system, pattern or style, but as the codes and rules according to which observed systems of interrelations are produced. Several archaeological studies have made a contribution to the analysis of structure as code, and some examples are discussed here.

Within studies of Palaeolithic cave art, Leroi-Gourhan (1965) has made specific interpretations of signs as male or female and has suggested various codes for the combination and relative placing of the signs within the caves. Marshak (1977) identified specific interpretations of symbols as dangerous and he related the structure associated with the meander in cave art to the general flow and participation in daily life. Conkey (1977) identified general aspects of the rules of organisation of Upper Palaeolithic art, such as 'the non-differentiation of units', and did not attempt to provide a specific meaning in terms of social organisation. All these analyses were concerned to identify codes or rules, but the nature of the interpretation of these structures and of their relationship to social structures varied.

Studies of later artefact and pottery design have often tended towards a still more formal emphasis in that little attention is paid to the social context in which structures are produced. The linguistic model has been developed most fully by Muller (1977) in his analysis of the grammatical rules of design. His work, and Washburn's (1978) definition of different types of symmetry, do not result in any attempt at translating cultural meaning and symbolism. Rather, Washburn uses symmetry simply as an additional trait for the discovery of population group composition and inter-action spheres. Such analyses can be, and have been, carried out without any major change in functionalist theories of society.

Some of the work on the identification of settlement structures has also involved little criticism of the New Archaeology. Clarke's (1972, pp. 828 and 837) identification of structural transformations (bilateral symmetry relating to male/female) in the Iron Age Glastonbury settlement appears as a peripheral component of a systems analysis. A clear link is made between the generative principles of the settlement design and the social system. Isbell's (1976) recognition of the 3000-year continuity in settlement structure in the South American Andes, despite major discontinuities in social and economic systems, raises more fundamental problems for systemic studies since structure is seen to continue and lie behind adaptive change. Fritz's (1978) interesting account of prehistoric Chaco Canyon in north western New Mexico shows that the organisation of houses, towns, and regional settlement can be seen as transforms of the same underlying principle in which west is symmetrical to east, but north is asymmetrical to south. This study is concerned to link the organisation of social systems to underlying structures. The

structuralist analysis of a Neolithic cemetery by Van de Velde (1980) has related aims. Fletcher's (1977*a*) work on the spacing between 'entities' – posts, walls, door posts, pots and hearths – in settlements is concerned less with social strategies and more with ordering principles which carry long-term adaptive value. Hillier *et al.* (1976) have identified a purely formal logic for the description of all types of arrangement of buildings and spaces within settlements.

The above examples are drawn from prehistoric archae-ology but structural studies have an important place in his-torical archaeology (Deetz 1967; Ferguson 1977; Frankfort 1951; Glassie 1975; Leone 1977). While many of the pre-historic and historic archaeology studies explain structure in terms of social functions and adaptive values, they also introduce the notion that there is more to culture than observable relationships and functional utility. There is also a set of rules, a code, which, like the rules in a game of chess, is followed in the pursuit of survival, adaptation and socio-economic strategy. In an ethnographic analysis of the Nuba in Sudan, it has been shown that all aspects of material cul-ture patterning (burial, settlement, artefact styles) must be understood as being produced according to sets of rules concerned with purity, boundedness and categorisation (Hodder 1982*a*). Individuals organise their experience according to sets of rules. Communication and understanding of the world result from the use of a common language – that is, a set of rules which identify both the way symbols should be organised into sets, and the meaning of individual symbols in contrast to others. Material culture can be examined as a structured set of differences. This structured symbolising behaviour has functional utility, and it must be understood in those terms. But it also has a logic of its own which is not directly observable as pattern or style. The structure must be interpreted as having existed partly inde-pendent of the observable data, having generated and pro-duced those data.

The concern with material culture as the product of human categorisation processes is described by Miller in chapter 2. It is sufficient to emphasise here that the various structuralist analyses of codes can be clearly distinguished from functionalist studies of systems. Both structuralists and functionalists are concerned with relationships and with the way things and institutions are organised. In other words, both are concerned with 'structure' if that word is defined in a very general way. But there is a difference in that the logic analysed by functionalists is the visible social system (the social relations) which exists separately from the per-ceptions of men. For Leach (1973*b*, 1977, 1978), structure is an ideal order in the mind. For Lévi-Strauss (1968), it is an internal logic, not directly visible, which is the underlying order by which the apparent order must be explained. But for Lévi-Strauss, the structure often appears to lie outside the human mind (Godelier 1977). Structuralists, including Leach and Lévi-Strauss, claim that adequate explanation of observed patterns must make reference to underlying codes.

Criticisms of structuralism

The problems and limitations of the different types of structuralism are discussed by, for example, Giddens (1979), and in this chapter only those criticisms will be examined which are particularly relevant to the themes to be debated in this book. A major problem concerns the lack of a theory of practice (Bourdieu 1977). The structuralism of Saussure, which uses a linguistic model, separates *langue* as a closed series of formal rules, a structured set of differences, from semantic and referential ties. The formal set of relationships is distinct from the practice of use. Similarly, Lévi-Strauss identifies a series of unconscious mental structures which are separated from practice and from the ability of social actors to reflect consciously on their ideas and create new rules. In both linguistic and structural analyses it is unclear how the interpretation and use of rules might lead to change. How an individual can be a competent social actor is not clearly specified. As in functionalism, form and practical function are separated.

The failure within structuralism and within structuralist analyses in archaeology to develop a theory of practice (concerning the generation of structures in social action) has encouraged the view within functionalist archaeology that structuralism can only contribute to the study of norms and ideas which are epiphenomenal. The gulf between normative and processual archaeology has been widened since, on the one hand, structuralist approaches could be seen as relating to ideas divorced from adaptive processes while, on the other hand, it was thought by processualists that social change could be examined adequately without reference to the structure of ideas. Some of the structuralist studies identified above, such as those by Muller and Washburn, make little attempt to understand the referential context. The notion of a 'mental template' can be criticised in a similar vein because it envisages an abstract set of ideas or pictures without examining the framework of referential meaning within which the ideas take their form. In other, more integrated studies, such as those by Fritz and Marshak, the social and ecological contexts of the structures identified are examined, but the link between form and practice is insecure and no relevant theory is developed. On the other hand, work such as that of Flannery and Marcus (1976), which fits better into the functionalist mould, relates all form to function and structural analysis is limited. Few archaeological studies have managed to provide convincing accounts of the relationship between structure as code and social and ecological organisation.

Other limitations of structuralism can be related to the above. As in functionalism, the role of the individual is slight. In functionalism the individual is subordinate to the imperatives of social coordination. In the structuralism of Lévi-Strauss the individual is subordinate to the organising mechanisms of the unconscious. The notion of a 'norm' in traditional archaeology implies a structured set of cultural rules within which the individual plays little part.

The dichotomy between synchrony and diachrony, statics and dynamics, exists in structuralism as it does in functionalism. Structural analyses can incorporate time as a dimension for the setting up of formal differences, but the role of historical explanation is seen to be slight in the work of Lévi-Strauss, and there is little attempt to understand how structural rules can be changed. Structures often appear as static constraints on societies, preventing change. Structuralism does not have an adequate notion of the *generation* of change.

While the main concern of reactions to structuralism is to develop an adequate theory of practice (Bourdieu 1977; Piaget 1971, 1972; Giddens 1979), other criticisms have concentrated on the methods of analysis. Structures, because they are organising principles, are not observable as such, and this is true whether we are talking about anthropology, psychology or archaeology. They can only be reached by reflective abstraction. Thus, structures of particular kinds could be said to emerge because the analyst is looking for them, trying to fit the data into some expected and hypothetical structural pattern. But how can such hypotheses ever be falsified (Pettit 1975, p. 88)? For structuralism to be a worthwhile pursuit, it must be possible to disprove a weak hypothesis. However, Pettit (ibid., pp. 88–92) feels that rejection of structuralist hypotheses is impossible, at least in regard to myths, for a number of reasons. For example, the initial hypothesis in structuralist analysis often is necessarily vague so that the analyst can give himself room to shift the hypothesis to accommodate the new transformations. Also, because there are few rules on the way in which structures are transformed into different realities, one can make up the rules as one goes along. By using sufficient ingenuity, any two patterns can probably be presented as transformations of each other.

Thus the structural method of Lévi-Strauss 'is hardly more than a licence for the free exercise of imagination in establishing associations' (ibid., p. 96). There is certainly a danger that archaeologists may be able to select arbitrary aspects of their data and suggest a whole series of unverifiable transformations. These criticisms are discussed in detail by Wylie in chapter 4. Here I wish to note that Pettit's attack is directed at those formal and structural analyses which take little account of the referential context of social action. Within a structuralism in which a theory of practice has been developed, Pettit's criticisms have less force because the structural transformations must 'make sense' as part of a changing and operating system. Abstract formal analysis must be shown to be relevant to a particular social and historical context, and it must lead to an understanding of the generation of new actions and structures through time.

All the above criticisms of structuralism have concerned the need to examine the generation of structures within meaningful, active and changing contexts. The criticisms of both functionalism and structuralism centre on the inability of the approaches to explain particular historical contexts and the meaningful actions of individuals constructing social change within those contexts. Archaeology in particular has moved away from historical explanation and has tried to identify cross-cultural universals concerning either the functioning of ecological systems or (rarely) the human unconscious. There is a need to develop a contextual archaeology which resolves the dichotomy evident in functionalism and structuralism between cultural norm and societal adaptation.

Archaeology as a cultural science

The approaches developed by the majority of the authors in this volume are not structuralist in that they take account of the criticisms of the work of, for example, Leach and Lévi-Strauss, made by various 'post-structuralist' writers (Harstrup 1978; Ardener 1978). Yet the insights offered by structuralism must be retained in any adequate analysis of social processes, and it is for this reason that I have not deleted the term structuralism from the papers in this book (e.g. Wylie, chapter 4; see also the term 'dialectical structuralism' used by Tilley, chapter 3). Even if structuralism as a whole is generally rejected, the analysis of structure has a potential which has not been exhausted in archaeology.

Structural analyses involve a series of approaches described by Miller (chapter 2). Important concepts which can be retained from structuralism include syntagm and paradigm. Syntagm refers to rules of combination, and to 'sets' of items and symbols. In burial studies it may be noted, for example, that particular 'costumes' can be identified which are associated with particular sub-groups within society. The rules of combination describe the way in which items or classes of item (e.g. weapons) placed on one part of the body are associated with other classes of item on other parts of the body. Similarly, sets of items may be found to occur in settlements. Syntagmatic studies can also be applied to the combination of attributes on artefacts, and in chapter 14 rules for the generation of Dutch Neolithic pottery decoration are described. Paradigm refers to series of alternatives or differences. For example, in the burial study, a brooch of type *A* may be found worn on the shoulder in contrast to a pin or a brooch type *B* placed in the same position on other skeletons. Each alternative may be associated with a different symbolic meaning.

But in all such structural analyses the particular symbol used must not be seen as arbitrary. 'High structuralist' analyses are directed towards examinations of abstract codes, and the content or substance of the symbol itself often appears arbitrary. However, the symbol is not arbitrary, as is seen by, for example, the placing of a symbol such as a crown, associated with royalty, on the label of a bottle of beer in order to increase sales. The crown is not chosen arbitrarily in a structured set of differences. Rather, it is chosen as a powerful symbol with particular evocations and connotations which make its use appropriate within the social and economic context of selling beer in England. The

content of the sign affects the structure of its use. Barth (1975) has demonstrated elegantly that material symbolisation cannot be described simply as sets of categories and transformations, however cross-cutting and complex one might allow these to be. Culture is to be studied as meaningfully constituting – as the framework through which adaptation occurs – but the meaning of an object resides not merely in its contrast to others within a set. Meaning also derives from the associations and use of an object, which itself becomes, through the associations, the node of a network of references and implications. There is an interplay between structure and content.

The emphasis on the symbolic associations of things themselves is not only a departure from purely formal and structuralist analyses. It also breaks with other approaches in archaeology. In processual analyses of symbol systems, the artefact itself is rarely given much importance. An object may be described as symbolising status, male or female, or social solidarity, but the use of the particular artefact class, and the choice of the symbol itself, are not adequately discussed. Similarly, traditional archaeologists use types as indicators of contact, cultural affiliation and diffusion, but the question of which type is used for which purpose is not pursued. The symbol is seen as being arbitrary. In this book an attempt is made by some of the authors to assess why particular symbols were used in a particular context. For example, in chapter 14 the shape of Neolithic burial mounds is seen as having been appropriate because the shape itself referred back to earlier houses, and such references and evocations had social advantage in the context in which the tombs were built.

The structural and symbolic emphases lead to an awareness of the importance of 'context' in interpretations of the use of material items in social processes. The generative structures and the symbolic associations have a particular meaning in each cultural context and within each set of activities within that context. Although generative principles such as pure/impure, or the relations between parts of the human body (see chapter 12), may occur widely, they may be combined in ways peculiar to each cultural milieu, and be given specific meanings and associations. The transformation of structures and symbols between different contexts can have great 'power'. For example, it has been noted elsewhere (Hodder & Lane, in preparation) that Neolithic stone axes in Britain and Brittany frequently occur in ritual and burial contexts, engraved on walls, as miniatures or as soft chalk copies. The participation of these axes in secular exchanges would evoke the ritual contexts and could be used to legitimate any social dominance based on privileged access to these items. In a study of the Neolithic in Orkney (Hodder 1982*a*) it has been suggested that the similarities between the spatial structures in burial, non-burial ritual, and domestic settlement contexts were used within social strategies to legitimise emerging elites.

So far, it has been suggested that material items come

to have symbolic meanings as a result both of their use in structured sets and of the associations and implications of the objects themselves, but that the meanings vary with context. It is through these various mechanisms that material items and the constructed world come to represent society. But what is the nature of representation in human culture? In particular, how should social relations be translated into material symbols? For New Archaeologists these questions are relatively unproblematic since artefacts (whether utilitarian, social or ideological) are simply tools for adaptive efficiency. Symbols are organised so as to maximise information flow and there is no concept in such analyses of the *relativity of representation*. It is in studies of representation that concepts of ideology play a central role, and although there is considerable divergence of views within this book on the definition and nature of ideology, it is at least clear that the way in which structured sets of symbols are used in relation to social strategies depends on a series of concepts and attitudes that are historically and contextually appropriate. I have demonstrated elsewhere (1982*b*), for example, that social ranking may be represented in burial ritual either through a 'naturalising' ideology in which the arbitrary social system is represented as occurring in the material world, or through an ideology in which social dominance is denied and eradicated in artefacts and in the organisation of ritual. This example demonstrates two extremes in the representation and misrepresentation of social relations, but it serves to indicate that all material patterning is generated by symbolic structures within a cultural matrix.

Burial pattern, then, is not a direct behavioural reflection of social pattern. It is structured through symbolically meaningful codes which can be manipulated in social strategies. Archaeologists must accept that death and attitudes to the dead form a symbolic arena of great emotive force which is employed in life. Similar arguments can be made in relation to other activities in which material culture is involved (Hodder 1982*a*). Throwing away refuse and the organisation of dirt are used in all societies as parts of social actions (see, for example, the use by Hippies of dirt and disorder in the 1960s and 1970s in western Europe and North America). Equally, the preparation of food, cooking and eating have great symbolic significance in forming, masking or transforming aspects of social relations. Pottery shapes and decoration can be used to mark out, separate off or conceal the social categories and relationships played out in the context of food preparation, storage and consumption. There is no direct link between social and ceramic variability. Attitudes to food and the artefacts used in eating activities play a central role in the construction of social categories (as is seen, for example, in the use by Hippies and Punks of natural 'health' and unnatural 'plastic' foods in contemporary western Europe). Similar hypotheses can be developed for the wearing of ornaments on the body, the organisation of the production of pottery and metal items, and the organisation of space within settlements and houses. Before

archaeology can contribute to the social sciences, it must develop as a cultural science. The concern must be to examine the role of material culture in the ideological representation of social relations. Excavated artefacts are immediately cultural, not social, and they can inform on society only through an adequate understanding of cultural context.

Material symbolisation is not a passive process, because objects and activities actively represent and act back upon society. Within a particular ideology, the constructed world can be used to legitimise the social order. Equally, material symbols can be used covertly to disrupt established relations of dominance (see Braithwaite, chapter 8). Each use of an artefact, through its previous associations and usage, has a significance and meaning within society so that the artefact is an active force in social change. The daily use of material items within different contexts recreates from moment to moment the framework of meaning within which people act. The individual's actions in the material world reproduce the structure of society, but there is a continual potential for change. The 'power' of material symbols in social action derives not only from the transformation of structures between different contexts or from the associations evoked by particular items or forms. It resides also in the ambiguous meanings of material items. Unlike spoken language, the meanings of material symbols can remain undiscussed and implicit. Their meanings can be reinterpreted and manipulated covertly. The multiple meanings at different levels and the 'fuzziness' (Miller, chapter 2) of material symbols can be interpreted in different ways by different interest groups and there is a continuing process of change and renegotiation. It is essential to see material symbols as not only 'good to think', but also 'good to act'. Artefacts, the organisation of space and ritual are embedded in a 'means-to-end' context. The effects of symbols, intended and unintended, must be associated with their repeated use and with the 'structuration' of society. Symbolic and structural principles are used to form social actions, and they are in turn reproduced, reinterpreted and changed as a result of those actions.

The dichotomy between normative and processual archaeology is thus by-passed by the notion that symbolic structures are in a continual state of reinterpretation and change in relation to the practices of daily life. Because of the emphases on context and on the continual process of change which is implicated in material practices and symbolisation, archaeological enquiry is of an historical nature. Artefacts and their organisation come to have specific cultural meanings as a result of their use in particular historical contexts. The examples of the crown and the Neolithic barrows have been provided above. The enquiry is also historical because the intended and unintended consequences of action affect further action. They form a setting within which future actors must play.

The approaches explored in this book are neither idealist nor materialist. They attempt to bridge the gap between these extremes. On the one hand, it is hoped that the major criticisms of structuralism, as outlined above, are avoided. The aim is not to identify cognitive universals. It is not intended to encourage the notion that material items are simply reflections of categories of the mind, nor to develop abstract linguistic analyses of material symbolism. Archaeology is seen as an historical discipline concerned with the active integration of cultural items in daily practices. Structures are identified in relation to meaning, practices and change. Verification is aided by the use of models concerning the ways in which structures are integrated in action. The models identify the components which make up cultural contexts. They suggest relevant causal relationships within adaptive systems.

On the other hand, attempts are made to answer the various criticisms of functionalism described earlier in this chapter. It is clear that the approaches outlined here can be described as extensions of the New Archaeology in that there is a continued concern with social processes and with the use of material items in those processes. Since processual studies in archaeology have been so closely linked to functionalism it is necessary to indicate that the suggestions made here can avoid the various criticisms of that school. A significant development is that the culture/function and statics/dynamics dichotomies are denied since meaning and ideology are inextricably tied to daily practices. In addition attempts are made to locate the individual as an active component in social change, since the interests of individuals differ and it is in the interplay between different goals and aims that the rules of the society are penetrated, reinterpreted and reformed. The cross-cultural generalisations which are to be developed are concerned less with statistical levels of association in summary files of modern societies and more with careful considerations of relevant cultural contexts. Finally, all aspects of archaeological endeavour become infused with the same social and cultural theories, the same models of man. Theories concerning the relationship between material residues and the non-material world are placed within overall theories of society and social change.

The historical context of a symbolic and structural archaeology

The above outline of various aspects of a structural (but not structuralist) and symbolic archaeology will be expanded in the other chapters in this first part of the book. While the ideas put forward here can be seen to provide an extension of the New Archaeology, an asking of additional questions, it would be misleading to claim that the aims of a contextual or cultural approach are altogether new. The views are reactionary in the sense that they have certain similarities to the attitudes of an older generation of British prehistorians. Writers such as Childe, Clark, Daniel and Piggott placed a similar emphasis on archaeology as an historical discipline, they eschewed cross-cultural laws, and they saw material items as being structured by more than func-

tional necessities. They saw artefacts as expressions of culturally framed ideas and they were concerned primarily with the nature of culture and cultural contexts.

Many traditional archaeologists acknowledged that artefacts were ultimately expressions of ideas specific to each cultural and historical context. These archaeologists were 'normative' in the sense described by Binford. But British prehistorians often found it difficult to apply their aims in practice since the ideational realm was seen as being unrelated to the practical necessities of life. Daniel (1962, p. 129) asserted that, although prehistory used scientific methods, it was a humanity (an art or human science) partly because it was concerned with man as a cultured animal, with a transmittable body of ideas, customs, beliefs and practices dependent on the main agent of transmission, language. Thus, artefacts such as Acheulian handaxes 'are cultural fossils and the product of the human mind and human craftsmanship' (ibid., p. 30). On the other hand, archaeologists have access only to the 'cutlery and chinaware of a society' (ibid., p. 132), not to its ideals, morals and religion. Since 'there is no coincidence between the material and non-material aspects of culture' (ibid., pp. 134–5), prehistorians cannot speak of social organisation or religion. It is this belief in the lack of integration between the different aspects of society and culture which prevented a development of the humanistic aims that Daniel had set up. There was no theory according to which the structure and cultural form of all actions within each context could be considered.

Similar problems were accepted by many British archaeologists. Piggott (1959, pp. 6–11) agreed with Hawkes (1954) that it was difficult for archaeologists to find out about past language, beliefs, and social systems and religion. He used megalithic burial in western Europe as an example of the limitations of archaeological data (ibid., pp. 93–5). An archaeologist can reconstruct the ritual such as successive burials, making fires at entrances to the tombs, the offerings of complete or broken pots placed outside the tomb, the exposure of the corpse before interment, the moving aside of old bones. But having reconstructed the ritual, noted its distribution, and suggested that the dispersal could indicate a common religion, 'it is at this point that we have to stop' (ibid., p. 95). While it is certainly true that the detailed beliefs connected with the ritual are unlikely to be recoverable archaeologically, it is not the case that no further inference can be made about the place of the described megalithic ritual in Neolithic society. The chapters by Tilley and Shanks, Shennan and Hodder in the last part of this volume use generalisations from ethnographic and anthropological studies to link Neolithic megalithic ritual into other aspects of archaeological evidence. Piggott was prevented from following his historical and humanistic aims by a lack of theory linking idea to action.

The difficulties encountered by Hawkes, Piggott and Daniel in their pursuit of an historical and humanistic discipline concerned with culture and ideas resulted from a lack of theory concerning the links between different aspects of life — the technological, economic, social and ideological rungs of Hawkes' (1954) ladder. Grahame Clark and Gordon Childe had similar aims, but also employed theories concerning the relationships between the different subsystems. Their work could less easily, I think, be described as 'normative' in Binford's sense.

By 1939 Clark was already employing an organic analogy for society which has continued into his more recent writings. In 1975 material items were described as parts of organic wholes adjusting within an environment. Every aspect of archaeological data 'forms part of a working system of which each component stands in some relationship, usually reciprocal, to every other' (1975, p. 4). Man and his society could be seen as the products of natural selection in relation to the natural environment. But this ecological and functional stance has, throughout Clark's writings, been coupled, sometimes uncomfortably, with an awareness of the importance of cultural value within historical contexts. He was at pains to emphasise that the economic organisation of prehistoric communities was not conditioned by, but was adjusted to available resources, and could not be understood outside the social and 'psychic' (1975) context. 'Most biological functions — such as eating, sheltering, pairing and breeding, fighting and dying — are performed in idioms acquired by belonging to historically and locally defined cultural groups . . . whose patterns of behaviour are conditioned by particular sets of values' (1975, p. 5). Clark's greater willingness to discuss social and 'psychic' aspects of archaeological data is consonant with, but also contradicts, his use of a functional theory. Unlike Daniel, for example, he saw the material and non-material worlds as functionally related. On the other hand, it was difficult to see how a generalising and functionalist approach could be used to interpret specific historical contexts and cultural values.

Clark, like Daniel and Piggott, accepted that artefacts were not only tools of man, extensions of his limbs, 'they were also projections of his mind and embodiments of his history' (Clark 1975, p. 9). Gordon Childe was prone to make similar statements. Also, and again like Clark, he began with a functionalist view of the relationship between ideas and economies. But during his life he questioned whether an anthropological functionalist approach based on general laws of adaptation could be used to explain particular historical sequences.

In the 1920s, Childe had already espoused the view that culture was an adaptation to an environment. By 1935 and 1936 he could state clearly that culture could be studied as a functioning organism with material culture enabling communities to survive. Material innovations increased population size and so aided selection of successful communities. Magic, ideas and religion could be assessed in terms of their adaptive value (1936). But Childe also criticised natural and organic models, and he acknowledged the importance of cultural styles and values. In his earliest work particular

patterns of behaviour were seen simply as innate characteristics of specific peoples. Thus in Germany there had been a 'virile' Stone Age, European cultures had 'vigour and genius', and 'stagnant' megalithic cultures were not European (Trigger 1980, p. 51).

But in *Man Makes Himself* (1936) Childe began to give more careful consideration to the structure of ideas and its relationship to social action. He noted (p. 238) that the achievements of societies are not automatic responses to environments, and that adjustments are made by specific societies as a result of their own distinctive histories. The social traditions and rules, shaped by the community's history, determine the general behaviour of the society's members. But these traditions can themselves be changed as men meet new circumstances. 'Tradition makes the man, by circumscribing his behaviour within certain bounds; but it is equally true that man makes his traditions' so that man makes himself. Yet at times in *Man Makes Himself* ideas act only as a constraint on social change. A functional/non-functional dichotomy is set up and ideas do not take a full part in the practice of economic and social actions.

In later writings Childe further resolved some of the contradictions between an ecological functionalist stance and a concern with the form and content of cultural traditions. In 1949 he emphasised that different conceptions of the world framed archaeological evidence in different terms. He began by saying that the meaning that is given to the outside world, and one's perception of it, is socially and culturally determined. The environment of man is not the same as the environment of animals since it is perceived through a system of conventional symbols (p. 7). Man acts in a world of ideas (p. 7) collectively built up over thousands of years and which helps to direct the individual's experience (p. 8). If the environment of man can only be understood by reference to his mind, so too must past 'laws' of logic and mathematics be studied as part of culturally variable worlds of knowledge. Geometrical pattern in space and concepts of space vary in different societies, and 'any society may be allowed its own logic' (p. 18).

Even basic distinctions between mind and matter, society and nature, subject and object were seen by Childe as having varied through time. In Neolithic Europe these distinctions were not made. For example, the ritual burial of animals and the use of miniature axes and amulets were seen as suggesting mental attitudes which did not separate society and nature, practice and ritual (p. 20). The conceptual separation of man from nature was envisaged (p. 20) as being first apparent in the writings of Egyptian, Sumerian, and Babylonian clerks. But nature was still personal; it was an I—thou not an I—it relationship. Social relations were projected onto nature. It was only with the arrival of the machine age that causality could become fully depersonalised and mechanistic; our own distinctions and views are part of this latest stage.

Thus, 'environments to which societies are adjusted are

worlds of ideas, collective representations that differ not only in extent and content, but also in structure' (p. 22). While it could be claimed that Childe never developed these various components of a general theory so that they could be used successfully in archaeology, and while he never developed structural analyses, never gave the individual sufficient place in social theory and never gave an adequate account of the recursive relationship between norm and practice, he did, more than any other archaeologist, recognise the contextual nature of social action and material culture patterning. He tried to develop a non-functionalist conception of man and his culture by emphasising the relative nature of functional value and by concerning himself with historical contexts. 'Whether Childe saw beyond the New Archaeology or mere mirages in the Promised Land remains to be determined' (Trigger 1980, p. 182). While there are clear differences between the work of Childe and the viewpoints put forward in this volume, the papers do develop many of the themes he espoused.

Whatever the other differences between traditional British prehistorians, all claimed archaeology as an historical discipline. 'Archaeology is in fact a branch of historical study' (Piggott 1959, p. 1). 'Prehistory is . . . fundamentally historical in the sense that it deals with time as a main dimension' (Clark 1939, p. 26). In both these quotations archaeology is referred to as historical simply because it is concerned with the past. Daniel, however, gave additional reasons why prehistory should be viewed as part of history (1962, p. 131). Prehistory suffers from all the problems found in historical method – the difficulty of evaluating evidence, the inability of writing without some form of bias, and the changing views of the past as the ideas and preconceptions of prehistorians alter.

But the term 'historical' can be used to refer to more than the study of the past or the subjective assessment of documents. Prehistoric archaeology and history are idiographic studies which provide material for generalisation about man (Radcliffe-Brown 1952). Historical explanation describes an institution in a society as the end result of a sequence of events forming a causal chain. Of course, generalisations are used in this type of explanation, but the particular and novel structure of the cultural context is emphasised (Trigger 1980). Within such a viewpoint there is no absolute dependence on cross-cultural generalisations and laws, and Childe did not see archaeological inference as a deductive process.

Childe was wary of the use of cross-cultural laws and he rarely referred to ethnographic generalisations. Daniel (1962, p. 134) also doubted the possibility of identifying immutable laws concerning man, his culture and society and he denied the deterministic use of ethnographic data. Indeed the only traditional British prehistorian who has frequently used ethnographic data, Grahame Clark, is the one scholar who has accepted most readily the functionalist stance and has referred to cross-cultural laws of adaptation and selection.

If archaeology was to be accepted as being concerned with historical explanation, the viewpoint of most traditional archaeologists that cross-cultural ethnographic correlations should be used with caution was correct. But ethnographic analogies could be used if the relevant context for the comparison could be specified. Childe did use ethnographic analogies when he thought that the total context was comparable (Trigger 1980, p. 66) and in his later writings he emphasised the importance of close links between archaeology and ethnography. But the general paucity of detailed studies of particular ethnographic contexts severely hampered the development of historical explanation by traditional prehistoric archaeologists. There were few analogies and little general theory concerning the use of material symbols in social action and within different ideologies. It will be possible to reuse the traditional definition of archaeology and prehistory as history if contextual ethnoarchaeology continues to expand and if a general theory of practice is further developed. The use of analogies associated with an emphasis on a general understanding of the nature of the links between structure, symbolism and action allows the idiographic aspect of historical explanation to be retained, in line with the viewpoints of traditional archaeologists, without accepting the existence of immutable behavioural, ecological or functional laws.

There is some evidence that the contextual and cultural archaeology proposed here and some traditional British prehistorians have a common direction, as least in comparison with the deterministic functional laws and positivism of much of the New Archaeology. But traditional prehistorians such as Childe found difficulty in pursuing their aims, partly because the careful collection of large amounts of primary archaeological data and the resolution of chronological issues had only just begun. But their work was also hampered by the lack of an adequate theory of social practice wherein the role of material culture in the relation between structure, belief and action could be described. In pulling archaeology 'back into line', it is necessary greatly to expand, alter and develop the earlier approaches.

Conclusion

The theory discussed in this chapter and in this book is reactionary in that it accepts that culture is not man's extrasomatic means of adaptation but that it is meaningfully constituted. A contextual or cultural archaeology is also reactionary in that it sees archaeology as an historical discipline. Man's actions and his intelligent adaptation must be understood as historically and contextually specific, and the uniqueness of cultural forms must be explained. It is only by accepting the historical and cultural nature of their data that archaeologists can contribute positively to anthropology, the generalising study of man. The papers in this volume also react against the rigid logico-deductive method that has become characteristic of much New Archaeology. Explanation is here not equated solely with the discovery of predictable law-like relationships but with the interpretation of generative principles and their coordination within relevant cultural contexts.

In this chapter I have attempted to demonstrate that archaeology could profitably explore the notion that the severe and absolute rejection by some New Archaeologists of many traditional emphases hampered the development of a mature discipline. In particular, the dichotomies set up by Binford and various of his associates between culture and function, norm and adaptation, history and process, altogether impeded an adequate understanding of the very aim of their enquiry — social and economic adaptation and change. I have tried to show that the New Archaeology can be extended by a reconsideration of the issues outlined by traditional and historical archaeologists, and that culture, ideology and structure must be examined as central concerns.

This book outlines some avenues of exploration, but it would be incorrect to suggest that a single viewpoint is here espoused or that we have got very far along the road. There are many differences of opinion concerning, for example, the nature of ideology, the degree of determinacy in social change, the types of structure that should be analysed, and the value of any reference to structuralism. There is disagreement about epistemology and about whether positivist approaches should be used. But the variety of different views indicates the importance and breadth of the questions being asked by the authors in this volume and by the Cambridge seminar. While little more than a beginning has been made in answering the questions, the fact that they have been raised at a theoretical level is encouraging for the development of archaeology as a discipline integrated within the social sciences.

In the remaining chapters in this first part, theoretical issues are further explored. Miller (chapter 2) examines the primary and fundamental proposition that material culture is organised by processes of human categorisation. The articulation of generative principles in the representation and reproduction of society is discussed by Tilley in chapter 3. Tilley develops further the concerns with the individual and his role in social change, and with ideology, that have been introduced here. As in structuralism, it is necessary to posit relationships that are not directly observable. The epistemology of the New Archaeology is, paradoxically, a hindrance to the development of a scientific archaeology as Wylie demonstrates in chapter 4. The scientific enterprise may involve making hypotheses beyond observed phenomena.

But, in addition to the general theory and the epistemology it is necessary to build models that can be applied in a rigorous archaeology. Because so little is known of the generative principles used in the production of material residues, of the relationships between material culture and ideology, of the discursive and non-discursive dimensions of material symbolisation, or of the ways by which material culture is structured within and yet structures daily prac-

tices, the main response to the new questions has naturally been to turn to ethnoarchaeology. It is desired to develop a theory of practice in which culture and function are integrated and which provides analogies and models which are usable in archaeology. Information must be provided which allows the testing of structural analogies in that a large amount of different types of archaeological data (economic, settlement, burial, pottery decoration, refuse, etc.) can be seen as being meaningfully constructed in relation to each other within each cultural context as part of social processes. The chapters in the second part of this book describe cultural studies in modern societies which aim to examine the use of material items within social strategies.

In the final part of the book archaeological studies are presented which examine the structure and use of material items and patterned residues within social change. They show the potential contribution that archaeology could make, as an historical discipline, to an understanding of the manipulation of cultural forms within social strategies. Archaeology can be defined as a distinct discipline both in terms of its concern with the material world constructed by man and in terms of the long periods of time to which it has access. A symbolic and structural archaeology investigates both these components and thus realises the full strength of archaeology as an independent discipline, contributing to and being well-integrated into the social sciences. Our concern must be with cultural studies, today and in the past.

References

Allen, W.L. & Richardson, J.B. (1971) 'The reconstruction of kinship from archaeological data: the concepts, the method, and the feasibility', *American Antiquity* 36: 41–53

Ardener, E. (1978) 'Some outstanding problems in the analysis of events' in E. Schwimmer (ed.) *The Yearbook of Symbolic Anthropology* 1, Hurst, London

Barth, F. (1975) *Ritual and Knowledge among the Baktaman of New Guinea*, Universitetsforlaget, Oslo

Binford, L.R. (1965) 'Archaeological systematics and the study of cultural process', *American Antiquity* 31: 203–10

Binford, L.R. (1972) *An Archaeological Perspective*, Seminar Press, New York

Binford, L.R. (1977) 'General introduction' in L.R. Binford (ed.) *For Theory Building in Archaeology*, Academic Press, New York

Binford, L.R. (1978a) *Nunamiut Ethnoarchaeology*, Academic Press, New York

Binford, L.R. (1978b) 'Dimensional analysis of behaviour and site structure: learning from an Eskimo hunting stand', *American Antiquity* 43: 330–61

Bourdieu, P. (1977) *Outline of a Theory of Practice*, Cambridge University Press, Cambridge

Carneiro, R. (1968) 'Cultural adaptation' in D. Sells (ed.) *International Encyclopaedia of the Social Sciences* 3: 551–4

Childe, V.G. (1935) 'Changing aims and methods in prehistory', *Proceedings of the Prehistoric Society* 1: 1–15

Childe, V.G. (1936) *Man Makes Himself*, Collins, London

Childe, V.G. (1949) *Social Worlds of Knowledge*, Oxford University Press, Oxford

Clark, J.G.D. (1939) *Archaeology and Society*, Methuen, London

Clark, J.G.D. (1975) *The Earlier Stone Age Settlement of Scandinavia*, Cambridge University Press, Cambridge

Clarke, D.L. (1968) *Analytical Archaeology*, Methuen, London

Clarke, D.L. (1972) 'A provisional model of an Iron Age society and its settlement system' in D.L. Clarke (ed.) *Models in Archaeology*, Methuen, London

Clarke, D.L. (1973) 'Archaeology: the loss of innocence', *Antiquity* 47: 6–18

Conkey, M. (1977) 'Context, structure and efficacy in Palaeolithic art and design', Paper presented at the Burg Wartenstein Symposium, 74

Daniel, G.E. (1962) *The Idea of Prehistory*, Penguin, Harmondsworth

Deetz, J. (1967) *Invitation to Archaeology*, Natural History Press, New York

Deetz, J. (1968) 'The inference of residence and descent rules from archaeological data' in S.R. Binford & L.R. Binford (eds.) *New Perspectives in Archaeology*, Aldine, Chicago

Deetz, J. (1977) *In Small Things Forgotten*, Anchor Books, New York

Doran, J. (1970) 'Systems theory, computer simulations and archaeology', *World Archaeology* 1: 289–98

Ember, M. (1973) 'An archaeological indicator of matrilocal versus patrilocal residence', *American Antiquity* 38: 177–82

Ferguson, L. (ed.) (1977) *Historical Archaeology and the Importance of Material Things*, Society for Historical Archaeology, Special Series Publication, 2

Flannery, K.V. (1972) 'The cultural evolution of civilisations', *Annual Review of Ecology and Systematics* 3: 399–426

Flannery, K.V. (1973) 'Archaeology with a capital S' in C. Redman (ed.) *Research and Theory in Current Archaeology*, Wiley, New York

Flannery, K.V. & Marcus, J. (1976) 'Formative Oaxaca and the Zapotec Cosmos', *American Scientist* 64: 374–83

Fletcher, R. (1977a) 'Settlement studies (micro and semi-micro)' in D.L. Clarke (ed.) *Spatial Archaeology*, Academic Press, New York

Fletcher, R. (1977b) 'Alternatives and differences' in M. Spriggs (ed.) *Archaeology and Anthropology*, B.A.R. Supplementary Series 19, Oxford

Frankfort, H. (1951) *The Birth of Civilisation in the Near East*, Ernest Benn, London

Friedman, J. & Rowlands, M. (eds.) (1977) *The Evolution of Social Systems*, Duckworth, London

Fritz, J.M. (1978) 'Paleopsychology today: ideational systems and human adaptation in prehistory' in C. Redman *et al.* (eds.) *Social Archaeology Beyond Dating and Subsistence*, Academic Press, New York

Fritz, J.M. & Plog, F.T. (1970) 'The nature of archaeological explanation', *American Antiquity* 35: 405–12

Giddens, A. (1979) *Central Problems in Social Theory*, Macmillan Press, London

Gifford, D.P. (1978) 'Ethnoarchaeological observations of natural processes affecting cultural materials' in R.A. Gould (ed.) *Explorations in Ethnoarchaeology*, University of New Mexico Press, Albuquerque

Glassie, H. (1975) *Folk Housing in Middle Virginia: a Structural Analysis of Historical Artifacts*, University of Tennessee Press, Knoxville

Godelier, M. (1977) *Perspectives in Marxist Anthropology*, Cambridge University Press, Cambridge

Gould, R. (1980) *Living Archaeology*, Cambridge University Press, Cambridge

Harstrup, K. (1978) 'The post-structuralist position of social anthropology' in E. Schwimmer (ed.) *The Yearbook of Symbolic Anthropology* 1, Hurst, London

Hawkes, C. (1954) 'Archaeological theory and method: some suggestions from the Old World', *American Anthropologist* 56: 155–68

Hill, J.N. (1970) *Broken K Pueblo: Prehistoric Social Organisation in the American Southwest*, Anthropological Papers of the University of Arizona 18

Hill, J.N. (1971) 'Report on a seminar on the explanation of prehistoric organisational change', *Current Anthropology* 12: 406–8

Hill, J.N. (ed.) (1977) *The Explanation of Prehistoric Change*, University of New Mexico Press, Albuquerque

Hill, J.N. & Gunn, J. (eds.) (1977) *The Individual in Prehistory*, Academic Press, New York

Hillier, B., Leaman, A., Stansall, P. & Bedford, M. (1976) 'Space syntax', *Environment and Planning B* 3: 147–85

Hodder, I.R. (1979) 'Social and economic stress and material culture patterning', *American Antiquity* 44: 446–54

Hodder, I.R. (1981) 'Towards a mature archaeology' in I. Hodder, G. Isaac & N. Hammond (eds.) *Pattern of the Past*, Cambridge University Press, Cambridge

Hodder, I.R. (1982a) *Symbols in Action*, Cambridge University Press, Cambridge

Hodder, I.R. (1982b) 'The identification and interpretation of ranking in prehistory: a contextual perspective' in C. Renfrew & S. Shennan (eds.) *Ranking, Resource and Exchange*, Cambridge University Press, Cambridge

Hodder, I.R. & Lane, P. (in preparation) 'Exchange and reduction' in T. Earle & J. Ericson (eds.) *New Approaches to Exchange Studies in Prehistory*

Hymes, D. (1970) 'Comments on Analytical Archaeology', *Norwegian Archaeological Review* 3: 16–21

Isbell, W.H. (1976) 'Cosmological order expressed in prehistoric ceremonial centres', Paper given in Andean Symbolism Symposium Part 1: Space, time and mythology, International Congress of Americanists, Paris

Leach, E. (1973a) 'Concluding address' in C. Renfrew (ed.) *The Explanation of Culture Change*, Duckworth, London

Leach, E. (1973b) 'Structuralism in social anthropology' in D. Robey (ed.) *Structuralism: an Introduction*, Clarendon Press, Oxford

Leach, E. (1977) 'A view from the bridge' in M. Spriggs (ed.) *Archaeology and Anthropology*, B.A.R. Supplementary Series 19, Oxford

Leach, E. (1978) 'Does space syntax really "constitute the social" ' in D. Green, C. Haselgrove & M. Spriggs (eds.) *Social Organisation and Settlement*, B.A.R. 47, Oxford

Leone, M.P. (1977) 'The new Mormon temple in Washington D.C.' in L. Ferguson (ed.) *Historical Archaeology and the Importance of Material Things*, Society for Historical Archaeology, Special Series Publication 2

Leone, M.P. (1978) 'Time in American archaeology' in C. Redman *et al.* (eds.) *Social Archaeology Beyond Subsistence and Dating*, Academic Press, New York

Leroi-Gourhan, A. (1965) *Préhistoire de l'Art Occidental*, Mazenod, Paris

Lévi-Strauss, C. (1968) *Structural Anthropology*, Allen Lane, London

Longacre, W. (1970) 'Archaeology as anthropology', Anthropological Papers of the University of Arizona, 17, Tucson

Marshak, A. (1977) 'The meander as a system: the analysis and recognition of iconographic units in upper Palaeolithic compositions' in P.J. Ucko (ed.) *Form in Indigenous Art*, Duckworth, London

Martins, H. (1974) 'Time and theory in sociology' in J. Rex (ed.) *Approaches to Sociology*, London

Muller, J. (1977) 'Individual variation in art styles' in J. Hill & J. Gunn (eds.) *The Individual in Prehistory*, Academic Press, New York

Pettit, P. (1975) *The Concept of Structuralism: a Critical Analysis*, Gill and Macmillan, Dublin

Phillips, P. (1971) 'Attribute analysis and social structure of Chassey – Cortaillod – Lagozza populations', *Man* 6: 341–52

Piaget, J. (1971) *Structuralism*, Routledge and Kegan Paul, London

Piaget, J. (1972) *The Principles of Genetic Epistemology*, Routledge and Kegan Paul, London

Piggott, S. (1959) *Approach to Archaeology*, McGraw Hill, Harvard

Plog, F.T. (1975) 'Systems theory in archaeological research', *Annual Review of Anthropology* 4: 207–24

Radcliffe-Brown, A.R. (1952) *Structure and Function in Primitive Society*, Cohen and West, London

Renfrew, C. (1969) 'Trade and culture process in European pre-history', *Current Anthropology* 10: 151–69

Renfrew, C. (1972) *The Emergence of Civilisation*, Methuen, London

Renfrew, C. (1973) *Social Archaeology*, Southampton University Press, Southampton

Sahlins, M. (1976) *Culture and Practical Reason*, University of Chicago Press, Chicago

Salmon, M.H. (1978) 'What can systems theory do for archaeology?', *American Antiquity* 43: 174–83

Schiffer, M.B. (1976) *Behavioural Archaeology*, Academic Press, New York

Stanislawski, M.B. (1973) 'Review of *Archaeology as anthropology: a case study* by W.A. Longacre', *American Antiquity* 38: 117–22

Thomas, D.H. (1974) *Predicting the Past*, Holt, Rinehart and Winston, New York

Trigger, B. (1980) *Gordon Childe: Revolutions in Archaeology*, Thames and Hudson, London

Velde, P. Van de (1980) *Elsloo and Hienheim: Bandkeramik Social Structure*, Analecta Praehistorica Leidensia 12

Washburn, D.K. (1978) 'A symmetry classification of Pueblo ceramic designs' in P. Grebinger (ed.) *Discovering Past Behaviour*, Academic Press, New York

Watson, P.J., Leblanc, S.A. & Redman, C.L. (1971) *Explanation in Archaeology: an Explicitly Scientific Approach*, Columbia University Press, London

Wobst, H.M. (1977) 'Stylistic behaviour and information exchange', *University of Michigan Museum of Anthropology, Anthropological Paper* 61: 317–42

Yellen, J. (1977) *Archaeological Approaches to the Present*, Academic Press, New York

Chapter 2

**Artefacts as products
of human categorisation
processes**
D. Miller

Some aspects of the debate over the primary contention that the world is organised by people into sets of categories are introduced. The material world is produced as a series of ordered relationships using principles such as hierarchy and contrast. There has been considerable work in philosophy, psychology, linguistics and social anthropology on meaning and categorisation and the limitations and value to archaeology of studies in these different disciplines are assessed. For example, the structuralism of Lévi-Strauss, generative or transformational grammars and componential analysis are considered. The problem associated with these approaches concerns the relationship between form or structure and the social context in which it is generated. Studies which link categorisation to pragmatics are described, and there is a suggestion that we deal with the 'fuzziness' of categories directly, rather than treating categories as discrete groups.

Introduction
This paper is a discussion of the proposition that 'material culture sets reflect the organisational principles of human categorisation processes, and that it is through the understanding of such processes that we may best be able to interpret changes in material culture sets over time'. 'Material culture sets' refers to pottery, field systems, temple architecture or indeed anything in the archaeological record that we can interpret as being the result of human productive processes. The term 'sets' means that we are not concerned with individual forms but always with series of forms that share attributes common to the series as a whole, while a further

group of attributes discriminate between the members of the series and give them definition or 'meaning'.

The organisation that results in such patterning is the process of categorisation. This may take many forms, including subtractive strategies in which a recognisable stone tool is formed by the removal of parts of an amorphous pebble or block. It may be additive, building up complex shapes from relatively homogeneous clays, in pottery production, and it may be selective as in the choice of 'edible' or domesticated forms from the range of plants and animals in the environment. In all these cases, natural substances are being transformed into cultural categories, and as such they can be studied as processes of expression which carry meaning.

These terms 'expression', 'meaning' and 'categorisation' have been extensively studied in philosophy and psychology, but the overwhelming concentration of effort has been on linguistic expression and semantic categories. Anthropologists have studied social behaviour as systems of meaning, but there has been comparatively little attention given to material forms. This may seem surprising, when we consider that material objects are a concrete lasting form of human categorisation, that provides not only a fundamental medium of expression but also, to a substantial extent, forms the very environment in which we live. There are therefore substantial rewards in any demonstrable validation of our proposition. We might develop a theory and methodology that could explain the detailed variability in the artefactual record in terms of those processes that created it. These remain quite beyond the explanatory powers of even the most extravagant form of functionalism. A further reward would be the emergence of a model of categorisation processes as an alternative to that emanating from linguistic studies, and there is also the prospect of using artefacts to study the evolution of cognitive processes if the expected patterns fail to operate as we explore back into the early prehistoric record.

Most studies of categorisation tend to be predicated at least in some form on the philosophical position outlined by Kant (1934, 1953). Kant demonstrated that there must be essential dimensions of our knowledge of the world that are transcendental, that is prior to experience, but which are necessary preconditions for experience to take place. These include fundamental dimensions such as space and time. Commonly, studies of categorisation posit underlying mechanisms which are not in themselves observable but which generate through transformational processes the actual observable categories. The complexity of the processes and the relationships that are postulated mean that some of the more rigid epistemological principles of validation that have been proposed by archaeologists may be inappropriate, and a shift is required in these principles if we are to obtain more useful validatory procedures (Miller, forthcoming; Wylie, chapter 4).

Still more important than the problem of validation procedures is the model of man and rationality implied in current archaeological research and its inadequacy for the problems that will be discussed. The emphasis on external ecological factors as causative, with man and society reduced to passive respondents reacting to these external stimuli, suggests a behaviourist model. In contrast to this, we can examine the work of Jean Piaget who is responsible for the most elaborate and systematic attempt to provide candidates for human categorisation processes. In his genetic epistemology (Piaget 1971, 1972; Turner 1973) Piaget adopts an interactionist view of man, who is seen to develop categorisation processes through his active searching out and construction of his world. A stimulus only becomes constituted through interaction, which may be characterised by two processes: assimilation and accommodation. Assimilation is the 'inward directed tendency of a structure to draw environmental events towards itself', while accommodation is 'an organism's outward tendency of the inner structure to adapt itself to a particular environmental event' (Furth 1969, p. 14). Using a category as an example, we might suggest that an object that looks a bit like a table might be interpreted as such with no profound effect, but if enough odd-looking objects, which we recognise as serving the same purpose as tables, but which were not well-integrated into our previous category of table, enter our experience, then our category of table might shift accordingly to accommodate them.

One archaeologist has attempted to utilise directly Piagetian processes in studies of artefacts. Wynn (1977)

employed those processes that deal with spatial organisation, and attempted to examine the minimum competence in terms of these processes that would have been demanded by the manufacture of various Palaeolithic stone tools, in order to argue for the early evolution of several of Piaget's more complex processes. There are a number of critiques of Piaget's more specific propositions (e.g. Donaldson 1978; Seigel & Brainard 1978), but his general model of interaction may stand for our understanding of man in his generation of culture.

If we follow Piaget's argument that categorisation processes are developed in interaction with the world, then it seems reasonable that these processes should in some way reflect the organisational principles that characterise the external world itself. The extreme form of this view was that taken by the logical-positivists that the order of the world could indeed be known through those axiomatic systems of logic and mathematics by which an ideal descriptive language could be constructed. This assumption, and the strong form of empiricism that accompanied it, are not generally accepted today. On a more prosaic level, however, there are a number of attempts to demonstrate 'salience' or some necessary relationship between the order we create and that which we find. Some of the strongest examples arise from the proposition of a physiological basis for categories such as colours (Berlin & Kay 1969; Bornstein 1975; Miller & Johnson-Laird 1976). Berlin and others concerned with the nature of folk taxonomies point out the relationship between these and the classifications derived from botanists and zoologists (Berlin 1978), while Rosch proposes a more general relation to the correlational structure of the real world (1976). In contrast to these writers are the propositions of Leach (1976) and Sahlins (1976) who argue that while the external world is not an undivided or random configuration and that physiological salience may be demonstrated in certain areas, these factors do not determine how the world is divided up in human categorisation, which may be quite arbitrary with respect to them.

Both sides of this debate would agree, however, that the order in the natural world is a vital model for the construction of cultural order. Whilst Durkheim and Mauss (1963) argue the importance of basic social divisions as a model for classification in general, Lévi-Strauss provides many examples of the use of natural classes such as animals for symbolising social categories, as in totemism (1964). In chapter 12 Shanks and Tilley discuss in detail the use of another important natural model — the human body — in the creation of cultural order. These studies suggest that a consideration of categorisation processes has to include not only the material which is subject to that order, but also the structure of the relationships by which these appear to be ordered and their possible impact upon the process of categorisation itself. The ontological problems faced by such a proposal will, however, be obvious.

In the review of approaches to categorisation that follows, extensive use is made of linguistic and psychological models. Both of these are subject to criticism. Gardin (1965) and Hymes (1969) have pointed out some of the problems of a too literal interpretation and application of linguistic models to archaeological data. Language is a very particular medium, whose processes of articulation and patterns of formulation work at a relatively autonomous level, although the ways in which these rules relate to the world that language in turn refers to have been studied in semantics. While language is bound to provide a powerful analogy for the processes of categorisation in production, being a prime example of a categorisation process, the precise model has to be worked out through the analysis of the material objects themselves. In particular, just as linguists are finding that questions of pragmatics must be dealt with in order to understand 'everyday' language (Bar-Hillel 1970), so some equivalent to pragmatics must play an important part in any applications of these ideas to material artefacts. Ideally, the notion of a category itself should incorporate the flexibility necessitated by a consideration of context.

The proper use of psychological models depends upon making clear that such models need not necessitate any of the several reductionisms of which they are commonly accused. The examples given here are derived from scholarly work in cognitive science and are quite unrelated to the rather vague reductions to needs, drives and other vulgarised versions of psychoanalysis that have sometimes been taken as representing psychology (e.g. Wallace 1971). Secondly, we must ensure that such models relate to social processes and the products of society and do not remain at the individualist level in which much psychological writing is couched. This depends on a clear notion of the relationship between social convention and its individual interpretation, and the methods to be described may provide a systematic basis for the evaluation of this relationship. Thirdly, such models do not depend on relating material variability either to an emic level (that which can be verbally expressed) or a conscious level (that of which the subject is aware). As an example, if we were to study the detailed variability in sherry bottles, we would agree that individuals had no problem in recognising the characteristic shape, but the subtleties of curve and line that act to differentiate these from other bottles are extremely hard to describe in verbal form and do not impinge on conscious knowledge. Finally, although I will use terms such as intention and strategy, these should not be interpreted as being reducible entirely to purposive explanations. Popper's model of 'world three' (1972, pp. 106–53), which notes the autonomy of the creations of man with respect to his intentions in creating them, is an important counter to any such reductionism and plays a major part in any account of the development of these creations (Steadman 1979).

Structuralism and semiotics

The most influential attempt to provide a theory of the nature of categorisation that might apply to non-linguistic phenomena is that of structuralism and, in particular,

semiotic studies. These approaches are derived from Saussure's study of linguistics (1959) and the four essential dichotomies which he proposed. The first of these dichotomies, between 'substance' and 'form', is that which provides the basis for Leach and Sahlins' stance stated above, that the natural world provides only the material for categorisation and does not determine the way in which it is divided up. One society may have a single term for snow, but will discriminate various varieties of a type of rock, while in another these rock forms are generalised in a single term, although there are several terms for snow. In material production, one society may build sixteen kinds of structure for different activities such as temples and cooking-huts, while another society may perform the same range of activities in a single structural form. The essential point is that no object has an intrinsic meaning; its meaning depends upon the place it is assigned within this dividing up and active creation of the material world.

The second dichotomy between 'syntagmatic' and 'paradigmatic' forms of articulation provides a basis for the organisation of objects into meaningful patterns using sequential and alternate groupings. Thus we might divide up a pot into zones, and then select from a series of alternative appropriate motifs the filling of each zone (e.g. Clarke 1970; Hardin 1970), or we might divide a house into a series of rooms, such as lounge and kitchen, and then decide whether to have armchairs or beanbags in the lounge.

The third dichotomy is between 'langue', or the formal rules that allow expression to take place, and 'parole', the examples of the actual products of these rules. A possible analogy might be between the competence of a manufacturer of stone tools, in terms of his knowledge of the materials, his ability and the principles for the production of the conventional forms, as compared to the actual products of his hand. In linguistics, Chomsky's grammars (1957) as opposed to the products of everyday speech provide a clearer example. The final dichotomy is between 'synchronic' and 'diachronic' investigation. The etymology of a word does not provide us with its contemporary meaning, just as it is the turkey's relationship to Christmas rather than its origin and domestication that provides the key to its present significance.

All these dichotomies were presented by Saussure for the study of linguistics, but I have given examples using objects to illustrate how in semiotics these principles have been extended to anything that can be said to carry meaning. Eco provides examples from a range of fields through stories to architecture, that have received analysis as meaningful sets or codes (1977). It is through social convention that something comes to stand for something else. A stone that has the attribute red may acquire the attribute sacred if red is in a relationship of evocation with sacred. There is said to be a triangle of signification between a concept, a symbol or representation of that concept and the referent or object. Discussion of these relationships can, however, easily become highly convoluted and there is not even agreement on the terms that should be used (Lyons 1977, pp. 95–119 and

175—245). We can appreciate the reason for such complexity if we consider a term like dragon that has meaning but no apparent reference, or the use of symbols in dreams, or the question of the distinction between relationships that have some natural basis such as smoke standing for fire, called a sign or indexical link, and purely arbitrary relationships known as symbols (Leach 1976; Pierce 1931—58). In modern studies by French scholars, these ideas have become extended into re-examinations of Freud (Lacan 1979), the history of the construction of knowledge (Foucault 1970) and relativism (Derrida 1973) and a general concern with the ways by which relations of power and institutional thought are expressed.

It may, therefore, be more useful to archaeologists if we restrict the implications of structuralist thought to its practice as anthropological methodology and interpretation. Some studies have followed Saussure fairly closely in using syntagmatic and paradigmatic modes of articulation. Humphrey applies these to the study of Mongolian spirit figures (1971) which are produced through different combinations of elements that may be meaningful in themselves. Leroi-Gourhan's analysis of Palaeolithic cave paintings depends on the division of the caves into areas and subsequent identification of alternative animals that can be used to fill them (1968).

If Saussure exemplifies the derivation of structuralist thought in linguistics, it is Lévi-Strauss who has come to exemplify its practice in anthropology. Lévi-Strauss has been concerned with the forms of articulation and principles of organisation which generate cultural patterning, but he has insisted that in itself such work should be characterised as formalism, and should be contrasted with structuralism which includes a consideration of the social context in which such patterns are generated and of their social implications (1977, pp. 115—45). This difference can be illustrated in approaches to spatial patterning. Dickens' analysis of historical house plans (1977) and the first half of Hillier *et al.*'s elaborate examination of 'space syntax' (1976) would count as examples of formal approaches, but where, as in the second half of the 'space syntax' paper, there is a concern for the social basis for the selection of different patterns, we have the emergence of a structuralist approach. Ideally, these should be closely integrated as in Turner's analysis of body design (1969) or Munn's analysis of Walbiri iconography (1973). Symmetry has been a favourite medium of articulation of the formal and social in the study of design both by ethnographers concerned with northwest coastal American Indian art (Holm 1965; Lévi-Strauss 1963; Vastakos 1978), and by archaeologists (Shepard 1956; Washburn 1978; Zaslow & Dittert 1977).

Lévi-Strauss has also emphasised the way in which the relationship between a pattern and its expression in another medium or its use as social expression may not be direct but accomplished through various transformational processes. These ideas have recently been used for an elaborate material culture study using a group of masks (1975). For example, a mask with bulbous eyes and sunken cheeks is taken as the inverse of one with sunken eyes and blown cheeks. From the interest in the use of contrast and the division between categories has come a further set of studies that examine the space created between categories and the ambiguous nature of objects that do not easily fit within the resultant groups. Douglas' work on dirt (1966) and Leach on terms of abuse (1964) illustrate these approaches, while Braithwaite applies them to material objects (chapter 8).

Notwithstanding Lévi-Strauss' comments, the examples of his own work, where elaborate analyses of formal patterns and transformation have been reduced to relatively minor contradictions within social relations, have resulted in his studies being criticised as highly formalist. It has become evident that there is a tremendous emphasis on systems of art and ritual. These are areas that are relatively autonomous, being held to comment at a 'higher' level on the more mundane aspects of society, and therefore more amenable to formal analysis. Both Bourdieu (1977) and Tyler (1978) provide major critiques of this formalist tendency, and the assumption that relations of meaning can be adequately studied outside of the consideration of pragmatics. This is a crucial point for those wishing to use such an approach in the study of artefacts.

A second critique of concern to archaeologists stems from the fourth of Saussure's dichotomies, that between synchrony and diachrony. Some structuralist studies have been concerned with processes of change. Munn (1973) and Humphrey (1971) both investigate the way in which a system of meaningful symbols may generate and also constrain the acceptance of new forms. Using archaeological data, Wheatley has undertaken an extensive study of the possibility that there is a stage of 'ceremonial centre' embedded in the process of urban genesis (1971). Most theoretical treatments of change have attempted to move beyond the 'classic' form of structural studies and attempted to give process a more central position in studies of categorisation. Examples include Ardener's post-structuralism (1971, 1978), Piaget (1968) or Giddens' notion of structuration (1979). These would stress the way material production changes the context within which it takes place as well as reflecting it.

In their more extensive applications in anthropology, the original insights that structuralist thought provided may have become somewhat overstretched. We find ever more deft and elegant demonstrations that one area of social expression appears to act as a metaphor for another, through ever more complex systems of transformations. The criterion for judging the results has become almost their aesthetic value, and analyses appear to suggest that almost any two aspects of society can be so related. In this case the result would have been anticipated in various studies that emerged in psychology, but are most often used today in marketing research. These approaches include Osgood's semantic differential testing (1957) and Kelly's grids (Bannister & Fransella 1971). By these methods it can be shown how if we map the attitude of an individual along certain dimensions, we can predict the associations that virtually any other mode of expression would have for him/her. Thus, we might find that there is a relation between those colours a person takes to be strong or weak and their political affiliation. These studies are less well-known and less theoretically developed than structuralist approaches, but if archaeologists wish to see how the material objects of our own societies form patterns of associative meaning, then the use by marketing researchers of these methods provides numerous examples.

Most of the approaches outlined in this section have been used by archaeologists, and a reading of structuralist literature is unlikely to leave unchanged our understanding of the nature of material objects, and the factors that may be responsible for their patterning. The tendency to remain within formal systems of expression in the use of structuralism may, however, suggest that it has failed to develop a sufficiently clear and flexible notion of category, which must remain the essential first step in any systematic study of material objects as categorisation processes.

Alternative approaches to categorisation

The approach that in recent years has proved most effective for the study of linguistic organisation has also been highly specific to linguistic form and therefore may be problematic when translated into the analysis of other media of expression. Nevertheless, Chomsky's various grammars include a powerful analogy for material production and at least one possible technique. In its most developed form, transformational-generative grammar illustrates how human beings, using a relatively small set of rules and units, can build up a virtually infinite variety of new structures even at an early age. If it is the case that patterns of linguistic expression can best be understood by postulating the rules that generate them, it may be that material production might also be approached through the analysis of possible generative mechanisms. Unfortunately, it seems unlikely that the division within linguistics of syntax, semantics and pragmatics, which is in any case hard to maintain, would be at all plausible in the study of material forms, and the actual use of any such 'grammar' would probably be limited in archaeology and social anthropology to the study of formal systems such as designs. Attempts to use a transformational model are, however, already quite diverse in anthropology and archaeology, examples ranging from shell gorgets (Muller 1977) through wall decoration and pottery (Hodder 1982), to body designs (Faris 1972), with a recent extension to the manufacturing processes posited for pottery production (Krause 1978). In essence, these have been concerned to demonstrate that the generation of observed patterns may be summarised by the application of certain basic (usually space filling) rules to some fundamental units. These may then serve as a basis for more conventional archaeological study, such as the comparison between two areas in terms of the structural rules they hold in common instead of merely the comparison of the design attributes themselves.

Anthropological study has itself exerted a powerful influence in the development of formal methods in semantic analysis. Componential analysis was formulated in the 1950s by Lounsbury and Goodenough, but was dominant in the 1960s with compilations of its applications by Kimball and D'Andrade (1964), Hammel (1965) and Tyler (1969). Essentially, this approach and its near neighbour, folk taxonomy, utilise three main ideas: hierarchy, field and contrast. The principle of hierarchy provides for the relationship between a major area of the categorised world and some small section of it. One of the best areas for studying hierarchy is in the organic world. The studies of Berlin and his co-workers (Berlin *et al.* 1973; Berlin 1978) suggested that a series of distinctive levels might be identified cross-culturally, starting with a 'unique beginner', a term for all animate forms, down to varieties such as *western white pine*. In such a series, a higher term like *fish* is called superordinate to lower terms included within it, such as *perch* or *bream*, which are termed hyponyms of fish (Lyons 1977, pp. 317–35).

These levels of hierarchy in turn create fields which are defined by Lehrer (1974, p. 1) as 'A group of words closely related in meaning and often subsumed under a general term'. Lehrer also provides an elaborate examination of one such field, that of cooking terms. Within a field items contrast, so that the superordinate term *furniture* establishes the contrast between *chair* and *table*, the meaning of the term *table* being then at least in part defined by being that which is not a *chair*. In componential analysis the emphasis is on the dimensions which may establish these contrasts subdividing the field into their units. A favourite example is that of domestic animals, where the young may be discriminated from the old as calf from cow, or colt from horse, and the female from the male as cow from bull, or mare from stallion. We can then establish a matrix of terms in which gender and age are set against species. It then becomes apparent that these contrasts are not always employed, and we have no term in English for a female cat or a young rabbit. The goal was to establish those contrasts which were both sufficient and necessary to account for all the terms in a given field, and this led on to further questions as to the possible salience and cross-cultural validity of some of these dimensions of contrast.

These ideas influenced archaeology through a number of routes. The basic sets of patterns employed, such as keys and paradigms, have been incorporated by Dunnell (1971) and others in general approaches to classification studies. Arnold (1971) uses an emic analysis of this type to compare perceptual divisions potters make of their clays with mineralogical studies. The idea of determining the sufficient and necessary contrasts for generating a series of material forms would find parallels in older approaches such as that of Boas, who demonstrated how northwest coastal Indian art emphasised certain such attributes to promote recognition of the intended form. So the beaver was recognised by its long incisors, large round nose, scaly tail and stick held in its paws (1955). An equivalent is found in modern attempts by archaeologists using numerical taxonomy to identify the idiosyncratic features that differentiate otherwise formalised motifs, as in Roaf's work at Persepolis (1978). Saxe employed Goodenough's notion of role identification to suggest that items of grave furniture might, using componental analysis, be used to discriminate levels of social status (1973); finally a series of pottery might be seen as the recombination of certain basic units as suggested by De Boer and Lathrap in their presentation of Shipibo–Conibo ceramics (Kramer 1979, pp. 102–38).

Clearly, these ideas have been found useful by archaeologists, and the obvious links to approaches from semiotics reflect in part parallel influences and in part parallel conclusions. Since the 1960s, however, severe problems have emerged. As Keesing suggests (1972), the extensive use of componental analysis has revealed its potential and also its limitations. This approach relates to an idealised logical language, in which something either is or is not a member of a category. While suited to abstracted semantics, it ignores real variability both in words and in the things words refer to. The analysis provides a mould into which examples are fitted, but the challenge of variability is not fully met. Like the 'mental template', componental analysis thereby becomes a normative approach subsuming rather than explaining variability, and this problem is aggravated when dealing with material forms. Further, it does not fit the increasing evidence that psychologists have provided on category structure.

In opposition to the principles of formal logic that characterises the above approach is the tradition that stems in its modern form from the later work of the philosopher Wittgenstein. In his *Philosophical Investigations* (1958), Wittgenstein concentrated on the everyday use of language and showed its divergence from an abstracted ideal form. His best known examples come in passages 66–71 where he demonstrated the absence of any single attribute connecting all the items subsumed under the term 'game', and he goes on to deal with many of the implications for communication, experience and relativism that arise from this point. Attempts to deal with categories have run into the same problem in almost every discipline. Archaeologists will be familiar with Clarke's advocacy of polythetic sets in numerical taxonomy (1968, pp. 37–8). In mathematics and logic there has been increasing concern with what are known as 'fuzzy sets' and 'fuzzy set theory' (Zadeh 1965). The problem appears whenever one can argue that objects are not just members of a set but better or worse members. Lakoff (1973) illustrates this point in linguistic behaviour with what

he calls 'hedges' – phrases such as *A* is in some ways a *B* or is a sort of *B*.

Fortunately this point has been further developed using a very familiar set of data – pottery. The linguist Labov produced a series of vessel profiles with measured variance, such as a gradual increase in width as a ratio to height (1972). It was possible graphically to illustrate how the shift from cup to bowl occurs, when asking people to draw a line between all those shapes they would call one and those they would call the other. Obviously as a cup becomes wider it looks more like a bowl, until the point of shift is reached. Labov showed, further, how this shift can be altered by other factors such as the number of handles or whether the vessel contained mashed potato. Labov comments that 'in the world of experience all boundaries show some degree of vagueness, and any formal system which is useful for semantic description must allow us to record, or even measure, this property' (ibid., p. 342). It is this 'fuzziness' in categories that is met with whenever we attempt to apply our ideas to the investigation of social phenomena. This has been demonstrated in an analysis of the concept of function (G. Miller 1978) and, as the ethnomethodologists would point out, is true of the processes of analysis itself (Garfinkle 1967). In our everyday consideration of material objects we commonly consider them as better or worse examples of the type they represent.

This variability expressed in material categories may be related to various factors. Archaeologists have suggested that there is inevitably some variability produced by individual style (Hill & Gunn 1977). This is probably only a minor factor in observed variability. Other archaeologists have stressed the notion of function. Function in the form of some absolute externally generated constraint, as opposed to 'needs' that are based on social convention, is also unlikely to impinge very far upon observed variability, even in the ecologically most marginal areas. Rather, we might expect that as a category in its material form is expressed within a social and pragmatic context, itself highly differentiated, then observed variability may derive in large part from this contextual base. If this is the case, then we would expect that category variability would be systematically related to (though not necessarily directly reflective of) contextual variability. Kempton (1977) has attempted to use sets of drawings of pottery shapes to demonstrate this principle. His work shows that, in Mexico, categories can be shown to vary systematically between males and females or rural as against town dwellers. I have developed a method by which a computer draws systematically varying pottery profiles, and have been using these to study category variability in an Indian village.

The most sustained study of categories as sets of focal points with fuzzy boundaries is that by Rosch (1978). Her work amongst the Dani showed how the key factor in the formation and use of colour categories was their focal point.

This core region of a category has become known as a 'proto-type' which is 'just those members of a category which most reflect the redundancy structure of the category as a whole' (ibid., p. 36). Rosch used a series of tests such as recall and pairing experiments to demonstrate which items were most characteristic of a prototype on the basis that 'the better examples of a category should come closer to the core meaning of the superordinate term than the poorer examples' (ibid., p. 25). Her studies of the implied hierarchical organisation of categories lead her to propose a basic level as that which best compromises between generalisation and discrimination. Although most of Rosch's work was on lexical behaviour, it is of note that the basic level can be determined through perceptual features. Thus, in the field of *furniture*, that term generalises a group that perceptually contains little in common. Its hyponym 'chair' generalises a relatively coherent set while discriminating well against contrastive terms such as *table*. *Kitchen-chair*, a hyponym of *chair*, generalises a still more coherent set, but there is little that is perceptively distinctive about its features. *Chair* is therefore a basic level term. Rosch's ideas have been utilised in artificial intelligence programmes that are designed to replicate the kinds of everyday understanding of the external world that we employ, and with KRL (Bobrow & Winnograd 1977, 1979) we can follow through the implications of these organisational principles in dealing with semantic evocation and practical recognition in a variety of contexts.

The implications of these ideas for the organisation of material culture sets may be illustrated with reference to variability in our own society. Perhaps the most familiar set of containers to most archaeologists are those used to hold alcoholic beverages. An 'off-licence' may contain hundreds of varying shapes, all of which serve essentially the same function, that of storing liquids. An inspection of this material would reveal patterns in the variability that may be related both to bottles as a referential system standing for their contents, but also to their place as an autonomous system of meaning employing hierarchy, contrast and gradation. If we examined sherry bottles we might find one shape that was easily recognisable as that used by the best known brand or 'brand leader'. This might well be the bottle we would image if asked in the abstract to describe a sherry bottle. The shape might serve as a proto-type that has to be taken into consideration in the manufacture of other sherry bottles that will derive their meaning in part from their variation from this bottle. This variation might in turn relate to differentiation within the social context of consumption. We might suggest certain bottles as cheap as against expensive, classic as against modern, or we might even identify bottles as appealing to male as opposed to female. None of these associations are intrinsic to the shape, and all such dimensions of variance might be employed in the gradation of other bottles, say vermouth or claret, from their own prototypical forms.

Even this superficial inspection would appear to affirm our initial contention that material production reflects the organisational principles of human categorisation processes. Categorisation is seen to imply a relationship between formal organisational principles and pragmatic considerations. The processes of categorisation are realised through social strategies. Manufacturers are aware of and manipulate bottles as systems of meaning. 'Pomagne' is a cider whose foil-topped green bottle is a pun on champagne in a precise parallel to its name. Consumers are also concerned to manipulate this series in expressing attitude and status. Douglas and Isherwood (1980) provide many examples of the relationship between variability in goods and their use as modes of expression in contemporary society. In chapter 9 I develop this aspect of categorisation in more detail in order to demonstrate how the active manipulation of categories may affirm the second part of our initial proposition, which is that we can use our understanding of these processes to study change in material culture sets. The methodology is still being developed but already some of Rosch's ideas and the related 'golden section hypothesis' have been employed by Alan Tuohy to provide an alternative explanation for the patterning found by Leroi-Gourhan in his study of Palaeolithic cave art (Alan Tuohy, pers. comm.), while further work continues which uses pottery as an example of a material culture set. In chapter 3 Tilley examines theories which link social action and change to material forms.

Categorisation studies may be held to subsume rather than to oppose the notions of function and adaptation. The external ecological environment impinges through its interpretation and interaction with social beings. Adaptation becomes explanatory when the concept of the environment becomes understood as socially created rather than externally given (Steadman 1979). Function is not absolute but reflects the conventional division of needs and activities. 'Langue' and the rules of structural generation may be subject to large-scale generalisation. 'Parole' or evidence for the results of productive activity are clearly not, thereby rendering functionalist approaches as they stand incapable of explaining the variability of the archaeological record. Categorisation studies focus on the mechanisms that generate the detailed variability, the intrinsic 'fuzziness' that characterises material forms, and can thereby link 'langue' and 'parole' and provide explanations in a 'realist' mould (Miller, forthcoming). Categorisation processes mediate and organise the social construction of reality, and may be our best means for understanding and interpreting the remains of material production.

References

Ardener, E. (1971) 'Introductory essay: social anthropology and language' in E. Ardener (ed.) *Social Anthropology and Language*, Tavistock, London

Ardener, E. (1978) 'Some outstanding problems in the analysis of events' in E. Schwimmer (ed.) *The Yearbook of Symbolic Anthropology*, Hurst & Co., London

Arnold, E. (1971) 'Ethnominerology of Ticul, Yucatan potters; etics and emics', *American Antiquity* 36: 20–40

Bannister, D. & Fransella, F. (1971) *Inquiring Man*, Penguin, Harmondsworth

Bar-Hillel, Y. (1970) *Aspects of Language*, Magnes, Jerusalem

Berlin, B. (1978) 'Ethnobiological classification' in E. Rosch & B. Lloyd (eds.) *Cognition and Categorisation*, Lawrence Erlbaum, New Jersey

Berlin, B. & Kay, P. (1969) *Basic Colour Terms*, University of California Press, Berkeley

Berlin, B., Breedlove, D. & Raven, P. (1973) 'General principles of classification and nomenclature in folk biology', *American Anthropologist* 77: 214–42

Boas, F. (1955) *Primitive Art*, Dover, New York

Bobrow, D. & Winograd, T. (1977) 'An overview of KRL-O a knowledge representation language', *Cognitive Science* 1: 3–46

Bobrow, D. & Winograd, T. (1979) 'KRL: another perspective', *Cognitive Science* 3: 29–42

Bourdieu, P. (1977) *Outline of a Theory of Practice*, Cambridge University Press, Cambridge

Bornstein, M. (1975) 'The influence of visual perception on culture', *American Anthropologist* 77: 774–98

Chomsky, N. (1957) *Syntactic Structures*, Mouton, The Hague

Clarke, D. (1968) *Analytical Archaeology*, Methuen, London

Clarke, D. (1970) *Beaker Pottery of Great Britain and Ireland*, Cambridge University Press, Cambridge

Derrida, J. (1973) *Speech and Phenomena*, Northwestern University Press, Evanston

Dickens, P. (1977) 'An analysis of historical house-plans' in D. Clarke (ed.) *Spatial Archaeology*, Academic Press, London

Donaldson, M. (1978) *Children's Minds*, Fontana, London

Douglas, M. (1966) *Purity and Danger*, Routledge and Kegan Paul, London

Douglas, M. & Isherwood, B. (1980) *The World of Goods*, Penguin, Middlesex

Dunnell, R.C. (1971) *Systematics in Prehistory*, Collier-Macmillan, London

Durkheim, E. & Mauss, M. (1963) *Primitive Classification*, Allen and Unwin, London

Eco, U. (1977) *A Theory of Semiotics*, Macmillan, London

Faris, J. (1972) *Nuba Personal Art*, Duckworth, London

Foucault, M. (1970) *The Order of Things*, Tavistock, London

Furth, H. (1969) *Piaget and Knowledge*, Prentice Hall, London

Gardin, J.-C. (1965) 'On the possible use of componential analysis in archaeology' in E. Hammel *American Anthropologist* 6 part 2

Garfinkle, H. (1967) *Studies in Ethnomethodology*, Englewood Cliffs, New Jersey

Giddens, A. (1979) *Central Problems in Social Theory*, Macmillan, London

Hammel, E. (1965) 'Formal semantic analysis', *American Anthropologist* 67 part 2

Hardin, M. (1970) 'Design structure and social interaction: archaeological implications of an ethnographic analysis', *American Antiquity* 35: 3

Hill, J. & Gunn, J. (eds.) (1977) *The Individual in Prehistory*, Academic Press, New York

Hillier, B., Leaman, A., Stanhall, P. & Bedford M. (1976) 'Space syntax', *Environment and Planning B* 3: 147–85

Hodder, I. (1982) *Symbols in Action*, Cambridge University Press, Cambridge

Holm, B. (1965) *Northwest Coast Indian Art*, University of Washington Press, Washington

Humphrey, C. (1971) 'Some ideas of Saussure applied to Buryat magical drawings' in E. Ardener (ed.) *Social Anthropology and Language*, Tavistock, London

Hymes, D. (1969) 'Linguistic models in archaeology' in J.-C. Gardin (ed.) *Archaeologie et Calculateur*, C.N.R.S., Paris

Kant, I. (1934) *Critique of Pure Reason*, J.M. Dent, London

Kant, I. (1953) *Prolegomena*, Manchester University Press, Manchester

Keesing, R. (1972) 'The new ethnography and the new linguistics', *South-western Journal of Anthropology* 28: 219–32

Kempton, W. (1977) 'Grading of category membership in the folk classification of ceramics', University Microfilms, Michigan

Kimball Romney, A. & D'Andrade, R. (eds.) (1964) 'Transcultural studies in cognition', *American Anthropologist* 66 part 2

Kramer, C. (ed.) (1979) *Ethnoarchaeology*, University of New Mexico Press, Albuquerque

Krause, R. (1978) 'Towards a formal account of Bantu ceramics' in R. Dunnell & E. Hall (eds.) *Archaeological Essays in Honour of Irving B. Rouse*, Mouton, The Hague

Labov, W. (1972) *Sociolinguistic Patterns*, University of Pennsylvania Press, Philadelphia

Lacan, J. (1979) *The Four Fundamental Concepts of Psycho-Analysis*, Penguin, Middlesex

Lakoff, G. (1973) 'Hedges and meaning criteria' in R. McDavid & A. Druckert (eds.) *Lexicography in English*, Academy of Sciences, New York

Leach, E. (1964) 'Anthropological aspects of language: animal categories and verbal abuse' in E. Lennenberg (ed.) *New Directions in the Study of Language*, M.I.T. Press, Cambridge

Leach, E. (1976) *Culture and Communication*, Cambridge University Press, Cambridge

Lehrer, A. (1974) *Semantic Fields and Lexical Structures*, North Holland, Amsterdam

Leroi-Gourhan, A. (1968) 'The evolution of Palaeolithic art', *Scientific American*

Lévi-Strauss, C. (1963) *Structural Anthropology*, Allen Lane, London

Lévi-Strauss, C. (1964) *Totemism*, Merlin Press, London

Lévi-Strauss, C. (1975) *La Voie de Masques*, Edition Albert Skira, Geneva

Lévi-Strauss, C. (1977) *Structural Anthropology 2*, Allen Lane, London

Lyons, J. (1977) *Semantics Volume 1*, Cambridge University Press, Cambridge

Miller, D. (forthcoming) 'Explanation and social theory in archaeological practice' in C. Renfrew (ed.) *Explanation in Archaeology Revisited*, Academic Press, London

Miller, D. (ms) 'Material production as human categorisation'

Miller, G. (1978) 'Practical and lexical knowledge' in E. Rosch & B. Lloyd (eds.) *Cognition and Categorisation*, Lawrence Erlbaum and Press, New Jersey

Miller, G. & Johnson-Laird, P. (1976) *Language and Perception*, Cambridge University Press, Cambridge

Muller, J. (1977) 'Individual variation in art styles' in J. Hill & J. Gunn (eds.) *The Individual in Prehistory*, Academic Press, New York

Munn, N. (1973) *Walbiri Iconography*, Cornell University Press, Ithaca

Osgood, C., Suci, G. & Tannenbaum, P. (1957) *The Measurement of Meaning*, University of Illinois Press, Urbana

Piaget, J. (1968) *Structuralism*, Routledge and Kegan Paul, London

Piaget, J. (1971) *Biology and Knowledge*, Chicago University Press, Chicago

Piaget, J. (1972) *The Principles of Genetic Epistemology*, Routledge and Kegan Paul, London

Pierce, C. (1931–58) *Collected Papers*, Harvard University Press, Cambridge

Popper, K. (1972) *Objective Knowledge*, Oxford University Press, Oxford

Roaf, M. (1978) 'A mathematical analysis of the Persepolis reliefs' in M. Greenlaugh & V. Megaw (eds.) *Art in Society*, Duckworth, London

Rosch, E. (1976) 'Classification of real-world objects: origins and representations in cognition' in S. Ehrlich & E. Tulving (eds.) *La Memoire Semantique*, Bulletin de Psychologie, Paris

Rosch, E. (1978) 'Human categorisation' in N. Warren (ed.) *Advances in Cross-Cultural Psychology*, Lawrence Erlbaum and Press, New Jersey

Sahlins, M. (1976) 'Colours and cultures', *Semiotica* 16: 1–22

Saussure, F. de (1959) *A Course in General Linguistics*, Philosophical Society, New York

Saxe, A. (1973) 'The social dimensions of mortuary practices', University Microfilms, Michigan

Seigal, L. & Brainard, C. (eds.) (1978) *Alternatives to Piaget*, Academic Press, London

Shepard, A. (1956) *Ceramics for the Archaeologist*, Carnegie Institute of Washington, Washington

Steadman, P. (1979) *The Evolution of Designs*, Cambridge University Press, Cambridge

Turner, T. (1969) 'A Central Brazilian tribe and its symbolic language of bodily adornment', *Natural History* 78: 1–8

Turner, T. (1973) 'Piaget's structuralism', *American Anthropologist* 75: 351–73

Tyler, S. (ed.) (1969) *Cognitive Anthropology*, Holt Rinehart and Winston, New York

Tyler, S. (1978) *The Said and the Unsaid*, Academic Press, New York

Wallace, A. (1971) 'A possible technique for recognising psychological characteristics of the ancient Maya from an analysis of their art' in C. Jobling (ed.) *Art and Aesthetics in Primitive Societies*, Dutton, New York

Vastakos, J. (1978) 'Cognitive aspects of North-West Coast art' in M. Greenlaugh & V. Megaw (eds.) *Art in Society*, Duckworth, London

Washburn, D. (1978) 'A symmetry classification of Pueblo ceramic designs' in P. Grebinger (ed.) *Discovering Past Behaviour*, Academic Press, New York

Wheatley, P. (1971) *The Pivot of the Four Quarters*, Edinburgh University Press, Edinburgh

Wittgenstein, L. (1958) *Philosophical Investigations*, Blackwell, Oxford

Wynn, T. (1977) 'The evolution of operational thought', University Microfilms, Michigan

Zadeh, L. (1965) 'Fuzzy sets', *Information and Control* 8: 338–53

Zaslow, B. & Dittert, A. (1977) 'Pattern mathematics and archaeology', *Arizona State University Anthropological Research Papers*: 2

Chapter 3

**Social formation,
social structures
and social change**
Christopher Tilley

In this chapter Tilley outlines aspects of a general social theory which has implications for all archaeological processes – the use and deposition of material culture and its analysis and interpretation. The concern is to situate archaeology securely within the social sciences to which it can contribute positively as a discipline defined by a distinctive body of information.

According to the theory presented, societies have a dual nature. They consist of individual people, but also of social structures. Individual acts are orientated according to principles or rules which in turn are reproduced by the actions. Man makes himself within a particular spatial and historical context in which he 'knows how' to act, even if he is unaware of all the structuring principles employed. Action has consequences (intended and unintended) which form the social structure.

Material culture has a central role in the relationship between the individual and the social structure. Material items are structured according to principles or rules, but they also structure further individual actions as part of a particular ideological framework. Finally, the nature and causes of social change are considered and emphasis is placed on contradictions between the interests and orientations of individuals and groups within society.

Introduction

The position put forward here for an understanding of the nature of social formations and of changes within them is defined as *dialectical structuralism*. The term is used to distance the approach from orthodox structuralism as it is normally understood in anthropology and sociology, largely being related to the work of Lévi-Strauss, as well as from the currently fashionable structural-Marxist orientations. The stance taken is structuralist in the sense that a consideration of social structures plays a central part in the analysis, and dialectical in the emphasis it places on the relationship between structures and the activities of individuals and groups situated within social formations. An attempt is made to chart the difficult course between the Scylla of positivism, functionalism and reductive materialism and the Charabydis of idealism. It is not intended to engage in a detailed exegesis of other positions or authors within archaeology. Critical comments on some of these may be found elsewhere (Tilley 1981*a*, 1981*b*) and are only introduced where they may serve to clarify or highlight the relevance of the arguments expounded.

The individual and society

My initial question concerns the amount of theoretical space we should give to the intersubjective context of human interaction in societal change. There has been relatively little discussion of this in the archaeological literature. For example, Hill and Gunn's book *The Individual in Prehistory* (1977) is primarily directed towards the methodological techniques required to identify the artefacts produced by specific individuals in prehistoric social systems, but does not touch upon the point at issue here. Two polarised positions concerning the relationship between the individual and society have been taken in much of the philosophical and sociological literature, those of methodological individualism and holism. Needless to say, no unitary view may be associated with either but we may draw out the essential arguments. Methodological individualism (Brodbeck 1966; Lukes 1970; Popper 1966; Watkins 1970*a*, 1970*b*) asserts that social phenomena can only be analysed and successfully explained in terms of the subjective dispositions (desires, wants, intentions, motives) of the individuals that constitute societies. For instance, Popper states that 'all social phenomena, and especially the functioning of all social institutions should always be understood as resulting from the decisions, actions, attitudes etc. of human individuals . . . we should never be satisfied by an explanation in terms of so-called "collectivities" ' (1966, p. 98). Weber makes a similar point (1964, p. 101). The paradigmatic objects of social knowledge may only be individual social actions, their meaning and causes. On this basis social change must come about as a result of changes in the motivational referents underlying the actions and interactions of individuals, without any consideration of wider structures or social institutions (that is, standardised modes of behaviour as in ritual activities). In such analyses institutions and structures are merely regarded as abstract models of collectivities of individuals. The only concessions made to holism are in such examples as the hysteria of a rioting crowd.

Counterposed to this position is the holism of Durkheimian sociology (Durkheim 1915) and, in a guise familiar to archaeologists, of systems theory (Clarke 1968; Hill 1977; Renfrew 1972). The whole, society, is greater than the sum of its parts, that is, it is not in principle reducible to the sum of the individuals which comprise it. Society is treated in a totally reified way and change takes place 'behind the backs' of social actors who become largely irrelevant to the analysis. The sole theoretical function of the individual is as a counterpoise to the social realm, thus serving to establish, in this difference, the existence of the specific realm of the social (Hirst 1975, p. 98). This position owes much to the old Hobbesian problem of order, or how is society possible in the struggle between competing individuals, in the battle between all against all? This problem becomes resolved by the internalisation of social facts, norms or rules into the individual consciousness in the form of needs dispositions which create specific motivational referents for individual action: 'the ideal is for the man to act without dislocation because dislocation, as opposed to permissive disjunction, results in an act which communicates a set of contradictory values — capable of causing confusion, loss of cohesion and ultimately social anarchy' (Clarke 1968, p. 97).

Both positions would seem to be equally unsatisfactory. In the methodological individualist perspective, society assumes the form of an unreal logical atomism, change resulting solely from new motivations for situated action, while in holism the individual is effectively screened out of the analysis and becomes powerless in the face of general causality in the overall system so that change becomes a reified mechanical process. Clearly, some resolution is required between these two positions. One solution is simply to regard the relationship between the individual and society as a dialectical one. The results of individual actions form society which, in turn, reacts back and shapes individual actions (Berger 1966; Berger & Luckmann 1967). This dialectical process is comprised of three synchronous moments: externalisation, objectification and internalisation (Berger & Luckmann 1967, p. 149). The individual internalises features that are given to him from outside and these become contents of his own consciousness which he externalises again as he continues to live and act in society. Society is an objectification or externalisation of man, and man internalises or appropriates, in his consciousness, society. Social structures are produced by individual actions and these in turn constrain future actions. It can be argued that this position, while appearing to avoid reification on the one hand, and a voluntaristic idealism with respect to human actions on the other, in fact incorporates the worst aspects of both methodological individualism and holism. Man does not produce social structures any more than he produces gravity. Social structures and society always appear as prior forms to the individual who can only reproduce or transform them through his practical activity, on and in the world. Social structures are not just alien features which constrain human actions. They are also enabling, and form a medium for action. As a concomitant of this we must regard the social totality as having a *dual* nature. The fundamental truth in the methodological individualist position is that societies can only be composed of people; without individuals society would simply not exist. People act in terms of intentions, motivations and choices between different courses of action. As a consequence of these actions society exists; it is not consciously produced by individuals any more than these individuals are predetermined in their actions or 'programmed' by society. Social structures depend upon the activities of individuals but have different properties. They are for the most part the unintended results of the activities of individuals. As Bhaskar notes (1979, p. 44), people do not marry to sustain the nuclear family or set out to work in order to sustain capitalism. However, these are the inevitable results of their activities. We should regard societal change, therefore, as having dual aspects. Change occurs as a result of both changes in the actions of individuals and changes in social structures. An adequate account of societal change requires a theory of social structures as well as one of social actions. The link between the two may be found in the Marxian notion of *praxis* and in the notion of *structural principles* underlying actions. These are considered below.

Social structures

Detailed discussions of what social structure might be are virtually non-existent in the archaeological literature. It is too often assumed that we know what social structure is, that the concept is in no need of further grounding in theory and that as a consequence may be applied in our analyses without too many problems. Social structure may be defined, to risk an oversimplification, in two fundamentally different ways. Divergent interpretations of the concept have direct implications for archaeological research as they are founded on different epistemological notions with regard to the nature of social reality, the ontological status we confer to that reality and the level of abstraction at which we work. Furthermore, the concept of social structure is always allied to a particular methodology. Unless we have a clear understanding of the implications of different interpretations of the concept, our analyses will be inadequate and lead to misleading conclusions.

The most usual conception of social structure adopted in the archaeological literature is largely derived from structural-functionalist and role theory, as developed in sociology and anthropology (Evans-Pritchard 1940; Firth 1971; Dahrendorf 1968; Goodenough 1965; Merton 1957; Nadel 1957). Social structure is considered to reside in the network of observable patterns of interactions between individual actors. The notion of structure employed becomes equivalent to pattern. Social structure arises either from an analysis of empirically given realities in social life, or from abstractions based on these. The notion of structure is therefore directly analogous to anatomical patterns in biology where the skeleton and the organs exist in a visible way as supports for the body and may be reasonably conceived to be independent of the functioning of that body. To Radcliffe-Brown (1952) the basic unit of structure was the elementary family, consisting of a man, his wife and their children. From this starting point he deduced what were termed first order structural relationships: (a) that between the man and his spouse, (b) that between the children, (c) that between parent and child. Second order structural relationships were those linking two families with a common member (brother's spouse etc.). This was presented as a basic analytical position from which the matrix of any society's social structure could be built up. This led Radcliffe-Brown to consider all social structures in terms of three basic problems: (i) what kinds of social structures are there, and by what means may we classify them in a consistent way which adequately accounts for their similarities and differences? (ii) how do social structures function and maintain themselves? (iii) how do social structures of a different form come into existence? These were the problems, respectively, of social morphology, social physiology and social change (Radcliffe-Brown 1952, pp. 178–80).

A more abstract conception of social structure is based on role theory. Social structure consists of the ordered arrangement of social relationships which occur between people as a consequence of their playing different roles in different contexts. The theatrical imagery is apparent and the role system becomes the matrix from which social structure

is formed. A number of different roles forming an actor's social persona are enacted in different situations. The role changes in relation to whether it has been ascribed or achieved and in terms of temporal enactment and context. In any such role system there will be various degrees of role summation (the number of roles enacted by any one person), role coherence (the interrelatedness of roles within the social system), and role dependence or independence, within society, or with regard to other specific roles. The methodological effects of this position in relation to mortuary practices are discussed in chapter 12 of this book. Here we might note that the concept of social structure, when reduced to social pattern, as in both structural-functionalist and role theory, can be seen to lose all explanatory power. It becomes merely a descriptive device, almost superfluous to the overall analysis. Since, in social life, patterns of structures exist only so far as they are actively reproduced in human action, logically, structure cannot exist independent of system, and in fact the two terms are either conflated or used interchangeably. Tainter (1975, p. 1, 1977, p. 131) only refers to structure in systemic terms. Structure is only important as a means of description and consequently has no real theoretical importance. Function rather than structure plays the explanatory role as human society can only exist in its activity. The possibility that underlying principles of operation exist, not directly discernable in terms of perceived relationships or roles, simply does not exist within this framework, and structure has importance only as a descriptive and classificatory device. Leach (1961, p. 7) is critical of this position: 'our task is to understand and explain what goes on in society, how societies work. If an engineer tries to explain to you how a digital computer works he does not spend his time classifying different kinds of nuts and bolts. He concerns himself with principles not things.' Archaeological attempts to infer past social organisation have invariably tried to classify societies and infer social 'facts', in a Durkheimian sense, from their tangible manifestations rather than the underlying principles at work in society. Consequently the work has little explanatory force. To describe something as a chiefdom tells us very little about that society, particularly as the concept has no precise definition. On the other hand to use a quantitative measure (Binford 1972; Tainter 1975, 1977) is equally unsatisfactory. At best this can only lead us to limited inferences about general societal form. Of course, social structure resides in the interrelationships of individuals but this does not mean that the interactions of individuals explain its nature and form adequately, an explicit assumption often made. A correct explanation may consist in the discovery of systems of relationships existing at a more abstract level which govern the observed social relations. We need to pay attention to the underlying logic behind the apparent visible logic.

Role theory is an inadequate conception because, to use Gidden's phrase, 'the stage is set, but the actors only perform according to scripts which have already been written out for them' (Giddens 1976, p. 16). Role theory provides a model of the relationships between individuals and groups in an implausible and deterministic manner. A person's role is regarded as given, fixed and determinate, rather than negotiated and renegotiated; actors are viewed as slotting into a variety of roles and acting in conformity with them. To the extent that they do not do so this is regarded as deviant behaviour. Any social relationship would seem to involve a redefinition of expectations on a more or less continual basis and cannot be regarded as static and fixed. In particular, there is no analysis, in role theory, of meaningful structures at the level of interpersonal encounter or in relation to the wider social group or plural subject. The approach fails to take account of the fact that it is people and not roles which constitute society. Again, society becomes reified as the roles are detached from human purpose and expression (Keat & Urry 1975, p. 93).

An alternative view of social structure is adopted by Saussure (1960) in structural linguistics and by Lévi-Strauss in his theoretical discourses (1966, 1968). Using Saussure's basic distinction between language, 'langue', and speech, 'parole' (see chapters 1 and 2), we might conceive of social structure as a set of relations which underlie the observed patterns of interrelationships that we perceive between individuals in society. As such, the structure is not open to direct empirical observation. Nevertheless it is real, that is to say it has ontological status. Lévi-Strauss' writings echo many of the fundamental tenets of Saussurian linguistics. In particular, priority is given to the study of the universal and the collective rather than of the determinate and individual. The study of social phenomena is, in essence, no different from the study of language. Social structures are only constituted through difference, through the relations between the elements, so that form becomes more important than content. Different empirical instances of social relations and activities in different societies may be conceived as being variations of each other so that by a logical or mathematical operation one can be seen as the transformation of the other. The underlying structure is what relates these different instances. Lévi-Strauss asserts the priority of the logical operations of the mind. Human actions are determined by models of intelligibility projected onto the world in an endless series of combinations and recombinations. Individual changes in the way in which mankind organises his existence are not really important because these are only transformations of the same underlying logic. Men are players in a card game in which the rules (logical operations of the mind) are always laid out in advance. Of course, each deal of cards is contingent, and the individual players may change tactics, but the outcome of each game can only be a transformation of the games which preceded it.

This conception of structure has been criticised in chapter 1. Here I would like to emphasise that the position involves functionalism since there is no sense of any internal incompatibility between the elements of the structure, of contradictory relations existing between them. Also, as in structural-functionalist theory, conceptions of system and structure become entirely conflated.

A more adequate conception is to see structures as dialectically related entities. Structures must be regarded as being dynamic entities, embracing contradictions and non-correspondences. The nodes within a structure are as important as the relations between these nodes. There can be no structures common to all mankind but only particular structures with a particular locus in space and time. We need to distinguish clearly between structures and systems or social formations. Structures go to make up a social formation but do not themselves constitute it, as social formations can only be present by virtue of the activities of human agents. Structures may be regarded as internally related sets of structural principles, the medium through which the actions of individuals and groups within the social formation are mediated and given meaning. As such, a structure should only be seen as being present through its effects (Althusser & Balibar 1970, p. 188). Structural causality is the existence of a structure *through its effects*. Internal contradictions occur within a structure because structures must be viewed as a unification between opposites. Without contradictions, structures can only be characterised by their self-sameness, and have no potentiality for change. The internal contradictions are a necessary source of change, and they may only be dissipated through change. Giddens (1976, pp. 118–29, 1979, pp. 69–73) stresses the duality of structure, relating to the recursive quality of social life and the interdependence of structures and the actions of individuals and groups. Structural principles form both the medium and the outcome of the activities of individuals, and as such they may be reproduced or transformed. They are always in a continual state of *structuration*. Human actions are mediated by structures, and in turn the structures are actively reformulated and reconstructed by the agency of individuals (Bhaskar 1979, p. 44). Structures are constructs which produce or orientate action and are in turn reproduced. They do not just hold man prisoner and constrain his future actions, they are also enabling. All human actions should be regarded as being structured and no social phenomena may be interpreted outside these structures. Social structures should be regarded as being related to each other through complex linkages of autonomy and interdependence. They do not predetermine social form in any simple causal way, although they may constrain the nature of its developmental trajectory and particular spatial contexts of human interaction. Structures are irreducibly social in their nature. As Piaget puts it: 'whereas other animals cannot alter themselves by changing their species, man can transform himself by transforming the world and can structure himself by constructing structures; and these structures are his own, for they are not entirely predestined from within or without' (Piaget 1971, pp. 118–19). The fact that these structures are in a continual state of structuration enables us to do away with the synchrony/diachrony distinction which has beset such positivist analyses of change as systems theory. Here stability and change become polarised, and the problem becomes, given the deviation counteracting tendencies of the system in the form of negative feedback mechanisms, how can change come about? The usual resort is to explain the social by the non-social, by the environment in relation to a determinant economic base or by such means as population pressure. However, a social formation, through the stocks of knowledge of its constituent actors and the structures which they reproduce 'has the capacity to define itself and thus, through the knowledge and investment it has achieved, to transform its relations with its environment, to constitute its own milieu' (Touraine 1977, pp. 3–4). Because social activities, social structures and the products of material action on the world are all irretrievably social products, social change must be given a social explanation, and non-social parameters can, at best, set down general constraints. This conception of structure obviously requires a clear formulation of the nature of social action, to which we will now turn.

Social action

Action, as opposed to movement, goes beyond itself. Actions may be characterised on the basis of their intentional nature. They are motivated by reasons to bring about some goal, aim or purpose. Digging a hole requires a coordinated set of bodily movements. What makes these movements intelligible is their subsumption under the end to which they are directed. The explanation must be cast in terms of the way an agent sees himself, his situation and the meanings it has for him. Intentionality is a crucial concept which distinguishes mental from physical phenomena. It involves a conception of persons who can (a) make preferred distinctions, (b) understand and follow rules, (c) impose normative constraints upon their conduct, (d) judge reflexively or monitor their actions, (e) be capable of deliberation and choice. This is a very different perspective from the usual view of behaviour espoused in much of the archaeological literature where actions are treated in a behaviourist perspective, propelled by various external stimuli, needs and role expectations (cf. Plog 1974, pp. 49–53, 1977, pp. 16–17; Schiffer 1976; Higgs & Jarman 1975; Saxe 1970). When we conceive action as being cognitively informed, it becomes impossible to avoid the assumption of a model of purposiveness and of certain standards of rationality (always relative to specific social formations) in terms of which the conduct of an agent in relation to his natural and social environment may be specified (Pettit 1978). In particular, we should regard agents as possessing causal powers, within themselves, by means of which they can alter the conditions of their own existence and what they regard as constraints upon their activities. Actions are not simply induced by the external stimuli to which they are subject (extrinsic conditions) but, perhaps more fundamentally, by the nature of the agent or the constitution of the social group (intrinsic conditions). In

one sense the ascription of such powers, by itself, provides a schema for an explanation or understanding of the manifestation of such powers on any particular occasion. We can understand causation as the active production of effects by agents. Such actions are not performed because they 'had to be' as a result of being instances of causal laws (Harré & Secord 1972, pp. 240–62; Harré & Madden 1975, pp. 82–90).

There are a number of ways in which we may conceive of the link between reasons and intentions or properties of the mind and the movements of the body in the world, which together characterise the actions of agents. One is to assert a mind/body dualism. Reasons are said to cause actions, they are viewed as being external to the action, and the notion of causality is the classic Humean one employed in the positivist philosophy of science. According to the Humean view of causation, two events C and E are related as cause and effect, if, and only if, they are members, respectively, of classes C and E of observable events. Thus each member of E regularly follows and is contiguous with a particular member of C, and an observer experiencing E will be led to expect the presence of the former (Sayre 1976, p. 65). Popper states that 'to give a causal explanation of an event means to deduce a statement which describes it, using as premises of the deduction one or more universal laws, together with certain singular statements, the initial conditions' (Popper 1959, p. 59). Davidson's (1968, 1976) attempt to use this framework to explain actions only results in an entirely unsatisfactory position of 'anomalous monism'. Monism occurs because he holds that psychological events must be interpreted as physical events. The position is anomalous because such events cannot be linked under strict psychophysical laws since the realm of the mental does not constitute a closed system. This entire view of causality, which many archaeologists have embraced with open arms, has many limitations (Tilley 1981b). The extension of this model to the study of man denies that he is in any way unique. If we accept the primacy of sentience, intentionality, linguistic and symbolic communication, man is not a natural entity. It is far more realistic to treat him as a culturally emergent entity that is physically embodied (Margolis 1977, pp. 23–5). The admission of such terms as 'culture', 'tradition' or 'style' spotlights the inadequacy of this form of reductive materialism. The position that men are sentient social actors capable of controlling their own destinies is far more scientific than the traditional conception of the embodied automaton.

Pritchard (1968) suggests that we should restrict action to the process of the activity of willing itself, and that this process, though normally having a physical movement as its result, cannot be accurately considered to have caused that result. An action must be identified with the 'willing', rather than with the result. The willing is the cause of the physical movement (Pritchard 1968, p. 61). Action, in this perspective, is a mental event and it is a mistake to confuse the result of the action (movement of some kind) with the event itself. This is the converse of Davidson's position where action is the physical result of the mental state. A more satisfactory position is to demolish the mind/body dichotomy altogether. Actions are neither mental states nor physical events, and the intentions and reasons may be conceived as being embodied in movement of the body. In this way we can eschew causality in the sense of a direct cause → effect relationship, and say that persons embody *causal powers* or the ability to act on and in the world. This conception is non-Humean and depends upon the practical judgments of actors in relation to situational context. In other words, it is generative. Edgley argues convincingly that there is a logical connection between the practical reasoning of an agent and his movement in the world, forming an action:

> Practical judgments are practical, i.e. related to action ... in accordance with the following three conceptual truths: if from the fact that p it follows that q, then from the fact that p one can infer that q; if from the fact that p one can infer that q, the fact that p is a (conclusive) reason for thinking that q; and if the proposition that q is a practical proposition, e.g. that one ought to do x, then a reason for thinking that q is a reason for doing x. The connection stated in this last truth, between a reason for thinking something and a reason for doing something, is the connection mediated by the possibility of an action being consistent or inconsistent with a practical judgment.
>
> (Edgley 1969, p. 124)

Now, this discussion is not an irrelevant diversion into the realms of action philosophy alien from a consideration of societal change. If it is conceded that the realm of the social has a dual nature, as argued above, we must involve in our discussions a clear formulation of the nature of agents and their actions before we can link these up with the wider concerns of structure and structuration or structural change. Individuals have reasons, purposes and intentions, and society or social formations may not be properly said to possess these features, nor may they be characterised as 'goal seeking' as Clarke suggests (1968, p. 52).

All action may be considered to be social action, whether directly orientated to others or not. Marx and Engels express this position well: 'not only is the material of my activity given to me as a social product (as is even the language in which the thinker is active): my *own* existence *is* social activity, and therefore that which I make of myself, I make of myself for society and with the consciousness of myself as a social being' (Marx & Engels 1975, p. 298). Action can be conveniently encompassed by Ryle's distinction between 'knowing how' and 'knowing that' (Ryle 1949, pp. 30–4). 'Knowing that' refers to propositional knowledge which can be discursively formulated, so that the actor would be able to tell us his reasons for a particular pattern of behaviour. 'Knowing how' relates to knowledge which an actor possesses but cannot put into propositional form, in

that he is unaware of the principles upon which he is acting. This does not mean his action is unintentional. This form of practical activity can be considered to make up the vast majority of the stream of ongoing activities in any society. Speaking a language without being aware of the grammatical rules involved, is a particularly apposite illustration. Bourdieu places particular stress upon this form of social action and relates it to what he calls the *habitus* of a social group. The habitus, especially in small-scale, relatively undifferentiated societies, is all embracing in its nature: 'a system of schemes of perception and thought which cannot give what it does give to be thought and perceived without *ipso facto* producing an unthinkable and unnameable' (Bourdieu 1977, p. 18). The actors perform as they do because the social world in which they find themselves is, above all, a symbolically structured reality which is inherently meaningful. The stocks of knowledge which agents draw upon in their activities in the reproduction and transformation of their social world depend upon knowledge which is largely taken for granted or implicit. Social life largely consists of the constitution and transformation of the frames of meaning through which agents orientate and reorientate their conduct to others and the natural environment.

An important feature of all action, whether it can be discursively formulated or not, is that it has consequences which the agent(s) did not intend as well as those that were intended, and this has important implications for the study of societal change. The activities of individuals and groups inevitably produce social conditions which in some respects constrain and set limits to the possibility for future actions. These become independent of the will of individuals and this fact means that we can describe all social reality as a form of contradictory reality. Material production in most cases requires a division of labour, and this must be seen as a result of man's productive practices and by no means a consciously intended result. The link between social action and social structures may be made by a consideration of the Marxian concept of praxis and by reference to generative or structural principles.

Praxis, structural principles

Praxis refers to an important property of doing or acting; a series of causal interventions in the natural and social world. Any determinate social formation is characterised by distinct practices, temporally, spatially and socially situated. Particular social practices are contextually situated within the totality and consequently have a relative autonomy in such forms as ritual or economic production. Nevertheless they are orientated and structured in relation to other practices which form the whole. A concomitant of this is that a doubly contextual archaeology results — contextual in that explanations can only relate to the totality of the practices of a particular sociocultural formation, a point to which we will return, and contextual in the sense that it must consider the moments which go to make up this formation. Space and time are not merely backdrops to actions, they are active elements involved in action. Form and sequence impose themselves on content, they structure action and are in turn structured by it. Praxis has a dual nature and involves both the production and, simultaneously, the reproduction or transformation of the conditions of existence for future activity. Social praxis should not be understood in the narrow sense of economic production, which a narrow technical reading of Marx might give, but of economic, political, ideological and theoretical practice (Althusser & Balibar 1970, p. 58). Althusser stresses the notion of transformation which is involved in all social practices:

> By practice in general I shall mean any process of *transformation* of a determinate given raw material into a determinate *product*, a transformation effected by a determinate human labour, using determinate means (of 'production'). In any practice thus conceived, the *determinant* moment (or element) is neither the raw material nor the product, but the practice in the narrow sense: the moment of the *labour of transformation* itself, which sets to work, in a specific structure, men, means and a technical method of utilizing the means. (1977, pp. 166–7)

All products of labour, such as material culture, embody properties of mind. They are the results of intentional activity in relation to purposes and beliefs, and embody meanings (cf. Clarke on attribute and artefact systems: 1968, pp. 134–45). Praxis mediates between consciousness and activity, and the link between the two must be essentially dialectical, each serving to redefine the other. Praxis produces not only a means for subsistence but also men and their social world. In the process of transforming the world through practical activity, man transforms himself and alters the conditions for his own future existence. Social being does not determine consciousness (*contra* Williams 1977, p. 75) since consciousness, conceived as a body of structured ideas, transcends the conditions of its own production. It would be more accurate to say that social being sets limits to consciousness. Change in both must be seen as aspects of the same process: 'thus thought and existence are not identical in the sense that they "correspond" to each other, or "reflect" each other, that they "run parallel" to each other or "coincide" with each other (all expressions that conceal a rigid duality). Their identity is that they are aspects of one and the same real historical process' (Lukács 1971, p. 204).

The notion of praxis as a mediation between activity and consciousness leads to an understanding that ideational systems are not just abstract features of consciousness and consequently of little importance for archaeology, but that they are embodied in material culture. As a result, material culture is not just passive. In its role as an embodiment of ideologies it is an active element within social life. It structures and is structured by the perception of actors of their social world and may be a powerful means of legitimating the existing social world. It has a dual effect, as both a creation and a creator of social practice.

Structural principles are components of structures, but they are also the principles drawn upon by actors in the reproduction and transformation of their social and material conditions of existence in and through praxis. This leads to either the reproduction and transformation of structures, usually as an unintended consequence of the activities of agents, although as an important theoretical limit, the actors may, at a discursive level, consciously change these themselves. These principles should normally be regarded as being embedded in the practical consciousness of actors rather than being formally located within the social formation in the form of laws or customary sanctions, hence the importance of Bourdieu's use of the term habitus, discussed above. The principles are embedded in praxis and are therefore subject to change, since praxis involves transformation of the world. The principles are akin to the term *rule* as this is employed in sociology. A distinction is normally made between constitutive and regulative rules. The former generate certain actions, the latter stipulate the form they should take. Structural principles should be seen as involving both aspects simultaneously. The regularities in social life depend on the application of these principles and are not akin to the 'laws' of natural science since there may be considerable indeterminacy in their effectiveness from one context to another. The outcome of their application depends upon decisions as to 'how to go on' in a particular context; in other words, they are mutable. Winch (1958, pp. 32–3) suggests that whether an item of conduct is governed by a rule depends upon whether or not it makes sense to distinguish correct and incorrect ways of carrying out a particular action, and this does not require discursive availability. These principles should be seen as generating practices rather than as being a generalisation of existing practices. They give actions their *meaning*. The principles should be seen as being more like the rules of children's games than the rigid rules of chess (Giddens 1979, p. 68). It is an important characteristic that there can be no rigid definition and that the principles are subject to a considerable degree of interpretation and as such are chronically subject to change through the medium of praxis.

Social formations, contradictions, social change

There is no point in attempting to formulate a general model of change since all changes take place within the context of determinate social formations, and the structures, structuring principles and conditions for social action, will differ from one particular case to another. Rather than attempting to deduce low level propositions which are good for all times and places but which at best are trivial and at worst false and misleading, we need to consider each case in all its particularity. There is a clear need for a much greater emphasis on regional archaeology, which Binford correctly stressed almost two decades ago (Binford 1964). As Gregory argues, spatial structures cannot be theorised without social structures, and vice versa. Social structures are only practised within spatial structures, and vice versa (Gregory 1978, p. 121). Both are deeply implicated in each other. The position that we can hope to explain change or understand material culture only in relation to specific social formations depends on one of *epistemic relativity*. Reality is always socially constructed and defined. Men in specific situations agree on a form of life and play particular kinds of language games (Wittgenstein). This agreement is a product of time, place and circumstances. No game can have any further justification other than that it has been agreed upon. So, the question whether *X* or *Y* is an appropriate act becomes unintelligible outside the particular game being played. For instance, whether suicide is an appropriate act can only be judged within the framework of particular belief systems. To the Roman Catholic, life is regarded as a gift of God, and this is one example of the agreement of the Catholic community on a form of life. On the other hand, to commit *hari-kari* in order to save face within a traditional Japanese community was perfectly acceptable. 'Right' and 'wrong' only make sense within the moral game that is being played. All actions of individuals within a particular social formation are mediated and structured in relation to the whole. Men live in symbolic universes of their own making which are objectified in such forms as language and material culture. This position should not be confused with the much stronger one, sometimes linked with it, that all our judgments are relative, and that there are no rational grounds for accepting one statement or explanation rather than another.

The Marxist conception of the social formation is broadly equivalent to 'society' in social theory, the social formation being the specifically Marxian treatment of social form. The concept, as elaborated by Althusser in *For Marx* and Althusser and Balibar in *Reading Capital* (Althusser 1977; Althusser & Balibar 1970) in their anti-humanist 'reading' of Marx, is that it is a structural combination of a number of levels or 'instances' (the latter is a preferable term as it goes some way to avoid the problems posed by Marx's base/superstructure analogy in which the latter might be conceived as merely a reflection or an effect of the former). The instances (minimally the economic, political and ideological) are conceived as being relatively autonomous from each other. The economic instance is made up by a mode or modes of production which are internally constituted by an articulation between the social relations (relations between individuals in production, division of productive labour, mode of appropriation and distribution of surplus) and the forces (technical conditions) of production in which the relations are always dominant. The elevation of the forces of production to any kind of determinant role can, in this perspective, only result in a materialist reductionism in the interpretation of social life. The mode of production

may contribute to the overall make-up of the social formation with varying degrees of determinancy, depending on its position, in respect to its degree of dominance or of subordination in relation to the other instances.

The social formation is conceived as a complex, or 'over-determined', 'structure in dominance' (Althusser 1977, pp. 96–107). It is a system of relations linking a number of levels or 'instances'. Within the system as a whole certain elements are held to predominate in determining the relations between the instances. The type of causality which makes any particular social formation 'move' must be considered to be metynomic. The instances of the social formation, ideological and juridico–political (superstructure), and the mode of production (base), are linked in a complex web of autonomy and interdependence. Nevertheless, the economy is considered to be 'determinant in the last instance', hence the relative autonomy of the other instances.

The structure of the social formation is only imminent in its effects and is not concretely present, so that structural causality is the existence of a structure *through its effects* (Althusser & Balibar 1970, p. 188). The relations of production become a 'regional structure', inscribed within the structure of the social totality. This regional structure is held to determine its own elements. Consequently the structure of the relations of production determines the places and functions occupied by the agents of production who are merely the 'supports' (*Träger*) of these functions (Althusser & Balibar 1970, p. 180). A similar position is adopted by Friedmann (1974, 1975; Friedmann & Rowlands 1977) and Godelier (1977).

This formulation involves a number of inadequacies which would seem to make it untenable as a conception of the social totality. Either the connections between the instances must be conceived as embodying some sort of imminent necessity, as in the Althusserian position, or there is no connection of this type. There can be no middle way. The relative autonomy of the superstructural instances is ambiguous in Althusser's scheme, as their autonomy is contradicted by the determination of the economic instance, whether this is a last or a first instance. The relative autonomy of the other instances cannot be maintained if the economic must hold sway ultimately. Althusser fails to distinguish clearly between structure and system, or the social totality, so that the latter becomes reified and individuals and groups are only important insofar as they remain props for the structure.

It can be posited that it is only the articulated combination of the instances that is determinant, that the social formation is determinant of itself, as a distinct totality and that no level within it may be considered to possess a privileged causality. This must be so if we conceive of the social formation as comprising only individuals and groups and the conditions of existence for their interrelations, namely praxis and structuring principles (considered above). We should conceive of the articulation between the instances in terms of the connections, given through the process of structuration, between social actions. Hindess and Hirst are surely right to suggest that

> the social formation cannot be resolved into the classical Marxist formula of economic base and its political–legal and ideological–cultural superstructures. Legal and political apparatuses and cultural and ideological forms provide the forms in which the conditions of existence of determinate relations of production are secured, but they are not reducible to their effects and they are not organised into definite structural levels which merely reflect the structure of an underlying economic base. This means that political forces and ideological forms cannot be reduced to the expression of 'interests' determined at the level of economic class relations. (Hindess & Hirst 1977, p. 57)

It is a trivial truism that people must eat and extract resources from the environment, but the environment itself and the specific nature of the resources which are actually exploited are themselves constituted in the ideological instance as part of man's active self-construction of reality. The nature of economic activity and the form of environmental constraint are given their specificity and effectiveness, their conditions of existence, by the ideological order. Relations of production have specific conditions for existence in the overall matrix of social relations. They cannot, themselves, secure these conditions nor determine the nature in which they are fulfilled. So the social formation should be conceived as a determinate set of productive relations and the other social relations (ideological production and so on) in which their conditions of existence are satisfied. Structures conceived as sets of generative or structural principles are implicated in these social relations, forming both the medium and the outcome of actions. As such of course, the structures do not constitute the social formation, but they are the largely unintended and inevitable consequences of social action, present at their moments of constitution, through structuration. Man is inseparable from the meanings he gives to his existence. He orders his activities in the world and simultaneously effects an ordering of the *representation* of those activities, as a symbolic scheme, apart from which those activities may not be understood. Meanings are not simply the reflection of the extant material conditions of existence and the social relations necessary for social reproduction. On the contrary, the ability to use, meaningfully constitute, and manipulate symbols is a distinctively human quality which makes ideation and consciousness possible, the basis for all social interaction.

In sum, the social formation is a totality of human experience and action, the entire *ensemble* of the relations between individuals and groups and of their relationships with their natural and social environment. It is a dynamic whole, always in the process of structuration; there can be no elements outside it, nor can the elements within it be understood without dialectically referring them to it. The possibility of transformation embedded within the social totality can now be discussed.

We may suggest that, appropriately formulated, contradiction and conflict provide an adequate basis for the study of change in specific social formations. Marx uses the term contradiction somewhat ambiguously throughout his writings, and the exact position he wished to take is further complicated by the principles of the 'dialectic'. Dialectical thought proposes that all things are constantly in motion, in a state of being and becoming and ceasing to exist, that contradictions are universal and that no distinctions may be fixed. In Engels' classic statements in the *Anti-Durhing* and the *Dialectics of Nature* (Engels 1939, 1940) the concepts of the dialectic and the 'laws' involved with their use are proposed as constituting a separate outlook on the world, a materialist philosophy of the dialectic. These dialectical laws are thus held to be of general relevance, as applicable to the study of natural science as to the study of man — the negation of the negation, the transformation of quantity into quality, the unity and interpenetration of opposites, development through contradiction. Use of the dialectic is not difficult to find in Marx's writings, for example his introduction to the *Grundrisse* where we are told 'production is simultaneously consumption as well . . . each is simultaneously its object . . . each of them by being carried through creates itself as the other' (Marx 1971, quoted in Ruben 1979, p. 47). It would appear to be misplaced to suggest that the language of the dialectic itself constitutes a separate philosophy. Ruben (1979) suggests that these ideas may be translated into a position where entities are regarded as being necessarily connected in terms of development, dependence, opposition and structure which is a far more satisfactory position than the much stronger thesis advanced by Engels. As Colletti is at pains to demonstrate, the laws of the dialectic, formulated by Engels, from Hegel's *Science of Logic* (Hegel 1969), may not be separated from their logical conclusion, an idealist philosophy of nature (Colletti 1973, pp. 40–51). It is suggested here that a successful translation of the language of the dialectic into the more ordinary language of necessary connection (through structure) and development (through contradiction) provides a powerful alternative conception of change to positivist and empiricist positions.

Marx's most explicit statements on contradiction occur in the 1859 Preface to *A Contribution to the Critique of Political Economy*, an unfinished work which embodies a reductionist conception of societal change. Four main theses may be drawn out from the exposition (Cutler *et al.* 1977, pp. 136–7):

1. 'The totality of these relations of production constitutes the economic structure of society, the real foundation on which arises a legal and political superstructure.'
2. 'At a certain stage of development, the material pro-

ductive forces of society come into conflict with the existing relations of production . . . from forms of development of the productive forces these relations turn into their fetters.'

3. 'Then begins an epoch of social revolution. With the change of the economic foundation the entire immense superstructure is more or less rapidly transformed.'

4. 'No social order ever perishes before all the productive forces for which there is room in it have developed, and new higher relations of production never appear before the material conditions of their existence have matured within the womb of the old society.'

(Marx & Engels 1968, pp. 182–3)

The contradiction between the forces and relations of production is viewed as being a general mechanism of societal change. This is based on an assertion of a privileged economic causality which works its way throughout the structure of the social formation. Thesis 1 involves a correspondence between the infrastructure and the superstructure of the social formation. At least, the former constrains the possible forms of the latter. Thesis 2 suggests that the dynamics promoting change may be located in a contradictory relation between the forces and relations of production, which becomes inscribed in a change in the entire superstructure (thesis 3). The non-correspondence between the forces and relations of production serves to negate the correspondence between the infrastructure and the superstructure. Thesis 4 asserts the primacy of the forces of production. The relations of production become an obstacle for the future development of the forces of production because they have created conditions which necessitate a new set of productive relations.

As Cutler *et al.* point out (ibid., p. 137), this conception of contradiction works because the social formation is divided into distinct classes; infrastructure/superstructure, forces/relations and the infrastructure and the forces are given a privileged causality in relation to the superstructure and the relations. They are linked by an external relation of causality: forces → relations/infrastructure → superstructure/ forces → totality. This perspective forms the basis for Marx's materialist conception of social development. It is not intended here to enter into the debate over the extent to which Marx actually subscribed to this apparently reductionist position, or to whether or not, as Althusser claims, there is an 'epistemological break' between Marx's earlier writings (which include the *Contribution*) and his 'mature work'. An almost infinite variety of 'readings' of Marx may be made and this is, perhaps, because his words are like bats: one can see in them both birds and mice (Pareto 1902, quoted in Ollman 1971, p. 3). What is important is that Marx claims that social reality is a contradictory reality, a claim which has considerable importance. In the *Contribution* this contradictory reality is played out in the relation between the

forces and the relations of production, with the former being regarded as determinant.

Marx also discusses social contradictions in relation to the Capitalist Mode of Production (CMP), upon which a far more satisfactory conception may be grounded. Social relations, within the CMP, are, for Marx, always based on a contradictory relationship which exists between the dominant and the dominated classes. The structural interests of these classes of agents are incompatible with each other, yet they form a unity. On the one hand are the agents who are in possession of the means of production, who purchase labour power, which becomes a commodity form, and who convert money into capital. On the other hand are the agents who are forced to sell their labour power and produce exchange value for the capitalists. The interests of these classes of agents are incompatible with each other as the expansion of profits is at the direct expense of those who provide the labour power. This is because, as Marx demonstrated, the value of a commodity is not inherent in itself. It is actually made up by the social labour that goes into its production. Profit is unpaid labour, mystified within the CMP as a property of the commodities themselves. The CMP depends on socialised production but this principle is entirely incompatible with the private appropriation of the capitalist, a structural contradiction existing *within* the relations of production which threatens the continued existence of the CMP.

Althusser (1977, pp. 106–16) suggests that this contradiction between capital and labour is never simple, since it is overdetermined and is always dependent on the historically concrete forms and circumstances in which it takes place, in the particular forms of the superstructure and the base. The contradiction is 'inseparable from the total structure of the social body in which it is found, inseparable from its formal *conditions* of existence, and even from the *instances* it governs; it is radically *affected by them*, determining, but also determined in one and the same movement, and determined by the various levels and *instances* of the social formation it animates' (Althusser 1977, p. 101). The concept of overdetermination has nothing whatsoever to do with the empiricist use of the term in which an event is said to be overdetermined if there occurs a whole series of conditions which are causally sufficient for it to take place. A contradiction within the economic instance, between the forces and relations of production is never sufficient to bring about change in the overall social formation. The effects of this contradiction, or of contradictions in the other instances, play through the other instances of the social formation, and in turn, 'react' back on the initial contradiction. There can be no simple opposition of contradictions as in Engels' dialectical materialism.

To Althusser, contradictions are firmly located within and between the structures and instances of the social totality. We have already rejected the position that the social formation can be conceived as a definite series of structural levels or instances, so that the term contradiction must be considered as being a property of structures. It may be defined as an opposition of the structural principles which go to make up a structure. These principles form part of a structure and therefore must work in terms of each other but also exist in opposition to each other. Giddens points out that the CMP is by its very nature contradictory because its operation, which results in private appropriation by the few, presumes a structural principle which negates it: socialised production (Giddens 1979, p. 142). Change is more likely to take place, as Althusser suggests, when there is a multiplicity of these contradictions between structural principles. Recalling that structural principles orientate the actors of a social formation through praxis, contradictions between structural principles will result in competing beliefs and reasons for actions by individuals. These, ultimately, change the conditions of existence for social relations and so the nature of these relations themselves changes. Contradiction at the level of structure is translated into a clash of interests between actors within the social formation. Now Marx conceived this conflict of interests as being essentially a feature of the class relations of the CMP which is obviously inapplicable to pre-capitalist modes of production, in which archaeologists have their primary interest. This position can be considerably broadened. As a basic axiom we may suggest that conflicts of interests operate in all social formations because they are characterised by differential access to power and control over resources, both material and non-material (knowledge). This power, and the manner in which it is exercised, depend upon the structural characteristics of the particular social formation under consideration. The fact that this power exists obviously entails a conflict of interests between those in possession of this power and those who are controlled by it. When contradictions between structural principles become antagonistic this will coincide with conflicts of interest between actors, resulting in changes in social relations which serve to alter the overall social formation.

This position entails a radical break with the conception of 'traditional societies' as being 'cold' and in some sense impotent to change, a position which has much to do with the 'snapshot' pictures anthropologists take and on which archaeologists have based their presuppositions with regard to 'primitive' social organisation. The seeds of change are always present within social formations in that the structures which characterise them are a unity of oppositions, chronically subject to change through structuration. Whether or not the opposition between the structural principles becomes antagonistic depends upon the particular context of social action in terms of relationships between individuals and the intended and unintended consequences of action. Every social action is in one sense a new action and may take on a slightly different form, or temporal structure, and there will always be doubt as to the consequences of an action until it has been carried out. The change will normally be slow and incremental, but it may, under particular circum-stances, be rapid. Rapid changes are more likely to take place where clashes of interests become discursively available. The fact that this can occur depends on the axiom put forward by Giddens that all social actors have some degree of penetration of the social conditions of their existence:

> the *production of society* is a skilled performance, sustained and 'made to happen' by human beings. It is indeed only made possible because every (competent) member of society is a practical social theorist; in sustaining any sort of encounter he draws upon his knowledge and theories, normally in an unforced and routine way, and the use of these practical resources is precisely the condition of the production of the encounter at all.   (Giddens 1976, p. 16)

In one sense the position taken in this paper stands systems theory on its head; the problem becomes *not* why change should occur but why there is stability, why structures are reproduced rather than transformed, why the conditions for social action remain the same. The degree, and the nature of the legitimation of the social order, would appear to be a key element in maintaining social reproduction rather than transformation and the strongest form of this legitimation is likely to involve ideological forms of manipulation, which serve to justify the social order (see chapter 12).

Conclusions

This paper has attempted to expound a conception of social formations, social structures and social change which avoids both positivist reductionism and idealism. The position taken is rooted within social theory and the problems tackled are essentially problems grounded within philosophy and sociology. Archaeology, conceived as the study of man, and hence man in society, is irretrievably a social science. It can hardly lay claim to any independent existence with respect to the development of its own particular philosophy, methodology or explanatory framework as, for instance, Clarke asserted (1968, p. 13). Failure to tackle problems within sociology and philosophy can only result in a blind, unsystematic, groping towards an understanding of the past. It is sheer dogmatism to suggest otherwise, to suggest that problems within philosophy and social theory can be neatly circumvented in the practical business of carrying out research. In tackling these problems archaeologists can, themselves, contribute towards a wider understanding of social form and social dynamics.

The conclusions of the paper are embodied throughout the text and here the threads will be drawn together and stated in propositional form:

1. We can do no better than to adopt Weber's transcendental presupposition of any cultural science, that men 'are *cultural beings* endowed with the capacity and the will to take a definite attitude toward the world and to lend it *significance*' (Weber 1959, p. 81). A positivist perspective directly eschews such a position as the very nature of

positivism is to ignore intentionality, and thus man, insofar as human nature is mental and not physical in character.

2. Social formations have a dual nature. They can only be conceived as being constituted by individuals and groups, which, as a consequence of their activity, reproduce or transform the bases for their future action (social structures). Consequently the individual in society is of greater theoretical significance than has been recognised.

3. Social structures form both a medium for action and its outcome, and may be conceived as sets of structuring principles. These principles, through the medium of praxis, are the inevitable outcome and condition for social action. Concomitantly, a consideration of the structures and the structuring principles which go to make up, but do not themselves constitute, the social totality, must play a central part in archaeological analysis.

4. We may make a conceptual connection between the mental and physical events in an action sequence, between reasons for an action, which may be linked up with structural principles (although they are not directly reducible to these), and the physical movement of acting in and on the world by actors in a particular social formation.

5. Men live in a symbolically constructed social world which is of their own making. They transform this world through their practical activities, and as a consequence change themselves. Social change can only be explained in terms of the social. Non-social factors, at best, set down parameters. They have no *direct* explanatory power.

6. Archaeology is doubly contextual in that it must consider determinate social formations and the socially, temporally and spatially situated moments within the totality, through which the social formation is either reproduced or transformed. Material culture, as a human production, embodies meanings. It is not just a passive element but is an active element in the reproduction and transformation of social form. There is little point in attempting to formulate general models of societal change since the conditions of social reproduction and transformation differ so much from one situation to another.

7. Social reality is a contradictory reality. This follows from the conception of social structure as a unity of opposites and from differences of interests between individual agents and groups. Contradiction and conflict of interests provide an initial basis for an understanding of change, domination and legitimation of the social order through ideology, and stability.

Some of the theoretical and methodological effects of this discussion are worked through in relation to archaeological data in chapter 12 of this volume. The present discussion is only a beginning in a much needed reorientation of archaeological theory and inevitably raises many more issues than it attempts to resolve. Nevertheless, the effort is worthwhile if archaeology is to develop as a social science,

critically aware of man as a sentient social actor, participating in collective social worlds, apart from which the material products of his actions may neither be understood nor explained.

References

Althusser, L. (1977) *For Marx*, New Left Books, London

Althusser, L. & Balibar, E. (1970) *Reading Capital*, New Left Books, London

Berger, P. (1966) 'Identity as a problem in the sociology of knowledge', *Archives Européennes de Sociologie* 7: 105–15

Berger, P. & Luckmann, T. (1967) *The Social Construction of Reality*, Penguin, Harmondsworth

Bhaskar, R. (1979) *The Possibility of Naturalism*, Harvester, Hassocks

Binford, L. (1964) 'A consideration of archaeological research design', *American Antiquity* 29: 425–41

Binford, L. (1972) 'Mortuary practices: their study and their potential' in L. Binford *An Archaeological Perspective*, Seminar Press, London

Bourdieu, P. (1977) *Outline of a Theory of Practice*, Cambridge University Press, Cambridge

Brodbeck, M. (1966) 'Methodological individualisms: definitions and reduction' in W.H. Dray (ed.) *Philosophical Analysis and History*, Harper Row, London

Clarke, D.L. (1968) *Analytical Archaeology*, Methuen, London

Colletti, L. (1973) *Marxism and Hegel*, New Left Books, London

Cutler, A., Hindess, B., Hirst, P. & Hussain, A. (1977) *Marx's Capital and Capitalism Today*, Routledge and Kegan Paul, London

Dahrendorf, R. (1968) *Essays in the Theory of Society*, Routledge and Kegan Paul, London

Davidson, D. (1968) 'Actions, reasons and causes' in A.R. White (ed.) *The Philosophy of Action*, Oxford

Davidson, D. (1976) 'Psychology as philosophy' in J. Glover (ed.) *The Philosophy of Mind*, Oxford

Durkheim, E. (1915) *The Elementary Forms of the Religious Life*, Allen and Unwin, London

Edgley, R. (1969) *Reason in Theory and Practice*, Hutchinson, London

Engels, F. (1939) *Herr Eugen Dührings Revolution in Science* (Anti-Dühring), trans. E. Burns, London

Engels, F. (1940) *Dialectics of Nature*, New York

Evans-Pritchard, E.P. (1940) *The Nuer*, Oxford University Press, Oxford

Firth, R. (1971) *Elements of Social Organisation*, Tavistock, London

Friedmann, J. (1974) 'Marxism, Structuralism and vulgar materialism', *Man, New Series* 9: 444–69

Friedmann, J. (1975) 'Tribes, states and transformations' in M. Bloch (ed.) *Marxist Analyses and Social Anthropology*, A.S.A., London

Friedmann, J. & Rowlands, M. (1977) 'Notes towards an epigenetic model of the evolution of civilization' in J. Friedmann & M. Rowlands (eds.) *The Evolution of Social Systems*, Duckworth, London

Giddens, A. (1976) *New Rules of Sociological Method*, Hutchinson, London

Giddens, A. (1979) *Central Problems in Social Theory*, Macmillan, London

Godelier, M. (1977) *Perspectives in Marxist Anthropology*, Cambridge University Press, Cambridge

Goodenough, W. (1965) 'Rethinking "status" and "role": toward a general model of the cultural organisation of social relationships' in M. Banton (ed.) *The Relevance of Models for Social Anthropology*, A.S.A., London

Gregory, D. (1978) *Ideology, Science and Human Geography*, Hutchinson, London

Harré, R. & Madden, E. (1975) *Causal Powers*, Blackwell, Oxford

Harré, R. & Secord, P. (1972) *The Explanation of Social Behaviour*, Oxford University Press, Oxford

Hegel, G. (1969) *The Science of Logic*, trans. A.V. Miller, London

Higgs, E.S. & Jarman, M.R. (1975) 'Palaeoeconomy' in E.S. Higgs (ed.) *Palaeoeconomy*, Cambridge University Press, Cambridge

Hill, J. (1977) 'Systems theory and the explanation of change' in J. Hill (ed.) *The Explanation of Prehistoric Change*, University of New Mexico Press, Albuquerque

Hill, J. & Gunn, J. (eds.) (1977) *The Individual in Prehistory*, Academic Press, London

Hindess, B. & Hirst, P. (1977) *Mode of Production and Social Formation*, Macmillan, London

Hirst, P. (1975) *Durkheim, Bernard and Epistemology*, Routledge and Kegan Paul, London

Keat, R. & Urry, J. (1975) *Social Theory as Science*, Routledge and Kegan Paul, London

Leach, E. (1961) *Rethinking Anthropology*, Athlone, London

Lévi-Strauss, C. (1966) *The Savage Mind*, Weidenfeld and Nicholson

Lévi-Strauss, C. (1968) *Structural Anthropology*, Allen Lane, London

Lukács, G. (1971) *History and Class Consciousness*, Merlin, London

Lukes, S. (1970) 'Methodological individualism reconsidered' in A. Ryan (ed.) *The Philosophy of the Social Sciences*, Macmillan, London

Margolis, J. (1977) *Persons and Minds*, D. Reidel, Dordrecht

Marx, K. (1971) *The Grundisse*, translated and edited by D. McLellan, Macmillan, London

Marx, K. & Engels, F. (1968) *Selected Works*, Lawrence and Wishart, London

Marx, K. & Engels, F. (1975) *Collected Works*, Vol. 3, Lawrence and Wishart, London

Merton, R. (1957) *Social Theory and Social Structure*, Free Press, Chicago

Nadel, S. (1957) *The Theory of Social Structure*, Cohen and West, London

Ollman, B. (1971) *Alienation*, Cambridge University Press, Cambridge

Pareto, U. (1902) *Les Systèmes Socialistes*, II, Paris

Pettit, P. (1978) 'Rational man theory' in C. Hookway & P. Pettit (eds.) *Action and Interpretation*, Cambridge University Press, Cambridge

Piaget, J. (1971) *Structuralism*, Routledge and Kegan Paul, London

Plog, F. (1974) *The Study of Prehistoric Change*, Academic Press, London

Plog, F. (1977) 'Archaeology and the individual' in J. Hill & J. Gunn (eds.) *The Individual in Prehistory*, Academic Press, London

Popper, K. (1959) *The Logic of Scientific Discovery*, Hutchinson, London

Popper, K. (1966) *The Open Society and its Enemies*, Vol. 2, Routledge and Kegan Paul, London

Pritchard, H. (1968) 'Acting, willing, desiring' in A. White (ed.) *The Philosophy of Action*, Oxford University Press, Oxford

Radcliffe-Brown, A.R. (1952) *Structure and Function in Primitive Society*, Cohen and West, London

Renfrew, C. (1972) *The Emergence of Civilisation*, Methuen, London

Ryle, G. (1949) *The Concept of Mind*, Penguin, Harmondsworth

Ruben, D.-H. (1979) 'Marxism and dialectics' in J. Mepham & D.-H. Ruben (eds.) *Issues in Marxist Philosophy*, Vol. I, Harvester, Hassocks

Saussure, F. de (1960) *Course in General Linguistics*, Peter Owen, London

Saxe, A. (1970) 'Social dimensions of mortuary practices', unpublished doctoral dissertation, University of Michigan

Sayre, K. (1976) *Cybernetics and the Philosophy of Mind*, Routledge and Kegan Paul, London

Schiffer, M. (1976) *Behavioural Archaeology*, Academic Press, London

Tainter, J. (1975) 'Social inference and mortuary practices: an experiment in numerical classification', *World Archaeology* 7: 1–15

Tainter, J. (1977) 'Modelling change in prehistoric social systems' in L. Binford (ed.) *For Theory Building in Archaeology*, Academic Press, London

Tilley, C. (1981a) 'Conceptual frameworks for the explanation of sociocultural change' in I. Hodder, G. Isaac & N. Hammond (eds.) *Pattern of the Past*, Cambridge University Press, Cambridge

Tilley, C. (1981b) 'Economy and society: what relationship?' in G. Bailey & A. Sheridan (eds.) *Economic Archaeology: Towards an Integrated Approach*, B.A.R., Oxford

Touraine, A. (1977) *The Self Production of Society*, University of Chicago Press, Chicago

Watkins, J. (1970a) 'Ideal types and historical explanation' in A. Ryan (ed.) *The Philosophy of the Social Sciences*, Macmillan, London

Watkins, J. (1970b) 'Methodological individualisms and social tendencies' in M. Brodbeck (ed.) *Readings in the Philosophy of the Social Sciences*, London

Weber, M. (1959) *The Methodology of the Social Sciences*, Free Press, New York

Weber, M. (1964) *The Theory of Social and Economic Organisation*, Free Press, New York

Williams, R. (1977) *Marxism and Literature*, Oxford University Press, Oxford

Winch, P. (1958) *The Idea of a Social Science*, Routledge and Kegan Paul, London

Chapter 4

**Epistemological issues
raised by a
structuralist archaeology**
M. Alison Wylie

Insofar as the material residues of interest to archaeologists are cultural and, as such, have specifically symbolic significance, it is argued that archaeology must employ some form of structuralist analysis (i.e. as specifically concerned with this aspect of the material). Wylie examines the prevalent notion that such analysis is inevitably 'unscientific' because it deals with a dimension of material culture which is inaccessible of any direct, empirical investigation, and argues that this rests on an entrenched misconception of science; it assumes that scientific enquiry must be restricted to observables. It is clear, as realist critics of this view have argued, that scientific (explanatory) understanding depends fundamentally on theoretical extensions beyond observables; extensions which bring into view underlying and inaccessible causal structures or mechanisms responsible for the manifest phenomena through a procedure of analogical model construction. In consideration of realist models of these procedures and of the potential of linguistic modes of analysis for archaeology, it is proposed that archaeologists might (and, in fact, often do) effectively grasp the symbolic, structural order of surviving material culture through analysis governed by a rigorous and controlled use of ethnographic analogy. It is claimed, moreover, that the archaeological record can provide empirical bases for evaluating these theoretical constructs if a procedure of recursive and systematic testing is adopted in research, but the standard hypothetico-deductive model is seriously flawed as an account of an ideal for this procedure. Glassie's analysis of Middle Virginian folk housing is an example of research along these lines which illustrates the potential for a rigorous structuralist alternative.

There seem compelling reasons why archaeologists should adopt some form of structuralist approach, and yet even advocates of a structural archaeology sometimes assume that since it would concern itself with a radically inaccessible dimension of past cultures, it can claim to be no more than an exercise in creative speculation. I will want to argue that this presupposes a false dilemma with regard to the options open for 'scientific', empirical research and that, in principle, structural archaeology need not be consigned to the speculative horn of this dilemma simply because its theories are empirically under-determined. I will suggest, moreover, that the most promising and successful structuralist analyses of material culture do exploit a methodological option that escapes the dilemma and that seems open to a structural archaeology. Glassie's study of Virginian folk housing (1975) is a case in point and I will rely on it for an illustration of how this option might be brought into archaeological practice. My main concern in this paper is, then, with the epistemological questions that a structural archaeology raises about the kind of scientific or other knowledge that archaeologists should be striving to realise.

Let me first draw on a recent philosophical review of structuralism, Pettit's *Concept of Structuralism* (1977), for a suggestion of what structuralism has to offer archaeology and why archaeologists should take such an approach seriously. In broad outline, Pettit's thesis is that structuralism is a research programme characterised by a particular way of conceptualising a field of phenomena which 'draws us to an entirely new perspective on the subject' (1977, p. 109) and thus serves to raise new questions and to open up promising new directions for enquiry in that field. In particular, it involves the systematic extension of a framework of linguistic concepts (a linguistic metaphor) to non-linguistic fields so that they are seen to be like language in important respects and hence a proper subject for systematic, linguistic-type analysis. The framework of concepts functions as an analytic model, that is, a model which serves to guide analysis by providing a broad definition of the nature of the phenomena in question, and in this case it suggests that objects in the new field (e.g. cuisine, fashion, 'customary arts' or the material record) are 'semiological'; they are cultural constructs which are analogous to sentence structures in that they have definable meanings (or, in Pettit's terms, 'meaning effects') due to the arrangement of their component word-like elements. They are, that is, meaningful constructs whose significance (meaning) is determined by the contrasts set up between distinct classes of elements subject to specific principles of structure, i.e. the syntagmatic ordering constraints that determine what articulation of elements (or classes of elements) will comprise a 'well-formed', meaningful 'string' and what paradigmatic alternatives there are within a given structure by which meaning content may be varied. A structuralist analysis is initiated when this original analogy is extended and it is claimed that something like a linguistic mechanism of articulation (*qua* governing competence or set of structuring principles) must be operating in the non-linguistic field and must be postulated to account for the systematic way in which well-formed, meaningful objects are constructed in the new field. The structuralist view of a field as meaning-structured or meaning-bearing thus raises the question of how meaning is encoded in non-linguistic constructs and suggests that enquiry, perhaps modelled on linguistic analysis, should be concerned to define the articulating mechanisms involved.

While Pettit's account captures the essential character and promise of structuralism as a general research programme (i.e. as defined by its commitment to a particular (linguistic) analytic model in terms of which a field may be 'set up' for semiological analysis), he glosses the real difficulties involved in extending a linguistic metaphor to non-linguistic fields. In general, it does not seem that non-linguistic, cultural phenomena produce 'meaning effects' in the sense of conveying specific messages of states of mind on strict analogy to sentences or speech acts, and it has already been suggested (chapter 1) that linguistic models and the semiological approach may be of limited value in archaeological analyses. There does, on the other hand, seem to be an important sense in which cultural items are meaningful constructs inasmuch as they often represent a definable tradition whose distinctive structures of articulation (i.e. of the elements comprising the constructs in the field) embody a set of intuitions about what constitutes a well-formed construct

comparable to the intuitions identified in linguistics as a governing competence or body of structuring principles. They represent, that is, various aspects of material reality that have been 'made cultural', appropriated by a cultural system and, in this, transformed, made orderly and inter-subjectively meaningful through the imposition (or objectification) of established 'models of intelligibility' or 'innate logics of classification'. Cultural constructs may, then, be considered 'meaning-determined' and in this, they may embody a particular world view. But however much they express and reinforce this world view, they cannot be said to have distinctive, unambiguous 'meaning effects' in the same sense that a linguistic expression of a world view would have. The linguistic analogy holds primarily, I suggest, on the level of the encoding process; meanings (and a mediating 'competence') may govern the structuring of non-linguistic items.

The significance of this qualification of the underlying analogy of the structuralist programme is two-fold. First, lacking clear-cut 'meaning effects' (such as communicated messages), the would-be structuralist in a field like cuisine or fashion (or archaeology) must demonstrate that the structures manifest in the phenomena in question are, to a significant extent, meaning determined. Second, even where it seems clear that the basic analogy of meaning-determined structure holds, Pettit is quick to acknowledge that intuitions about proper (meaningful) form are generally much less 'firm' where non-linguistic constructs are concerned, perhaps because, I suggest, they may not be intended to produce 'meaning effects' of the specificity of the messages conveyed by linguistic constructs. This means that the articulating mechanisms involved cannot be assumed to be strictly analogous to the sharply defined competences and sets of recursive structuring principles identified in analysis of linguistic phenomena. The archaeological structuralist may be able to demonstrate that something like a syntax or competence must be postulated to account for the structured variability observed in surviving material culture but cannot expect that models of specifically linguistic articulating mechanisms will apply directly to their field; the mechanisms involved may be quite different. The onus is, then, on the structuralist operating in a non-linguistic field to define the specific sense in which the phenomena involved are meaningful and to develop appropriate explanatory models (i.e. which capture the particular kind of structuring principles that assure such meaningfulness and the systematic structure of constructs in that field).

This latter qualification simply reaffirms the point that the linguistic metaphor operates as an analytic model; it provides a general conceptual framework for research and though it may suggest the kinds of specific explanatory models that would be appropriate for the field in question, it does not necessarily provide them 'ready-made'. While this, in effect, defines the task that confronts a structural or contextual archaeology, it is the first qualification that presents the immediate challenge to the archaeologist who must make a case for viewing her/his data as meaningful and for framing research under the guidance of the linguistic metaphor. The sort of argument which can be used to set a field up for structuralist analysis is suggested by Chomsky's demonstration, against behaviourism, that innate cognitive capacities must be postulated to make sense of the human ability to acquire and use language – his 'poverty of stimulus' argument. In general terms, the argument is that whenever the output of a system is much more complex than the input or stimulus, you should look within the system itself for the responsible factors. In an archaeological context this suggests that where the richness and variability of the material record is too great to be explicable solely in terms of response to environmental constraints or stimuli, factors internal to the cultural system must be considered. An example of where structuralists dealing with material culture do, in fact, frequently rely on an argument like this to establish that structural analysis is appropriate to their field is Bourdieu's analysis of the Berber house structure. He is quite explicit on the point that he was drawn to a structuralist mode of analysis because the organisation of space within the Berber house is never completely due to technological imperatives or functional requirements (1977). They manifest such a complex of boundaries and articulating parts that an adequate explanation of their form must, in his opinion, involve some account of the governing cognitive factors involved.

Variants of this poverty of stimulus type of argument occur frequently in the archaeological literature, emerging wherever dissatisfaction with the techno-ecological paradigm leads to the demand that social or other aspects of past cultures be considered by the archaeologist. As this suggests, however, such a line of argument does not, in itself, establish the need to adopt a structuralist approach; for structuralist purposes it must be supplemented by a further argument to the effect that cognitive factors are uniquely significant where the structure of material in the archaeological record is concerned. Leach makes such a case when he insists that archaeologists have good reason to believe that they are dealing with intentional beings who have unique cognitive capacities for self-determination, the proto-type of which is the ability to acquire and use language. Where this is the case, Leach argues, it cannot be assumed that these cultures, or individuals, responded directly to environmental stimulus; their behaviours must be understood as involving a unique capacity to 'engage in work' (praxis) and thus deliberately to manipulate and transform the environment to which they were adapting through the projection onto the material world of certain 'cognitive maps'. Consequently, Leach concludes that 'Archaeologists must appreciate that the material objects revealed by their excavations are not things in themselves, nor are they just artifacts – things made by men – they are representations of ideas' (1973, p. 763).

This argument establishes that the archaeological record is at least a potential subject for a linguistic type of analysis; that it is reasonable to attempt to disembed the underlying ideas, or at least the principles of articulation by which ideas effectively structured the materials encountered in the archaeological record. In fact, however, it establishes considerably more. It introduces the linguistic source model as, in effect, a metaphysical theory which claims to have brought a crucial and otherwise overlooked dimension of the phenomenon into view, namely, that it is meaningful in the sense that systems of meaning are instrumental in its formulation. If this model is applicable to archaeological material, as the Chomsky and Leach arguments suggest, it demonstrates that formal variability in the archaeological record is due, to a significant extent, to structuring mechanisms operating on a cognitive and ideational level and that enquiry into this dimension of past cultures is not merely an interesting option opened up by a novel perspective; the researcher *must* be concerned with such factors if an adequate account is to be given of the material record as a cultural record.

Structuralism, then, offers archaeology a way of conceptualising its data backed by particularly compelling arguments to the effect that, insofar as material culture is a genuinely cultural phenomenon, it can only be understood as meaningfully constituted and, in the sense outlined above, semiological (i.e. the arguments that set the field up for structuralist analysis have strong prescriptive import). The difficulty is, however, that as a research programme, structuralism characteristically directs attention to an underlying cognitive reality, presumed responsible for manifest patterning in the record; it seeks to get at 'that on which an understanding of immediate, surface reality depends' (Glucksmann 1974) and in this, to disclose a 'structural domain' which, by definition, is not itself directly, empirically accessible. This is seen to raise serious epistemological problems for archaeology as a whole by many who would take a structural archaeology seriously. The core issue is that raised by Leach; the structuralist programme demands that the material record be understood in terms of the complex inner workings, particularly the cognitive workings of past cultural systems, yet these, Leach insists, constitute the interior of a black box that is decisively closed to the archaeologist because they are never accessible to direct inspection. He takes the position that 'as soon as you go beyond asking "what" questions' and 'start asking "how" and "why" questions' then 'you are moving away from verifiable fact and into the realm of pure speculation' (1973, p. 764), particularly when the 'how' and 'why' questions are directed at the details of how 'the prehistoric game of social chess was played out'. Leach goes on to say that though speculations about the content and structure of the archaeologists' black box 'can never rate better than well-informed guesses', it is still important, indeed essential, that archaeologists should make them: 'All I am saying is that you should recognise your guesses for what they are and not delude yourselves into thinking that, by resort to statistics and computers you can convert your guesses into scientifically established facts' (1973, p. 767).

This scepticism sets up a profound dilemma for the archaeologist; if the structuralist argument is taken seriously and it is recognised that the cultural black box and its cognitive and ideational content must be dealt with (i.e. because its material output cannot realistically be considered a direct functional-adaptive response to environmental input), then there is no recourse but to abandon empirical enquiry and take up precisely the type of non-scientific guessing that was rejected with nineteenth-century anti-quarianism and more recent forms of idealistic conventional-ism. And, in fact, structuralists like Glassie have been fully prepared to accept the terms of this dilemma, despite a strong commitment to rigorous standards of empirical analysis, and to represent their results as pure guesswork. He comments that 'Once the artifact, whether document or house, has been analysed, the student has a choice. He may stop; from the angle of scientific method he cannot go farther. Or, he may adopt the risky sort of explanation tra-ditional to history and move from assembled facts to hypo-thetical causes, thus eschewing methodological purity for understanding' (1975, p. 185). The sense is that, insofar as archaeologists are sensitive to the richness of the record as a cultural record, they will be forced to adopt non-scientific, speculative modes of reasoning which, the converted struc-turalist will say, may as well allow themselves to be guided by intuitions and methods drawn from linguistics as by any other interpretive source model.

This, I would claim, is a false dilemma created by a scepticism about the possibility of any reliable, empirically grounded knowledge of the cultural past which only arises if it is assumed that scientific knowledge is characteristically reducible to observational data and that only observables are knowable. This, however, is tantamount to accepting an extremely restrictive form of empiricism which, if consist-ently held, would rule out physics as a scientific enterprise and would call most established explanatory theory into question. It assumes that fact and theory may be sharply distinguished and that theory is, if meaningful and scientifi-cally acceptable, parasitic on a stable base of observation statements. The difficulty with this, which is relevant here and has been widely acknowledged in the archaeological literature, is that facts in any field are always and necessarily constituted within a theoretical context.[1] Even observation involves a theoretical element where a principle of con-nection must be introduced to constitute objects of per-ception out of discrete bits of visual experience. On a higher level, the theoretical principles that make explanatory sense of a field of perceptually constituted facts generally do this by specifying connections among facts which are not them-selves observable, that is, by referring them to underlying

productive mechanisms or causal relations which are assumed to have generated them. These principles, which may be said to 'colligate' or give form to a body of disparate facts, are rarely simply a shorthand description of the facts themselves so that virtually any scientific knowledge (even descriptive knowledge of fact) involves some theoretical extension beyond the observable. A 'realist' theory of science, which acknowledges (indeed, emphasises) this aspect of scientific knowledge, can, in fact, make a strong argument to the effect that it is just this extension beyond observables, this attempt to bring into view the mechanisms and processes responsible for manifest phenomena, that characterises science and gives scientific theory its unique explanatory power.

The point of this is simply that it is not unique to archaeology or to structuralist enquiry that the interesting theories should be under-determined by all available data or that unobservable dimensions of the cultural reality in ques-tion should be the primary object of enquiry. Mellor (1973) brought this point home in his criticisms of Leach's scep-ticism (described above) and he concludes that 'While the data will always be flimsy, the tests inconclusive, the scope for imaginative alternative theories great, none of this reduces archaeological theorizing to the level of guesswork' (1975, p. 670). In particular, I might add, it does not estab-lish that a structural archaeology is, in principle, unscientific and limited to arbitrary speculation.

It would seem, then, that there should be some epis-temological options open to the structural archaeologist that escape Glassie's dilemma. One suggested by the realist con-ception of science, mentioned above, is that the structuralist programme be treated as a procedure of constructing models which, on the linguistic metaphor, attempt to bring order to disparate bits of cultural phenomena by providing an account of the cognitive and ideational factors assumed to have been instrumental in generating them. While these models will inevitably be under-determined by the accessible empirical data, they purport to represent mechanisms or processes that actually existed and produced the phenomena in question. They are not, that is, constructed as convenient or conven-tional fictions; they are formulated on the basis of an explicitly realist presupposition that such mechanisms or processes did exist and operate independently of our knowl-edge (or lack of knowledge) of them and are indirectly accessible to us through their tangible, surviving effects. Because they therefore carry quite specific ontological com-mitments (i.e. they make claims about actual past conditions responsible for the record), these models will be subject to two sets of constraints which set them decisively apart from the products of purely speculative interpretation: (a) plausi-bility considerations introduced by the analytic model (as a model of the nature of the phenomena in question) and mediated by background knowledge of how such phenomena could have been generated, and (b) empirical constraints on what may reasonably be claimed about the cultural past adduced from the material record of conditions and processes that actually existed in the past. These constraints do, I suggest, impose significant restrictions on the content of explanatory models (even when they refer to such intangibles as cognitive factors) assuring some measure of confidence in their claims about the past and providing strong grounds for resisting Leach's (and Glassie's) scepticism about the possibility of any non-speculative knowledge of the cultural past.

Pettit's account of structuralism as a research programme captures the overall form of the methodology by which these constraints are brought to bear on explanatory theory inasmuch as its point of departure is a conceptual restructuring of the field in the light of a general theory (i.e. an analytic model) defining the nature of the material in question. It is within this conceptual framework that the archaeologist can begin to construct potential explanatory models by a procedure of drawing on background knowledge as a 'source' of models of the mechanisms that could have produced the 'subject' phenomena (i.e. it is a procedure of analogically constructing explanatory models which necessarily draws on sources different from the subject; see Harré 1970, chapter 2). This construction is closely controlled conceptually, on one hand, by the analytic model which, in effect, delimits a search space for candidate models, ruling out, for example, models which represent ecological or technological factors as the primary determinants of variability in material culture and directing attention to source contexts in which articulating mechanisms of a cognitive sort are known to operate (especially those contexts in which, as in the Bourdieu example cited earlier, their operation is expressed in a material dimension). The use made of these sources, i.e. the actual construction of candidate explanatory models, may be controlled, on the other hand, by certain formal and substantive criteria that, contrary to New Archaeology rhetoric (which rules the use of scientific contexts as a categorically unreliable form of inference), can effectively control the credibility or strength of the inference by which information is transferred from source to subject. They require, in the first instance, that conjectures about real, though unobservable, conditions or processes be informed by detailed analysis of the accessible (relevant) source contexts which serves to identify a range of causal mechanisms necessary for or capable of producing the effects in question and which, most importantly, defines the conditions under which they may be expected to operate. The analogical inference itself is, then, a *selective* projection onto the past of those features of known (or imaginable) mechanisms which, on the basis of a systematic comparison of source and subject contexts (i.e. in light of the parameters established concerning the conditions governing the operation of these mechanisms), could or most likely would have been present in the past and have produced the existing archaeological record. No assumption need be made that specific known source contexts are uniquely comparable to the past or that, as a whole, they exhaust the possibilities of

past cultural forms. The general methodological principle involved is simply that known contexts may be expected to provide guidelines for the reconstruction of mechanisms or conditions that would have been capable of producing a given body of data.

It is at least more plausible to expect that something like known mechanisms, or mechanisms governed by the same parameters as known mechanisms, operated in the past than to postulate such total discontinuity that the past is considered completely unreconstructable from its material record and knowledge of contemporary cultural phenomena. The slide from reasonable doubt that any modern context directly corresponds to past ones, to radical scepticism about the possibility of gaining any insight into the past (necessarily based, to some extent, on knowledge of contemporary cultural phenomena) occurs only if radical discontinuity between past and present is assumed (i.e. such that past cultural reality is assumed to be so totally different that it is not reconstructable from present cultural contexts and is probably not even recognisable as cultural in any current sense of the term), and if the modelling process is represented as an arbitrary projection of whole, actualised ethnographic contexts onto the past. As the discussion here indicates, analogical inference need not be uncontrolled and arbitrary in the sense frequently assumed by archaeological positivists who reject it out of hand as unscientific. Failure to specify the (usually limited) points on which an analogy holds (i.e. to specify the positive, negative and neutral aspects of an analogical comparison of items or contexts) and an indiscriminate carrying over of all features of the source to the subject exemplify bad analogical argument. Though analogical inference will always be ampliative and therefore less than logically certain, it need not be misleading and speculative; there are definable degrees of reliability and strength in analogical argument and criteria of formulation by which it may be controlled.

The assumption of radical discontinuity, the other presupposition of radical scepticism, only holds if it is denied that there are any natural (cultural) connections or processes governing the correlation of cultural attributes and the generation of new cultural forms, which is, in effect, to accept a Humean analysis of causal relations (applied to the cultural world) whereby they are held to be purely formal, hence radically contingent and unreconstructable (or, unprojectible) associations among attributes or events. Such denial would undermine the possibility of any anthropological knowledge and seems, in any case, largely unwarranted (in fact and practice). Though there may be fairly extreme variability in cultural forms, it is not entirely fortuitous or arbitrary; there remains the possibility of a cautious, controlled reconstruction of cultural possibilities given knowledge of actual generative processes operating in the cultural realm. Ironically, Leach defends this possibility when he argues that, in fact, all humans (as humans) share certain fundamental cognitive structuring capabilities (primarily a propensity for binary structuring on all dimensions of their behaviour and material production) such that it is reasonable, he says, to assume that 'there may well be characteristics of that archaic mental landscape that we can recognise' (1977, p. 169) and that would provide a basis for grasping the cognitive, semiological significance of their surviving material culture. Thus, while he rejects simple-minded uniformitarianism (that fails to acknowledge the creative capacity of the human actor), he provides the conceptual basis for adopting a methodology of controlled reconstruction similar to that developed by nineteenth-century geologists who postulated an anti-deluvial model of the history and formation of existing geological features on the principle that it is at least more reasonable to assume that processes (or, in the cultural case, cognitive capacities) similar to those observable in the contemporary geological world, operated in the past to generate these features than to postulate a completely novel formation process (such as instantaneous, divine creation and/or floods). It is to be recognised that this methodology can accommodate the selective use of a range of sources so that the model of basic cognitive capabilities or cultural processes may be amended in the light of knowledge of other sorts of phenomena where the populations or contexts in question are recognisably different from known 'cultural' contexts (i.e. guidelines for reconstruction are not limited to ethnographic background knowledge).

Depending on the archaeologist's knowledge of the field under study, the analytic model and background information about the kinds of mechanisms capable of producing the effects in question will provide either a range of candidate models for selection or a general idea of the kind of mechanism involved which needs to be refined to fit a given situation. The collection and analysis of data in the field is then carried out as a systematic observation of the effects of the postulated mechanisms which serves to introduce a further type of constraint; empirical constraints imposed by the archaeological record as surviving evidence of the conditions that actually existed in the past. Though the record may not select for a unique solution to the problem of reconstruction or explanation, archaeological research does, as a whole, bear out the operative, realist assumption that the data are sufficiently independent of superimposed interpretation to challenge, to force revision and even rejection of the theoretical constructs intended to explain them.[2] The import of this is that the archaeological record can be expected to provide good empirical grounds for selecting among candidate models or for forming a general idea about the type of mechanism involved so that it accounts for a particular range of phenomena; though there will inevitably be some ambiguity, archaeologists are not in the position of having no recourse but to speculate and to rely on purely conventional criteria for the selection of theory which makes explanatory sense of their data as cultural (i.e. meaningful) phenomena.

Archaeological information is empirically constraining of what archaeologists can meaningfully say about it as a record of past cultural contexts in two respects. It is constraining, in the first instance, as an intractable subject which does not always obligingly accommodate the models that are intended to give it form and explanation. It may also, however, be engaged in an active dialogue and in this it provides a test of theories built up after its cultural antecedents. The hypothetico-deductive model of scientific procedure has traditionally been invoked as an account of this testing procedure and though it is minimally adequate, it has one serious flaw; it treats the test situation as one of confrontation between theory, constituted in a context of discovery, and a body of independently gathered fact. Given the close formative relation between fact and theory established earlier, it does not seem reasonable that facts could ever confront theory in this way; observation is constituted as fact and facts acquire significance as relevant evidence only within a theoretical framework, generally the one which is under test (see reference to Binford, p. 46). The empirical constraint seems, then, to make itself felt through a subtle, mutually conditioning interaction between fact and theory more like that described by Collingwood's logic of question-and-answer than by the hypothetico-deductive model (Collingwood 1939, chapter 5).

The procedure by which empirical constraints are brought to bear on theory is not, however, necessarily or viciously circular for all its reflexiveness. It is a process of 'trying out' different explanatory ways of conceptualising the data suggested by the analytic framework to see if, when the data are conceived as the outcome of one type of mechanism rather than another, they are better integrated or take on a more intelligible form. Internally, this is a process of continually asking whether an invoked mechanism accounts for the range of data involved or, more important, whether it anticipates or brings to light further specific facts of association among the phenomena that could only be expected if the given mechanism had, in fact, been responsible for the structure of items in the record.[3] The empirical constraints operate when, in the course of this process, some among the explanatory models are held, amended or rejected according to their effectiveness in establishing an inherent structure of connection or principle of unity in the data.

It is important to recognise, in this connection, that, as Mellor has commented, 'such intellectual bootstrap operations are not in principle ad hoc, nor are they peculiar to archaeology ... [they are] a corollary of theories inevitably going beyond all the data they can explain and against which they can be tested' (1973, p. 479). They are, in effect, unavoidably common scientific practice and represent the sort of methodological option that, I suggest, is open to a structural archaeology. The procedure of 'bringing a rich idea to sparse data to govern its description' and thus make explanatory sense of it (as Pettit describes it, 1977, p. 88) only becomes unscientific, coercive speculation if the explanatory model is so vaguely formulated that it will accommodate any body of data or if the description of 'fact' is manipulated so that any body of data can be fitted into the given theoretical framework. This, Pettit suggests, is the weakness of Lévi-Strauss' method of analysis which he characterises as 'little more than a license for the free exercise of imagination' (1977, p. 92) but it is not, he insists, a shortcoming which need characterise structuralism as a research programme.

Pettit's suggestion is that if the postulated explanatory models are sharply formulated and description controlled (i.e. such that there is a genuine possibility of the data challenging claims of the models), then the theories which emerge confirmed, or at least reinforced and sustained, by an active probing of the record may legitimately be said to have been conditioned and selected for by the empirical data to which they give form. Though they will never enjoy conclusive confirmation, there are, at least, compelling reasons for accepting them as an account of the past over arbitrary speculation which has not been subject to these constraints. Consequently, structuralism in general and archaeology in particular need not acquiesce in the face of charges that they are restricted to non-empirical, non-scientific forms of enquiry; there are methodological options by which they may rise above the dilemma posed by Glassie and Leach. In the final analysis, however, the potential and value of a structuralist archaeology depends on the ability of the structuralist researcher to move beyond the arguments which establish, in general terms, the need to consider cognitive variables, opening up the field to structuralist analysis, and to develop, within this rubric, sharply defined, empirically plausible models of the kinds of articulating mechanisms capable of structuring material culture, and a methodology of controlled scientific inference and recursive question-and-answer testing whereby these can be refined into explanatory models appropriate to specific archaeological contexts.

To illustrate in closing how this challenge might be met and how the methodological options beyond speculation might be effectively exploited by a structural archaeology, let me briefly review Glassie's analysis of Middle Virginian folk housing which I take to be an example of structuralist procedure applied to a non-linguistic field at its best and which, despite Glassie's official scepticism, does suggest how structural analysis of material culture may be governed by empirical constraints such that the explanatory model proposed as its outcome has strong empirical claims for acceptance.

As Pettit might expect, Glassie opens his analysis with an account of the sort of timeless conventions that live on in Virginian culture which serves to challenge the way we would ordinarily see the architecture, suggesting that it, too, embodies these conventions and is to be regarded, along structuralist lines, as 'meaning-determined' material. The linguistic nature of the analytic model introduced at this point only becomes clear when Glassie begins to exploit its inherent standards of plausibility and to draw out what he calls a 'general idea' with which to approach the data. This

idea is essentially that, where the folk architecture comprises a recognisable tradition and, in this, manifests quite a definite, limited range of forms, it must be assumed that something like a linguistic competence — he calls it an architectural competence — governed the design process.

Glassie's objective in research is, accordingly, to develop an explanatory model of the specific competence, the 'unconscious cultural logic', that informed Virginian designers and defined the architectural tradition that they generated. In this, he is concerned to form his 'general idea' into an explanatory theory which would, he says, 'enable the analyst to locate an unexpected abundance of information in discrete things — things floating free of their contexts — and to relate apparently unconnected phenomena into a system' (1975, p. 41). That is, he seeks to disembed the governing, cognitive and cultural principles, to reconstruct the context which, once grasped, would effectively 'colligate' the surviving fragments of an architectural tradition, giving them coherent, explanatory form and meaning.

Though he frequently represents the processes of data collection and theory or model formulation as separate aspects of research (consistent with the empiricist view of science mentioned earlier) the accumulation of data for his study seems to be clearly a process of constituting facts, that is, of giving them form and significance as the outcome of a (postulated) design process governed by specific structuring principles in the course of which the explanatory model of a Virginian architectural competence is more and more closely defined. He observes, in this connection, that the general idea which initiated his search for an architectural competence, in fact, served him as a 'useful guide in the accumulation and interpretation of information' and, in practice, he constructed his model of competence through a process of probing the data that closely approximates the logic of question-and-answer described earlier. That is, he framed his investigation as a search for answers to the question, 'what principles must have guided Virginian designers such that they generated the observable (limited) range of architectural forms in question?', thus refining the general idea that Virginian architecture is semiological and using the constraints of standards of plausibility introduced with the analytic model itself and the empirical data which were to be explained. As a whole, then, his research programme failed to preserve the sharp separation of 'scientific', empirical enquiry and speculative theoretical interpretation described in the discussion cited earlier; theory enters directly into the procedure of data collection and is, itself, closely and deliberately controlled by the factual evidence thus recovered.

The model of competence with which Glassie emerges at the end of his analysis defines a basic inventory of geometric forms (diagonally defined squares and a series of regular extensions of them into rectangles) and a set of structuring rules which Virginian designers must presumably have followed in order to have added, massed, pierced and otherwise elaborated these forms into traditional, 'well-formed' houses. This model deserves acceptance as a non-arbitrary, empirically grounded explanatory theory, first, because it was formulated in a process of probing the data in which the model was directly responsive to empirical constraints. In this, the model was specified closely enough to risk being challenged by the data and where this occurred, Glassie revised the model rather than altering his descriptions to fit it.[4] Second, the model itself seems, in the end, to be assimilated to the data it fits closely and in this, it successfully draws out a governing 'fact' of structural unity among the details of the field. The presence of this unity is good evidence that the kind of competence proposed did, in fact, generate the regular, traditional structures observed among Virginian houses. Though there may be other explanatory alternatives, since this one is not uniquely reducible to or determined by the data, it does have strong empirical claim for acceptance and, *contra* Glassie himself, it is considerably more than pure guesswork or arbitrary speculation. Finally, it is to be noted in this connection, that the explanatory model enjoys this credibility precisely because of the integration of fact and theory in the research process which Glassie had resisted in his statements of methodological policy. While a certain (untenable) 'objectivity' on the observational level (required of science by empiricist theories) may have been sacrificed, the explanatory model that emerges of the interactive procedure described is closely tied to and supported by its empirical basis, thus warranting the claim that it approximates to a subject reality. It is, in fact, only when theory is constituted in a separate interpretive stage of research and superimposed on the data (such that it is detached from and an extrapolation beyond 'fact') that it may legitimately be impugned as 'pure speculation'.

Though most archaeologists will not have access, as Glassie did, to linguistic expressions of the world view embodied by an architectural (or other material culture) tradition, the first level of Glassie's study, his reconstruction of the mediating competence, does seem to exemplify a viable strategy for dealing with symbols and cognitive variables as they figure in archaeological contexts. Consideration of beliefs or world views simply represents an extension of the structuralist method to deeper levels of the cognitive reality in question and, in fact, there will always be further possibilities for explanation whenever one level of generative mechanism has been brought into view and demands explanation in terms of other, underlying conditions; archaeologists are in the position of grappling with that level of cognitive reality most immediately presupposed by their data. The general thesis here has been that, while structuralism offers a compelling but epistemologically problematic conception of archaeological data (i.e. demanding consideration of enigmatic cognitive factors), it is, in addition, a (potentially) scientific approach inasmuch as it resists the appeal of cautious restriction of enquiry to observation, and endorses a process of reaching beyond what is or has been made accessible that characterises distinctively scientific enquiry and is, in large part, the key to its success. Its great

value is that it challenges archaeologists to come to terms with the cognitive, semiological and symbolic significance of their data as distinctively cultural material and, in this, forces them to explore methodological options which, successfully developed, promise to carry the discipline decisively beyond the scepticism and narrow empiricism that has comprised the controlling epistemological frame of research.

Notes

1 Binford makes this point in a particularly interesting discussion of archaeological theory when he observes that 'the scientist must use conceptual tools to evaluate alternative conceptual tools that have been advanced regarding the way the world works' (1978, p. 3). Here he acknowledges the essential reflexiveness of scientific enquiry and the interpenetration of theoretical and observational levels of enquiry.

2 One instance in which a case is made quite explicitly for the importance of empirical constraints is W.D. Strong's (1939) defence of the possibility of using the archaeological record as a testing ground for reconstructions of prehistory when his own research in Nebraska had effectively overturned the established theories about plains cultures. This illustrates the sense in which the record is capable of passively resisting superinduced interpretive models.

3 As Collingwood describes it, this is a process of asking, 'if the phenomena were produced in *x* way' or, 'for *x* purpose, would this not have generated a particular "*y*" type of pattern or output?' and then checking to see how far the data bear out these expectations.

4 This responsiveness is most clear when he describes how his original idea about the basic geometric forms involved had to be revised (the units proved not to be defined by their end measurement but, as indicated, by the diagonal measurement) and it is evident throughout his discussion of how the structuring principles articulate with observable architectural form.

References

Bhaskar, R. (1975) *A Realist Theory of Science*, Harvester Press, Leeds

Binford, L.R. (1978) *For Theory Building*, Academic Press, New York

Collingwood, R.G. (1979, originally published in 1939) *Autobiography*, Oxford University Press, Oxford

Glassie, H. (1975) *Middle Virginian Folk Housing*, University of Tennessee Press, Knoxville

Glucksmann, M. (1974) *Structuralist Analysis in Contemporary Thought*, Routledge and Kegan Paul, London

Harré, R.H. (1970) *Principles of Scientific Thinking*, Macmillan, London

Leach, E. (1970) *Lévi-Strauss*, Fontana, Glasgow

Leach, E. (1973) 'Concluding address' in C. Renfrew (ed.) *The Explanation of Culture Change*, Duckworth, London

Leach, E. (1977) 'A view from the bridge' in M. Spriggs (ed.) *Archaeology and Anthropology*, B.A.R. Supplementary Series 19, Oxford

Lévi-Strauss, C. (1972) *Structural Anthropology*, Penguin, Harmondsworth

Mellor, D.H. (1973) 'On some methodological misconceptions' in C. Renfrew (ed.) *The Explanation of Culture Change*, Duckworth, London

Pettit, P. (1977) *The Concept of Structuralism: A Critical Analysis*, University of California Press, Berkeley

Strong, W.D. (1939) *Introduction to Nebraska Archaeology*, Smithsonian Miscellaneous Collections 93 (10)

PART TWO

The search for models

Chapter 5

**Matters material
and ideal**
Susan Kus

In her introduction, Susan Kus emphasises culture as being meaningfully constituted within historical and intersubjective contexts, and describes the need for a greater dialogue between the social sciences and philosophy. The question of the legitimation of a sociopolitical order in complex societies is seen as concerning the relationship between the social order, a natural order and the individual. It is the 'naturalisation' of the social order which is taken up as the focus of the discussion. A distinction is made between legitimating strategies, a distinction between the confounding of the social and natural spheres of activity and representation on the one hand, and the bringing of order different from that inherent in physical nature on the other. Means for the constitution of a legitimating order in spatial relationships are examined in relation to ethnohistorical evidence from the Merina of Madagascar. The spatial layout of the regional settlement pattern and within settlement pattern is shown to play a role in a legitimation of the social order in which the natural and the socially constructed are both involved.

Philosophy is nature in us, the others in us, and we in them. Accordingly, we must not simply say that philosophy is compatible with sociology, but that it is necessary to it as a constant reminder of its tasks, and that each time the sociologist returns to the living sources of his knowledge, to what operates within him as means of understanding the forms of culture most remote from him he practices philosophy spontaneously.   (Merleau-Ponty 1974, p. 107)

One can immediately appreciate the problem that any notion of idea or individual presents to the archaeologist confronted with the anonymous material remains of a society. Yet, it is these apparently methodologically elusive issues that are theoretically critical to the understanding of archaeology as a social and historical science and of the archaeologist as participant in meaningful discourse.

The methods of the natural sciences would appear to be of use to the archaeologist in the description of archaeological materials and of the relations between such materials in an archaeological context. Yet, this methodological facility does not entail unmistakable theoretical directives. The 'objects' confronting the archaeologist fit the assumptions of an empirical science that wishes to see physical objects as completely specified in objective space and time even less adequately than do the 'objects' confronting the natural scientist.[1] Merleau-Ponty, though far from having been an archaeologist or having been specifically interested in the discipline of archaeology has, nonetheless, remarked with insight on the theoretical dilemma facing the archaeologist: 'The animals painted on the walls of Lascaux are not there in the same way as the fissures and limestone formations' (1974, p. 285). The material remains of a given culture are both produced and specified in a field of human perception and conception, that is, such material items are aspects of a meaningfully structured configuration, a configuration which includes not only matters material but matters ideational as well. They exist and have existed in a context of structures of 'natural' and 'social' systems within a field of symbolic interaction. Meaning, rather than being incidental or contingent to, is constitutive of culture, 'culture' being understood here in the most inclusive sense of the term.

Simply giving credence to a concept of collective consciousness or ideology as traditionally understood, or even examining a concept of knowledge defined as socially shared pragmatic information, as suggested by Childe (1956), is theoretically insufficient to handling a concept of meaning in social theoretical discourse. This is because the dimensions of meaning include not only the social dimensions of 'symbol' and 'structure', but also the dimensions of subjective 'experience' and 'representation', dimensions of an inescapable human scale. Though this is to argue that the final context and thus the final dimensioning of meaning is in subjective experience and representation, it is not the case that meaning is simply subjective intention and expression. Meaning necessarily encompasses the consequences of expressive action, for ideally the individual is capable of not only acting through volition, but of taking responsibility for the consequences of such actions as well, consequences which are aspects of the intersubjective context and of material processes. It is only within the dialectical relationship between subjective experience and expression and the intersubjective context that meaning is possible.[2] Too often the social sciences have denied the dialectical nature of this

relationship by reifying and opposing the categories of individual and society. Such a forced dichotomy can only lead to academic exercises such as reductionist explanations or normative descriptions, to a simple choice between conformity or non-conformity in social praxis (Spurling 1977, p. 95), and, perhaps more importantly for the social scientist, to the forfeiture of meaning in individual experience and expression by rendering such meaning as idiosyncratic, anonymous, or epiphenomenal to sociocultural processes.

In beginning to handle any constellation of concepts when arguing that culture is meaningfully constituted, it becomes clear that the issue then is *not* one of a simple exchange of a materialist or empiricist stance for an idealist or rationalist argument; the issue is displaced beyond the conventional controversies of a positivist—romantic debate (Brown 1978). To argue that subjective experience and expression is inseparable from an intersubjective context is to argue, more importantly, that consciousness is inseparable from an historical and an existential context. Neither side of the traditional contrasts, such as materialist and idealist, or empiricist and rationalist, positions which have served to underpin most theoretical discourse in archaeology, adequately handle the critical dimensions of history and the existential. Within such traditional perspectives either history is viewed as simply the progressive actualisation of the pre-ordained or the existential is considered as contingent to the 'real'. To thus strip the force from the concepts of history and the existential is to render culture just one more object for the sciences and to alienate meaning from the individual at the final level by rendering meaning as external to history, inconsequential to existence, or as incomplete or unattainable as it regards the individual.

If we are willing to accept some form of the proposition that a culture is meaningfully constituted, and if we further take the position that meaning is not simply a presupposition to social theory, but that the problem of meaning is central to social theoretical discourse (Brown 1978, p. 24), then we open such theoretical discourse to themes encompassed by traditional philosophical discourse. In particular, the concepts of history and the existential context must be open to re-examination in our social theoretical discourse insofar as they are dimensions critical to a concept of meaning.

To suggest that the social sciences and philosophy have words to exchange is neither novel nor new to either domain. Modern European literature, philosophy and social science recognised early a common interest in problems connected with the question of meaning (Douglas 1973), recognising that a concept of meaning is as critical to the understanding of a social 'object' of study as it is to decisions of individual praxis. The correlate theme of the 'social construction of reality' is a point critical to many social theoretical discussions going back to Hegel and Marx, as well as to Durkheim and Mauss. This intellectual and artistic current eventually places epistemological issues squarely within the field of a sociological theory of knowledge (Douglas 1973, p. 9).

One individual to have addressed such philosophical issues in archaeological discourse is V. Gordon Childe. In a very immediate way Childe's theoretical directions pulled him towards a recognition of the critical theoretical burden that knowledge, belief and epistemology carry in the social sciences. Childe specifically addressed the questions of individual, society and history in a philosophically reflective manner in two works: an article entitled 'The sociology of knowledge' and a short book entitled *Society and Knowledge*. Suffice it to say that these two works, which illustrate the penetrating and intricate nexus of arguments underpinning his theoretical contributions to archaeology, merit more attention than the cursory remarks that are to follow. It is the basic assumption of these two works, the assumption that the objects confronting the archaeologist must be treated 'always and exclusively as concrete expressions and embodiments of human thoughts and ideas' (1956, p. 1), which allowed Childe to understand epistemological problems as involving a concept of society, as well as a concept of knowledge held by individuals.

Childe began with an empiricist epistemology but his insistence upon a reading of Marx and a concern for archaeological data, that is, an insistence on the intersubjective context and on history, allowed him to overstep traditional stumbling blocks of a strict empiricist definition of epistemology. Yet, the cost of this introduction of society and history into epistemology was the cost of embracing a strong normative and utilitarian definition of knowledge.[3] (It should be noted, however, that Childe himself judged such a definition as adequate to the needs of social theory in archaeology.) Childe recognised society as the final arbitrator of any definition of knowledge, arguing that a notion of absolute knowledge is meaningless in practice, for the 'best of reasons' upon which a notion of truth is based are those reasons society declares as 'best', as a society provides the reference and the only effective means of correcting error: 'Conceptual errors can be exposed in precisely the same way as perceptual error — only in practice, only by human co-operative action' (Childe 1956, p. 117). Childe's arguments, in effect, recognise a concept of knowledge as dependent on a social and historical context.

The socialisation of knowledge by Childe is based ultimately upon a central proposition in Marx's argument, that 'social being determines consciousness' (Williams 1977, p. 75). However, it will be noted that Childe formalised this concept into the apparently correlate argument that knowledge possessed by the individual is socially determined. The effect of this correlate was to wrest knowledge from its roots in subjective experience, and thus to avoid the threat of psychological reductionist arguments in epistemology and the social sciences, by containing it theoretically in the intersubjective context. Childe's theoretical strategic coup is to be admired; this argument guarantees that the inventory of archaeological data can be mapped perfectly onto that part of the cognitive domain which carries social theoretical relevance. Yet, if we look closer at this correlate argument, it is clear that it is not faithful to the original proposition of Marx. The original proposition that 'social being determines consciousness' places subjective experience and expression in a very immediate dialectical relationship with the intersubjective context. Childe's correlate on the other hand reifies and separates the individual from society at a critical juncture of being by classifying personalised judgement as belief and anonymous consent as knowledge. If we as social scientists and as historians, despite a primary theoretical focus on the intersubjective context, wish to avoid 'setting society up as an abstraction over and against the individual' (Marx as quoted in Fromm 1961), as well as alienating ourselves from our theoretical discourse (both are implications of Childe's arguments), then we must recognise a concept of meaning as going beyond the bounds of an epistemology preoccupied with the historical development of 'scientific' knowledge. We must also be willing to pose further questions on the forms and limits of subjective experience and expression within the historical and existential context eventually leading to the re-examination of our definitions of knowledge and belief as they relate to a concept of meaning.

Recognising the dialectic of the intersubjective and the subjective, it becomes obvious that we cannot continue to 'reify science as something external to humans rather than seeing it as symbolic human creation through and through' (Brown 1978, p. 20). Further, philosophy, as well as science, must be recognised as a product of, and grounded in, subjective experience and expression. Consequently, the suggested dialogue between the social sciences and philosophy is not simply a question of common themes. Rather, the dialogue possible and necessary between the social sciences and philosophy is quite radical within the outlines of the perspective sketched above. In this dialogue not only do concepts and conceptual structurings stand to be reformulated in the light of the dynamics of history and the lived experience (rather than remaining unquestioned in the stasis of the absolute), but science and philosophy stand to be redefined. This latter project of redefinition has been repeatedly suggested by authors from Marx to Merleau-Ponty.

In essence, the project of history is a philosophical project where the lived human drama, and not a postulated transcendental cosmological order, is recognised as the subject of philosophy. In an interesting twist the more our social theoretical arguments seek to encompass history the more they become dependent on philosophical arguments. Where social—historical contexts contrast dramatically is where we are forced to give fuller attention and expression to those issues that we consider to be common to the human situation, to questions concerning form and variation in experience, as well as to the means of expressing and understanding being-in-the-world. Yet, the domain of philosophy is not only a domain encompassing themes of eternal fascination.

Philosophy is also a method of reflective thought, that is, of critical consciousness. This method is of crucial importance in addressing questions concerning an historical context, for the only means we have to understanding history are indirect. History does not speak for itself and neither is the social scientist removed from an historical context. As Merleau-Ponty (1974, p. 313) has said: 'We can never be the past, it is only a spectacle before us which is there for us to question. The questions come from us, and thus the responses in principle do not exhaust historical reality, since historical reality does not depend upon them for its existence.' Social theoretical discourse and our understanding of history thus depend on the poetry or poverty of our questions. Philosophy, both as generalisations drawn from immediate human experience and as self-reflective thought upon our representations of the human drama, is the only tool we have to evaluate critically the validity and to assess the limitations of these questions which we bring to history in our attempt to create a context of meaning which seeks to extend itself beyond our specific social and historical context.

When we set ourselves the specific task of reflecting upon social—theoretical arguments, we can begin to trace through the lines of suppositions that underpin our more specific arguments and uncover their philosophically generalised base. However, when we concentrate our attention on a specific social—historical context, it is easy to lose sight of the encompassing scale of theoretical frameworks. This is because it is easy to confuse representation with a notion of description at the most specific level of an experiential and representational context. If we recognise the social—historical context as the major determining factor of experience and representation, then it is the case that the closer the alternative social—historical context which we are examining approximates to our present social—historical context, the more specified and concrete in social—historical content appear the vocabulary and the questions we bring to history. Questions that preoccupy our own socio-political discourse are easy to pose and seem equally valid given the similarities of vocabulary and institutions within the context of other complex societies. This is to say that social scientists interested in the study of complex societies have a certain possibility of posing questions which are at the same time personal and socially generalisable. Because such individuals are investigating contexts which are close to their own social and historical contexts of meaning, they can pose questions at a very specific level of vocabulary, conceptual organisation, and material experiential context. Yet, since the contexts they are investigating are, in fact, different contexts, the refraction rather than replication of their questions offers the possibility of demonstrating their generality or of discovering the conceptual means to their generalisation. However, the proximity of contexts has the very real risk that the apparent concreteness and immediacy of the issues under examination facilitate their reification as social and

historical 'facts' obscuring their position within a conceptual framework upon which their existence and meaning is dependent.

Our contemporary experiential social context is overwhelmingly determined by the institutions and structurings of a state-organised society. The scale and comprehensiveness of this social—historical environment as argued above necessarily colour the questions we bring to a field of social theory, particularly when reinforced within the context of alternative complex social forms. Questions concerning the origins, organisation, and operation of complex societies are an understandable theoretical preoccupation. Yet, in this preoccupation it is easy to lose sight of the individual and the subjective level of experience and representation in society. In certain cases social theoreticians have gone as far as investing society with goals, with the *elan vital* of 'reproduction' and 'growth', leaving the individual as a means to accomplish society's ends. However, if we leave the individual as a means to an end, and if we deny the subjective as a necessary scale in our social theory, then we once again leave meaning as epiphenomenal to a social formation.

To avoid unnecessary reification of the social form we might insist on the human scale of our social—theoretical questions by recognising them as being ultimately based on our own individual experience and representation. To be clear, this is not to deny their contextualisation in a social—historical or intersubjective context. In fact, we must insist on the recognition of this context to allow a personalisation of our theoretical questions while avoiding idiosyncratic forms. It is precisely at the juncture of the subject within the social—historical context that we might profitably begin social—theoretical questioning, recognising a repertoire of questions that not only includes those addressing the character of society, but also those addressing the character of individual experience and representation within society. Here it is important not to confuse a theoretical or representational scale with the dimensions of methodological exigencies. Archaeologists have traditionally approached the individual in the archaeological context either through the reconstruction of modal behaviour or through idiosyncratic identification. Yet, our theoretical enquiry is not necessarily limited to the identification and description of extremes of generalised, anonymous and depersonalised behaviour and of unique acts as materially manifested. Rather, if an understanding of history is possible then the questions we ask of history must be ultimately based on the recognition and exploration of the elements of the subjective human situation shared between our present context, the only frame of meaningful reference we have, and from which we cannot stand aside,[4] and the historical situation we are investigating.

Anthropological archaeology has made substantial contributions to our understanding of the operations of complex societies. Yet, social change is not simply characterised by changes in the volume, form and organisation of material production; such changes are contingent upon changes in meaning and ordering in the representational sphere. An order of meaning and representation is inextricably interwoven with an order of activity in society and is thus equally critical to the understanding of the self-production of society (Touraine 1977). There is a complementary series of questions yet to be fully and adequately addressed by anthropological archaeology, precisely the questions posed at the level of the dialectic of the subject within such a social context. One such question is the formulation of a concept of legitimacy as it relates to a socio-political order. Legitimacy is not an inherent attribute of society. It is a question posed within a human order of meaning and perhaps a question only possible in the dialectic of the subject within the social and historical context of a complex society.

It is perhaps only the context of complex societies wherein the possibility of a high degree of material manifestation and conceptual reification and abstraction provides an experiential and representational field for the emergence[5] of a particular conceptualisation of society. This is a debatable point, but at the risk of oversimplifying the distinction between complex and non-complex societies, it could be said that within complex societies we begin to see dramatic increases in the degree of objectification of social production, institutionalisation of social activity, and consequently conceptual reification and abstraction of social relations. The distinction of complex societies from non-complex societies is also characterised by a certain level of social discourse that is both possible and necessary in the former context. The complex differentiation of activity and representation in complex societies manifests itself as potential disorder needing resolution, not only at the level of activity but at the conceptual level as well (Bourdieu 1977). The need for the re-constitution of order within such contexts 'permits and requires the development of a body of specialists charged with raising the level of [social] discourse, so as to rationalize and systematize [experience]' (Bourdieu 1977, p. 233, n. 16).

What is being argued here, in part, is that aspects of a field of social discourse are thematically re-aligned in complex societies in comparison to a field of discourse in non-complex societies; the form and 'nature' of society or of the socio-political order find increasing need to be specifically addressed in social discourse in complex societies. Questions on the 'nature' of society find their formulation in a conceptual field that potentially recognises the positing of a concept of a social or a socio-political order in contradistinction, both to a concept of the individual participant in this social order and to a concept of physical nature.[6] In a conceptual field which recognises a concept of a socio-political order that stands above the individual and is distinguishable, in part, from the natural order, a number of concomitant themes of social discourse present themselves. One of the more interesting problematic themes to arise in this context is the question of the 'legitimation' of a socio-

political order. 'Legitimation' is used here in the most encompassing sense of the term, a sense which invokes such topics as tradition, pattern and authority, as well as lawfulness.[7] This question of legitimation is the question of the definition and justification of the social order in its activities as it relates both to the activities and goals of individuals and to a natural order of items and events. That is, the question of legitimacy is posed not simply in the *recognition* of a concept of society, but in the definition of a social order in *relation* to a natural order and in *relation* to the individual.

The meaningful dimensions that a society assigns to concepts of a natural order, a social order and the individual are major determinants of the character of the society's self-production[8] (Touraine 1977), its capacity for action upon itself and its environment. Where there exists an historical materialist understanding of the constitution of a social order, this creative capacity opens onto an enlarged field of individual and historical choice. That is, Marx recognised nature as a societal category, but he further understood human society as included in nature (Schmidt 1971). It was with this awareness and the dialectical understanding that nature, the sole object of knowledge, is only presented to consciousness in social formulations, along with the further understanding that society is ultimately constituted by individuals entering into social relations with one another, that Marx hoped to confront humanity, and thus society, with historical choice. Within such a perspective the legitimation of social action can have no recourse to dictates of an authority external to society, that is, to an authority beyond the individuals engaged in creative social praxis.

In societies where critical consciousness holds no authority and praxis no final creative force, the question of the legitimation of a social order is posed and solved differently. Such social orders must appear arbitrary[9] to their participants unless sustained by an appeal to principles of authority of a different order. Such ordering principles which have 'authorised' social convention vary historically. They have invoked such sanctionings as divine mandates and cosmological harmonies. More recently, the image of ordering principles which define industrialised societies has made reference to the conceived principles of society (society understood as reification), to arguments on human nature, or to an appeal to the dynamics of history (Touraine 1977, pp. 16 and 50). To these principles which 'subordinate social action and analysis to laws that transcend them', Touraine has appropriately given the name of 'metasocial warrants' (1977, p. 462). By way of clarification Touraine (ibid.) has suggested that 'The metasocial warrant of agrarian society is religion, that of mercantile society state-centered, that of industrial society economic.' This simple historical and cultural sketch of beliefs, religion, politics and economics, however suggestive, is nonetheless inadequate to a concept of metasocial warrant as a challenging and meaningful theme in the investigation of social discourse in complex societies. To reduce the question of metasocial warrants in anthropology to a gross historical outline of dominant ideologies is insufficient to a theoretical perspective which seeks both to accommodate an understanding of the richness and historical specificity of social discourse in individual complex societies and to reference such an understanding in subjective experience and expression. Any attempt to look closer at the conceptual fields that characterise social discourse in complex societies will demonstrate that unquestioned appeals to gods and kings do not constitute the entirety of the subject matter of such discourse. The conceptual fields invoked in such discourse, rather, overlap the conceptual field invoked in our contemporary social and philosophical discourse to a more significant degree than would be admitted by our traditional myths of the history of ideas. Very specifically as regards the discussion that follows, it can be demonstrated that social discourse in certain complex societies invokes concepts of progress (history), social practice and social contract, concepts which, within a certain field of theoretical argument, underpin our contemporary social discourse. Any examination of the 'definitions' of such concepts and their implementation in conceptual structurings in alternative social contexts would enhance our own philosophical reflections both on society and on history.

Returning to the specific argument on legitimation sketched earlier, it was argued that with the increasing reification of a concept of social or socio-political order, the question of legitimation of such an order presents itself as involving at least two conceptual facets: the relation of the social order to individual participants in this order and the relation of the social order to an order of physical nature. It is the second facet of the question of legitimation, the question as it arises in the conceptual field of social order and natural order, that is of primary interest to this present discussion. With a concern for the eventual application to the archaeological record of arguments on the question of legitimation, it is the focus on the perceived relationship of these two orders that might be most methodologically convenient to this initial stage of problem formulation.

If we consider western society for the moment, the question of legitimacy of a social order can be seen to create a field of argument that makes reference to a natural order in a very interesting manner. The definition of 'nature' in the western tradition involves two pivotal dimensions, nature as category and nature as norm. The philosopher Hepburn has offered the following definition of 'nature' as understood in the western philosophical tradition:

> In its widest sense 'natural' can mean 'the totality of things', all that would have to appear in an inventory of the universe. It can also refer to the laws and principles of structure by which the behavior of things may be explained. These two senses cannot be kept independent of each other at any sophisticated level of inquiry . . .   (1967, p. 454)

The tradition of western philosophy further demonstrates this dichotomy of meaning in the very revealing parallel of

the development of epistemological and ethical arguments. (Some philosophers have gone as far as to assert that epistemological statements are, in fact, ethical statements (Brandt 1967, pp. 6–8).) Obviously, one of the most powerful reconciliations of the double pivotal thrust of the concept of nature, as well as the relationship between the concepts of nature and society is to be found in Marx's thought. The reconciliation is effected dialectically; while human society is understood as included in nature, nature is understood as a societal category. Whereas the possibility of such an understanding has important consequences for contemporary social discourse and praxis, for the anthropologist there remains the more basic question as to whether this double thrust of a concept of nature is relevant and revealing to a concept of legitimation in complex societies. I think we can answer this question affirmatively. The ethnographic and historical literature provides, through a fascinating inventory of the forms that the relationship of nature to culture takes, evidence that this general thematic focus is crucial to understanding organisation and meaning in non-western societies. Further, such major themes as those of order, structure and pattern prove crucial to both a concept of nature and society, and if we recognise that time and space are the overriding dimensions critical to the definition of any social order as lived and thought, then the rhythms and patterns observable in physical nature are necessarily going to be critically involved in the conceptualisation and structuring of a social order.

As suggested above and as Bourdieu (1977, p. 164) has remarked: 'Every established order tends to produce (to very different degrees and with very different means) the naturalization of its own arbitrariness.' The 'degree' to which and the 'means' by which complex societies address the problem of naturalisation and thus legitimation of the social order are the backdrop to the tension of change and stability in the order of activity and the order of representation in such societies. The 'degree' of this 'tendency' is, in part, an aspect of the formalisation of the question of the legitimacy of a social order of representation in such societies. The 'means' of this naturalisation involves, in my opinion, among other issues, the interplay of two 'logics' that address the definition of the social order in relation to a natural order: the 'socialisation of nature' and the 'naturalisation of the social order'.

At the risk of simplification, the expression 'socialisation of nature' is meant to characterise the legitimation of a social order by its association with a natural order. In this confounding of the principles and representation of the two orders, the social order partakes of the ahistoric inevitability and self-evidence of the natural order. Legitimacy of the social order is guaranteed within a pre-eminent natural order, admitting of no alternatives and manifested in the lived experience of natural cycles and phenomena. This aspect of an order of representation can be seen in the embedding of social harmony in the natural or cosmological order. Within this ahistoric order the question of change becomes ambiguous, absorbed in the illusion of cyclic order, reincarnations and the actions of mythological predecessors, giving the illusion of reinterpretation rather than innovation. The price of inevitability is its very rigidity which does not admit of the manipulation of the social order save by 'sacred' ruse or cosmological intervention.

The 'naturalisation of the social order' is meant to characterise the delimitation of a social order in partial contradistinction to a natural order of domain. Though this affords a greater flexibility to the social order, that order must seek its naturalisation, not in the first sense of 'natural' — 'inherent in physical nature', but in the second sense of the term — 'in the self-definition of the qualities and characteristics intrinsic or natural to the social domain'. That is, the question of the legitimacy of the social order is answered in the conceptual field which serves to distinguish the social order from the natural order by way of the prerogatives of the social order. These prerogatives, grossly speaking, must include those very issues which are denied in the ahistoric repetitiveness of the natural order, the issues of temporality and of change. Yet, for these prerogatives to become a source of legitimacy they must incorporate some principles of ordering, thus giving rise to particular notions of the authority of history and the creation of order. It can perhaps be further argued that it is in the conceptualisation and experiencing of a social order as partially distinguished from an order of physical nature that concepts of history and social praxis (an aspect of the existential context) as understood in modern philosophical systems begin to take shape.

We might look to Frankfort's observations on *Kingship and the Gods* as a first illustration of these arguments in a definite cultural context. In this book Frankfort examines the concept of kingship in early Egyptian and Mesopotamian civilisations through texts and as manifested in the institutional character and the ritual accoutrements of the office of king. The work of Frankfort may be justly criticised for historical telescoping — for speaking of several centuries of social flux in terms of cultural continuity and elaboration. This criticism does not detract, however, from the suggestive quality of Frankfort's remarks taken at their most general level for the purposes of this present work. The major thesis of Frankfort's work is directly stated in the following quote:

> The Mesopotamian king, was like Pharaoh, charged with maintaining harmonious relations between human society and the supernatural powers, yet he was emphatically not one of these but a member of the community. In Egypt, on the other hand, one of the gods had descended among men.

> The significance of this divergence is clear. In Egypt the community had freed itself from fear and uncertainty by considering its ruler a god. It sacrificed all liberty for the sake of a never changing integration of society and nature. In Mesopotamia the community retained considerable independence, since its ruler was but a man. It accepted as correlate the never ending

anxiety that the will of the gods might be misunderstood and catastrophe disturb the labile harmony between the human and the divine sphere. (1948, p. 6)

The Egyptian menagerie of gods, ritual emphasis on the agricultural cycle and renewal and rebirth, the mythical exegesis of contemporary events are among the features of the Egyptian order of representation that point to the confounding of the social and the natural spheres of activity. In contrast, Mesopotamian myths of origin 'knew neither single origin nor single authority' (Frankfort 1948, p. 232); order and form were brought to the world, they were not characteristic of the universe. The king as lawgiver, as diplomat and as warrior — as active social force — brought order to social chaos, and such deeds are historically witnessed and recorded, not simply mythically foreshadowed.

The Mesopotamian and the Egyptian civilisations as portrayed by Frankfort present an important example of the contrast between 'strategies' of legitimation of a social order vis-à-vis the natural order. However, the contrast between these strategies is far from black and white, and it is not a simple contrast *between* the orders of representation of different cultural contexts. It is the particular dialectical balance of the 'socialisation of nature' and the 'naturalisation of society' that constitutes a thematic focus within the order of representation in a given society.

It is easy to understand how a social order which finds legitimation in an order of physical nature would show a high degree of conformity in its representational elaborations with items and events, with patterns and structures in nature. The representation of a social order which stands part way distinguished from an order of physical nature by invoking prerogatives of the social domain presents, perhaps, the more intriguing subject. In particular, the mapping of such a social order onto the dimensions of time and space, dimensions which already exhibit the superabundant patternings of physical nature, becomes a crucial problem in the legitimation of a social order which sees the social or the sociopolitical order in dynamic terms of the constitution of an ordering. One area from which we, as archaeologists, can glean evidence of the representation and structuring of a social order is the symbolic organisation of activity and space.

The cultural and symbolic organisation of space is a theme well ensconced in the traditions of the archaeological discipline. Outside this tradition, psychologists, geographers and architects have been equally fascinated with this multifaceted dimensional field, a dimensional field which is minimally tactile (Lynch 1960), visual, and conceptual (Bachelard 1964; Matoré 1962). The critical importance of the pervading experience of spatial orientation to human perception — both sensory and emotional — and to human activity has not eluded scholars across the various disciplines (e.g. Bloomer & Moore 1977; Doxiadis 1972; Lynch 1960; Soleri 1973). Given the fact that a spatial ordering presents itself as one of the most dominant experiences of ordering, it must necessarily be a decisive element in the definition of a social order. It is in the spatial order that a social order might be both experientially and visibly reinforced and thus attain a high degree of self-evidence. Not every aspect of spatial ordering, however, necessarily transforms the character of the social order in the same way, and to specify the levels and sectors of spatial organisation where one finds a high degree of legibility in the mapping of a social or a socio-political order onto spatial considerations is an interesting question.

Clarke, in his survey article on 'Spatial information in archaeology' (Clarke 1977, pp. 1–32), provides a general scale of resolution of spatial structuring with three levels (micro, semi-micro and macro) which is extremely useful in approaching the question of the symbolic organisation of space. Briefly, the micro level refers to within-structure focus, the semi-micro level to within-site focus and the macro level to between-site focus. Each of these levels permits a degree of creation (e.g. architectural) and manipulation (e.g. mapping) of spatial ordering that can be directed toward the symbolic schematisation and experiential reinforcement of a recognised social ordering.

At the micro level it is often possible to speak of public and private domains. Although structures and divisions of spaces within structures associated with individual households can be, in certain cases, differentially designated as public and private sectors (e.g. drawing room and boudoir), it is in the more obvious social domain of public architecture that the character of a social order should be highly visible and legible. The realm of public architecture is fascinating in the sense that it is an attempt at spatial organisation which potentially involves a high degree of conscious conceptualisation (and thus attendant discourse and questioning) of a social order previous to its transformation into material–spatial order. Needless to add, public monuments of complex societies as symbolic mappings have long drawn the attention of archaeologists.

At the semi-micro level one most promising area of investigation is the spatial organisation of complex and urban centres. The high degree of urban planning characteristic of certain early states is highly significant to an argument of the mapping of a social order onto space. Not only is there the occasion for the conscious and deliberate organisation of space, as is the case with public architecture, but this organisation of space goes beyond schematisation to a high degree of actualisation in the physical arrangement of activities and individuals which provide the experiential counterpart to the conceptualisation and symbolisation of a particular social order. In a sense, urban space is potentially social space par excellence.

Too often spatial studies at the macro level have concentrated exclusively on geographic and economic models (Clarke 1977, p. 13). The importance of such considerations is not to be denied, but traditional ethnographic and archaeological literature points to the social mapping of space at this level as well. This level is particularly interesting in that the scale of mapping is potentially 1:1 and thus the map can become most easily confounded with the territory.

Each level must be seen as a transformation of the others, and two considerations which appear to be critical to all levels are: (1) the creation of boundaries and (2) the social valuation of space.

1. One of the major characteristics traditionally used to describe complex social organisation is the superseding of principles of kinship organisation by territorial organisation at the political level. This territorial organisation not only facilitates an administrative overlay, but reinforces the socio-political quality of such a mapping. Boundaries carry with them potentially the social obligation of the unification of the parts generated. The dialectical relationship of ordering to unity in the social context of complex societies is perhaps an important facet of the definition of the social order.

2. The possibility of the differential social valuation of space is an extremely challenging theme. Space can be invested with historical weight, for example, in the form of commemorative structures and associated tales. The realisation of this possibility in the attempt to legitimise specific claims of individuals and dynasties to the role of representatives of the social order is an important consideration in the manipulation of the social order. Another aspect of the social valuation of space is the actual 'putting into value' of land through recognised social effort. The creation of colonies, large-scale transformations of land surfaces (e.g. clearing of forests, draining of swamps, construction of complex irrigation systems and so on), and the creation of markets, for example, raise questions not only regarding the assignation of the use and profits of such lands, but also questions on initiative and authority in the creation of such value. The above comments are suggestive and incomplete rather than definitive of considerations that might be taken into account when looking at the symbolic organisation of space as it relates to the creation and legitimation of a social order within complex societies.

Where an overwhelming majority of the traditionally recognised 'characteristics' of state organisation possess a very marked component of physical spatial organisation (e.g. increasing emphasis on territorial organisation as opposed to kinship organisation in the definition of a polity, monumental architecture, urban organisation, large-scale agricultural projects), the theme of the symbolic organisation of space would appear more conceptually nuanced and challenging than the traditional 'checklist' formulations of a definition of the state. We must recognise, however, that if we direct attention to such issues as public architecture, urban organisation, and territorial mappings as symbolic orderings, we are looking at features of an objectified material social context that serves as the context of subjective experience and representation. It is important to recognise further that this is one pole of a complex dynamic of symbolic and conceptual ordering which finds its necessary complement at the other end of the scale, so to speak, in the embodiment of meaning in subjective experience and representation. This places archaeological information in the context of a more encompassing theoretical perspective than that of Childe's pragmatic definition of material cultural remains as 'concrete expressions . . . of knowledge' (1956, p. 1); it is a theoretical perspective which precludes any simple opposition or identity of matters material and ideal. This theoretical reflection leads to qualifying remarks on the discussion to follow.

The social order of Central Imerina (Madagascar) during the fifteenth to the nineteenth centuries AD provides a specific cultural context in which certain of the issues discussed above concerning the symbolic organisation of space and the legitimation of a socio-political order might be examined. During this period Central Imerina witnessed an increasing conceptual specification of a political ideal significantly manifested in the social mapping and valuation of space. It can be argued that an intimate tie between land and polity was central to the legitimation of the Merina sociopolitical order. The major evidence for this argument is gleaned from ideological fields of representation; the oral tradition and the symbolic organisation of space. Thus the discussion which follows is not a full sketch of the dynamics of an order of representation and an order of activity in Central Imerina. Such a sketch must await further archaeological and historical investigation. The following discussion is rather an initial attempt to characterise certain elements of

a field of social discourse in the early Merina state of the late eighteenth century. An understanding of these elements should eventually contribute to an understanding of the self-production of Merina society.

The Malagasy and Madagascar are one of those peoples and places whose name, though exotic, rings familiar, but whose geographical and ethnological character remains elusive. Seemingly adrift somewhere in the Indian Ocean, one Malagasy poet[10] has called his homeland 'l'île au bout du monde'. It is an island that has offered refuge as easily to the lost tribe of Israel as to the lost primates of Africa (the lemurs). Unfortunately, the limitations on the present work do not allow a comprehensive introduction to the island's history and population. The interested reader is initially referred to the classic works of Grandidier (1892), Dandouau & Chapus (1952), and Deschamps (1972).

What follows is a brief introductory sketch of one area of the island that saw the rise of an indigenous complex socio-political organisation. The central highlands area has often been referred to as the 'hauts-plateaux', but such a description is inadequate to the considerable relief in this area. This relief is visually impressive, as well as geologically interesting. There are numerous hills interspersed with higher mountains of volcanic origin. There are steep-sided valleys and lacustrine and alluvial plains. In the central area of Imerina (fig. 1), the region of particular interest to this study, recent faulting and uplift along the western edge of the area has blocked the flow of rivers and created a vast expanse of lakes and marshy plains. The traditional core of Imerina was restricted to an area of about 30 km radius around Antananarivo (fig. 2). This region witnessed indigenous 'state(s)' development somewhere between the

Fig. 1. Early states in Madagascar.

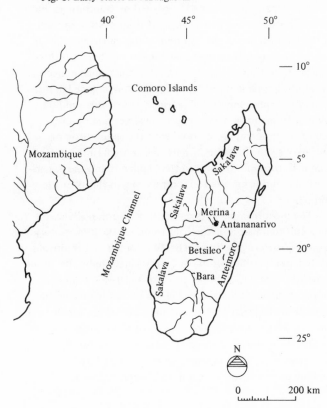

Fig. 2. Central Imerina.

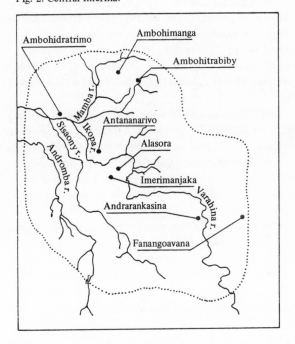

sixteenth and the eighteenth centuries AD. (Though this is not the only area on the island to have witnessed complex social development. See fig. 1.)

During the reign of the historically renowned unifier of Imerina, Andrianampoinimerina (1787–1810), the agricultural base of the Merina state was both rich and complex. The main staple was wet rice. The dependence on this crop today is overwhelmingly obvious to the casual observer of the Merina countryside as it was obvious to the eighteenth- and nineteenth-century visitor to Imerina. Not only did the rich soil of the valley floors offer well-irrigated land for rice cultivation which was easily put into crop with small-scale terracing, but a series of major drainage projects initiated or expanded under the auspices of Andrianampoinimerina, involving tracts of marshland in Imerina, brought into cultivation a large amount of additional paddy area. These large-scale irrigation projects, besides opening up new land to cultivation, allowed the possibility of a second (and in some cases, even a third) planting of rice each year. According to the geographer, Raison (1972) and others, the linguistic evidence points to a late introduction of the techniques for the large-scale cultivation of wet rice into the plateau area, though dry rice cultivation and the cultivation of wet rice in marshy areas may have been practised earlier. One might also note that *taro*, which is sometimes referred to in the oral traditions as the original food source of the Merina, would have been as easily cultivated in the valley floors and marshy areas. The archaeological evidence available at present on the earliest settlements in Imerina shows such sites as located on low-flanking ridges always close to the smaller marshy valleys ideal for small-scale wet rice or tuber cultivation (Wright & Kus 1980).

Besides the valley floor areas, hillsides were also put into cultivation. According to Raison, the evidence points to a practice 'd'une agriculture soigneuse et savante à sa manière' (1972, p. 417). The various crops cultivated on hillside slopes included roots and tubers such as manioc, potatoes, sweet potatoes and yams, and various legumes. Obviously, the finer questions of introductions, techniques and emphases await palaeo-ethnobotanic and archaeological study.

Oral traditions and ethnohistorical accounts (e.g. Callet 1974; Deschamps 1972; Dandouau & Chapus 1952; Boiteau 1958; Isnard 1953) present an extensive sketch of Merina views of their proper history in the eighteenth and nineteenth centuries. To familiarise the reader with the gross outlines of this history, the following brief summary is offered.

The Merina are said to recognise three periods of their history: *fony vazimba ny tany* or the period when earthly power was held by the Vazimba, the *fanjakana hova* or government by the Hova and the Merina kingdom(s). The legendary aboriginal inhabitants of Imerina are called the Vazimba. In some accounts they are said to be forest-dwelling hunters and gatherers, in others they are reputed to be fishers, cattle herders and yam growers. The acknowledged ancestors of the Merina, the Hova, are said to have entered Imerina from the south. They supposedly first occupied the sites of Fananagoavana and Andrarankasina, then moving closer to Antananarivo through successive occupations of Imerimanjaka and Alasora (see fig. 2). Through marriage and warfare the Vazimba were absorbed or displaced by the new arrivals. The Vazimba, who are said to have possessed only clay tips for their spears and to have been politically disparate, were no match for the Hova who carried iron weapons and the seeds of statesmanship.

The Hova began to show socio-political initiative during the reigns of the queens Rangita and Rafohy who reigned at Imerimanjaka (approximately early sixteenth century AD). Rangita is credited with bringing order to political rule among the Hova when she designated an order of succession to office thus creating the possibility of political unity and continuity. She passed the reins of office to her eldest son, Andriamanelo, and further indicated that he was to be succeeded by his younger brother, Andriamanitany.

Andriamanelo, whose reign is traditionally placed in the sixteenth century, was the first Andriana (as evidenced by his name) or noble in Imerina, thus giving form to the socio-political hierarchy characteristic of the Merina state. The term Hova was subsequently used to designate the commoner 'class'. Andriamanelo's and succeeding reigns of various Andriana are characterised in the literature by assorted material and political innovations in a continued and concerted push towards political unification.

Andrianampoinimerina is regarded by tradition as the great unificator of the Merina state. It is interesting to note that the list of innovations credited to this ruler reads like a checklist of state institutions drawn from the classic anthropological definition of the state. They include such concerns as taxation, permanent military organisation, corvée labour, population displacements and colonisation of surrounding areas, not to mention major irrigation projects. Upon the death of Andrianampoinimerina, with the assumption of power by his son, Radama I, there began in 1810 the period of major European influence in the highlands and the expansion of the Merina empire to incorporate two-thirds of the island.

The most invaluable documentary source available on Merina cultural history is the four tomes of the *Tantaran'ny Andriana* (*Histoire des Rois*). The *Tantara* are oral traditions collected and recorded in the Malagasy language by the Jesuit missionary, Père Callet, between 1868 and 1883. Callet's informants included Malagasy elders who had witnessed the final days of the reign of Andrianampoinimerina. Yet these traditions refer not only to the events of this period, but to the entirety of Merina history as conceptualised by these local inhabitants. This information provides an important complement to archaeological investigation in Central

Imerina for these traditions permit a finer dimensioning of conceptual issues at play in Merina sociocultural organisation.

The *Tantara* has recently been the subject of a brilliant sociocultural analysis by Delivré (1974), an analysis which goes beyond the traditional readings of the oral traditions of the *Tantara* as a quasi-historical sketch of events involving the central dynasty of the Merina kingdom. Delivré's work is an attempt to understand the sense given by Merina of the nineteenth century to their own history. Whether this sense of history can be legitimately projected back to earlier periods is moot, but even if restricted to nineteenth-century Imerina, Delivré's arguments are important for the elaboration of the theme of the legitimation of a socio-political order in Central Imerina.

The *Tantara* is a fascinating document in that it is organised with greater complexity than a simple collection of genealogies, origin myths, folk tales and historical scenarios. It is possible, as Delivré has demonstrated, to read the *Tantara* as a structured socio-political discourse on the creation of a social and political order in Imerina. Merina history is not simply preoccupied with regarding and examining the genealogical credibility of various pretenders to political power. It is a history preoccupied with the very concept of 'history' seen as a critical dimension in the creation and evolution of a social order. As Delivré has argued, the *Tantara* speaks of 'an intimate relation between a political ideal and a vision of history that serves as concrete model of this ideal' (my translation of Delivré 1974, p. 116). History was not simply a temporal dimension for the Merina; it was a dynamic principle that linked the past to the present in the sense of an unfolding of a political ideal through social praxis.

The concept of *fanjakana* is central to an understanding of the political ideal of Merina society. *Fanjakana* has been traditionally translated as kingdom (*royaume*) in the ethnographic literature, but the semantic field of this term is considerably more complex than the word 'kingdom' implies (Delivré 1974, p. 159). The recurrent expression found in the *Tantara*, *ny tany sy ny fanjakana* ('the land and the kingdom'), draws a tight association between territory and government. Yet, as Delivré argues, the spatial dimension is not the only dimension critical to understanding *fanjakana* as a concept, there is a temporal dimension as well, the dimension of history (1974, pp. 159–61).

> The Imerina past is understood as a gigantic cultural history, where the present society has gradually found its exemplary models and its mode of functioning, thanks to royal initiative and to it alone: because there existed nothing at the beginning but chaos and the absence of *fanjakana*.
>
>   (my translation of Delivré 1974, p. 167)

The term *fanjakana* is both a structure of socio-political order and a political ideal, an ideal of unification which becomes increasingly specified and predominant in the *Tantara* and finds its actualisation in the accomplishments of Andrianampoinimerina. The political ideal of *fanjakana* does not imply a simple static maintenance of order, but rather a dynamic principle of the creation of order, dialectical in its implication of both continuity (tradition) and directional change: '*fanjakana* presupposes a history and a progression' (my translation of Delivré 1974, p. 161).

Continuity is a critical element in the Merina concept of history as mentioned above. It is a notion tied to concepts of custom (e.g. *didin-drazana* signifying 'law of the ancestors') and taboo (*fady*) (van Gennep 1904, p. 126). The classic study of custom and taboo as structuring elements in Malagasy society is the work of van Gennep on *Tabou et Totemisme à Madagascar*. Though this work assumes that the social institutions of custom and taboo can be most effectively studied at the level of a cultural area (i.e. Madagascar) rather than at the level of socio-political groupings, van Gennep's generalisations are not without value in considering Merina society.

Custom and taboo guarantee social stability and integration. As van Gennep points out, when conceptually and experientially the customary and the habitual have been invested with the guarantee of stability and order, it follows logically that the abnormal and the extraordinary appear as elements of instability and disorder, and thus as dangerous. For the present discussion, the more critical feature of a conceptual field that surrounds a notion of social custom in Madagascar is not the contrast of the abnormal but, rather, the enigma of the new. As van Gennep recognised: 'La notion de *nouveau* n'est qu'une nuance de la notion d'anormal' (1904, p. 37). Whereas twins and chickens that crow like roosters can be dispensed with if found threatening, the building of a new house and the undertaking of a new project is more problematic. Within this conceptual field a notion of change and novelty must involve the interpretation and limitations of such concerns as innovation, political prerogatives, and history. Where such issues become most critical and most explicit in Merina society is in the actions of individuals occupying pivotal social positions, more precisely, in the individual of the king standing at the apex of the social order. The genius of the Merina society lies in the escape of the logical conclusion of the hemming-in of the actions of the king through the rigid notions of ritual and sanctity necessary to maintaining an ahistoric order. Instead, Merina society elaborated a dynamic notion of continuity which guaranteed order through directional change. The Merina elaborated what is, in effect, an evolutionary principle of the creation of social order. What is even more fascinating in the elaboration of this dynamic concept of history is that whereas the king is charged with the conceptualisation necessary to historical movement, the role of society is recognised in the actualisation of history.

For the Merina the creation of political order invoked

a notion of 'social contract'. One of the most striking examples of this theme is the Merina practice of formal public discourse. The royal *kabary* (interestingly enough, said not to have been known to the Vazimba) is an address by the ruler to his people, ideally taking the form of a dialogue and ideally a prerequisite to the making of major policy decisions on war and public works, the institution of new laws, and the levying of special taxes.[11] In reality, the *kabary* was often the presentation of a *fait accompli* to the populace. Nevertheless, the royal *kabary* traditionally began with such statements as 'It is not I who command, it is we who command, you and I' (my translation of Delivré 1974, p. 60), or 'It is to the people that the king owes his right to govern, because if it is the case that the king wields great power in his position as sovereign, it is also the case that the people hold great power as the people' (my translation of Dandouau & Chapus 1952, p. 144).

The issues of history and the creation of political order through social action guided by royal initiative, issues critical to the 'naturalisation of society' in Merina social discourse, can also be seen in various aspects of spatial and temporal ordering in Central Imerina (Kus 1979). One most striking example is in the reconstruction of the sacred capital of Ambohimanga (see fig. 2) under Andrianampoinimerina after his pacification of Central Imerina. The reconstruction of Ambohimanga is interesting in that there appears to be an interplay, rather than a clean separation, between a cosmological ordering and a political ordering. This may be seen in the double internal spatial organisation of the site. This interplay would seem to be in accordance with the argument presented earlier that it is the particular dialectical balance of the 'socialisation of nature' and the 'naturalisation of society' that constitutes a thematic focus within the order of representation in a given complex society.

Height is perhaps the most obvious spatial dimension to invest with social value, and Imerina's rich topography of hills and valleys was not ignored according to the *Tantara*. A central and elevated position was symbolically related to social hierarchy according to tradition. Ambohimanga, along with other sites associated with noble or royal residence, was located on a fortified hilltop. Yet, the more interesting aspects of spatial ordering concerning the purposes of this paper are based on two major overlapping systems invoking a twelve-part and a four-part division of the planar surface.

The twelve-part division is, in fact, to be understood as the spatial mapping of a temporal ordering. *Vintana* is the Malagasy concept of destiny. It is necessary to the success of individual and social undertakings to take into account the forces of destiny; to begin a new undertaking on an unlucky day will only result in disaster or failure. Individuals, as well, according to the time of their births, possess *vintana* which will determine the major character of success and failure in their lives. A system of astrological calculation (with reference to the sun and the moon in exclusion of most other celestial bodies) is common to the island as a whole, but

interpretations of different aspects of this system vary. The temporal divisions used in the calculations of *vintana* begin with a division of the year into twelve months, the week into seven days, and the day into twenty-eight periods. (Fig. 3 presents the common arrangement of the twelve *vintana* of the year.) Each month has a characteristic destiny associated with it. The first destiny, *Alahamady* in the northeast corner, for example, is considered a noble period associated with the king, for it is *Alahamady* 'that accords dignity and sovereignty and thanks to which all can be undertaken' (my translation of Callet 1974, Volume 1, p. 54). *Adalo*, on the other hand, is a destiny associated with tears and unhappiness. The interplay of the destinies of the months, days, and divisions of the day adds considerable complexity of calculation and subtlety of interpretation to this system which finds its full exploitation in the hands of specialists, the *mpanandro*.

The numbers twelve and seven, significant to the temporal order in Central Imerina, also appear in ritual invocations and social divisions. For example, there are seven noble (*andriana*) groups in the Merina social hierarchy and there are seven royal tombs at the capital of Antananarivo. There are twelve royal talismans, twelve sacred mountains, twelve kings of Imerina and Andrianampoinimerina had twelve royal wives. The mapping of this temporal order onto the spatial dimension is evident in both house and village layout. It is important to note that in a large number of cases where the number seven is employed, reference is made to genealogical depth and affiliation or to social hierarchy. Other cases, as the twelve sacred mountains or twelve royal

Fig. 3. *Vintana*.

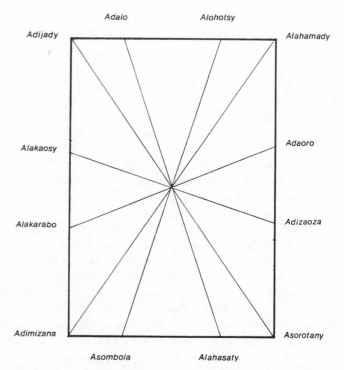

talismans, seem to make reference to a primal order or grouping. There is, however, a second order of possible spatial partitioning employed in Imerina that is overtly political in its references to an ideal of political unification.

The symbolic significance of the four cardinal directions and the centre point (sometimes translated into the relationship between four corners and the centre) in the Merina order of representation cannot be overstressed. Each set of opposing directions is conceived as a contrast of qualities. The North is the noble direction while the South is lowly or humble. The East is considered sacred and the West profane. It is the centre, as union and as transcendance of the four directions, that represents the political ideal of unification. The story of Andriamasinavalona is the pre-eminent political tale of the *Tantara*. It was Andriamasinavalona who originally brought unification to Imerina, but it was also Andriamasinavalona who brought division and warfare again to Imerina by partitioning the kingdom and assigning each of his four sons to administrative posts without designating one as heir to the united kingdom. Under Andrianampoinimerina Imerina attained once more the political ideal of unification in the reunification of the four original districts of Imerina: Avaradrano, Marovatana, Amibodirano, and Vakinisisaony (see fig. 4).

The Northeast direction is the most honoured direction as it combines the character of the noble and the sacred. Appropriately enough, the dual capitals of Imerina under Andrianampoinimerina, Ambohimanga and Antananarivo, are located in the northeast district of Avaradrano. Located in the district of Avaradrano are also the three major com-

moner social groups (i.e. Tsimahafotsy, Tsimiamboholahy and Mandiavato) who originally backed Andrianampoinimerina in his claim to the throne of Ambohimanga and in his eventual drive to unite Imerina.

The two systems of spatial division, the twelve-part astrological system and the four cardinal directions plus the centre, are superimposable, and this fact is not without import for the structural layout of the capital of Ambohimanga. As mentioned above, when the centre of Imerina was pacified, Andrianampoinimerina undertook the reconstruction of the defensive ditches and main gates of the sacred capital of Ambohimanga. The division of social labour in these tasks and the spatial layout of the *rova* (royal quarters), town, ditches and gates are discussed in the *Tantara* (Callet 1974, Volume 2, pp. 278–323). The investment of social labour and spatial configuration with symbolic value is obvious upon reading the description in the *Tantara*. The construction of the seven major gates of the town was assigned to the three major groups of the Avaradrano district (i.e. Tsimahafotsy, Tsimiamboholahy and Mandiavato) along with the other social groups of the Merina kingdom divided into three units according to residence in the three additional districts of Central Imerina (i.e. Marovatana, Vakinisisaony and Ambodirano). In designating the division of labour and the eventual functions to be served by these seven gates, Andrianampoinimerina made reference to the four cardinal directions. Thus the Tsimiamboholahy were to dig the ditch and build the gate of Ambatomitsagana at the East. Correspondingly, the Mandiavato were assigned to Amboara at the North, the Tsimahafotsy to Andakana at the West, the Marovatana to Miandravahiny to the West, the Vakinisisaony to Ampitsaharana at the South and the East and the Ambodirano to Andranomatsatso at the South (fig. 5). In

Fig. 4. The districts of Imerina. 1: Avaradrano. 2: Marovatana. 3: Ambodirano. 4: Vakinisisaony. 5: Voninzongo. 6: Vakinankaratra. 7: Imamo.

Fig. 5. The districts of Ambohimanga. Source: Razafintsalama 1973.

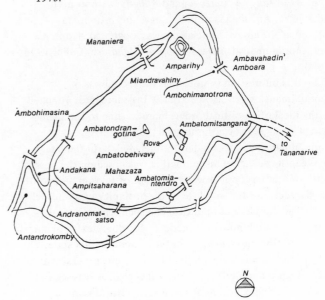

the assignment of tasks, the groups of Avaradrano were honoured above the other three districts. The Tsimiambo-holahy and the Tsimahafotsy were assigned to construct the two gates considered as 'the gates of the State' (Callet 1974, Volume 2, p. 279). The Mandiavato were assigned the only door to the North or noble direction.

The evaluation of the spatial configuration of Ambohimanga was the re-duplication and re-confirmation of the ideal of political unity through the united social action of the four original districts of Imerina under the direction of the king. The site of Ambohimanga was, further, invested with a sense of historical continuity. The organisation of Ambohimanga under the auspices of Andrianampoinimerina was, according to tradition, the *re*-construction of the ditches and gates built by an earlier ruler, Andriantsimitoviaminan-driana. Yet, upon completion the social symbolic re-valuation through renaming makes not only overt reference to progress and ordering, but in dialectical fashion also makes allusion to continuity for it is, in fact, *re*-valuation and *re*-naming.

Besides conforming to the political ideal of the union of the four cardinal directions through the centre, the spatial layout of Ambohimanga was the subject of cosmological ordering as well. Where the *rova* stood as political centre to four directions, the village of Ambohimanga stood as social centre of the astrological chart. The *Tantara* speaks of Andrianampoinimerina's consultation of astrologers when undertaking the construction of the gates of Ambohimanga. In a revealing passage, the seven gates of the city, referred to originally with regard to the four cardinal directions, were referred to a second time with regard to the scheme of *vintana*. For this second spatial mapping it is the village, rather than the *rova*, that serves as point of orientation. Thus Ambatomitsagana was located with reference to the village at *Alahamady*, the great and noble destiny of the Northeast. At the other three major destinies (the corner locations of fig. 3) of *Asorotany*, *Adimizana*, and *Adijady* were located Antsolatra, Andakana, and Miandravahiny. Amboara was located at *Alohotsy*, Amitsahana was located at *Asombola* and Andranomatsatso was located at *Alahasaty* (Callet 1974, Volume 2, p. 281).

It is interesting to note that the sacredness of Ambohimanga was very specifically the sacredness attached to the ideal of a political order, more so than to the sacred-ness of a religious or cosmological theme. Entry to Ambohimanga was forbidden to foreigners until the late nineteenth century. This injunction was based on the possi-bility of sacrilege, but it was a sacrilege of treason and politi-cal disorder, not the sacrilege of the profanity of an infidel.

The double socio-political and socio-cosmological mapping of Ambohimanga points to the complexity of social representation and discourse in the ancient Merina state. The urban space is not simply a field for mapping generalised cosmological and mythic schemes; it is also, as realised in the case of Imerina, a potential social and political symbolic

space as well. The re-construction of Ambohimanga under Andrianampoinimerina was a symbolic re-construction, invoking a conceptual field that included notions of history and social practice (themes which are still critical to con-temporary social, political and philosophical discourse) and their articulation with a cosmological order.

The position of society within the Merina concept of history appears pivotal. Society, as symbolised in the centring of the village of Ambohimanga in the order of *vintana*, is the guarantee of social stability and harmony within the Merina cosmology. But society as named political groups, unified under the central direction of royal auth-ority, is the active force of history and thus of progressive change. The king appears as privileged participant in the social order and creator of political order. As the *rova* stands both to the northeast of the village and as centre to Ambo-himanga, so the king and the political order would appear to be articulated with the cosmological order by occupying the most privileged and potentially transcendent position in that order. As noted earlier, the northeast corner, or the first destiny of *Alahamady*, is the noble and sacred position 'that accords dignity and sovereignty and thanks to which all can be undertaken' (my translation of Callet 1974, Volume 1, p. 54). Where all are subject to *vintana*, the influence of *vintana* is not potentially equivalent for all individuals; status

Fig. 6. Military camp of Andrianampoinimerina.

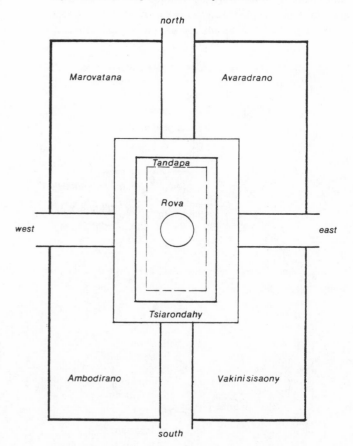

is an important determinant in one's ability to bear the weight of the forces of *vintana*. There is the suggestion in the *Tantara* that the king cannot deny *vintana*, yet the king possesses a capacity to channel and actualise the forces of destiny for the benefit of the kingdom. This capacity places him in a vital rather than in a subservient relationship to this principle of ordering forces.

Where the spatial organisation of Ambohimanga is revealing as to the articulation of the twelve-part division of *vintana* and the political ideal of the four cardinal directions united by the centre, the military camps of Andrianampoin-imerina demonstrated the real potential for the schematis-ation and abstract symbolisation of the political ideal of unity in the spatial dimension. As overtly political in func-tion and carrying restricted historical investment, the military camp presents the most forceful image of four corners united by their centre (fig. 6). The *rova* at the centre of the camp was surrounded by the Tandapa or royal attend-ants, who were in turn surrounded by the Tsiarondahy or royal guards. At each of the four corners were located the soldiers of the four original districts of Imerina. The soldiers of the Vonizongo and Vakinankaratra districts, districts subsequently added to Imerina (see fig. 4) were later given specific spatial locations in military camps. The Vonizongo were located north of the Marovatana and the Vakinank-aratra to the south of Ambodirano. Yet, despite the addition of these two districts, the ideal of the four corners and the centre remained as spatial core and ideal of the military camp according to the *Tantara*.

The brevity of the above discussion and the limitation of its focus are certainly inadequate to an effective under-standing of the complexity of the interwoven orders of representation and activity that defined the self-production (Touraine 1977) of Merina society. Yet, the discussion does point to the symbolic valuation and organisation of space as critical to the historicity of Merina society, as a theme worthy of fuller exploration in Merina archaeology and oral tradition, and as a theme with implications for generalised arguments on organisation and change in complex societies. Yet, in any move toward an understanding of history through the generalisations of philosophical inquiry, we must realise that despite its potential for comprehensiveness, any social—theoretical scheme must find its touchstone in the lived human drama — that is, we must come to realise that the cosmological and the quotidian are of the same human scale.

Notes

1 Childe has made this point most dramatically in his statement: 'As an archaeologist I deal with concrete material things as much as any natural scientist. But as a pre*historian* I must treat my objects always and exclusively as concrete expressions and embodiments of human thoughts and ideas — in a word of knowledge' (1956, p. 1).

2 Spurling has remarked: 'All action is understood as a dialectic

between subjective intentions (in the ordinary sense) and their intersubjective consequences or results, so that the actual meaning or significance of an action will emerge from this interplay' (1977, p. 86).

3 Childe has defined 'knowledge' in the following passage: 'in my title "knowledge" is coupled with "society". To deserve the name, I contend knowledge must be communicable and in that sense public and also useful. I mean, capable of being translated into successful action' (1956, p. 4).

4 Merleau-Ponty has remarked 'we are not in a situation like an object in objective space. Our situation is for us the source of our curiosity, our investigations, and our interests in first other situations as variants of our own and then in our own life illuminated by (and this time considered as a variant of) the lives of others. Ultimately our situation is what links us to the whole of human experience, no less than what separates us from it' (1974, pp. 106—7).

5 To employ the term 'emergence' without qualification is to court philosophical and social—theoretical objection. As critics have repeatedly noted, the most obvious difficulty arising in the use of this term is the potential for the indiscriminate theoretical mingling of radically different phenomena such as life, structuring and consciousness. The implications of the use of the term 'emergence' in the present work are severely restricted 'cosmologically' speaking. The term is employed initially in its descriptive sense to phenomena in a conceptual field. The theoretical—philosophical sense in which the con-cept is employed in this text specifically alludes to Bachelard's concept of epistemological 'rupture' (*coupure*). An epistem-ological rupture in Bachelard's sense occurs at various points in the history of scientific discourse when, given new factors in the experiential milieu, a theoretical reconceptualisation and a reformulation of a *problématique* become imperative.

6 In non-complex societies it may be the case that a concept of nature stands in contradistinction to a more general concept of 'humanness', where 'humanness' implies the embedding of a definition of the individual in a nexus of social relationships.

7 Consider the American Heritage Dictionary's definition of 'legitimate': '1. In compliance with the law; lawful. 2. In accordance with traditional or established patterns and stan-dards. 3. Based on logical reasoning, reasonable. 4. Authentic; genuine . . . 6. Of, relating to, or ruling by hereditary right . . . '

8 Touraine (1977) recognised society as *self*-producing rather than simply reproducing, arguing that society is not equivalent in definition to the state of its productive forces. Besides the 'intellectual' ('knowledge' in Touraine's vocabulary) and material means at its disposal (productive forces) for activity, society's actions are also dependent upon 'the image it [society] has of its capacity to act upon itself' (Touraine 1977, p. 4). This image of creative capacity arises from the symbolic capacity of society which allows, besides the posit-ing of an order of activities, the positing of an order of repre-sentation (Touraine 1977). These two orders, however, are not separate orders of material situation and of idea. An order of representation is critical to the constitution and structuring of an order of activities.

9 The recognition of concepts of critical consciousness and praxis does not eliminate the apprehending of the social order as arbitrary, such a recognition does, however, provide for a creative and positive confrontation of this arbitrariness.

10 Flavien Ranaivo

11 Delivré has said of the *kabary*: 'Il est essentiellement dialogue entre le roi et le peuple, où le premier a sans doute dès le début ses idées en tête, mais où le second ne les apprend que pro-gressivement. Se déroulant parfois sur plusieurs journées, les dialogues manifestent une progression dans l'exposition, sans

crainte des répétitions ni de redites, selon une logique essentiellement persuasive' (1974, pp. 93–4).

Acknowledgement

I would like to thank Drs Henry T. Wright III and Christopher S.
Peebles for reading and commenting on earlier drafts of this paper.

References

American Heritage Dictionary of the English Language (1971) William
    Morris (ed.), American Heritage Publishing Company, New
    York

Bachelard, G. (1934) *Le Nouvel Esprit Scientifique*, Librairie Felix
    Alcan, Paris

Bachelard, G. (1964) *The Poetics of Space*, translated by Maria Jofas,
    Orion Press, New York

Bloomer, K. & Moore, C. (1977) *Body, Memory, and Architecture*,
    Yale University Press, New Haven

Boiteau, P. (1958) *Contribution à l'histoire de la nation Malagache*,
    Editions Sociales, Paris

Bourdieu, P. (1977) *Outline of a Theory of Practice*, Cambridge
    University Press, Cambridge

Brandt, R.B. (1967) 'Parallel between epistemology and ethics' in
    The Encyclopedia of Philosophy, Volume 3: 6–8, Macmillan
    Company and the Free Press, New York

Brown, R.H. (1978) 'Symbolic realism and sociological thought:
    beyond the positivist romantic debate' in R.H. Brown &
    M.L. Stanford (eds.) *Structure, Consciousness and History*,
    Cambridge University Press, New York

Callet, F. (1974) *Histoire des Rois (Tantaran'ny Andriana)*, trans-
    lated from Malagache and edited by G.S. Chapus & E.
    Ratsimba. 3 vols. Editions de la Librarie Madagascar,
    Tananarive

Childe, V.G. (1949) 'The sociology of knowledge', *The Modern
    Quarterly*, New Series, 4: 302–9

Childe, V.G. (1956) *Society and Knowledge*, George Allen and Unwin
    Ltd, London

Clarke, D.L. (1977) 'Spatial information in archaeology' in D.L.
    Clarke (ed.) *Spatial Archaeology*, Academic Press, London

Dandouau, A. & Chapus, G.S. (1952) *Histoire des Populations de
    Madagascar*, Larose, Paris

Delivré, A. (1974) *L'histoire de Rois d'Imerine, Interpretation d'une
    Tradition Orale*, Klicksieck, Paris

Deschamps, H. (1972) *Histoire de Madagascar*, Editions Berger-
    Levrault, Paris

Douglas, M. (1973) (ed.) *Rules and Meaning*, Penguin, Suffolk

Doxiadis, C. (1972) *Architectural Space in Ancient Greece*, translated
    by Jacqueline Tyrwhitt, The MIT Press, Cambridge

Frankfort, H. (1948) *Kingship and the Gods*, University of Chicago
    Press, Chicago

Fromm, E. (1961) *Marx's Concept of Man*, F. Ungar Pub. Co., New
    York

van Gennep, A. (1904) *Tabou et Totemisme à Madagascar*, Ernest
    Leroux, Paris

Grandidier, A. (1892) *Histoire Physique, Naturelle et Politique de
    Madagascar*, Volume 1, L'Imprimerie Nationale, Paris

Hepburn, R. (1967) 'Philosophical ideas of nature' in *The Encyclo-
    pedia of Philosophy*, Volume 5, 454–8, Macmillan Company
    and the Free Press, New York

Isnard, H. (1953) 'Les bases geographique de la monarchie hova' in
    Eventail de L'histoire Vivante: Hommage à Lucien Febvre,
    195–206, Librairie Armand Colin, Paris

Kus, S. (1979) *Archaeology and Ideology: The Symbolic Organisation
    of Space*, Ph.D. thesis, University of Michigan, Ann Arbor

Lynch, K. (1960) *The Image of the City*, The MIT Press, Cambridge

Matoré, G. (1962) *L'espace Humain*, Editions du Vieux Colombier,
    Paris

Merleau-Ponty, M. (1974) *Phenomenology, Language and Sociology:
    Selected Essays of Maurice Merleau-Ponty*, John O'Neill (ed.),
    Heineman, London

Raison, J.P. (1972) 'Utilisation du sol et organisation de l'espace en
    Imerina ancienne' in *Etudes de Geographie Tropicale Offertes
    à Pierre Gourous*, 407–25, Mouton, Paris

Razafintsalama, A. (1973) *Les Tsimahafotsy d'Ambohimanga:
    Organisation Familiale et Sociale en Imerina-Madagascar*,
    Universite de Madagascar, Cahier 1

Schmidt, A. (1971) *The Concept of Nature in Marx*, Ben Fowkes,
    transl., NLB, London

Soleri, P. (1973) *The Bridge Between Matter and Spirit is Matter
    Becoming Spirit*, Doubleday, New York

Spurling, L. (1977) *Phenomenology and the Social World*, Routledge
    and Kegan Paul, London

Touraine, A. (1977) *The Self-Production of Society*, University of
    Chicago Press, Chicago

Williams, R. (1977) *Marxism and Literature*, Oxford University Press,
    Oxford

Wright, H.T. III & Kus, S. (1980) 'An archaeological reconnaissance
    of Ancient Imerina' in R. Kent (ed.) *Madagascar in History*,
    Foundation for Malagasy Studies, Berkeley

Chapter 6

House power:
Swahili space and
symbolic markers
Linda Wiley Donley

Donley introduces an ethnographic analysis of settlements and houses on the East African coast which aims to increase our knowledge of how settlement space is integrated into other aspects of life. An important component of the cultural context considered is the Islamic religion, but the particular relationships between Indian Ocean traders, middlemen and local tribes, and the use of material items in the social and economic strategies of these groups also play their parts. The specific models identified concern the use of house form and appearance in the relationships between trading groups and in the control of women. The high, blank, fortress-like exteriors of the houses protected the position of the Swahili middlemen and their control over 'pure' women who played an essential role in the trading system. The analysis also concerns the use of decoration to maintain the purity of women and to protect men and women from defiling activities within the house, in the innermost room and in the toilet. The use of ethnoarchaeology to study the location of material items within a symbolically organised settlement space is emphasised.

Traders have built coral settlements on the eastern coast of Africa from at least the ninth century AD until the present day. Archaeologists have excavated some of these Swahili sites and described the finds, house-plans, mosques, tombs and walls of the towns. The periods of occupation have been established by dating the imported Chinese and Islamic wares, by inscriptions and coins, and by noting the stylistic seriations (Kirkman 1964; Garlake 1966; Chittick 1967; Wilson 1979, 1980).

This paper will consider the coral houses in Lamu town. The island of Lamu lies off the northern coast of Kenya where I was engaged in ethnoarchaeological research from April 1979 to September 1981. The oldest standing coral houses in Lamu town date to the eighteenth and nineteenth centuries AD. They have been chosen for study because they are still inhabited by the families who claim that their ancestors built the houses. The houses are clearly linked in form to the earlier houses found at many of the archaeological sites along the coast of Africa, from Somalia to Mozambique. Therefore, the way they are used today, and the reports on how they were used in the days of slavery, should be useful in the interpretation of at least the later archaeological periods.

Coral houses have been taken as the unit of study because they are durable and the locations of birth, child-rearing, marriage, death, burial and many business, social and religious activities. Houses are richest in artefacts (and thus in durable symbolic markers) and are used by all ages, both male and female, free-born and slave. In comparison, mosques are most often used by men, and tombs may be restricted to a select group.

The coral houses were built and lived in by an elite class of Swahili people called the *wa-ungwana*, but the power of the house affected all of the people living in its shadow. The *wa-ungwana* (free-born of a high station) also called themselves *wa-Amu* (the people of Lamu), and they are a part of a larger group called the Swahili. *Swahili* is a collective term that has long been used by outsiders to refer to the people who live on the coast of eastern Africa, and is derived from the Arabic word *sahil*, meaning coast. *Swahili* was not used by the people themselves until very recent times, and even now it is used only in some areas. Many of the *wa-ungwana* families also refer to themselves as local Arabs, but many mixed generations often separate them from their Arab ancestors. They also freely admit that most of their families have African blood, a result of the practice of taking local women as concubines. Most of these people only have a vague idea about the Arabian origins of their clan, and present-day Arabs from the recognised Arab world consider the *wa-ungwana* to be Africans. This study is basically concerned with the *wa-ungwana*, and not with the larger group referred to as the Swahili people. This distinction is not unique to Lamu and has complicated discussions in the past about the Swahili culture (Pearce 1920, p. 248).

The *wa-ungwana* were the owners of the plantations, and of the slaves who worked there. The *wa-ungwana* not only controlled the surplus from these plantations; they also obtained the indigenous raw products (ivory, animal skin etc.) from the other coastal people by trading imported goods with them. The imported goods themselves were secured through international trade, in return for the raw products. Thus the *mw-ungwana* set himself up as a middle-man. The imported goods came in the form of cloth and beads needed for the local trade, and imported porcelain, furniture and finer textiles that were to become the symbolic markers of the trader's high station.

How did the coral houses and their contents affect the *wa-Amu*, and the people who came into contact with the settlement and its material culture? The *wa-ungwana* came into contact with three categories of people: (1) free hunters (Boni or Awera), pastoralists (Galla or Orma and Somali) and agriculturalists (Pokomo), (2) slaves and (3) foreign traders.

The first category lived on the mainland opposite Lamu, and were considered to be inferior and 'pagan'. They lacked the material culture that the *wa-ungwana* required as a prerequisite to superior status. The *wa-ungwana* controlled the distribution of the material goods, and by association determined the symbolic values of these goods. Some people like the Orma, who were also Muslims, were considered 'pagan' only on the grounds that they did not share the same material culture. It was these so-called 'pagans' who produced the material which directly and indirectly supported the urban *wa-ungwana* before, and even to some extent after, the later development of large slave plantations in the nineteenth century. The hunters provided the ivory and other animal by-products, the pastoralists provided some of the meat for the settlement, and the agriculturalists' surplus reached the town. These tribal groups (see above)

Fig. 1. Roof-top view of Lamu on the Indian Ocean.

traded with the *wa-ungwana* for the goods to which the more powerful group decided to let them have access. But how did the *wa-ungwana* prevent the 'pagans' from trading directly with the Indian Ocean traders who brought the full range of goods?

The house and settlement had features which projected a barrier to the other coastal people, as well as to the foreign trader, who came to the Swahili towns to trade. It will be explained later why the traders came to the towns to trade, and did not go to the countryside in search of the producers of the raw products which they had come to buy. But for now we will explore why the 'pagans' did not come to deal with the foreign traders in the Swahili towns. The clue lies in the belief of the *wa-Amu* that they *owned* Lamu town. They traded with the other coastal people but did not want them in their town in case they decided to demand by force a share of the full range of imported goods or to deal directly with the foreign traders. The goods would then lose their 'value' and the *wa-ungwana* would lose their system of material symbolic markers which helped them to establish and maintain their superior economic position (although perhaps no one was aware of the symbolic system of which they were a part).

A town wall was needed as a boundary to mark off the limits of what the *wa-ungwana* could control and defend. With a wall there could be no doubt about the nature of the visit if a group of tribesmen appeared in town. The town gates were open during the daytime to people who dressed and talked like town dwellers. Historically, we know that the *wa-Amu* traded with the other coastal people in the sixteenth century and that there were also times of conflict. A Portuguese traveller, Duarte Barbosa, noted in about 1517 that 'going forward along the coast is a town of Moors, Arabs named Patee (Pate) and then another named Lemon (Lamu). These carry on trade with the inland country, and are well-walled with stone and mortar, inasmuch as they are often at war with the Heathen of the mainland' (Freeman-Grenville 1975, p. 134). Even the houses that could be seen over the walls must have appeared fortress-like compared to the grass or mud and thatch houses in which other coastal people were living. The houses were perhaps intended to protect the inhabitants and the goods stored and used within.

The houses (see fig. 2) were linked by connecting bridges, *wikio*, and internal passage-ways, *kipingee*, which gave a picture of a 'united front' to any outside group (marked *A* on the house-plan, see fig. 3). But even an individual house reflected the image that the *wa-ungwana* still try to project – proud, tall, powerful and reserved, at least on the exterior. The tribesmen may have been unaware that the house form was not unlike the style that the foreign traders visited in other ports around the Indian Ocean (Beaumont, Gerald & Wagstaff 1976, p. 196). To the foreigner the house was a symbol of credit-worthiness, permanence and cultural affiliation (Allen & Wilson 1979). Thus the foreigner felt safer within the city walls, dealing with fellow Muslims. In

this way he was discouraged from venturing into the hinterland. This observation partly answers the earlier question of why the Indian Ocean traders did not 'cut out' the Swahili middleman, and trade cotton cloth for ivory with no 'overhead' costs. Houses, it would seem, served to provide more than shelter.

The second category of people were brought into the *wa-ungwana* house and system by force; they were the slaves. They were not stopped by the boundary of the city wall. They were in fact needed within the town to build and repair the walls and houses. They also made the items which were not imported, with only a few exceptions, such as the men's embroidered caps, *kofia*, made by free-born men and women. The male slaves lived outside town on the plantations and only a few had special skills that brought them into town. Most of the women slaves also lived and worked on the plantations, but a few female domestic slaves, called *madada*, were chosen by the master to live not only within the town wall but within his house. The areas marked *B* and *C* on the house-plan (fig. 3) were the slave quarters while *D* and *E* were the storage areas. There were also large room-sized spaces, approached by trap doors, that were located between the floor and the lower ceiling of some of the houses. These

Fig. 2. Lamu street with connecting bridge, *wikio*.

areas were used for the secret storage of valuable trade items, ivory and slaves. None of the rooms on the ground floor had plaster on the coral rag walls and the pit toilet in the room marked *F* was undecorated. This room contained only a hole in the floor and no washing facilities. Slaves were considered unclean in every way and therefore to have little need for elaborate arrangements which they would not know how to use, having been accustomed to the 'bush' from which they came. This arrangement was very different from the one created for the master's toilet and bathroom upstairs, which will be described later.

Some two-storey houses have plaster decorations on the lower level because not all *wa-ungwana* had two-storey houses to begin with, and thus first lived in a decorated single storey house. Later, a second upper floor was added and the lower level was then used for storage and slaves. The slaves were never, in any context, located above or ahead of their masters. The master slept on a bed, the slave on a mat on the floor. A slave never walked in front of a master, always

behind. A slave was taught his or her inferior position by being placed below, or behind. The *wa-ungwana* use of space taught them their place within the elite-controlled society.

A slave girl did sometimes have a chance to move upstairs within her master's house or to acquire a house of her own if she became his concubine (called *souriya* in Swahili). Her offspring might be considered lower class, but they were free because their father was an *mw-ungwana*. Even the *souriya* was considered a freed person once she had begat a child by her master. Women in general were tightly controlled, but the *souriya* could become a midwife, a Koran teacher for girls, or a specialist on wifely duties for free-born brides-to-be. In many ways the master's free-born wife, called a *nana*, led a much more restricted life. In stories the *nana* are often portrayed as dull and materialistic. (But it should be noted that the story-tellers were often the *souriya*.) Regardless of this portrayal, the *nana* was always the more powerful woman. The *souriya* would not be given a bed upstairs if the *nana* objected strongly. If indeed she was not

Fig. 3. House plan. *Left*: upper storey. *Right*: lower storey.

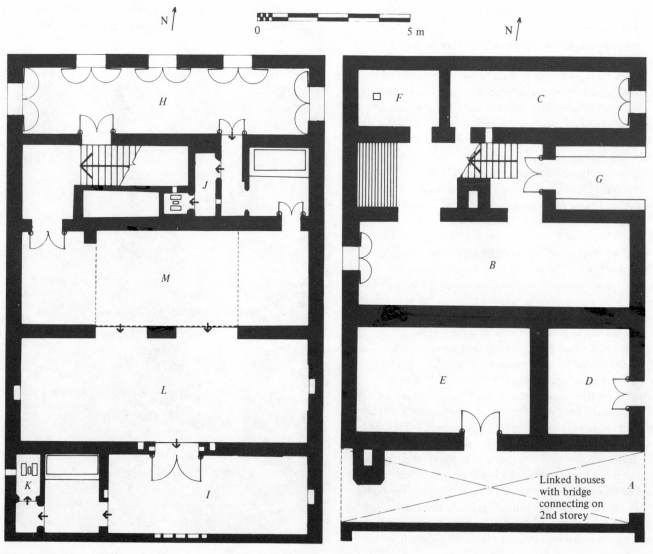

allowed in the house she could be given a house of her own by the master at the edge of the *mitaa* (ward) in which her master lived. Her house was not usually a coral rag with lime mortar house as was the master's main house. The *souriya* house was in fact more mud than lime, but it did have plaster walls that made it look like a respectable free-born house. The interior walls lacked the rich plaster decorations of the master's house. The decoration would have been viewed as a waste by the master because he certainly did not intend to hold large prestigious family weddings there, or any other occasions intended to impress others. It is also doubtful if he was concerned with her 'purity', an issue which will be introduced in the analysis of the decoration within the main house. And of course the master's free-born wife would perhaps not have been pleased to have a slave wife living in the same environment as herself. In more abstract terms: if the same decorations and objects were given to the *souriya*, they would have lost their value as symbolic markers for the upper class *wa-ungwana*.

The 'liminal' concept used by Victor Turner (1969) for people and places that are of a transitional nature can be used to understand the third category of people to be affected by the space created and controlled by the *wa-ungwana*. They have been mentioned earlier as the Indian Ocean traders who provided the imported goods. They were the people with whom the *wa-ungwana* wished to be associated, since their wealth depended on the Indian Ocean trade.

The open street was too public and was not thought to offer a setting conducive to conducting a good business deal between the trader from Arabia or India and the wholesale local *wa-ungwana* trader. The coral houses had a stone bench in a covered porch called a *madaka* (marked *C* on fig. 3), just outside a large impressive door. The carving above the door sometimes contained inscriptions from the Holy Koran. This carving, it was believed, gave the occupants added protection, in the same manner as charms, *hirizi*, containing Koranic inscriptions, gave protection to their wearers, or as *tilasm* (Arabic for talismen) protected buried treasure in Islamic lands.

Here in the *madaka*, just outside the carved door, men could come to discuss trade, while slaves provided coffee and sweetmeats for the master to serve to his guests. Many houses also had an entertaining room, *sabule* (*H* on fig. 3), which was separate from the main part of the house and if it was located on the upper level, often had a window that looked onto the street. The *madaka* and the *sabule* were as liminal and transitional as the respected foreigner was to the *wa-Amu* society. He could not be expected to do business in the street nor could he be invited into the house where he would see and perhaps threaten the honour of the wives and daughters of the family. He could not, since he was a cultured Muslim, be sent to sleep in the 'bush' where the pagans lived (and would be willing to trade), but he certainly could not be given a bed in the main part of the house. For the most part, the foreign trader just slept on his ship or on the floor of the mosque. Sleeping on the mosque floor was an approved practice for travelling Muslim traders, but the long stay sometimes enforced by the monsoon trade winds made the *sabule* a more attractive alternative.

In 1331 Iban Battuta wrote that 'when a merchant has settled in his host's house, the latter sells for him what he has brought and makes his purchases for him. Buying anything from a merchant below its market price or selling him anything except in his host's presence is disapproved of by the people of Mogadishu' (Freeman-Grenville 1962, p. 28). Old *wa-ungwana* trading families in Lamu say that if they were sure that a man had a respectable reputation, and he had traded with their family for a period of years, the foreigner would be allowed to stay in their *sabule*. The closer a wealthy foreign trader was to the family, the more powerful a local trader could become, both at home and abroad. The most obvious way a trader might be tied to a local family was if the foreigner asked to marry a free-born daughter. For such an alliance to have far reaching social and economic ramifications, the wedding had to be an auspicious social occasion. But the foreign trader would only be interested in marrying a free-born virgin of known lineage. He would not publicly risk his own lineage. The *wa-ungwana* were no exception, and, as in other Islamic societies, they believed that a man's honour and known lineage were important.

Women were to be kept 'pure' since they were the reproductive means of the *wa-ungwana* class. Some women were born within the walls of the house, and only left it to be buried. (There are three women in Lamu today who know this degree of seclusion.) The women were thus protected, and this strict seclusion can certainly be seen as a control. Why was the control so harsh? Perhaps because the *wa-ungwana* men *had* called their known lineage into question by having slave wives. If the free-born women were not strictly controlled the claim to a pure line could have been lost completely. No respectable man would then see it as an advantage to marry the daughter if any women in the family had brought shame to the family. After marriage all must be shared, honour and shame. Thus, women became a type of symbolic marker, as controlled as other highly valued goods. If a slave or anyone could have an elite daughter, who would then want one? Not a *wa-ungwana* or a wealthy foreign trader.

In the ethnographic present (Douglas & Isherwood 1979, p. 23) the *wa-ungwana* arrange marriages with economic and political purposes in mind. The daughter has to marry either an equal, for example, a cousin with a free-born mother, or a free-born trader, often a wealthy foreigner. A son, on the other hand, could take a socially inferior girl (as, for example, in the case of *souriya*). The family used to arrange their son's first marriage to strengthen local economic and political relationships. The first wife was a free-born *wa-ungwana* girl, but after that a son could have as many slave wives as he wanted. He could also have more free-born wives, up to a total of four, if he could afford to

keep them all in equal comfort, as was the Islamic require-
ment. The free-born daughters were used for important local
family unions, and to facilitate 'intercontinental' ties. (If the
father of a *wa-ungwana* could afford it, he had a house built
for his daughter, and her husband came to live with her in
this house.) The purpose of such marriages was to extend the
family alliances and prestige. Thus some marriages contributed to the integration of the family unit and its security
(Bourdieu 1977, pp. 58–71). The marriages to foreigners
could be more prestigious, but also more risky. These
marriages could provide rich pure Arab blood and good
business, but what if the foreigner married the girl and took
her back to his home in Arabia? How was this investment of
the prized, free-born, purest of daughters protected?

If a 'pure' daughter was married to a foreigner in a
small private wedding and taken from Lamu, the family
might well lose its investment. But if a coral house was built
for, and delivered with the bride, on the large and auspicious
occasion of an extraordinary wedding day, the foreign trader
was firmly tied to the family. The groom *could* sail away for-
ever, but without the bride, house and its contents. All this
was at least some incentive to return to Lamu with each
monsoon wind, if not to settle there. And often the outsiders
themselves did want to settle in Africa, and this was the
easiest way for an outsider to break into the *wa-ungwana*
hold on local property, exports and even political power.

One of the best known examples of such a process was
the marriage in the sixteenth century in Pate town (another
Swahili town near Lamu) between the local *wa-ungwana*
family, the Batawi, and the Nabahani family from Oman.
While the Nabahani retained the Batawi family name for a
period, they used the Nabahani name when they established
their own ruling dynasty (Chittick 1969).

Now we have come to see that while the house was a
barrier to outsiders, it could be entered by both the slave
women and the male foreigner through marriage unions with
the *wa-ungwana* class. Thick walls could only effect a certain
degree of protection, and defilement was always possible.
Sexual intercourse was seen as defiling, even with the 'purest'
of women. Women were defiling when in their menstrual
periods and impure for forty days after they gave birth. A
man could perform his ablution at home before going to the
mosque to pray, but if he were touched by a marriageable
woman on his way, he had to repeat his ablution before
prayers. Women were not the only source of defilement:
dead bodies had to be cleaned and their polluting properties
removed before burial. Sexual intercourse, birth and the
cleaning of a dead body all took place in the innermost
rooms of the house, the *ndani* (*I* on fig. 3 and see fig. 4).
'Purity' and protection of various kinds were great concerns
within this society. Women, as well as birth, death and body
wastes, were considered forms of defilement, perhaps
because they were regarded as potentially uncontrollable and
therefore threatening elements.

How then could the free-born *wa-ungwana* couple be

protected, if unavoidable defilement was to take place in the
innermost rooms of their houses? Protective charms and
carved inscriptions from the Koran, similar to those around
the front door (described above) are commonly used in the
Swahili culture. Coconuts inscribed with Koranic scriptures
are hung in the main section of some houses as protection
against evil spirits. Eggs are placed near new-born children to
protect them from harm. Ostrich eggs are sometimes hung in
the *mihrab*, the prayer niche, of the mosque as protective
charms (fig. 6). Iron objects can be used to protect a person
or a buried placenta from evil. Babies' faces are decorated
with a black substance to protect them from evil or danger.
Objects and decoration are seen in the Swahili culture as a
source of protection and of purification. They are symbolic
markers which attain protective qualities through use within
their cultural context.

Women were not allowed to pray in the mosque in
Lamu because it was, and still is today, believed that they
could defile the mosque. It was also believed, however, that
special blessings were received by those who prayed in the
mosque. A few houses contained a feature that solved this
problem for the secluded women, who evidently did not
want to be excluded from this extra blessing: a *mihrab* or
prayer niche like that in the mosque, to be used by those
people unable to go to the mosque (see fig. 6). It seems that
the *mihrab* decoration, which was not originally a religious
symbol within the tenets of Islam, and served merely to
indicate the direction of Mecca and prayer, had become for
the *wa-ungwana* a symbolic marker through association with
the act of prayer within the mosque. Informants also pointed
out that the traditional houses were orientated on the

Fig. 4. Interior of the main area of a *wa-ungwana* house: the
innermost room is the *ndani*.

north—south axis because this provided the correct direction for people saying their prayers in the house. There is thus evidence of mosque decoration and orientation with its related purposes being introduced into the domestic architecture. Porcelain plates were used to decorate *mihrabs* in some mosques, and also to adorn tombs and houses. Local people no longer know why this was done, but Marian Wenzel, in her book entitled *House Decoration in the Nubia*, writes that porcelain plates have been used to protect the house from the 'evil eye'. Before imported plates were available, cowrie shells were embedded in the walls for the same purpose (Wenzel 1972, p. 40). Cowrie shells are also embedded in Swahili houses. Mathew noted that 'it is probable that the Chinaware with which they were increasingly ornamented had some magical significance' (Mathew 1956, p. 68). He was speaking of the plates used to decorate Swahili tombs, but the principle could be applied to houses as well.

With these supporting data, two more examples of symbolic markers as protective decorations will be put forward for consideration. These are related to the earlier

question of how the *wa-ungwana* protected their 'purity' from unavoidable defilement.

Elaborate plaster decoration and porcelain plates were concentrated in the area of the house where protection from defilement was most needed, in the *ndani* (see figs. 7(a) to (c)). The main wall of this innermost room was virtually covered with small niches called *zidaka*. These niches closely resembled the larger niches, the *mihrab* in the mosque and the *mswali* in the house, both used for the purposes of prayer. The style of the smaller niches is so similar to the larger type that it is difficult to believe that there is no connection. It was after all not a 'pagan' decoration, and it was, as mentioned before, associated with prayer to Allah, the purest of pure. Perhaps these powerful symbolic markers (*zidaka* and plates) were needed as protection by the *wa-ungwana* in the focal and innermost point of their houses where defilement was most threatening.

If the *mihrab* niche style became a protective decoration for certain kinds of defilement (birth, death and sexual intercourse in the *ndani*), why could it not be used against defilement of another type in another room of the house?

Fig. 5. Prayer niche in a ruined house.

Fig. 6. Prayer niche: *mihrab* with ostrich egg.

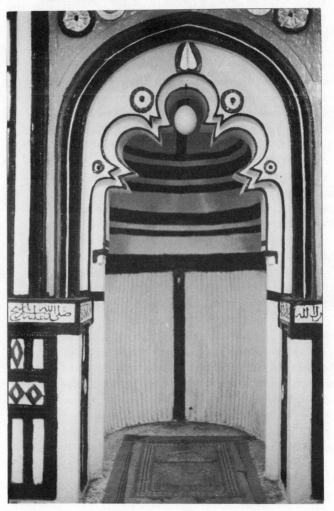

Thus, a large niche of the same style was used over the *wa-ungwana* pit toilet (fig. 8). People now say that by putting this arch and decoration over the toilet their ancestors committed sacrilege. This indicates that (a) they do see the arch as a *mihrab* and (b) the *mihrab* does have a religious association and is more than a decoration that gives the orientation for prayer for the Swahili. Although the *mihrab* was certainly not introduced into Islam as a religious symbol, it does seem to have become one by association. When other foreign Muslims see this toilet decoration in Swahili traditional houses they are invariably shocked.

It was perhaps difficult to adjust to the idea of such basic defilement as human excrement within the house. The custom, before women were restricted to the house, was to use the bushes away from the settlement for this function. Toilets were not found in all *wa-ungwana* coral houses until the eighteenth century, and then there could be as many as five in one house. Different toilets were provided for different categories of people that lived in the house (for example, there was one for the slaves on the ground floor).

Care was often taken to build the pit toilets on an east—west axis away from the direction of Mecca as directed by Islamic traditions. This can be seen in fig. 3 in the toilet marked *J*, shared between the *sabule* and the open courtyard. In this particular house-plan the toilet (marked *K*), in the most private part of the house near the *ndani* (marked *I*), was positioned on the north—south axis. This toilet was used by virginal daughters and their parents. Both toilets are decorated, and both pits are within niches that would be easily mistaken for a *mihrab* in any other context.

It was said above that symbolic markers can be established through practice. The following example will clarify how a ritual can reinforce or transmit symbolic markers. A ritual termed *kutolewande* takes place forty days after the birth of a male or female free-born child. The new-born baby, its face adorned with black protective decoration, is carried out of the *ndani*, and around the house. With the slaves looking on, the mother, midwife and female relatives and friends tell the child in song and verse about the activities appropriate to each area of the house. The child is told who is to use each item of furniture and on what occasions. The child is taken to each member of the extended family living in the house and told what relationship it has to that person. The child is told that the large ivory and ebony chairs, *kiti cha mpingo*, are only for special occasions, such as weddings. They are used solely by the honoured members of the household. The child's father was reported to have said that if a slave was found sitting in one of these chairs, the slave's head would be taken from his body. These are the only chairs in the house. Other respected people (i.e. free-born people) sit on beds, while slaves, if they are allowed to enter the main part of the house, are expected to sit on the floor. The beds are used by the free-born, and perhaps by the *souriya*. Slaves sleep on mats on the floor. The large canopy bed in the *ndani* is reserved for the master. The *ndani* is at the highest level of

this floor of the house. (Ten-inch steps mark the boundaries between the rooms.) At the lowest level is the open courtyard, *kiwanda* (marked *M* on fig. 3), where children play and a few domestic duties may be performed. The baby is also shown the dirt-floor kitchen, where the slaves were once supervised, and its many locally made cooking pots. She is told that the master of the house never goes there. It is not a very highly valued part of the house and its appearance transmits an inferior setting for inferiors. In contrast to this the child is taken to the *sabule*, which was used only by men, and sees that this is a beautifully carpeted room with furnishings to make a guest comfortable. As they have moved around the house, the women have sung or recited poems about each area, and have blessed the child in relation to the activity to be performed in it. Fried millet or popped maize has been thrown in each area as a blessing, and as an offering to the spirits, *shetwani*, who live in the house. The last place to which the baby is taken is the *teka*, a covered entrance just inside the front door. There, if the child is a girl, she is told that on the stone benches beyond (outside) only men are allowed to sit and talk. This is the boundary of her world.

Fig. 7. Below and opposite: rows of niches on the back wall of the *ndani*.

If the baby is male, the *kutolewande* would be suitably adjusted to a description of a boy's life in this society, and values would be given to people, places and things from a man's viewpoint.

Gradually, as the child's range of senses expands, it will begin to perceive the people in the physical environment around it. The house becomes its world, the very cosmos for several years. If the child is a girl, her father may want to guard her purity to the point that she will never go outside until the day she dies. If the child dies before reaching the age of six months it will be buried in the back room of the house and thus will never leave the house. Even when a daughter marries, she may stay in the house in which she was born, while her parents move elsewhere, or her father may connect two houses.

As the child grows up it will see that some people give orders and others obey. Some have nice clothes and wear shoes and others never do. Not everyone eats the same food, and there are some people who never sleep in the more prestigious beds. Space as well as objects and people begin to fit into categories and the child learns not only its place in

Fig. 8. *Wa-ungwana* pit toilet.

the household but its place within society. Thus, the child imbibes naturally and gradually that which it could not grasp when it was first symbolically spoken. Little boys are sent out to play games in the streets, girls are expected to play in the courtyard of the house. From an early age the child learns where and how to play its role in the context of the settlement and society. The *kutolewande*, a ritual associated with birth, demonstrates that the *wa-ungwana* rely on space and objects having values. The rite is purely symbolic for the baby, but for the people who share in the ritual it is a way of learning and forming the social order, through expressing the association of people with certain objects and areas of the house.

Swahili poetry and early travellers' reports can provide more ethnographic data, similar to that related above, but because of their secluded nature there are few descriptions of the *inner* workings of the households. The Zanzibar Sultan's daughter wrote, in 1888, a book entitled *Memoirs of an Arabian Princess*, which relates her childhood in the palace. This provides an excellent insight into a household, but the family was of course Omani and royal, and thus is not a typical example.

Oral accounts passed down through families about the slavery period are most valuable. The *wa-ungwana* society and social order were certainly weakened after the end of slavery. People are still, however, very much aware of the old classifications. Everyone knows who came from a slave or *wa-ungwana* family. There is reluctance for change. No *wa-ungwana* family would agree to a marriage between their daughter and an ex-slave family's son, no matter what other qualities he might possess. People are afraid to change too quickly, they fear chaos. Western culture is forcing change through imported objects, buildings and far-reaching value systems from which the Swahili can no longer remain as isolated as they have been until recent times. Today it is still possible to talk to people who know about the traditional ways and even to observe traditional activities within houses dating to the eighteenth and nineteenth centuries. Therefore, the modern and recent cultural system can be used to elucidate the local archaeological record in a way that an Eurocentric interpretation never will.

There are many contemporary systems of symbolic markers which, if traced back into past material culture, could add a greater time depth and a better understanding of cultural change. Cunningham (1973, p. 219), in his article 'Order in the Antoni house', writes that 'order in building expresses ideas symbolically, and the house depicts them vividly for every individual from birth to death. Furthermore, order concerns not just discrete ideas or symbols, but systems; and the system expresses both principles of classification and a value for classification *per se*, the definition of unity and difference' (see also Tambiah 1969 and Tuan 1979).

Humphrey, in her article on Mongolian tents, writes: 'present day Mongols persistently categorise objects in terms of their position in space. This characteristic of Mongol life was noted by travellers as long ago as the thirteenth century, and it was further observed that Mongols used this categorisation to define social position' (Humphrey 1974, p. 273). She stresses that the Mongols still have the same socially designated places in the tent for people and objects, and give them values. This structure, persisting from the thirteenth century until the present day, is perhaps of interest to archaeologists interested in the relationship between structural and socioeconomic change.

Directly relevant material is to be found in Mary Douglas' and Baron Isherwood's book entitled *The World of Goods* (1979). The examples in this book are taken both from our own Western culture and from traditional societies. The authors write about the social uses of goods, and go on to say that 'space is also harnessed to the cultural process, and that its divisions are heavy with meaning' (ibid., p. 66). 'Forget that commodities are good for eating, clothing, and shelter; forget their usefulness and try instead the idea that commodities are good for thinking, treat them as a nonverbal medium for human creative faculty' (ibid., p. 62). 'Abstract concepts are always hard to remember, unless they take on some physical appearance' (ibid., p. 4). 'Goods are neutral, their uses are social; they can be used as fences or bridges' (ibid., p. 12). 'Goods, then, are the visible part of culture. They are arranged in vistas and hierarchies that can give play to the full range of discrimination of which the human mind is capable. The vistas are not fixed: nor are they randomly arranged in a kaleidoscope. Ultimately, their structures are anchored to human social purposes' (ibid., p. 66).

This general view of material objects and space underlies the proposed approach to ethnoarchaeology. After understanding symbolic markers in the ethnographic present, it is possible to identify positioned artefacts as symbolic markers in the archaeological sites, and to use them as keys to understanding the culture of past generations, particularly where there is cultural continuity. Thus, the material links, by way of durable symbolic marker systems, provide a method of illuminating the past in view of the present, and of elucidating the present in view of the past.

Acknowledgements

I would like to thank the friends and colleagues who read earlier versions of this paper and whose critical comments have been most valuable. In particular, I am indebted to Dr Ian Hodder, Dr James Kirkman, Dr Ronald Lewcock, Ms Sheena Crawford, Mr Peter Avery, Dr G.E.R. Lloyd, Mr Mark Sacks and Ms Alice Welbourn. I am pleased to acknowledge assistance from the following sources: the L.S.B. Leakey Foundation, the Wenner–Gren Foundation for Anthropological Research, the Sir Bartle Frere's Memorial Fund, the Smuts Memorial Fund, the Crowther–Beynon Fund and King's College. The National Museums of Kenya have also been supportive of my research in Kenya and I am deeply grateful to many people within that organisation.

References

Allen, J. & Wilson, T.H. (1979) *Swahili houses and tombs of the coast of Kenya*, Art and Archaeology Research Papers, London

Barbosa, D. (1866) *A Description of the Coast of East Africa and Malabar*, Hakluyt Society, London

Beaumont, P., Gerald, B. & Wagstaff, J. (1976) *The Middle East: A Geographic Study*, Wiley, New York

Bourdieu, P. (1977) *Outline of a Theory of Practice*, Cambridge University Press, Cambridge

Chittick, H.N. (1967) 'Discoveries in the Lamu archipelago', *Azania* 2: 37–68

Chittick, N. (1969) 'A new look at the history of Pate', *Journal of African History* 10: 375–91

Cunningham, C. (1973) 'Order in the Atoni house' in R. Needham (ed.) *Right and Left Essays in Dual Symbolic Classification*, University of Chicago Press, Chicago

Donley, L. (1979) 'Eighteenth-century Lamu weddings', *Kenya Past and Present* 11: 3–11

Douglas, M. & Isherwood, B. (1979) *The World of Goods*, Basic Books, Inc., New York

Freeman-Grenville, G.S.P. (1962) *The East African Coast: Select Documents from the First to the Earlier Nineteenth Century*, 2nd edn, Rex Collings, London

Garlake, P.S. (1966) *The Early Islamic Architecture of the East African Coast*, Oxford University Press, London

Giddens, A. (1979) *Central Problems in Social Theory: Action, Structure and Contradiction in Social Analysis*, Macmillan, London

Humphrey, C. (1974) 'Inside a Mongolian tent', *New Society*, October, pp. 273–75

Kirkman, J.S. (1964) *Men and Monuments on the East African Coast*, Butterworth Press, London

Mathew, G. (1956) 'The culture of the East African coast in the seventeenth and eighteenth centuries in the light of recent archaeological discoveries', *Man* 56: 66–8

Pearce, F.B. (1920) *Zanzibar, the Island Metropolis of Eastern Africa*, T. Fisher Unwin Ltd, London

Salme, Princess (Emily Ruete or Salamah Bint Said) (1888) *Memoirs of an Arabian Princess*, Doubleday, Page & Co., London

Tambiah, S.J. (1969) 'Animals are good to think and good to prohibit', *Ethnology* 7: 423–59

Tuan, Y. (1979) *Space and Place: The Perspective of Experience*, Edward Arnold, London

Turner, V.W. (1969) *The Ritual Process: Structure and Anti-Structure*, Aldine, London

Wenzel, M. (1972) *House Decoration in Nubia*, Duckworth, London

Wilson, T.H. (1979) 'Takwa, an ancient Swahili settlement of the Lamu Archipelago', *Kenya Past and Present* 10: 7–16

Wilson, T.H. (1980) *The Monumental Architecture and Archaeology of the Central and Southern Kenya Coast*, privately published for the National Museums of Kenya, Nairobi

Chapter 7

The interpretation of spatial patterning in settlement residues
H.L. Moore

Moore argues, in the introduction to this paper, that the analogies suggested by ethnoarchaeology should be structural rather than formal. The category 'rubbish' in settlement studies must be located and understood within cultural contexts, including the archaeologist's own society. The notion of curation is shown to be culturally variable and to have varying significance. The organisation and categorisation of refuse must be linked to data on burial, settlement, decoration, formalised ritual and so on within a cultural context. Such relationships are identified by reference to an initial survey of the Marakwet of Kenya. This study demonstrates ways in which the archaeologist could link refuse organisation to other types of data within a cultural context.

Ethnoarchaeology is one of the fastest growing areas within archaeology, and its general development reflects some of the current problems in archaeological theory. The term ethnoarchaeology covers a broad range of interests but I would like to restrict my discussion here to those studies which are concerned with the interpretation of intra-site spatial patterning in material remains and with the cultural factors which affect the formation of the archaeological record.

Ethnographic analogy
One of the main problems in archaeological explanation with which ethnoarchaeology has been most closely associated is the use of analogy. Under the influence of the New Archaeology, analogy became a 'dirty word'; it became associated with culture historians and with attempts to provide an 'historical' rendering of the past. While it was grudgingly admitted that analogy could not be avoided, most New Archaeologists felt that its role in archaeological explanation should and could be reduced to a minimum. It is now widely agreed that ethnographic data do generate hypotheses about the past which can be tested against archaeological material, and thus avoid the charges of unsophisticated particularism levelled against the earliest uses of anthropological analogy. Whilst some still argue that ethnoarchaeology can furnish the discipline with general laws, many researchers feel that either these laws are too 'general' to be of real value, or that because they are derived from ethnographic situations, they lack validity for a discipline which is primarily concerned with broad expanses of time. In order to highlight some of the problems associated with recent archaeological uses of analogy, it may be instructive to consider part of the debate on analogy which has been conducted in social anthropology.

The use of analogy in anthropological interpretation has encouraged social anthropologists to ask such questions as: 'In what does anthropological explanation reside?' and 'How does an anthropologist make the practices and beliefs of an alien culture intelligible?' 'What is the so-called logic of the "primitive" mind?' and 'How does man make sense of the world around him?' These two questions are clearly related since they are both concerned with the role of analogy in explanation, the logical basis of constructed reality and with whether a 'scientific' orientation is or is not a superior mode of knowing. Anthropologists had to come to terms with the fact that rigorous description was not sufficient for making sense of 'native' classifications and that statements like 'twins are birds' (Evans-Pritchard 1956) were clearly not without sense. It was the recording of native taxonomies and of statements of identity which prompted anthropologists to compare different modes of thought and systems of knowledge and to enquire into how they were to 'explain' witchcraft beliefs, and the like, given that to a western observer such things appeared nonsensical. Discussions on these points have been varied, and although the extreme Frazerian view that 'magic is a bastard science' has been largely discarded in favour of a view which sees the processes of 'primitive' and 'modern' thought as essentially similar (with both magic/religion and science characterised by analogical reasoning), there are still many points of difference (Gellner 1974; Horton & Finnegan 1973; Tambiah 1969). The nature of the disagreements which persist and the detailed arguments which support them need not be paraded here; it will suffice to say that these debates forced anthropologists to the realisation that, on one level, explanation is fundamentally a process of explication based on translation. In other words, the meanings of events, terms, social practices and so on can only be grasped in relation to the world view or 'frame of meaning' (Giddens 1976, p. 142) of the culture concerned. This can produce a dangerous situation. On the one hand it becomes imperative that accounts are not ethnocentric and do not merely confirm our prejudices and predilections (i.e. superiority of a scientific orientation in the world). On the other, if we resign ourselves to the view that every culture is different and provides a coherent and finite province of meaning, then we are dangerously close to a doctrine of cultural relativism and this is a problem which must be faced if there is to be an emphasis on holism and 'contextuality' in explanation. This means that since we are forced to provide explanation using the categories of our own language (and consequently categories of our own experience) the result of good translation could either be the failure to recognise differences where they exist (i.e. ethnocentrism) or the failure to observe the nature and extent of similarities. Arriving at this point social anthropology was forced to recognise two things, both of which have important theoretical consequences: (1) the cultural background of the observer is a crucial element both in observation/ recording *and* in the development of theoretical models, and (2) in the process of explanation, which is fundamentally one of translation (i.e. rendering unfamiliar terms and concepts intelligible using terms and concepts which are our own), if one is to escape the charge of cultural relativism one must proceed not on the basis of formal similarities but on the basis of structural or organisational similarities.

On the whole archaeologists have assumed that the pre-

conceptions of the individual archaeologist employed in explanation are not relevant in a discipline which observes its data (i.e. the past) indirectly. The latter assumption is false since it views observation, description and explanation as a hierarchy of stages, whereas it can be argued that they are, in some very important sense, simultaneous. It is now common-place in archaeology to comment that observation is theory dependent; it is agreed that meaning does not inhere in the objects under study, that relationships are not intrinsic to the data and that these things have to be created by the observer. Yet archaeologists have not sufficiently considered the cultural background, categories and conceptions of the individual archaeologist as opposed to his 'intellectual' or theoretical predispositions (see, however, Leone 1978). Archaeological explanation currently employs (analogically) a large number of ethnocentric concepts which are never challenged for the simple reason that they seem so basic and such good common sense. In the following paragraphs I shall show how some of these ideas can be illustrated with regard to specific problems in archaeology.

Refuse

Nowhere has the lack of examination of the cultural background of the archaeologist been clearer than in studies of refuse disposal, discard and their spatial correlates. One of the main problems is the category 'rubbish' and its related category 'value' which in some cases may be seen as the inverse of the former. Researchers sometimes assume that all phenomena subsumed under our term 'rubbish' will be subsumed under the category 'rubbish' in other cultures and would have been subsumed under that category in the past. They may also assume that other cultures, both past and present, have a single category 'rubbish' and that this stands in the same relation to a postulated category of 'value' as it does in our own society. These problems arise simply because the main criterion for defining the category 'rubbish' is based on the action of discard. Rubbish is discarded and whatever is discarded is rubbish. (This argument is only relevant to intentional discard and is not concerned with problems of loss etc.) Placed in this bald fashion there are probably few archaeologists who would agree with the statement, but the fact remains that this is a common and implicit assumption in much ethnoarchaeological research.

There have been studies that have considered discarded faunal material which is clearly not classified as 'rubbish', but they have concentrated on explaining how symbolic and religious requirements may influence the patterning of material remains. Bulmer's study of the disposal of animal bone by the Kalam of New Guinea makes it clear that anomalies in the final distribution of certain bones cannot be explained either by post-depositional disturbance or by reference to 'activity' areas, although both these factors are important (Bulmer 1967). Similarly, Hodder's (1982) study of the highland Nuba illustrates that the spatial organisation of faunal remains cannot necessarily be related to the spatial organisation of functional activities. So far there has been no investigation of the possibility that all discarded objects may not fall into the same category and that objects so discarded may be organised according to several categories, none of which may be equivalent to our category 'rubbish'. I would like to suggest that it may not be profitable to view the spatial organisation of refuse as primarily governed by functional and practical requirements with occasional, inexplicable anomalies being attributed to the intervention of cognitive or 'religious' factors. It seems more probable that differential distribution of refuse types will always be the product of interaction between functional requirements and cognitive categories. Archaeologists cannot hope to be aware of the exact nature of these categories but they should realise that spatial variation in refuse disposal is likely to be the result of interaction between functional requirements and differing attitudes to various artefact types and by-products. In only a few cases is it likely to be possible to interpret the spatial patterning of refuse purely in terms of either functional or cognitive factors. These difficulties are also apparent in relation to the curation of certain artefacts.

As far as studies of curation are concerned, the notion of 'value', as it is most frequently applied, seems to be closely linked to western concepts of energy saving and efficiency. It is common for archaeologists to analyse curation in terms of the value of objects, this value normally being related to the amount of energy that would have to be expended in order to replace the artefact. Scarcity of materials or periodic non-availability are also thought to affect the value of objects (Gifford 1978). However, studies concerning curative tendencies have all so far been conducted among groups with a high degree of mobility and this seems likely to have produced evidence of a rather high degree of curation. Factors which influence the abandonment of sites associated with more sedentary groups may be more complicated. Apart from some unusual events (such as the Roman invasion and the Black Death) or natural catastrophe (Pompeii), it seems likely that such sites would run down over a period of years and the artefacts and parts of structures removed for curation might be of a rather different kind. Certain objects of symbolic or religious importance, whatever their physical form, might either be removed or left behind and the criteria which govern such decisions are unlikely to be based on how scarce the object is or on the amount of energy that will have to be expended to replace it.

I have recently begun an ethnoarchaeological study among a group of Marawet sedentary tribal agriculturalists in northwest Kenya, where, in recent years, there has been a slight increase in settlement mobility. Factors governing such mobility are varied but many younger people are abandoning their homes in the upper escarpment in favour of new houses on the lower slopes. If a house is abandoned in favour of a site nearer the fields, then a man will frequently take his roof poles with him. As long as that man lives or as long as people think there is any chance of him returning, they will not remove any other part of the house. However, once a man dies, whether he had abandoned his house before his death or not, anyone who is in need may come and help himself to any part of the house, except that no one may remove the fireplace. The fireplace symbolises both the house itself and ownership of that house; while the fireplace remains no one may claim that piece of land for rebuilding and the fireplace stands in remembrance of the deceased and of the deceased's lineage ancestors.

This fact is part of a complex series of rules governing choice of house plots, property rights, inheritance and so on, but the point here is that a fireplace is a very common object, made from unaltered local stone. It is easy to replace and requires very little expenditure of energy. Either one can view these objects as being uncurated and therefore their value only becomes clear because they have been left behind, or one can view them as being curated in a very special way. Curative tendencies, whenever they are observed, may well be related to some concept of 'value', but that concept will probably not be intelligible in terms of demand, energy saved or efficiency, all of which are modern, western ways of looking at the world. It seems that in any pre-monetary economy the real value of any object is likely to be closely linked to its social and cultural value and that this may on occasion correlate with high energy input etc., but there is no necessary correlation. Archaeologists must be careful that during the ordering process, which is a necessary part of explanation, they do not imbue their data with principles which they later rediscover analytically. In other words the activities of hunter—gatherers are likely to seem rational, logical and logistic if those are the principles which the archaeological observer uses to make sense of what he sees going on around him.

This is a very simplistic example of the unhindered use of an ethnocentric concept which governs and influences both observation and the formulation of models. However, the important point is that ethnocentricism can be operative on several levels and while archaeologists have been alerted to the problem of ethnocentrically ascribing functions to artefacts and structures, it is more difficult to realise that certain types of basic assumptions may be fundamentally ethnocentric and very pervasive and will not fall victim to the 'cautionary tales' which ethnoarchaeology is currently providing. It is clear that ethnographic data supply hypotheses that we could not generate from our experience in and observation of our own world and it is for this reason that archaeologists usually employ ethnographic and ethnoarchaeological analogues. However, although acquaintance with other cultures, both past and present, may aid the realisation that the world is not always ordered in ways that are familiar, when explanation is sought it will always be rendered in terms which are familiar (i.e. through the use of analogy) and which imply familiar concepts. Ultimately any observer in any discipline cannot avoid becoming embroiled in the translation question and will thus be forced, in some measure, to utilise familiar concepts to elucidate the unfamiliar. The trap to be avoided is the one of literal translation, since it is much more likely that similarities where they exist will be structural and organisational rather than formal.

Discard patterns must, then, be interpreted in their context. Refuse must be related to all aspects of social action, that is to burial, settlement, subsistence, formalised ritual, and so on, if a meaningful translation and explanation of spatial patterning are to be achieved. I would emphasise this point by a return to the Marakwet, and in particular to a sub-group of the Marakwet called the Endo.

The Marakwet

In spite of the fact that there is now a large amount of research being conducted in the Kerio valley, by the Institute of African Studies, Nairobi, there has, as yet, been very little work published on the Marakwet except for Kipkorir and Welbourn's *The Marakwet of Kenya* (1973). As a result, there is no general ethnography to which the reader could be referred. The basic social unit of the Marakwet is the individual family, composing a man and his wife, or wives, and their unmarried offspring. Unmarried sons often have their own houses, however, and these may or may not be near their father's compound. (The Marakwet say that if two people build within 20 m of each other, then they are almost certain to be close kin.) Each family lives in a compound, usually consisting of two wattle or stone and mud houses. Traditionally, one house would have been for the man and one for the woman; nowadays it is possible that one hut may be for sleeping and the other for cooking. Goats, which are now the principal livestock, are kept in houses which are often away from the compound down in the valley, or they may be built 50 m or so down the escarpment from the other huts. Sometimes there is no goat hut and the goats live in the man's hut. Alternatively, there is no hut for the man and he lives with the goats. In the latter case, if there is a compound fence it may only enclose the goat hut plus a small clear area. In this case, the woman's hut, although part of the same unit, is actually outside the fence. The presence or absence of a compound fence, as opposed to just a cleared area around the huts, and the area it encloses, is always governed by the presence or absence of goats. Choice of hut locations is governed by the contours of the Cherangani escarpment which runs almost north—south and huts are therefore normally perched on the edge of a rocky precipice facing each other, i.e. huts face north—south but never east—west (see fig. 1).

Settlement, refuse and burial

When a man dies he will be buried between his house and the escarpment edge, to the right-hand side of his hut, lying on his right side with his right hand under his right ear. Vice versa for a woman (see fig. 2).

The Marakwet are buried in shallow rock graves without any ornaments or grave goods of any kind. If a child dies he or she is buried in the same way as an old man or old woman. If a circumcised girl or boy dies this is considered unpropitious and some informants say that the corpse may have its hands and legs tied and will be tipped into the grave as opposed to being placed in the proper position. Even if this is not done, young people who die before they have had time to produce children themselves are buried further away from the houses and further to the right or the left, depending upon sex (see fig. 3). However, this may not be possible if the compound is very close to the edge, in which case they will just be buried further down the escarpment. Variation in the placement of graves is the product of various conceptual notions about the dead. Those who die in innocence, like children, and those who die at the end of their lives, like the elderly, are considered less 'harmful' than those who die young or 'out of turn'. Variation is also the result of proximity to the compound and especially to other men's goat houses or goats, and can also be due to topographical constraints.

Ideally, an old man should be buried under the goat *taka taka* (the Swahili word for rubbish) which has been thrown out of his house, or the goat house in which he was living, and down the escarpment. This will often be possible even if the goats' house is in the valley because under these circumstances it is normal for the man to keep a few young kids in his hut.

The Endo distinguish between three types of rubbish: ash from the fire, goat *taka taka* and chaff. These types of rubbish are conceptually and semantically distinct and are usually spatially segregated as well. Ash is always thrown behind the woman's house. Chaff is often mixed with compound and house sweepings and is usually dumped at some convenient point along the escarpment edge. Goat faeces are swept over the escarpment edge next to the man's or goats' house. Schematically these relationships can be represented as in fig. 4. This spatial separation clearly results from the spatial organisation of the compound, in that the refuse 'reflects' the activities carried out within each structure, e.g. all cooking is done in the woman's house and 'therefore' the best place to put ash is behind her house. However, the

Fig. 1. The positions of Marakwet huts in relation to the Cherangani escarpment.

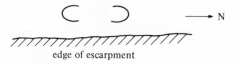

edge of escarpment

Fig. 2. The position of male and female graves in relation to huts.

woman's hut   man's hut

woman's grave   ×   ×   man's grave

positioning of the huts in the compound is in fact a 'reflection' of the ordering of the Marakwet world which also governs disposal of refuse and the burial of the dead.

Sometimes it is possible to find compounds where the ash is mixed with the chaff or compound sweepings, but this is relatively rare. The chaff rubbish area will always separate the ash from the goat faeces, that is, lie between them, and such mixing as does occur is usually the result of scuffing by goats and children. Deliberate mixing of ash and chaff does occur, however, because it is quite common to find the ash pile as far as 15 m away from the house, and it may frequently include maize cobs, banana skins, etc. which are normally included in the compound *taka taka*. However, the ash and goat refuse have not yet even been found adjacent to each other. When asked why they are kept so rigidly separated, the usual reply is that 'one should not mix good things with bad things'. Among the Marakwet, goats are associated with fertility and prosperity and this is why the dead of other families, particularly the inauspicious dead, should not be buried near the goats or goat house.

Both women and goats represent fertility, but they are in some sense opposing forces or sources of fertility. Goats are the main livestock of the Marakwet, they are also the animals slaughtered for all kinds of ceremonies and it is the innards of the goats which are inspected to foretell the future. Women have a subordinate place in social life amongst the Marakwet (at least until they are past the menopause). A woman cannot be an elder. She is a child compared to a man and *knows* nothing. Knowledge and access to it are the key points of status. Control is in the hands of a group of male elders whose authority rests on their personalities as much as on their economic wealth. A man must be wealthy but he must also command respect. He gains respect, as opposed to wealth, through control of knowledge and through having a large number of children. A man without children is shunned and an unmarried man of middle age may not even be greeted. A man without children cannot go through the final marriage ceremony which marks the attainment of full elderhood. A man is therefore reliant on two sources of fertility – goats and women – but it is important to realise that these two forces are in some senses opposed. The wealth obtained from goats differs from the respect obtained through women, but wealth is partly dependent on and subject to the subordinate women since it is children who

not only provide a man with the 'symbolic' means of acquiring respect but who also, through their labour potential, provide an essential 'physical' means of acquiring wealth. As an example of the opposition between goat fertility, controlled primarily by men, and the fertility of women, it is interesting to note that a woman who has had twins (i.e. she is too fertile) must perform a number of acts before entering a compound or goats will die. She must not walk through a herd of goats but must let them pass her or goats will die. She must also perform a special act before crossing a river or the water will dry up and the land will then no longer be fertile.

This conceptual opposition is also apparent in the spatial organisation of the houses. The woman is associated with the home and her house. Apart from 'modern' young men, men do not sleep in the same houses as their wives. The Marakwet explain that a man cannot sleep in the same house as his daughters once they are sexually mature. Boys stop sleeping in the same house as their mother from eight years onwards.

Women are linked to cooking and to ash. Only a woman can remove ash from the house and carry it to the ash place. The ash is associated with the centre of the woman's world and her children. Cooking and burning are processes whereby things are devoured and eaten. They destroy, but are also sources of life. Therefore, ash is also related to the threatening part of female fertility. Ash is the symbol of suicide. It is often placed behind the house so that children will not accidentally play in it. In some Marakwet groups when a woman wants to refuse marriage she covers herself in ash, threatening not only the death of fertility of the union of man and woman, but revealing the destructive potential of female sexuality. Ash is related to destruction and to life; woman's fertility is life-giving and threatening. Amongst the Marakwet, goat faeces and ash, and their placing around the settlement, are points in a network of associations and metaphors and they are closely linked to opposing forces and tensions in social strategies.

Conclusion

Thus the placing of the houses within the compound, the spatial positioning of refuse areas and the allocation of burial places are all actions which are enforced by the same set of functional and symbolic requirements. The spatial

Fig. 3. The position of the graves of old people and circumcised children in relation to huts.

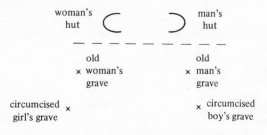

Fig. 4. The relationship between the distribution of rubbish and the position of huts.

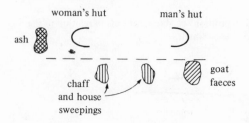

organisation of refuse is not merely the reflection of activities carried out within individual structures, but is in fact governed by a set of generative rules, which also govern the layout of the compound. There is no causal, unidirectional link between compound layout and refuse disposal. Both are mutually interdependent and recursively implicated and provide a mnemonic for day to day action within ordered space.

While it would not be possible archaeologically to reconstruct the world view of the Endo, it would clearly be possible, using the theoretical framework, to relate settlement, refuse and burial practices one to another and to identify the structuring principles. This preliminary piece of work illustrates that it is not possible to interpret aspects of the archaeological record in isolation from each other and that all aspects of that record are in fact governed by sets of structuring principles which generate social action. Human activities and their archaeological residues are only intelligible in terms of 'the objective conditions' which govern social action in any particular context.

Acknowledgements

Acknowledgements must go to Sheena Crawford and Ian Hodder for reading earlier drafts of this paper. Permission to carry out the fieldwork was obtained from the Government of Kenya and the Office of the President under Permit Number OP.13/001/10 C83/3. Thanks for hospitality and help go to Dr and Mrs Robertshaw, Richard Leakey, Neville Chittick, Joseph Kibowen and others. Special thanks to my interpreters Samuel Chebet and Josphat Kilimo, and to Dr and Mrs Carson and their staff. Lastly, gratitude to the Sisters and Fathers of the Catholic Mission at Chesengoch who not only proved themselves to be first-rate anthropologists, but also provided invaluable moral and logistical support.

References

Bulmer, P. (1967) 'Why the Cassowary is not a bird', *Man* 2: 5–25.
Evans-Pritchard, E.E. (1956) *Nuer Religion*, Clarendon Press, Oxford
Gellner, E. (1974) *Legitimation of Belief*, Cambridge University Press, Cambridge
Giddens, A. (1976) *New Rules of Sociological Method*, Hutchinson, London
Gifford, D. (1978) 'Ethnoarchaeological observations of natural processes affecting cultural materials' in R. Gould (ed.) *Explorations in Ethnoarchaeology*, University of New Mexico Press, Albuquerque
Hodder, I.R. (1982) *Symbols in Action*, Cambridge University Press, Cambridge
Horton, R. & Finnegan, R. (eds.) (1973) *Modes of Thought: Essays on Thinking in Western and Non-Western Societies*, Faber, London
Kipkorir, B.E. & Welbourn, F.B. (1973) *The Marakwet of Kenya: A Preliminary Study*, East African Literature Bureau
Leone, M.P. (1978) 'Time in American archaeology' in C. Redman *et al.* (eds.) *Social Archaeology*, Academic Press, New York
Tambiah, S.J. (1969) 'Animals are good to think with and good to prohibit', *Ethnology* 8: 423–59

Chapter 8

Decoration as ritual symbol: a theoretical proposal and an ethnographic study in southern Sudan
Mary Braithwaite

Relationships between the use of decoration and particular dimensions of social action are examined in Braithwaite's paper. A suggestion is made that covert forms of discourse, such as decoration, may express messages that are inconsistent with the legitimation of relationships of power. Through a study of the Azande of Sudan, it is shown that decoration occurs on objects that through their use involve encounters between opposed categories. Amongst the Azande the male/female dichotomy is particularly marked and the maintenance of this opposition, and of the dominant position of men, is problematical. The position of women is subordinate, but extremely powerful and certain ideological and ritual strategies are required to maintain the separation of the sexes and the dominant position of men. Items that through their use involve, either directly or indirectly, encounters between male and female are marked out with decoration, and it is suggested that decoration both covertly expresses and authorises the encounter between these opposed categories. Yet not all dichotomies between groups of people in Azande society require this form of ritual strategy. The study also shows that decoration may not be used on items involving opposed categories where other ideological strategies are employed to maintain the relationship of power. Through different kinds of ideological and ritual mechanisms the social order may be maintained, and also transformed.

This paper presents the results of an investigation into the contexts of decoration within the material culture and the social and cultural forms of some of the Azande people of southern Sudan. It outlines a general theory of a function of decoration in terms of the symbolic and ideological nature of human activity and phenomena, which, it is proposed,

may offer a new and additional model for the explication of decoration and archaeological data.

Theoretical framework

The theory I propose depends upon a particular view of humans and their nature and activities.[1] This view focuses on the conceptual nature of human action and the symbolic and semantic character of cultural phenomena. Action in, and understanding of, the world is effected within the framework of a conceptual order and by means of systems of signification, for example, speech, art, gesture, food or dress.[2] The meaning of semiotic items is dependent on their actualisation within social life and it is their recursive and subjective character which makes evident the dialectic nature of the conceptual order and social praxis, whereby the conceptual order both determines and is determined by social praxis.

Of the systems of signification apparent in any society I am primarily concerned here with non-verbal systems and their symbolic qualities. That is, I am concerned with the representation and association, through a sign, of concepts or things other than and secondary to the sign. Symbols and systems of symbols have the capacity not only to express and communicate, but also to guide and effect action. For Bourdieu, the symbolic system can be seen as having three functions; as a means of communication, as an instrument for the knowledge and construction of the objective world, and as an instrument of domination by establishing and legitimating, through its ideological effect, the dominant culture and concealing that culture's methods of division (Bourdieu 1979). As factors in social action, symbols and symbolic systems are associated with human interests, purposes, ends and means – and, as such, have a political and ideological dimension. This dimension is not a product of conscious human purpose, but rather, as Althusser suggests, it is through and within ideologies that conscious subjects exist (Althusser 1969). As an element of social formations ideologies are 'regions', whose form is determined by their articulation within the social whole, and which may thus express modes of class domination.

One of the ideological functions of discourse and communication is the production and reproduction of the established order through the misrecognition of the real relations of power within a social formation. As both Bourdieu (1977) and Giddens (1979) demonstrate, the modes and limits of discourse are geared to the legitimation and misrecognition of the real power relations and to the naturalisation and reproduction of the social order. I suggest, however, that this applies only to certain forms and contexts of discourse. Barth (1975, p. 1) suggests that different vehicles of expression have different potentials or strengths in what they can express, and that when knowledge is cast in a 'variety of simultaneous channels and expressions' these may be saying 'different things, with different clarity and implications'. Turner is also concerned with the plurality of meaning and behaviour associated with symbols. In a discussion of Ndembu ritual he shows that considerable discrepancy and contradiction exists between the interpretations of a certain ritual symbol offered by informants and the behaviour exhibited by Ndembu in situations dominated by this particular symbol (Turner 1967). I suggest that these contradictions and discrepancies between principle and practice, and the plurality of meaning of symbolic discourse are of considerable relevance to the functioning of symbols and systems of symbols within a society. Given the particular power relations in a social order, messages that are inconsistent with the naturalisation and legitimation of the relationships of power may be expressed in covert, implicit idioms, and those that sustain the order may be expressed in overt, explicit idioms.[3]

I have previously said that systems of symbols not only express and communicate, but also guide and effect action. They may have a ritual function within the social and conceptual order to 'facilitate passages and/or to authorize encounters between opposed orders' and to 'authorize . . . the necessary or unavoidable breaches of social order' (Bourdieu 1977, pp. 120 and 124). By the very nature of the unnatural conceptual order and of human social practices, problems of category definition and transgression of category boundaries are unavoidably entailed. Ritual practice serves not only to mark out, but also to authorise and transform

those forces of social disorder inherent in breaches of the conceptual order, in the ambiguous boundary areas between social categories. Thus rites of passage, such as ceremonies of circumcision or marriage, and taboos on certain activities and goods are part of a whole spectrum of practices and things which mark out and mediate encounters between opposed categories.

This marking and mediating effect of ritual practice may be extended to include the use of decoration. In a study of the philosophy of art and symbolism, Langer depicts a work of art as a symbol, expressing the verbally ineffable and negotiating insight and meaning. Decoration, she suggests, is also symbolic and makes more visible, by concentrating attention and vision to those surfaces or areas it adorns (Langer 1979). I suggest that decoration may function as a ritual marker of particular breaches of the conceptual order in contexts where covert expression of the messages or concepts involved is necessary or advantageous given the social order. Decoration may function specifically in contexts and about topics that may not be explicitly expressed, but must instead be restricted to the 'area of the undiscussed' (Bourdieu 1977, p. 168).

Analysis of the context and use of decoration within a particular social formation may inform not only about aspects of the content of the conceptual and symbolic systems, but also of the part played by these within the areas of ideology and of the relationships of power.

The study
The setting
The theory outlined above developed from attempts to understand the place and significance of decoration in the material culture of some of the Azande people of southern Sudan. The field research upon which this study is based was undertaken in two three-month periods in 1979 and 1980, in two areas of Western Equatoria Province, southern Sudan, lying within the Azande tribal region. One of these two areas, that of Chief Gangura near the border with Zaïre, lies within the old kingdom of Gbudwe where Evans-Pritchard conducted most of his anthropological research in the late 1920s. It is his subsequently published work on the Azande that provided me with an initial framework for understanding aspects of Azande social life and culture (for example, Evans-Pritchard 1937, 1967, 1971, 1974). Without this historical dimension any understanding of the 'ethnographic present', and particularly the Azande's own perceptions and images of it, would be substantially impoverished. I can do no more in this short paper than present a few facets of Azande life and culture that have a bearing on this discussion of decoration, its contexts and its functions.

The Azande live in the centre of Africa on the Nile–Congo divide. Their tribal region includes parts of southern Sudan, north eastern Zaïre and south eastern Central African Republic, although here I refer specifically to Azande of Sudan. They are a predominantly agricultural people, culti-

vating a variety of crops under a aystem of shifting cultivation, supplementing this diet with fish, wild game and
termites. Prior to the European conquest at the beginning of
this century, the Azande were divided into a number of
independent chiefdoms and consisted of an amalgam of
different tribes, assimilated under Avongara rule to one way
of life. The Avongara, the ruling clan, controlled almost all
military, political, economic and ritual systems by a hierarchy of headmen, deputies, sub-chiefs and chiefs — with
one chief at the centre of each chiefdom. Family life was
based on polygamous, exogamous marriage and patrilocal
residence and was characterised by the inferiority of women
and the authority of elder men. Under first European and
later under Arab administration the independent chiefdoms
were coalesced and the chiefs lost their dominant position in
the political structure as they were deprived of their military
and commercial power, and became agents of an external
authority.

Today the Avongara have in theory the same status as
any other Azande, although many of the government-paid
posts within the tribal structure are still occupied by Avongara, and memories of their former status still affect their
treatment and regard by Azande 'commoners'. The tribal
structure of a hierarchy of administrative posts with differing powers and responsibilities remains, and, although much
reduced in influence and functions, it is still a significant
aspect of Azande life and society, and retains much of its
former influence and involvement in the internal and personal affairs of the Azande people.

Marriage rules have remained unchanged and the household of one man and his dependents still occupies a crucial
position in Azande social life. Although the household
activities and appearance of the homestead have altered
relatively little since Evans-Pritchard's day, important structural changes have taken place within each household. Regulations concerning marriage and divorce procedures and the
introduction of money and wages have been most influential
in altering the structure of Azande life, with men being able
to marry at a much younger age, resulting in greater competition amongst men for wives. Of the three original distinctions between classes of people in Azande society —
between Avongara and commoner, elder and young men, and
women and men — only the latter remains as central to
present-day social life, although that between young and old
men is still felt as significant.

Native exegesis on social and cultural phenomena and
the significance of social activities is singularly lacking among
the Azande — at least of an explicit kind — and only by
observation of activities and actions can much of what is
orderly and significant be known and acquire meaning. The
differentiation between men and women, male and female,
dominates the Azande world. Public activities and behaviour
are geared to separation of, and contrast between, the sexes.
With few exceptions, tasks and activities are clearly divided,
in type, time and space, between men and women. The
greater prestige that is associated with men's activities and
products compared to women's is consonant with their
relative social positions and expectations. Nevertheless,
women are not without power and the dependence of
Azande men on women can be used to particular advantage
and gain. It is little surprising, therefore, that Azande men
see women as potentially troublesome, jealous and promiscuous. These feelings are a logical result of the inherent conflict
between the social separation of the sexes and the ambiguity
of the subordinate and yet powerful position of women.

In the presentation of the data in the following section
I shall talk much of the opposition and contrast between
women and men, and female and male. It is difficult to
avoid this in any discussion of Azande life since it is a basic
and central division and concern of the Azande symbolic
system and social praxis. Nevertheless, it is not the only
division and concern in the Azande world or between people.
Among Azande 'commoner' men there is now a general ethos
of equality and egalitarianism, with the sometime exception
of youths and elder men. Yet, in practice, there is a subtle,
but extremely complex system of representing and manipulating comparative status and relations, which varies from
situation to situation. For instance, one of the most important social obligations of men is to their kin, and most particularly to their in-law relations. These relationships involve
considerable respect, reserve and tension on both sides, and
necessitate careful manipulation of situations and practices
for the maintenance and creation of satisfactory relations.
The structure of relationships between people is not some
fixed, given entity, but is constantly being created and
recreated through social practices. The particular state of
social relations at any one time or place depends more or less
on the specific social context. The subordinate position of
women in the Azande social structure may be relatively
unchanging compared to, say, relative positions of men with
regard to each other, but it is only through social practices
that these positions are made manifest. The following discussion does not intend to present a thorough or representative view of Azande society or culture, but merely pin-
points particular aspects that help to clarify explication of
the data.

The data

For the sake of brevity and of clarity of presentation
of the data I shall consider only some of the classes of
material items used by the Azande. I shall also present in this
section only classes of items that either are or are not decorated by ornamentation or embellishment of a surface. Within
some classes of material items, some of the objects are and
others are not decorated. I have chosen to consider these in
a later section and initially to concentrate on the barer bones
of the data.

As an entry into the problem of decoration and the
material and non-material culture of the Azande, I shall at
first, and in some detail, consider just one type of material,

the pottery, and later present some of the other material forms made and used by the Azande. Although clay pots are made by men, they are used and owned almost entirely by women and in use clearly mark out and symbolise the domain of women and their major activity in the homestead, cooking. Each woman owns a range of, on average, about ten pots; cooking pots for porridge and sauces, water pots, beer-making pots and beer-serving pots (fig. 1). Ideally, each pot is used only for its assigned purpose. The pots are kept when in use, and also when out of use, either inside or immediately around her kitchen hut. This is an area which men should not enter and it is said by Azande that a man may become impotent or lose his hair if he does enter or if he disturbs any object in the hut. These pots are symbolic of women and women's activities and yet, by reason of some of their functions, they are sometimes associated with men. For example, a pot that is used to cook a sauce for a meal will also be used not only to serve the sauce, but also as an eating dish for the man or men. Since men and women always eat in different areas of the same homestead compound it can be seen that the transfer of a pot by the woman and from the female cooking area to the man and the male eating area could be of concern. It is a breach of the spatial separation of the sexes in this context.

But the situation is more complex than this since other types of pots are decorated that do not involve movement out of the female cooking area or use by men. They do, however, through the practices associated with them, enter into other actions of symbolic concern. In cooking a sauce for a meal, for instance, the woman has to prepare a range of foodstuffs which almost inevitably include at least one 'female' food and one 'male' food, which are mixed together in a pot and cooked with water and so changed from a raw state to a cooked state. The potentially confusing and transforming nature of these actions can only be understood in terms of the production, use and significance of foodstuffs in Azande social life and social relations.

The production and collection of foodstuffs is characteristic of the general sexual division of tasks and activities undertaken by the Azande. Many tasks are restricted to only one sex; hunting of wild animals and the production of cash crops, such as bananas, cotton, coffee and pineapples, to men, and the production of the various seeds, beans, vegetable and root crops used for domestic consumption to women. Even when the same foods are collected or grown by both the sexes there are, in other ways, distinctions between them. For example, although both the sexes go fishing they use different methods and equipment. Or, in

Fig. 1. Azande decorated pots. Left: beer-serving pot. Middle and right: water storage pots.

cultivating, each adult woman and man will normally have their own field and although many of the agricultural tasks are shared by the family unit, men and women are supposed to work in different and specified parts of the same field. Different stages of the production and preparation of crops tend also to be associated with a particular sex. Although reaping the eleusine is a man's task, weeding, threshing and winnowing it is women's work; although preparation of a new ground for cultivating is men's work, hoeing the cultivation is for women. The produce, mainly eleusine, maize, manioc, groundnuts, sesame, gourds and yams, from each field will be stored in separate granaries, and the ideal Azande homestead includes a granary for each man and for each of his wives. A woman's crops will normally be used for everyday consumption within the household, whereas the man's crops may be used either for sale or for the entertainment of guests and the fulfillment of social duties.

Food is an extremely significant and important part of Azande social life and, as in all societies, is used symbolically to mark out social relationships and to express things on many occasions. 'If food is treated as a code, the message it encodes will be found in the pattern of social relations being expressed. The message is about different degrees of hierarchy, inclusion and exclusion, boundaries and transactions across boundaries. Like sex, the taking of food has a social component, as well as a biological one' (Douglas 1975, p. 249). Raw food in contrast to cooked food, for instance, has a social and symbolic function in Azande society. A general rule is that raw food should not be given as a present or in a meal to a person whom one wants to show respect to, but it may be given without insult to someone of lower status and in some other circumstances.

I said earlier that among Azande men there is in theory an ethos of equality, but that in practice there is a complex system of representing and manipulating comparative status and relations. The giving and taking of raw or cooked food is just one small part of this system, which operates by a collectively maintained and approved pretence that these practices are insignificant and by a misrecognition of their real function. But the symbolic significance of the use of raw or cooked food is dependent upon a clearly defined contrast between the opposition of raw and cooked. A blurring of the categories would result in a less effective symbolic role in the definition of social relations; thus the necessity to mark out, and authorise, the points of transformation between raw and cooked.

These few examples should show that pots, as containers of food and drink, may have far more important connotations than we, or the Azande, may be aware. A pot used for serving beer involves the transfer of the beer, which is made and served only by women, from woman to man. A pot used for cooking porridge entails a transition from raw flour to cooked porridge. A water pot is used for drinking water for both men and women and is taken out of the female kitchen area to be filled at a communal water source.

These statements and events are not banal. All these types of pots so far discussed are decorated, with bands of simple incised, impressed and rouletted decoration between the neck and shoulder of the outer surface of the body of the pot (see fig. 1).

The point may be made clearer by looking at the contexts of use of the one kind of pot that does not have decoration applied to its surface. This is a small porous water pot used for cool drinking water and kept in the hut of the man. It is the only kind of pot used by men, and remains in the man's hut in the homestead. Moreover, it is only ever used by the man and although it is kept full by his wife or daughter, this is done when the man is not present in the homestead and so not seen. As Goffman's work suggests, the contrast between 'front' and 'back', or public and private regions in which social performances are carried out is of considerable relevance. Various potentially compromising features of interaction are kept hidden or absent by restricting them to 'back' or private regions (Goffman 1959). Giddens also suggests that 'performances in front regions typically involve efforts to create and sustain the appearance of conformity to normative standards to which the actors in question may be indifferent or even positively hostile, when meeting in the back' (1979, p. 208). Potentially compromising situations, given the symbolic and social order of the Azande, may be acceptable when done in 'private', for instance, when only the women of the homestead are present, but are unacceptable when the homestead becomes 'public' with the presence of men or visitors. This notion of the acceptability of certain things if they are not seen, but their unacceptability if seen is a particular feature of Azande actions and activities, as it is of our own, and separation in time and space is one of the main ways of preventing conflict or interaction between opposed categories. Given that the only possible compromising context of use of the man's water pot is 'not seen', there is no need ritually to mark the pot in any way – and this explains the complete lack of decoration on this type of pot.

Another example illustrates not only this ritual significance of decoration, but also shows how practices, and the practical, are geared to the symbolic system. Azande not only buy pots from their own potters, but also from the potters of another ethnic group, the Belanda, some of whom live within the Azande tribal region. The Belanda are very similar to the Azande in many aspects of their social activities and cultural forms, although certain forms and activities mark and reinforce their ethnic identity and difference. Likewise, Belanda pots are in some ways recognisably different from Azande pots, for instance in terms of a particular decorative effect and rim form, but also many features of the pottery are extremely similar. The structure, complexity, techniques, and content of the decoration are very similar, as are the overall forms and range of pot types. Whereas all types of Azande pots but one, the man's small drinking-water pot, are decorated, all but two of the Belanda pot types are decorated. One of these undecorated types is, like the Azande, the man's drinking-water pot and the other is the large beer-making pot type, which is similar in form and size but not in use of decoration to the corresponding Azande pot type. The Belanda do not apply decoration to this type of pot, whereas the Azande do. Although it is quite common to find other types of Belanda-made pots in use in Azande homesteads, I found no example in more than one hundred homesteads of a Belanda beer-making pot being used by an Azande. Azande say that they do not buy the large beer-making pots from Belanda, and Belanda potters say they do not sell them to Azande, although Azande buy all other kinds of Belanda pots. Belanda potters working in Azande areas tend to produce very few of these large pots and only make them to order because they say that they are more difficult to fire and to transport to market, while Azande potters say they prefer to make large pots because they can make more money from them than from smaller pots. All the Belanda and Azande potters I spoke to gave purely practical reasons for the discrepancy between Belanda and Azande beer-making pots and saw the difference in use of decoration only in terms of tradition or taste.

As is so in all societies, the explicit reasons given by the Azande for particular practices are often practical or functional, and, as for giving of food, there may be no recognition of the symbolic significance of the practices or of the sometimes inadequacy of the actual explanation offered. Yet it should not be surprising given the ideological nature of ritual and symbolic activity, that the practical fits so neatly with the symbolic. The nature of certain beer-making processes, such as the change from raw to cooked grains, is such that the pots concerned need to be ritually marked out. Belanda beer-making pots are undecorated and are therefore unsuitable for use within Azande practices although their undecorated state is appropriate for use in Belanda beer-making processes. The Azande only buy those types of Belanda pots that are appropriate given the need to mark out certain activities by the use of decoration. The practical dimensions of producing and selling pots are geared to the symbolic dimensions of their use.

The illustrations so far show that certain types of pots may be decorated if they are used in areas and actions of symbolic ambiguity and concern, and that the one type of pot that does not involve similarly ambiguous associations is not decorated. I have also shown, through the example of the Belanda pots, how the practical organisation of production, selling and buying is adapted to the symbolic and ritual needs of Azande activities. The pattern of the use and non-use of decoration in this one type of material culture of the Azande appears consonant with the use of ritual to mark out ambiguous boundary areas brought into being by the juxtaposition and encounter of opposed categories through social action. That female and male, woman and man, and raw and cooked are of particular social and symbolic significance in Azande life has, I hope, been sufficiently demon-

strated already. But why is decoration the ritual form chosen to mark these particular contexts? Part of the answer lies in asking another question. Why is there no awareness by the Azande of the significance of decoration?

By digressing for a moment and looking at another Azande ritual I can perhaps suggest an answer. Male circumcision is an important rite for the Azande, which, they say, is a recognition of social and personal maturity and marks the passage of a boy from the world of the child to that of men. The rite is undertaken by a group of boys and involves a period of seclusion in the bush. During this period the circumcision is performed and various taboos on food and activities are enforced for both the boys and their sponsors, who are adult men. For example, a sponsor must refrain from any sexual intercourse and the boys must have no contact or even set eyes on women for the duration of the seclusion. Azande do not explicitly acknowledge the extremely significant female dimension to the rite, although many of the activities and actions associated with it clearly indicate that this is so. The rite of circumcision is in practice not only a definition of the passage of the boy from child to man, but also from the world of women to the world of men. Prior to circumcision boys are brought up within the Azande female world. A boy's 'socialisation' into Azande life is dominated by women and female activities and orientations. It is little wonder, therefore, that the passage from this 'world' to that of men is defined by ritual. It is also unsurprising, given the explicitly subordinate position of women, that those aspects of the rite that are concerned with women's power and influence are implicit and not within the level of discourse, but in the 'area of the undiscussed'.

The dominant position of men in Azande society depends on emphasising the lack of power of women and making this appear 'natural'. That the power and influence a woman has is genuinely appreciated by men is typified by their statements about women. 'Women's thoughts are shallow, they need managing and controlling. They are fickle, unstable and, if given the chance, promiscuous.' Moreover, judging by many of the cases brought before the chief's courts the men's fears are not misplaced. It is at court, in fact, that both the women's structurally subordinate position and their considerable strength and influence is most apparent. Given this, it is perhaps more than necessary for the reproduction of men's dominant position to mark out those areas of ambiguity between significant categories with a relatively covert ritual effect, such as decoration. Although this only deals with the reasons for the use of decoration in certain encounters between female and male, a similar discussion and reason is applicable to all other encounters marked by the use of decoration. I have previously suggested, for instance, the importance of keeping the categories raw and cooked clearly defined, and of keeping their symbolic significance and function unacknowledged. Decoration serves to facilitate encounters between opposed categories and to authorise the breaches of the social and symbolic order inherent in the use of the objects concerned, but specifically in contexts and about categories that are not explicitly acknowledged.

It may be thought that the decoration of an item indicates something about its social value and status, or of the status of its owner. Yet some of the items owned and used by, and symbolic of, the person of highest status in Azande society are clearly undecorated. One example is a chief's wooden eating dish. This is of considerable value and indicates, by its form, his unique status, but is devoid of decoration. The dish is quite different in style and size from those used by other Azande and although other wooden objects are decorated with burnt and carved patterns the chief's dish is quite deliberately left undecorated. If we look at the contexts of its use, however, we may understand why decoration is unnecessary. The double-bowled dish is used for serving and eating the normal Azande meal of porridge and a sauce. It is only ever used by the chief, who eats privately and on his own, as his status demands. No other person is involved and although one of his wives will fill and later wash the dish this is done in another compound separate from the chief's and completely out of view. There seems to be little problem of encounters between opposed orders, whether of food or people, and no 'ambiguous boundary area' apparent during its use; no action that requires marking out by some ritual form. Indeed, one of the notable features of the material items associated with the chief is their general lack of ornamentation. His status is little apparent in his material associations, whether dress, dwelling or other belongings. I suggest that the reasons for the lack of display of status lie within the ideological framework of the Azande political structure.

The chiefdom system is still regarded by the Azande as 'natural' and although they may criticise and complain about it, their reliance on it for the making of decisions, the solution of complaints and problems, the means of legal action and for assistance and support is immeasurable. Most Azande do not perceive any alternative system and will not admit that they could make important decisions or effect social changes without reference to the chief. They will say that the chief is by the fact of birth into the chiefly clan and by his upbringing a 'natural' ruler. Even though the Azande now vote for a new chief through an election system introduced under British colonial rule, most Azande prefer to vote in line with the traditional system of succession. This is not just for reasons of tradition, but because they genuinely feel that the man chosen will be best suited for the position. This 'naturalisation' of the political structure means that the chief is in a remarkably secure political and social position. There is perhaps, therefore, less problem of boundary maintenance or of conflict between his position and others. Through the particular ideological effect that naturalises the political structure, breaches of social order are contained.

The chief's position is not seen as being in conflict with other groups in Azande society and is never in question or open to doubt in such a way that requires authorisation by a ritual practice or form. The use of decoration is unnecessary given the ideology that sustains the political system.

Analysis of the use or non-use of decoration in other forms of Azande material culture yields a similar interpretation. For instance, some of the other items used by women for the preparation of food are not decorated either. The woven sieves, made from strips of cane or reeds, that the women use for sieving the grain flours used for making porridge are undecorated, although they could easily be ornamented in some way. Chair backs and mats are also made of strips of cane or reeds and are decorated by weaving with dyed reeds and by contrasting naturally different shades to form patterns in the fabric. Not decorating sieves is as deliberate an action as decorating the mats and chair backs, especially as they are made by the same craftsmen who use the same methods. But whereas mats and chairs are sometimes associated with problems of boundary definition between categories, sieves are not since they are only ever used for foodstuffs in a raw state, are never used for the mixing of different foods, always remain in the female cooking area and are used only by women.

Many more examples could be noted, the lack of decoration on hut walls or the decorative and complicated hair styles of Azande women for example, but this would require more space than this paper allows. I shall later summarise the conclusions of this brief discussion of the possible function of decoration in the context of Azande life, but first I must present some apparent inconsistencies in the data and offer a possible solution.

Some necessary inconsistencies?

So far I have discussed certain classes of objects used by Azande that either always are or always are not decorated. To find this consistency in all classes of items would, however, be quite remarkable, and, indeed, within certain classes some of the items are and some are not decorated. One example is the chairs made and used by the Azande. There are three main types in use at present. One is a kind of deck chair with a frame of wood and a fabric back made of woven reed or cane strips; another is a simple wooden stool with cane slats for the seat, and the third type is a grander version of this with a light wooden back and arm support. The simple stools are regarded as a rather inferior type of seating, suitable for women to sit on, although many women say they prefer to sit on the ground rather than a chair. The stool with back and arm rests and the deck chair are types most commonly used by men; the deck chair usually being regarded as the most comfortable and will be used either by the most senior men in the homestead or for respected guests. Women will use chairs sometimes if men are not present in the homestead, particularly if they have female visitors, but will rarely use them if men are present. Stools and chairs are part of the few communal furnishings of the homestead, not usually owned by any one member. They can be used by anyone, although their use at any one time is often a reflection of the structure of relationships of the people present.

Chairs and stools are another small part of the complex of signifying practices associated with the production and maintenance of relationships of respect and deference. Taboos on the use of stools and chairs, for instance, show how significant seating arrangements may be. Widows and widowers in mourning and menstruating women, all potentially defiling and impure, are specifically not allowed to sit on any chair or stool that may be used by other people. The significance of stools and chairs, like other items, depends upon their use within the particular social context. This can alter considerably as, for instance, different people leave or enter an Azande homestead. The public nature of seats and their possible significations places them in a position of symbolic concern. How, therefore, can the inconsistency in the use of decoration be explained?

Bourdieu suggests that 'symbolic systems owe their practical coherence, that is their regularities, and also their irregularities and even incoherences (both equally necessary because inscribed in the logic of their genesis and functioning) to the fact that they are the product of practices which . . . bring into play . . . principles which are not only coherent . . . but also practical' (1977, p. 109). This is important for the interpretation of social and material data — not because it might enable me to sweep over the inconsistencies as simply part of the functioning of the system, but because they may provide an insight into the workings of the symbolic system and into the relationship between this and social praxis. Nevertheless what I am about to suggest is tentative and a statement of a possibly useful line of enquiry rather than a committed approach.

To understand some aspects of the relationship between the symbolic system and social praxis it is necessary to have a sense of the long-term changes in Azande society and material culture. As I noted earlier, substantial changes have occurred in the structure of Azande society, particularly during recent decades, such that the dichotomies between Avongara and commoners, elder and young men, and women and men have become increasingly less well-defined. Of possible correspondence with this is the fact that elder Azande say that stools and chairs were undecorated when they were young and that decoration has begun to be used on these items during their lifetimes.

If the changes that have occurred in Azande society have meant that the distinctiveness of the dichotomies between, particularly, elder and young men, and women and men have become increasingly less clear, it may well be that the boundary areas between the opposed categories of people have become of correspondingly more concern. Some of Douglas' work, for instance on couvade, suggests that when

the discreteness of categories and the definition of boundaries comes increasingly under question, the concern will be expressed by using 'whatever symbolic language is to hand for bringing the point home' (1975, p. 67).

So what may perhaps be happening with this increasing use of decoration on stools and chairs is a symbolic expression of concern over the weakening distinction and discreteness of such opposed categories of people as women and men or elders and young men. The inconsistency in the use of decoration in this particular class of objects is perhaps a stage in the gradual development over time of the Azande symbolic and social systems; the inconsistency being a practical effect of the gradual change.

Decoration and Azande culture: a summary

I have not, for brevity's sake, presented the full range of Azande material culture. Those forms I have chosen to discuss are, however, representative of the general findings of the full analysis and interpretation of decoration, its material contexts and social and symbolic associations. Nor have I presented a complete survey of Azande symbolic and ritual behaviour, for this would be a vast undertaking, and also unnecessary for the purposes of this paper. I have simply drawn a very few principles and aspects that are relevant to and apparent in the contexts of decoration discussed.

I have tried to show that decoration functions as a symbolic and ritual marker of particular areas of ambiguity and concern brought about by the actions of people in the course of everyday life. These areas of the conjunction of opposed categories are specifically those that are not' explicitly realised by the Azande. The reasons for this lie within the domains of ideology and the social order, in the masking of the real relations and possession of power and in the presentation of a particular social order, designed to disadvantage certain groups in favour of others. Particular ideological mechanisms function to present the Azande chiefdom system and the chief's position and person as 'natural', while others, such as decoration, function to authorise conflicts between opposed categories. Through these ideological and ritual mechanisms the social order is maintained, and is also transformed. It is through the symbolic order that both social change and the reproduction of the established order, if in a transformed form, is actualised.

Some conclusions

I have attempted in this paper to offer an explanatory framework for the analysis of decoration and its contexts in material and non-material culture forms. This framework is presented in the theoretical section at the beginning of this paper.

The theory is concerned specifically with certain contexts of the decoration of material items. It is not a contribution to theories of style or of the content of decoration. It is, however, an attempt to understand the part that the decoration of items may play within particular dimensions of human activity. I also propose that the theory has applications far outside the ethnographic context it developed in. Among the south eastern Nuba people of Sudan there is a highly developed tradition of body decoration. But as Faris points out, their 'personal art is not a semantic art in the sense that all design has some type of deeper symbolic meaning. The most meaningful element is the medium on which it is commonly produced' (1972, p. 50).

I suggest that this theoretical formulation of one function of decoration may form part of a far wider approach to the symbolic and ideational component of those activities, and products of activities, evidenced in the archaeological record. Decorative art is not merely some undynamic social product or representation, but may play an active part in the constitution, reproduction and transformation of societies. An analysis of decoration in terms of a symbolic and ritual function may offer additional information about social and ideational aspects of the archaeological record since it lays emphasis on the context of decoration within material and cultural forms. A construction and assessment of contextual associations of decoration with regard to its presence, degree of presence or absence is a practicable archaeological project. Taking a body of archaeological data it would be possible to construct a pattern of associations, for example with different types of objects or structures, different contexts or areas within sites, or different site types, which in addition may vary spatially and/or temporally. An interpretation of the resulting pattern of associations in terms of my theoretical formulation may suggest certain facets of the social life of the people responsible for, and evidenced in, the archaeological data. A more specific assessment of the explanatory value of this theory of decoration for archaeology will result from just such a project. This is presently being undertaken.

Notes

1 This 'view' is not novel in the field of social anthropology. My own presentation here is a result of ideas drawn from a range of work and is not necessarily true to the original contexts of the sources. Apart from the texts referred to in the paper I have also gained ideas from Clifford Geertz's *The Interpretation of Cultures*, Malcolm Crick's *Explorations in Language and Meaning* and Trevor Pateman's *Language, Truth and Politics* (Geertz 1973; Crick 1976; Pateman 1980).

2 Order is created by dividing and distinguishing, by emphasising and accentuating natural differences and creating false divisions and groupings, and also by juxtaposition of categories so that differences are manifest. Yet the order or system of distinctions that underlies and generates a person's understanding of the world is of a conceptual nature. It is both the source and the outcome of a subject's consciousness of, and action in, the world.

3 This is true in many contexts, but is a rather simplistic picture of the true complexity of the relationships between discourse and the presentation of the relationships of power. For instance, a contrast may be made between the explicit statement of heterodoxy or heresy in 'fringe' contexts and in 'establishment' contexts.

Acknowledgements

The fieldwork in Sudan was funded by the Scottish Education Department, and was made possible by the help and hospitality of many people in Sudan — Government officials in Western Equatoria Province and Azande alike. Especial thanks, however, go to Chief Thomas Gangura for his hospitality, to Natanyia for teaching me about the lives and tasks of Azande women, and to Daniel Kumbo and Benjamin Enosa for their interpreting work and valued advice.

I should also like to thank Henrietta Moore for sparing time to read and criticise the theoretical part of my work — the faults still in it are not due to her help. I also wish to thank Alan Lane for reading and commenting on various drafts and for proof-reading the final one, and for all his other help with my work.

References

Althusser, L. (1969) *For Marx*, Allen Lane, London
Barth, F. (1975) *Ritual and Knowledge Among the Baktaman of New Guinea*, Universitetsforlaget, Oslo
Bourdieu, P. (1977) *Outline of a Theory of Practice*, Cambridge University Press, Cambridge
Bourdieu, P. (1979) 'Symbolic power', *Critique of Anthropology* 13 and 14: 77–87
Crick, M. (1976) *Explorations in Language and Meaning*, Malaby, London
Douglas, M. (1975) *Implicit Meanings*, Routledge & Kegan Paul, London
Evans-Pritchard, E.E. (1937) *Witchcraft, Oracles and Magic Among the Azande*, Clarendon, Oxford
Evans-Pritchard, E.E. (1967) *The Zande Trickster*, Clarendon, Oxford
Evans-Pritchard, E.E. (1971) *The Azande: History and Political Institutions*, Clarendon, Oxford
Evans-Pritchard, E.E. (1974) *Man and Woman Among the Azande*, Faber & Faber, London
Faris, J.C. (1972) *Nuba Personal Art*, Duckworth, London
Geertz, C. (1973) *The Interpretation of Cultures*, Bacis Books, New York
Giddens, A. (1979) *Central Problems in Social Theory*, Macmillan, London
Goffman, E. (1959) *The Presentation of Self in Everyday Life*, Doubleday, Garden City
Langer, S. (1979) *Feeling and Form*, Routledge & Kegan Paul, London
Pateman, T. (1980) *Language, Truth and Politics*, Jean Stroud, Lewes
Turner, V. (1967) *The Forest of Symbols*, University Press, Cornell

Chapter 9

**Structures and strategies:
an aspect of the relationship
between social hierarchy
and cultural change**
D. Miller

Miller describes a model of emulation, in which material items associated with elites are copied by lower levels within society, so necessitating further symbolic elaboration by the elite in order to maintain structural and categorical contrasts. In the modern western world, the structure of society is reproduced in the strategies of individuals seeking reputation and status and one of the mechanisms used to achieve this is association with the language traits and material items of the elite. Material items are implicated in the emulation of higher castes within a village in India and an analysis of the pottery made and used in the village demonstrates that the organisation of pottery categories (in terms of colour and form) relates to the structure of the social hierarchy. This association is related to the emphasis on purity in the Hindu context, which, as in Braithwaite's study, is expressed in food and drink transactions. The proliferation of pottery types is not tied directly to utilitarian functions and may in fact decrease the efficiency of certain activities. Hierarchy may generate strategies of emulation, or the prevention of copying new forms, but only if a given set of material items is used to express and form status relationships. In a particular archaeological context, Miller shows how the process of emulation has structured the expression of rules of purity and pollution in material forms over two millennia.

Archaeologists have always been concerned with the processes that underlie cultural change: to identify patterns in dynamic processes and to postulate mechanisms that might give rise to these patterns. This paper is concerned with one such process that results from the interaction between the structure of society and the strategies employed by individuals or groups within that society. Unlike forms of

genuine structural change such as revolution, this is a process by which changes serve not to alter, but to preserve the major structural principles upon which society is organised. In a society where hierarchy or social differentiation has become a fundamental organisational principle, such differentiation is commonly expressed through symbolic elements, which may include many of the material products of that society. This results in both form and style becoming associated by the members of that society with higher or lower ranks within the hierarchy. If an individual or group wishes to improve its relative position within the hierarchy, it may seek to emulate the group above it by adopting certain of the products or styles associated with the higher group. If the group above wishes to maintain its superior position, it must seek either to prevent this, or to have new symbols of its differentiation adopted in order to maintain the previous contrast (fig. 1).

The process of emulation thereby results in items changing their symbolic association, and in new items being adopted, in a dynamic process, that proceeds quite apart from any actual change in the principle of hierarchy or even in the relative positions of the respective groups. It is proposed that emulation may be identified as a significant cause of change in material culture for many of the societies studied by archaeologists. This is not to accredit it any *a priori* status as an inevitable process. Emulation does not occur of necessity in any hierarchical society; it represents only one of several alternative strategies that may be employed by groups or individuals within such a society in order to improve upon their position. These strategies are in turn constrained and given meaning by their relationship to the structural organisation of society.

Various examples will be used to illustrate the nature of this process. The first will be taken from a study of language change in New York. The second will be a study based on the caste system of India and more precisely on innovations in pottery production in a contemporary Indian village. This will be followed by an investigation of changes in certain pottery vessels in India from the Early Iron Age to the present day.

New York

The work by Labov in diachronic sociolinguistics (1972), based on intensive fieldwork in New York, is an

Fig. 1. The process of emulation. While the social hierarchy remains constant, the process of emulation provides a dynamic force producing continual change in material items. Stage 1: highest status group adopts a change in conventional pottery form. Stage 2: second highest status group adopts innovation. Stage 3: third highest status group adopts innovation. Stage 4: lowest status group adopts innovation, but by this time highest status group has adopted another change and thereby maintained the contrast.

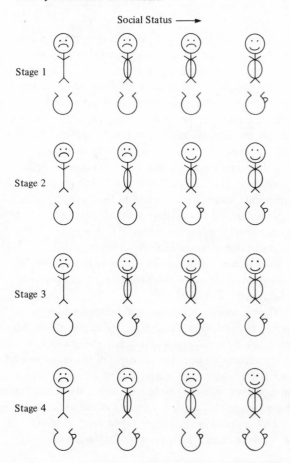

Social Status ⟶

Stage 1

Stage 2

Stage 3

Stage 4

attempt to bring precision to something of which we are all conscious and which we frequently remark upon: the way in which an individual's own interpretation of his language expresses his self-image as a member of society, and the way this results in changes in language itself. This phenomenon is often discussed in terms of social hierarchy as in Nancy Mitford's 'U' as opposed to 'non-U' speech, or with the associations of 'dropped-h's'. This is an area where prejudices are strongly held and we are aware that, as individuals we can — and do — shift our speech according to the social context of the communication.

Labov used the principle that process may be manifested in synchronic patterns to study the distribution of traits in samples of the contemporary population, and also employed some historical material from writings and tape recordings. His studies indicate that 'social attitudes towards language are extremely uniform throughout the speech community' (ibid., p. 248). The source of a linguistic shift may be any section of the speech community, but if the shift becomes associated with a high-status group it is frequently the case that a less prestigious group will tend to adopt it. Over a period of time, the variable may spread to all sections of the speech community; thus, the variable becomes an invariant, that is, the possibility of speaking in the alternative form fades out, and the variable becomes redundant as a contrastive feature. Labov notes, however, that some other shift is then usually employed to compensate for this change, and thus maintain the contrastive relationship. As an example, Labov found during his study that 'In every context, members of the speech community are differentiated by their use of (ing), so that higher and lower scores for this variable are directly correlated with higher and lower positions on socioeconomic indices' (ibid., p. 239). There may not always, however, be a direct correlation between speech use and social status, since, for example, we find hypercorrection: 'One of the most solidly established phenomena of sociolinguistic behaviour is that the second highest-status group shows the most extreme style shifting, going beyond that of the highest-status group in this respect' (ibid., p. 244).

New York society is hierarchical; its members have attitudes of respect and contempt through which they judge their fellow members. In order to preserve their elevated position, higher status groups must respond to encroachment upon their identity. They may try to prevent the adoption of a trait through their control of education or the communication network, but a linguistic trait has no inherent defence against being copied, and in New York society it is more efficient to generate new contrastive variables than to depend upon the preservation of old ones (different strategies are used, for example, in France). Though emulation is described here as a strategy, there are varying degrees to which we can ascribe conscious motivation to the groups involved: 'There are speakers in every community who are more aware than others of the prestige standard of speech, and whose behaviour is more influenced by exterior standards of excellence. They will show greater style shifting than those who do not recognise such a standard' (ibid., pp. 215—16). It is important to note that emulation can occur without being understood as a process, or the relevant groups even being aware of the changes that are taking place.

The process of emulation in modern American society has not only been studied in linguistics. In 1899, Thornstein Veblen published a critique of American society, in which the relationship between social hierarchy and patterns of production and, especially, consumption were detailed in a highly sardonic but telling manner (1970). Following from his general thesis that 'The motive that lies at the root of ownership is emulation' (ibid., p. 35), Veblen goes on to discuss topics such as 'The conservation of Archaic traits' (ibid., pp. 145—64) and 'Dress as an expression of the Pecuniary Culture' (ibid., pp. 118—31). This last section has been developed by Quinten Bell in a more refined and sustained analysis of the changing fashions in dress in Britain and America over several centuries, indicating the relationship between class and cultural change (1976). These works are concerned with precisely the kinds of communicative variables that archaeologists employ in their identification of specific sub-groups and periods.

The most recent attempt to forge a general theory of human behaviour from this tradition is the work of the social psychologist Rom Harré (1979). His study starts with the assertion that 'The pursuit of reputation in the eyes of others is the overriding preoccupation of human life, though the means by which reputation is to be achieved are extraordinarily various' (ibid., p. 3). Harré proceeds with an analysis of the relationship between structure and strategy; since social structure only exists through its reproduction in the individuals who make up society, structure is seen to be dependent upon the strategies employed by those individuals, whom Harré represents as actors interpreting their roles. This approach differs markedly from the dominant materialist interpretations of society. Harré claims that 'for most people at most times the expressive order dominates or shapes the practical order' (ibid., p. 5). Thus, in the analysis by Douglas and Isherwood (1979) of patterns of production and consumption, we find many examples of the ways in which these activities are organised through the categories by which hierarchy is expressed. They expand Veblen's original concern with conspicuous consumption to a more general theory of goods as categorisation. Their proposal for analysis seems appropriate for archaeological enquiry: 'We take consumption activities to be always social activities. It would seem then that the clue to finding real partitioning amongst goods must be to trace some underlying partitioning in society' (ibid., p. 97). We may note, however, that hierarchy itself must be seen as both a product and a cause of the differential distribution of power in social groups.

To conclude, if we reflect upon the variation in artefacts and behaviour evident within modern society — and this may include patterns of subsistence and production — then the tradition described here would suggest that much of this variation results from the expressive aspect of our society, and is particularly sensitive to processes such as emulation which may occur within or between what we generalise as social classes. The question arises, however, as to the extent to which this conclusion is influenced by the specific nature of capitalist society with its desire for an efficient relationship between production and consumption, and its ever increasing range of goods. To investigate these same principles as they might apply to the kinds of smaller scale societies more usually studied by archaeologists, we turn to more stable village-based farming communities, where there is a much more limited range of products, but where social hierarchy is very evident.

India

The caste system of rural India represents just such a village hierarchy. The origins of caste are a matter of controversy, and caste or its more abstracted justification *varna* are not strongly emphasised in the earliest Veddic literature. In the third century BC, Megesthenes, the Greek ambassador to the court of Chandragupta, records Indian society as comprising seven endogamous groups related to distinct professions. This appears to represent a reflection of a caste-like system, and certainly by the period of the Guptas in the third century AD we may consider most of the essential facets of the caste system to have emerged. Thus, we are dealing with a structural principle that is of some two millennia standing. Although there have been radical challenges to the caste system from the heretical and egalitarian religions of Buddhism and Jainism and the medieval Bhakti cult, it seems that the principle of hierarchy has always managed to emerge as the dominant organisational dimension of Indian society.

Caste has been described by Dumont as a structure within which the guiding principle of hierarchy gives meaning to the individual elements of the society by reference to the wider whole which it informs. He provides many examples of the way in which hierarchy is expressed in different facets of village life (1972). Essentially, caste is a social category to which all individuals are ascribed by virtue of birth, hence Weber's description of India as a land 'of the most inviolable organisation by birth' (1958, p. 3). The word 'caste' is usually a translation of the word *jati*, although, as Mayer has demonstrated (1960), it is actually the *biradari* or subcaste that represents the basic endogamous unit. The behaviour of an individual tends to be judged according to its appropriateness with respect to his caste. Patterns of production and consumption are strongly influenced by this system, most castes being associated with specific activities, and most of the village products being manufactured by the respective caste members, such as potters, carpenters and goldsmiths.

Castes are ranked, and various activities, such as food

transactions, can be used to symbolise the relative positions of each caste within the hierarchy, depending on whom they accept certain kinds of food from and who in turn accepts from them (Marriot 1968). There is not a precise correlation between caste ranking and secular power. The Brahmans, always the highest caste in ritual status, have a traditional aversion to agricultural labour, which may result in their controlling fewer economic resources than the dominant landowning caste. So powerful is the structure of caste that it dominates the strategies that can be enacted by individuals. The individual cannot hope to rise in rank within the village; only a caste can rise relative to other castes, and so the individual must rise by improving the lot of his whole caste. Caste ideology allows for mobility only outside of the individual's life. According to the doctrine of *karma* the caste into which a person is born is deemed to be a result of his activities in his previous life. If a person conducts his life in accordance with the expected behaviour of a person of his caste, he is bound to be born into a higher caste in the next life. Thus as Weber noted, 'A member of an impure caste thinks primarily of how to better his future social opportunities at rebirth by leading an exemplary life according to caste ritual. In this life there is no escape from the caste, at least no way of moving up the caste order. The inescapable on-rolling *karma* causality is in harmony with the eternity of the world, of life, and above all of caste order' (1958, p. 121).

The classical notion of *karma* notwithstanding, many individuals and groups have in practice tried to improve their position within society. To do so they have tended to concentrate on those groups with which they are immediately associated, trying to elevate themselves to the next rung on the ladder of hierarchy, and then improving their position further by forcing others below them. To understand this process, we must examine the symbols by which hierarchy becomes manifested in village life: through residential patterns, dress, professional activities and even sitting on particular mats or the sharing of a smoke. A rise in status cannot be achieved merely by the claim or self-conception of an individual caste, but only through changing activities and thereby becoming associated with materials and actions that reflect a higher group, and hoping that the caste will gradually attain the same level of respect as that higher group.

Srinivas has given the term 'Sanskritisation' to this process 'by which a "low" Hindu caste, or tribal or other group, changes its customs, ritual, ideology, and way of life in the direction of a high, and frequently "twice-born" caste. Generally such changes are followed by a claim to a higher position in the caste hierarchy than that traditionally conceded to the claimant caste by the local community' (1966, p. 6). Thus groups initially outside the caste system may become drawn into it through the process of emulation, which is also the basic strategy for groups struggling in their relative position within the system. There are, however, several models that may serve as the goals of emulation. A

caste may seek to emulate the Brahmans, become vegetarian and emphasise freedom from ritual pollution, or it may emulate a high status martial caste, such as the Rajputs, continuing to eat meat but taking on more aggressive mannerisms and features, such as a longer, more upturned moustache.

That emulation seems to be the characteristic response not only to mobility within the hierarchy but even of those who suffer outright rejection by the hierarchy is seen in the case of the Untouchables. Moffatt, in a recent study, has stated: 'Structurally, it is here shown that where the Untouchables are excluded they replicate. They recreate amongst themselves the entire set of institutions and of ranked relations from which they have been excluded by reason of their extreme lowness' (1979, p. 5). Srinivas records cases where low castes have been punished for assuming attributes considered unfitting for them by higher castes (1966, pp. 14–16) including, interestingly, a proclamation forbidding the use of metal as opposed to earthenware vessels.

This brief account of social mobility in Indian society forms the backcloth to a demonstration of the way in which it is related to changes in the use and meaning of pottery in the village of Dangwara, in Malwa, Central India. Dangwara is much like the hundreds of villages that stretch in every direction from it. A comprehensive account of the working of caste in one such village in a nearby area is given by Mayer (1960). Dangwara contains 265 households, divided into thirty castes. The potter's caste has seven families, six of whom make pottery. The dominant landowning caste is Jat. A description of the detailed relationships between the potter and his client households, and the manufacture, use and meaning of the pottery forms and paintings is to be given elsewhere. Here we are concerned to explain the logic behind innovation in pottery forms and the influence on this of social hierarchy. Any particular vessel derives its meaning as an example of a category, equivalent to a 'bowl' or 'cup', which has its own name and which is associated in the first instance with a particular function. There are well over fifty pottery forms produced in the village. These form a set such that the meaning and usage of one vessel is constrained by the other members of the set from which it is conceptually distinct and to which it provides alternatives in usage.

As a set of categories, the pottery can be related to the other sets of categories that make up village society, for example, the rules of purity and pollution, or to caste. We have noted the importance of food transactions for marking relative hierarchy between castes, and that the whole field of food preparation and consumption is one of the most important areas where rules of purity and pollution are in operation. Kane (volume 4, pp. 757–806) provides the background for these rules in classical Hindu texts, while two recent books by Khare (1976*a*, 1976*b*) provide a contemporary example of their practice amongst religious Brahmans. Not unnaturally, the symbolic associations of food and water have been extended to the vessels which are used for them, a second field of reference being derived from the material from which the vessels are made. The sharp contrast drawn between vessels of earthenware and of metal may be directly related to caste hierarchy: metal is deemed purer and less absorbent of pollution than earthenware, so that in Dangwara even the lowest castes would eat from metal, or leaves that can be thrown away, in preference to pottery. It is the use of vessel form and decoration to express differentiation, and particularly hierarchical differentiation, that has resulted in the production of such a wide range of vessels for relatively few functions, with up to nine vessels serving essentially the same purpose.

In examining change in pottery forms, we are not concerned with gradual shifts within a form, which when they occur are denied by the potter who claims all forms are produced according to traditional designs, but with more drastic changes such as the demise or introduction of whole categories of pot. A few remnant pieces may suggest the decline of a previously used form, but the Dangwara pots which are fired in the open are not robust, and many are not expected to last the year. Any firmly established pottery form may be closely related to a particular activity, and the decline of many forms comes when they are related to an activity that is becoming redundant. An extreme example of this is the *chillum* or pottery pipe which is completely tied to its purpose of smoking local tobacco. The Kumavat caste, whose traditional occupation was growing and curing tobacco, are still present in the village, but they have given up this work as imported cigarettes have become readily available. Thus, while there are many stories that relate to the manufacture and distribution of *chillums* by the potters' fathers, no example could be found in the village today. The introduction of electric mills has reduced the demand for *kundi*, a pot used for storing flour. The introduction of the metal bucket has changed the use of the main water pot, known as a *matka*, which is still used to carry water from the well. But according to the potters, this form may have lasted only a few days in former times when it was actually lowered into the well with a rope around its neck (a scene often depicted on Indian miniatures, as the well was a favourite place for arranging a lovers' tryst). In contrast to these are pots which have ritual associations and are thus included in a more formal and conservative set of categories. The *kulhari* is used mainly as a toy if at all, but it is still taken by all households (including, thanks to Sanskritisation, the Moslem households) on one of the Hindu holy festivals.

The link between a pottery form and a particular activity has not prevented the potters from introducing new forms that provide alternatives for that activity, leading to a potential decrease in the efficiency with which it is carried out, but an increase in the process of categorisation and subdivision. This may be considered as the first strategy which the potter as an agent of change can use to introduce new vessels. Thus the *surahi* and the *batloi* are made for water

carrying and storage, although several pots already existed that served this purpose. A second strategy is to produce an association between a vessel form and an activity that is on the increase. Thus the *kunda* for tree, also known as the *kunda* for mango, is taken as a recent introduction, although it is essentially a copy of the *gumla* or flower pot that has been produced in the local town from traditional times. This pot exploits the increasingly systematic planting of young fruit trees, which have now developed into a cashcrop rather than just a supplement to household supplies. When first made, this pot was taken up with alacrity by 'improving' farmers for planting their mango trees, and one potter claims to have sold 250 of these to two Brahmans and a Jat. Interest has, however, declined as the farmers await the results of their horticultural experiment, though the pot is still occasionally produced for its traditional role of planting decorative shrubs near to houses.

A third strategy is to attempt to make pottery for an area where earthenware was not previously employed. One potter has tried to do this with musical instruments, although so far he has only achieved one partial success and two failures. He has sold some of his *tabla* or hand drums, but no one has shown an interest in his *damru* and his attempt at a larger *dhol* drum broke in the firing. There is also the more general copying of vessels in other materials or the making of skevomorphs. Copies of metal vessels include the *batloi* and *bhartiya*, both of which are increasing in use. The *barni* is a copy of a glazed ceramic jug used for the storage of pickles, and the earthenware version includes the lid and handle of the original. A handle is also made for the rather crude versions of the china cup and saucer, but these have not been so successful and seem to be regarded with some amusement. A fourth strategy is to introduce a form that is used elsewhere but which was not hitherto produced in the village. The *surahi* is a water-holding vessel found in many parts of Northern India, but not previously made in Dangwara. Similarly, new forms of painted decoration are infused within the Dangwara tradition, often through the medium of brides coming from villages some distance away.

This description of the potter's strategies is somewhat over-simplified, since they represent single facets of a highly complex process. Firstly, many pots are subject to several of these strategies, so the *surahi* is both a sub-division within a previous group and an external importation. More important, we have not yet taken into account the symbolic associations of these forms, which as we shall see, provide the key to their acceptability. Already from these examples several points may emerge. All successful innovations are in some sense 'obvious', that is to say, they are not totally new shapes empty of meaning until they are described to the villagers, although the potter may still explain the specific purpose he has in mind. There are, therefore, no absolute innovations; all the introduced forms should have meaning for the villagers by virtue of their morphology alone, which may be familiar through use in other materials, or in other areas, or as recombinations of elements already in use. Some forms are learnt by the potters through relatives and especially affines, with whom the potters may work for a while following marriage, or the father of their children's spouses. A form such as the *surahi* may be spreading through many of the villages around Dangwara, and with brides being taken from villages up to 48 km away, new ideas may diffuse with comparative rapidity. No doubt some of these 'innovations' represent transient fashions that seem curious, will last for a while, to be forgotten and 're-invented' one or two generations later, while their model in metal continues to be used. In order to appreciate the relationship of innovation and symbolic association with village hierarchy, we will examine in detail a failure and a success.

The potter provides a major proportion of his vessels through what is known as the *jajman* system, whereby the potter stands in a fixed relationship with households within the village, to whom he supplies vessels on ritual occasions and who usually buy their ordinary secular pots from him. This results in a fairly loose form of reciprocity, in that the potter is reimbursed for his general services over the course of a year rather than for specific vessels. If a potter wishes to introduce a new form he is unlikely merely to keep it in an evident place in his courtyard in the hope that the curious will be attracted to it, since the higher castes will not enter the house of the middle-ranking caste potters, and the lower caste *jajman* who tend to come directly to the potter are unlikely to risk the taint of the unfamiliar. Rather, the potter will introduce the new form through those of his *jajman* who, being in high castes and wealthy, are respected by the rest of the community. He will give the pot as part of his general services with some suggestions as to its practicability and interest.

This strategy may not always succeed. During a caste-based census of pottery in village households, a vessel was found in the house of a wealthy Jat. The pot was black with an applique band around the rim that had then been impressed with a finger at regular intervals. It was a shallow form midway between a dish and a bowl, and was introduced as a vessel for frying. It seemed very well-suited to this purpose and filled a genuine gap, in that no similar vessel is found in the village. It had never, however, been used by the householder but placed straight onto the area where waste and redundant pots are stored. One of the possible reasons for the failure of this form was its similarity to a pot used elsewhere by Moslems for eating. This is unlikely, however, since if the potter was aware of this, the householder probably was not. The main problem was that the form with its unusual rim did not relate to anything else in the village; there was nothing that could provide it with positive associations apart from its functional advantages. It was for the village a genuine innovation and thus very unlikely to succeed.

In contrast to the frying vessel is the *bhartiya* (fig. 2*A*). Here we have a pot with absolutely no functional advantages.

It serves an identical purpose to traditional cooking pots, and the functional parts of its morphology are identical to them. Only the angularity of the top half and the shape of the rim marks the *dohni* cooking form as distinct (fig. 2*B*). The *bhartiya* is however, an exact copy both in size and morphology of a metal vessel of the same name in use in the village in some of the wealthier households. Yet this is the vessel that the potters regard as their most successful innovation in recent years; it is now well-established and is increasing in distribution. We can understand this through an examination of the associations of the *dohni*, and the history of the forms within this group of cooking vessels.

The *dohni* is the traditional and prime example of a black cooking vessel that is set on the hearth. Along with other such forms it has a different kind of clay to other village pots incorporated in the base during the beating process to improve its qualities on a direct flame. Cooking is an activity surrounded by ritual regulations: not only the ingredients of food preparation but even the order in which they are combined can change a food from a fit to an unfit state for high caste consumption according to the context in which it is to be eaten (Khare 1976*a*). The problem derives from the fact that the *dohni*, although intended for the preparation of milk products and pulses or vegetables, may be used for meat or other polluting activities by low castes that only have this form as their prime cooking vessel. Thus even though such pollution could not occur to the actual vessel used in a ritually pure vegetarian household, the pots as an example of a category have been rendered ambiguous. The *bhartiya* can best be seen as only the latest in a number of attempts to resolve this ambiguity.

The most blatant attempt at differentiation within the category is the presence of a vessel known as a *brahman dohni*. This is essentially identical to the *dohni* in form except that it has a sloping rim, and it is painted red and buff rather than black. There is diverse evidence to show the

Fig. 2. Pottery types in an Indian village. *A*: Bhartiya. *B*: Dohni. *C*: Chayra Dohni. *D*: Jhawalya. *E*: Tapeli.

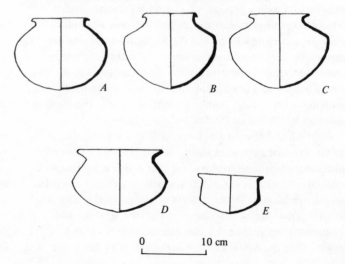

0   10 cm

association of red with high and black with low castes, including the results of the pottery census itself. Thus, the name may be seen as a kind of metaphor or pun. It may be, as some claim, that this vessel was once used by Brahmans who, perhaps with an increase in wealth, preferred to take metal vessels, but today the *brahman dohni* is a ritual vessel taken by the Gujar caste. It appears that the *brahman dohni* represents too extreme a strategy, in that although quite distinct from the *dohni*, it cannot be used on the hearth, because of the different clay used in its base.

The *brahman dohni* diverges from the *dohni* towards the higher end of the hierarchy; at the other side of the *dohni* are three further pots that tend towards the lower end (fig. 2 C to E). The first is the *chayra dohni*, whose name means sloping, indicating the form of the rim, which, together with a slightly greater angularity in the shoulder and thereby a slightly more squat appearance, is the only difference between this pot and the *dohni*. Then comes a pot called *jhawalya* or *chara* which has a longer sloping rim and is still more squat and angular. Where the *dohni* is ideally associated first with the purifying activity of boiling milk, a product of the cow, the *chayra dohni* is associated with the neutral activity of cooking vegetables and pulses, while the *jhawalya* is associated with the highly polluting activity of cooking meat. These are the ideals although they are not normally so explicitly expressed, and in practice the *chayra dohni* would still be used for cooking mutton in some households. The most squat and angular of all the black pots is the *tapeli*. This is a copy of a metal vessel commonly used in cooking and enjoys generally 'respectable' connotations. The pottery version, however, seems to have associations that fit its morphology, being used for among other things, urination, especially by elderly women, the most polluting function imaginable.

In this case, we have pots that seem intended to divest the *dohni* of its polluting associations by creating a morphological gradation away from it, that tends towards the polluting. Differences in morphology are, however, less obvious than differences in colour, and while the *brahman dohni* may represent too gross a shift, these may be too insubstantial in that, although the potters claim the villagers are aware of these distinctions, they admit that in practice they are often ignored, and villagers, unless specifically asked about them, refer to all such pots as *dohni*. But those castes who are most concerned about pollution and the maintenance of ritual status may have retained their unease about the *dohni*.

The *bhartiya* may then be taken as the third attempt at differentiation, and, although only a recent introduction, seems likely to be the most successful. It is a copy of a metal vessel which itself is used only for milk products and pulses and thus has no taint of meat. Its morphology is essentially neutral, sufficiently different from the *dohni* to be quite distinctive, but still recognisably within the same general category. Thus it provides for a cheap convenient black

cooking pot without the negative symbolic associations normally attributed to that class. Initially the *bhartiya* seems to have been introduced through the *jajman* system, but now it is used more generally and purchased directly from the potter's house. What happens to it will depend on the reaction of other castes. It is not only the potters who must be considered as agents of change; all castes become aware of the implications of the acceptance of a new form and all are engaged in carrying out their own strategies with respect to the castes directly above and below them.

The process of emulation is extremely complex today because there are several competing models. The traditional brahmanical mode is still the most important, and we find castes such as the Gujars who have taken to vegetarianism under a general caste agreement. Such a caste seems likely to favour the new pot, as do the more conservative of the Jats. The impact of westernisation has led to an alternative model that in many ways flows in the opposite direction to varieties of sanskritisation. This in combination with Ghandian principles has led to the dominance of a liberal political group in the village. The results of this innovation are therefore not predictable from either its major symbolic associations or the intentions of the potters, but depend on the working out of these competing strategies within the complex network of inter-caste relations. What does seem probable is that caste as social hierarchy will find its expression through this innovation.

The *bhartiya* is certainly not the only case in which hierarchy is manifested. The distribution of other pot forms such as the *dhatri*, used for making dough from sorghum flour, and a bowl known as *harawala*, indicate the influence of caste. This differentiation may also be expressed in the name rather than the form of a vessel, so that while the surahi is known by that name to most of the higher castes, it is called by the metaphorical name *badak* (duck) by the lower castes. This redundancy in the mode of expression of castes, suggests again that the relationship does not arise of necessity. Hierarchy does not depend on any particular medium of expression, but emerges rather through exploitation by actors for their various purposes. These examples are taken from aspects of material culture that villagers regard as of little importance.

The parallel between the situation in an Indian village and that in New York is evident in the process of emulation and the diffusion of an innovation from high status groups to low. More specific parallels may also be noted. In Dangwara a caste can be placed in an ambiguous position if there is a dichotomy between the traditional esteem given to that caste and the actual respect for the individuals that constitute it at that time. Thus, one middle ranking caste, a relative newcomer to the village, is represented by only a single family. The present head of the household is not known for his hard work, and has already lost two wives in second marriages, and is now being treated with a greater degree of contempt than is his right by virtue of his caste. The reaction to this is a form of hypercorrection. During the census of pottery, the householder drew attention to his complete lack of cooking pots and overall paucity of earthenware (which was not unrelated to his poverty and failure to establish a proper *jajman* relationship); he used this to argue that in caste ranking he was more than equal to the Brahmans, since they used more earthenware and he, claimed, used pottery for cooking as well.

The example from Dangwara illustrates further the relationship between structures and strategies. The production, use and distribution of a pot form is an act of social reproduction which expresses and forms the structure of society, not as mere reflection but through individual and group strategy. The potter wishes to enhance the reputation of his products and thereby of his caste, and to serve his ritual function as protector of separate categories through the pots he produces. Through these actions he also changes the context and thereby the meanings of pot forms. The new pot does not merely enter a system of relationships, it alters them. The *dohni* becomes a *dohni* as opposed to a *bhartiya*, a metal *bhartiya* is now opposed to an earthenware *bhartiya*, the user of the *bhartiya* is differentiated from the non-user, and the potter himself is now a person that produces *bhartiya*. These may seem trivial shifts but they are crucial if we consider pottery innovation overall, since the next introduction must take cognizance and may well exploit the gaps in the grid of meaning that is left by the last innovation. Insofar as structure is altered by the medium through which it is expressed, the relations of power and hierarchy are at least implicated in these changes. The process of emulation is inherently dynamic and produces a pressure for constant change and compensation for the maintenance of the structural contrast. In this we see the ambiguity of time itself, in its expression always conservative, arising from the past, in its impression always new, irrevocably altering the future.

The Indian Iron Age

In turning to the evidence from archaeology, we can identify one feature of archaeological methodology that is certainly related to the process of emulation. In the investigation of temporal sequences, seriation has become one of the most important tools developed in modern archaeology. This technique depends on the assumption of a pattern of gradual increase and then decrease in the frequency with which an artefact is found. The item is seen to come in to fashion and then to fade out. If we consider the first half of this sequence, it is clear that many processes may play a part in the gradual increase in numbers of a particular object found, the spatial as well as the temporal dimensions being involved (Deetz & Dethlefsen 1967). Insofar as the social dimension, that is, the particular organisation of the society in question, may influence the shape of the bulge, there may again be several processes at work, of which emulation could commonly be one, as would be suggested by modern research

on marketing patterns and in the diffusion of innovations (Engel *et al.* 1973, p. 598).

India might be a particularly valuable place to search for archaeological evidence for the long-term process of emulation, since with evidence for the existence of the caste system in at least some form for over two millennia, the fundamental principle of social hierarchy must have maintained some continuity for a considerable period. It is therefore possible to take features of the modern caste system as expressed in the distribution of material traits, and seek for evidence of their origins. As mentioned above, a nearly ubiquitous aspect of modern day Indian villages is the use by even the lowest castes of metal rather than earthenware vessels for taking their meals. The stated reason for this lies in the greater ability of metal to absorb pollution: a metal vessel need only be scrubbed after eating, whilst a pottery vessel must be broken, and when, as at some railway stations, earthenware is used for drinking or eating, the cup is broken afterwards by the user. Classical references to this distinction date back to at least the second century AD. The question to be asked then is whether the archaeological record provides evidence for a pattern of emulation that results in the abandonment of earthenware for eating vessels. One possibility is that metal, as a comparatively scarce resource, might have been used by higher castes to maintain a contrast between themselves and the lower castes, which had existed before in terms of earthenware.

The area of India in which the classical Hindu civilisation arose is the Gangeatic basin. In this area, remains prior to the Iron Age have only recently come to light in any detail, and are still not well understood. Most of the evidence for the Chalcolithic of South Asia comes from areas to the west and southwest. Similarly, the early Vedic texts which speak of a pre-iron using period refer to rivers and sites to the west. With the advent of a pottery style known as the Painted Grey Ware (PGW), we find the first clear evidence of a congruence between literary and archaeological sources since many of the associated sites feature in the major epic of Mahabharata. From the PGW develops, also in the Gangeatic basin, the Northern Black Polished Ware (NBP), which has still stronger associations with classical sites and dynasties. It seems quite clear, then, that these pottery traditions are directly ancestral to the classic civilisation of India. Recent appraisal of the radiocarbon dates and stratigraphic evidence for PGW-associated sites, suggests a time bracket of 1300–600 BC (Lal 1980), which may be compared to the traditional bracket which was several centuries later. NBP follows around 700–600 BC. To this period we may date the origins of the caste system with its associated rules of purity and pollution, and within a few centuries we find references to the comparative inferiority of earthenware.

PGW is a fine ware made of alluvial clay, which may be found in association with pots of other, coarser fabrics. The ware is dominated by two forms, one a shallow platter, with a convex base and shallow convex wall at an abrupt angle to the base, the other form having a much smaller diameter with higher walls forming a bowl. Sankalia states (1974, p. 401) that 'the shapes lack variety, but the *thali* (dish) and *katora* (bowl) seem to have been found so useful, that all these 2500 years and more these two have continued to form an essential feature in any Indian kitchen'. Sankalia is suggesting that these forms are the ancestors of the vessels used in meals today. This might at first seem unlikely, since on many later and medieval sites these forms do not appear.

Unfortunately, the records of the excavations where PGW is found are not such that we can tell if there is a pattern of emulation in its inception, with an initial association only with higher status groups. We do find, however, further emphasis on these forms in NBP, which is a very fine ware comparable in gloss to Roman Samian ware. With the decline of NBP these forms fade out and they are never again present as such fine wares. Where they do appear they tend to be represented by coarser fabrics. Early metal vessels are a rare find, but it may be noted that in period five (50 BC– 200 AD) at Nevasa, to the south, (Sankalia *et al.* 1960, p. 420) we find in copper a dish with a *lota*-like bowl inside it, much in the same relationship as the *thali* and *katora*, which is usually placed within the *thali* when served with a meal.

The sequence of events is summarised by Allchin (1959, p. 255):

> The repeated juxtaposition has led me to suppose that the two types were connected with a definite eating pattern and that they might be identified as *thalis* and *batis* respectively. At least in the finer wares the *thali* forms disappear at the beginning of the Christian era, and I had always supposed that this disappearance corresponded with the introduction of metal *thalis*. Today, the *thali* and *bati* are found in use, with only minor variations throughout India. The former is essentially a platter from which rice is eaten, the *bati* is used to hold liquid preparations, dal curd, vegetables etc. The earliest is the PGW black and red wares and these develop into the NBP *thali*. The tradition of fine earthenware *thalis* fades in the Ganges valley with the disappearance of NBP, although examples in coarse earthenware are met with in later assemblages.

The suggestion is that in the Early Iron Age certain fine wares were produced for eating vessels which may, at least initially, have been associated with higher status groups, but which, being made of earthenware, could well have diffused to lower status groups. The shift from pottery to metal then took place with the increasing ritualisation of activities concerned with food, part of the concern with rules of purity and pollution which provided the basis for caste differentiation into high and low, as can be documented from the classical literature. This shifting of medium from a common resource, such as pottery, to a comparatively rare resource, such as metal, may have helped to preserve this contrast as a result of the differential access to wealth and power associated with caste. Later, however (and in some areas this may have been quite recently), all castes were able to obtain metal eating-vessels, at which point this difference became redundant as a means of symbolising differentiation in social hierarchy, and eating off metal vessels became an invariant activity.

Conclusion

Although certain tendencies have been identified in the process of emulation, and the more expressive as opposed to the more utilitarian aspects of man's relationships have been stressed in order to explain changes in form and style, these are not proposed as general inviolable rules. The possibility of hierarchical organisation is only exploited by certain societies, and the materials through which this hierarchy is expressed are not to be predicted. At any given time, certain vessels, just as certain phonetic shifts, may be employed in this fashion, but it follows in the nature of emulation that, unless they can be affixed to some scarce resource unavailable to the whole population, then in time these elements will become redundant as social indicators. No doubt there are many societies where pottery is not exploited as a dimension of variance in this manner. If, however, individuals or groups within a society employ vessel form or decoration within strategies intended to improve their relative position within their society, then this material will take on symbolic associations of ranking, and a process of emulation is one process which may emerge. Emulation is characteristic of those processes by which the production and usage of material items represent both statements made within a social, temporal and cultural context, and factors that in turn alter that context.

Acknowledgements

I should like to thank the population of Dangwara village, and, in particular, the potters and their families, for their forebearance, and Dr Wakankar and Shri Kailash Pandey of the Vikram University, Ujjain, for their help. I am grateful to Dr Debbie Swallow for her extensive comments on this paper, and also for advice from Dr Raymond Allchin, Rickie Burman, Roger Blench and Keith Ray.

References

Allchin, F. (1959) 'Poor men's *thalis*, a Deccan potter's technique', *Bulletin of the School of Oriental and African Studies* 22: 250–7.

Bell, Q. (1976) *On Human Finery*, Schoken Books, New York

Deetz, J. & Dethlefsen, E. (1967) 'Death's head, cherub, urn and willow', *Natural History* 3: 290–7

Douglas, M. & Isherwood, B. (1979) *The World of Goods*, Allen Lane, London

Dumont, L. (1972) *Homo Hierarchicus*, Paladin, London

Engel, J., Kollatt, D. & Blackwell, R. (1973) *Consumer Behaviour*, Holt Rinehart and Winston, Illinois

Harré, R. (1979) *Social Being*, Blackwell, Oxford

Kane, P. (1930–1962) *History of the Dharmasatra*, 6 volumes,
    Bhandakar Oriental Institute, Poona

Khare, R. (1976*a*) *The Hindu Hearth and Home*, Vikas Press, Delhi

Khare, R. (1976*b*) *Culture and Reality*, Institute of Advanced Studies,
    Simla

Labov, W. (1972) *Sociolinguistic Patterns*, Blackwell, Oxford

Lal, M. (1980) 'The date of the Painted Grey Ware culture: a review',
    Bulletin of the Deccan College Research Institute 39: 65–77

Marriot, K. (1968) 'Caste ranking and food transactions: a matrix
    analysis' in M. Singer (ed.) *Structure and Change in Indian
    Society*, Aldine, Chicago

Mayer, A. (1960) *Caste and Kinship in Central India*, University of
    California Press, Berkeley

Moffatt, M. (1979) *An Untouchable Community in South India*,
    Princeton University Press, Princeton

Sankalia, H. (1974) *Prehistory and Protohistory of India and
    Pakistan*, Deccan College, Poona

Sankalia, H., Deo, S., Ansari, Z. & Ehrhardt, S. (1960) *From History
    to Prehistory at Nevasa (1954–6)*, Deccan College, Poona

Spaulding, A. (1960) 'The dimensions of archaeology' in G. Dole &
    R. Carneiro (eds.) *Essays in the Science of Culture in honour
    of Leslie A. White*, Thomas W. Crowell, New York

Srinivas, M. (1966) *Social Change in Modern India*, University of
    California Press, Berkeley

Veblen, T. (1970) *The Theory of the Leisure Class*, Unwin Books,
    London

Weber, M. (1958) *The Religion of India*, The Free Press, New York

Chapter 10

**Mortuary practices,
society and ideology:
an ethnoarchaeological
study**
Michael Parker Pearson

Recent accounts of the investigation of social organisation as reflected in mortuary practices have been based on role theory. If the notion of roles is deemed to be part of an inadequate conception of social systems, then it is necessary to reconsider existing archaeological approaches to burial data. Burial ritual is susceptible to ideological manipulation within the construction of social strategies. An analysis of mortuary practices in modern and Victorian England leads to an interpretation both in terms of the way the dead are seen by the living and in terms of the social relationships between competing groups. Since the Victorian era when burial ritual was a forum for the display of wealth and status, the dead have come to be seen more and more as unwanted matter to be disposed of quickly, without extravagance. This development, involving changes in the use of cremation and in the physical traces of the burial, is part of the increased use of hygiene, science and medicine as agencies of social control, and is related to a decrease in the use of conspicuous wealth consumption for social advertisement. Finally, a series of general propositions are advanced concerning the study and interpretation of mortuary practices.

Introduction

In the last ten years there have been many developments in the reconstruction of past social systems from the material remains of mortuary rituals. There have been several attempts to provide linking principles between the material culture associated with mortuary practices and the form of social organisation (Saxe 1970; Binford 1972; Brown 1971; Shennan 1975; Goldstein 1976; Tainter 1977; Peebles & Kus 1977). Although there is no 'cookbook' on the derivation of

social information from burial remains, certain major assumptions are generally shared by workers in burial studies. Firstly, the deceased is given a set of representations of his or her various social identities or roles when alive so that their status or social position may be given material form after death (e.g. gravegoods, monuments, place of burial etc.). Secondly, the material expressions of these roles may be compared between individuals. Thirdly, the resulting patterns of role differentiation may be ranked hierarchically as divisions existing within the society under study. Consequently, the social organisation of any society may be reconstructed and that society can be placed within a larger evolutionary framework according to its degree of organisational complexity. This procedure is very clearly illustrated by Saxe (1970) who uses role theory, componential theory, systems theory, information theory, and evolutionary theory to devise a set of hypotheses linking social complexity with mortuary practices. Studies of available ethnographic information on differentiation between individuals in death do seem to confirm the relationship between dimensions of disposal and the form of social organisation (Saxe 1970; Binford 1972; Goldstein 1976; Tainter 1978). The basic principles originally outlined by Saxe have been modified by later workers; Goldstein (1976) has considered the value of a spatial framework in the interpretation of mortuary differentiation; Tainter (1978) develops Saxe's quantitative measure of social complexity and introduces the notion of energy expenditure on deceased individuals for determining rank gradings; in their study of the archaeological correlates of 'chiefdom' societies, Peebles and Kus (1977) integrate the burial evidence with other archaeological forms (settlement hierarchy and placing, craft specialisation and society-wide mobilisation); O'Shea's study of nineteenth-century Plains Indians and Early Bronze Age communities in Hungary (1979) emphasises the importance of the specific cultural context and suggests that mortuary studies are most sensitive in the analysis of ranked societies (between egalitarian and advanced chiefdom/state societies).

The reconstruction of social organisation through the identification of roles (whether in burial, craft specialisation, settlement hierarchies etc.) can be challenged by the theoretical stance that social systems are not constituted *of* roles but *by* recurrent social practices.

The theoretical position adopted here comes from a tradition of social theory which considers power as central to the study of social systems. Social relations between humans take the form of relations of dominance and influence between groups of individuals who share mutual interests. These regularised relations of interdependence between individuals or groups constitute social practices. Practice is made up of individual actions which reflexively affect and are affected by explicit or implicit rules of conduct or structuring principles (which themselves are constantly being modified and changed).

These structuring principles, within which systems of domination are formulated, are legitimated by an ideology which serves the interests of the dominant group. Ideology hides the contradictions between structuring principles by giving the world of appearances an independence and an autonomy which it does not have. Larrain puts this simplistically but clearly when he states that 'In capitalist societies class differences are negated, and a world of freedom and equality re-constructed in consciousness; in pre-capitalist societies, class differences are rather justified in hierarchical conceptions of the world. In both, ideology negates contradictions and legitimates structures of domination' (1979, p. 48).

Ideology is a term which has proved remarkably hard to define. It can be seen as a system of beliefs through which the perceived world of appearances is interpreted as a concrete and objectified reality. It is the way in which humans relate to the conditions of their existence; their 'lived' relation to the world as opposed to their actual relation to the world (Althusser 1977, p. 252). As Hirst has pointed out, ideology is not false consciousness or a representation of reality but people's 'imaginary', lived relation to the conditions of their existence (1976, p. 11). In perceiving and explaining their surroundings, humans develop concepts which articulate with systems of signification (both verbal and non-verbal). Ideology is a form of signification, a 'pure ideographic system' where the signifier becomes the very

presence of the signified concept (Barthes 1973, pp. 127–8). That signification is carried out through a signifier (word, object etc.) connotating a signified concept.

The notion that material culture (defined here as man's transformed environment – portable artefacts, food, fields, houses, monuments, quarries etc.) is a part of human communication and signification is by no means new in archaeology – Childe stated that artefacts should be treated 'always and exclusively as concrete expressions and embodiments of human thoughts and ideas' (1956, p. 1). Material culture can thus be seen as a form of non-verbal communication through the representation of ideas (Leach 1977, p. 167). It is externalisation of concepts through material expression, a supposedly autonomous force which acts reflexively on humans as they produce it and is thereby instituted as a form of ideological control. It must be stressed that material culture is not a somehow 'objective' record of what is actually done as opposed to what is thought or believed (as in literary evidence or the testimony of the native subject); it does embody concepts but in a tacit and non-discursive way, unlike writing or speech. Archaeologists can study incomplete systems of material culture communication (which itself is fragmentary since it is all that is left of a fuller system of verbal and non-verbal communication) since the relationships and associations embodied by material culture can be reconstructed into a system of relationships between signifiers (see Sperber 1979, p. 28).

It is generally accepted that the context of death is one of ritual action and communication as opposed to everyday practical communication. Mortuary remains have to be interpreted as ritual communication if we assume the existence of ritual in all societies of Homo Sapiens (and probably even before). The definition and explanation of ritual have long concerned anthropologists; it can be very simply defined as stylised, repetitive patterns of behaviour (Keesing 1976, p. 566) in which a society's fundamental social values are expressed (Huntingdon & Metcalf 1979, p. 5). There is no clear boundary between ritual activity and other types of action, although ritual does have a peculiar fixity since it is clearly and explicitly rule-bound (Lewis 1980, p. 7); it is not necessarily 'irrational' and non-technical behaviour (Lewis 1980, pp. 13–16) and may constitute the communicative aspects of any action. Ritual can be seen thus as a kind of performance in the same way as a play where there is a pre-scribed routine of expression (Lewis 1980, pp. 10–11 and 33). Recent views have challenged the traditional explanation of ritual as the communication of social values which are expressed as unambiguous and believable statements. Bloch sees the formalisation of ritual action as resulting in a rate of change slower than other social actions with a consequent loss of propositional meaning and an increase in ambiguity (Bloch 1974); for Lewis, what is clear about ritual is how to do it but its meaning may be clear, complicated, ambiguous, or forgotten in different societies – it may mystify or clarify depending on cultural context (Lewis 1980, pp. 8, 10–11,

19 and 31). Whether or not the meaning of the performance is clear to the participants, mortuary ritual is a time when roles are clearly portrayed (Goody 1962, p. 29; Bloch 1977, p. 286): 'rites of passage are the rare occasions when it is possible to hear people giving lists of rights and duties, and even quite literally to see roles being put on individuals as is the case of ceremonial clothing or bodily mutilation' (Bloch 1977, p. 286). In ritual communication time is static and the past is constituted in the present:

> The presence of the past in the present is therefore one of the components of that other system of cognition which is characteristic of ritual communication, another world which unlike that manifested in the cognitive system of everyday communication does not directly link up with empirical experiences. It is therefore a world peopled by invisible entities. On the one hand roles and corporate groups . . . and on the other gods and ancestors, both types of manifestations fusing into each other . . .   (Bloch 1977, p. 287)

The roles that are portrayed in death ritual are expressions of status which must be seen as relating to, rather than 'reflecting', social position. Roles and corporate groups are, to Bloch, 'invisible halos' which must be appreciated within their specific context of death ritual rather than the wider framework of social hierarchy.

In any rite of passage the subject passes through a 'liminal' stage (Turner 1969) between two socially ascribed roles; in any analysis of status among the dead, the role of those individuals as members of the dead, as apart from the living, must be considered. Goody found that the Lodagaa dressed the corpse in the apparel of a chief or rich merchant, regardless of the person's social position in life (1962, p. 71). Among the Merina of Malagasy individuals are automatically classed as ancestors once dead. Status is expressed through membership of one of three 'castes' (nobles, commoners and slaves) and is manifested in the size and location of family tombs. However the significance of this form of ranking is severely diminished in social life (slavery was abolished in 1896, while the power of the nobles is not political but exercised through minor ritual privileges; Bloch 1971, pp. 69–70) and it has been replaced by a capitalist-influenced economic and political system. The old traditional roles are maintained in death as part of a reaffirmation of the past although the structure of power has shifted and new roles are economically important. Thus in death ritual it is not necessarily the case that the actual relations of power are displayed. It does not follow that those social identities which embody the greatest degree of authority will always be expressed (*contra* Saxe 1970, p. 6); however it is important to understand why certain roles are expressed in death as well as in other spheres of social life (e.g. house form, dress, display of material possessions etc.), and also to understand the extent to which they are used as social advertisements between competing social groups.

The use of the past to orientate the present has long been recognised in social theory: 'men make their own history, but they do not make it just as they please; they do not make it under circumstances chosen by themselves, but under circumstances directly encountered, given and transmitted from the past' (Marx 1970, p. 96). The past, especially through ritual communication (including the context of death), is often used to 'naturalise' and legitimate hierarchies of power and inequality which would otherwise be unstable. The dead are often an important part of the past in the present especially in the form of ancestors, deities and other supernatural beings. The construction of visible monuments, commemorating them collectively or individually, is one means of giving them material expression and recognition in the affairs of humans. The dead are consequently susceptible to manipulation by certain groups to maintain or enhance their influence over others. This can be done by idealising certain aspects of the past through the dead. Within this framework mortuary ritual, along with other aspects of tradition, ritual and custom, must be accommodated in theories of social and cultural change. The following case study of contemporary British mortuary practices and their development since the Victorian period attempts to place the treatment of the dead in such a framework.

The case study

This two-part study of British mortuary practices was based on data for Cambridge 1977, and involved 270 deceased individuals out of 3000 in that year in Cambridge and the surrounding area (15 km radius). Temporal variation in patterning could thus be controlled and connections between status among the living and status after death could be investigated. In the second part of the study these results were placed within a framework of social change over the last 150 years. Without the historical perspective the correlation could not be understood as relationships which had developed through time between mortuary practices, material culture and social trends.

A random stratified sampling strategy was used with stratification designated by the undertaker hired. In this way a cross-section of different funeral establishments, different disposal areas and the complete social spectrum in Cambridge could be analysed. The records of four funeral establishments were used to provide information on individuals relating to occupation, religion, rateable value of property, age, sex, notification of the death in the mass media, number of cars hired for the funeral, type of coffin and fittings, style of dress and treatment of the corpse, whether inhumed or cremated, place of inhumation or disposal of the ashes, and finally the construction, if any, of a monument. Unfortunately, the data on wreaths and flowers were incomplete and could not be included in the analysis.

Although a scale of income groupings has been devised for classifying professions within Britain (see Goldthorpe & Hope 1974), this could not be applied since the records of the profession of the deceased only permitted a two-fold division between males into blue-collar and white-collar workers. The funeral directors' information was given in the strictest confidence and I was expressly asked not to make enquiries with the bereaved families; consequently any more complete information on job and family background was unobtainable. There are a number of ways in which status may be expressed: through ownership of private wealth, type of occupation, family background and accent, and through material expression such as type and number of cars, size and location and internal decoration of houses and style of dress. In other words status should be regarded not as an innate quality inherited or achieved by individuals but as a collection of different forms of social expression and advertisement between groups as well as between individuals. For example, there need not be any correlation between class accent and ownership of private wealth yet both are important expressions of status. The most reliable measure of status which could be used in this study was another form of material expression – rateable value of private residential property. This is a measure of house size, type of neighbourhood and range of internal amenities. There were certain problems in relating this measure to 'status' – influential families might shun the ostentation of living in a large residence, elderly people might move into smaller, more manageable properties than those they had been living in, certain individuals might own several residences, and type of property owned might be different for different age groups.

The information gained from funeral directors, the council rates office and from graveyards and cemeteries was encoded as twenty-one variables which were divided into three groups; social position of the deceased, the form and expense of the funeral and the form and expense of the memorialisation of the deceased. These variables were cross-tabulated using the SPSS statistical package (Nie *et al.* 1975). However, there were very few correlations between the twenty-one variables. In correlating property value with funeral cost, memorial cost and total cost, r^2 equalled 0.002, 0.018 and 0.005 – there was no correlation at all, with rateable value accounting for little or none of the variance (fig. 1). Although the use of only one measure of status cannot be relied upon too heavily, this evidence ties in with statements made by funeral directors and other investigators regarding the simplicity and lack of ostentation involved in the purchasing of a 'funeral package'. Undertakers do not always agree on which classes of clients spend most on a funeral – one Cambridge funeral director denied any class differentiation (supporting the results above) and other undertakers have stated that members of the lower class often spend most on a funeral (Farthing 1977; Toynbee 1980, p. 8). Since it was considered that Cambridge might not be a representative sample, interviews were carried out with members of a London undertaker's firm who also stated that expenditure at funerals and on monuments did not correspond with social position.

There were however certain indications of class differentiation. Different funeral establishments catered for different classes of people even though fees were very similar – this was confirmed by the location of these establishments

Fig. 1. The cost of funerals in Cambridge in 1977 as compared with the rateable value of residential property inhabited by the deceased.

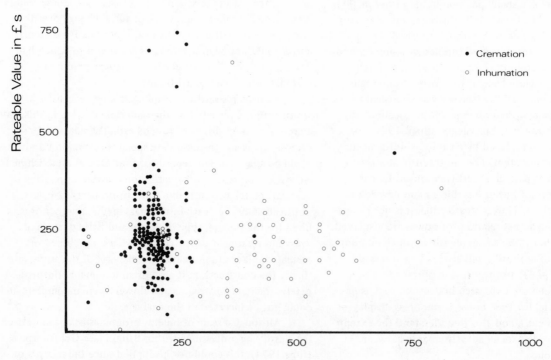

within certain areas of the town. One dealt with clients from the university and also with people from the more select areas of town. Two dealt mainly with middle and middle/upper class housing areas and two with the lower and lower/middle class housing areas on the east side of Cambridge (see fig. 2). Although the same basic materials were used by all funeral services (coffins, coffin furniture, hearses) and monumental masons (gravestones), there were certain differences in their use. One of the establishments in a lower class area apparently maintained the distinction of more 'delicate' O-ring coffin handles for women and bar handles for men. In 70% of the cases handled by establishments associated with the upper classes cremations took place, while these only accounted for 50% of cases handled by one of the firms employed by lower classes (in 1977 the national average of deceased cremated was 62%). This would suggest at least

some degree of class distinction in choosing between cremation and inhumation, although that relationship has become more complex and blurred. Financial outlay probably had little influence on this decision since at the time cremation was no cheaper. However, it would be more likely with inhumation to place a monument over the final resting place of the deceased and therefore to incur extra expense.

Religious affiliation did not directly match any class groupings although certain ethnic and religious minorities tended to go to certain undertakers and live in the less affluent areas of town (according to undertaker's remarks). Whereas all Roman Catholics have RIP inscribed in their nameplates and a crucifix attached to the lid, those Catholics that were members of the Polish, Italian and Irish communities in Cambridge displayed certain idiosyncratic characteristics; cremation was rare and burial monuments often

Fig. 2. Class distinctions in the choice of undertaker by households in Cambridge. ● Residence using services of middle/upper class undertaker. ✿ Residence using services of middle class undertaker. ✪ Residence using services of lower/middle class undertaker (a). ○ Residence using services of lower/middle class undertaker (b).

ornate and expensive. The stone type selected was mainly polished black or grey granite (two of the most expensive types) and decorative motifs were either religious 'pictures' cut into the stone or small marble angel statuettes (under 60 cm in height). Italians and Poles might also mount a small photograph of the deceased on the stone. Catholics, Jews and Moslems were buried in certain areas of the city cemetery which were separated from the main area (fig. 3). Moslems are also buried on a different orientation (northeast—southwest), diagonal to the closely packed, well-ordered rows of graves. Burials of members of nonconformist churches are not spatially differentiated within the city cemetery although certain graveyards separated from their churches in the rural centres around Cambridge were specifically for nonconformists (e.g. Melbourne URC burial ground, Cottenham Dissenters' burial ground; see fig. 4).

Within the city cemetery there were two groups of monuments which were not physically bounded from the other graves but were easily distinguishable by the style of monument. These were the gypsies and showmen (the latter are fairground owners and workers, often with kinship links to gypsies). They are generally recognised as occupying the lower levels of the British class system despite their often considerable accumulation of money stored as ready cash or converted into moveable valuables such as Rolls Royces, expensive china, large caravans and brasses (see Okely 1979).

Both groups use brick-lined graves and vaults for interment (only very rarely are they cremated although this will increase now that vaults may no longer be built). One showman's vault was decorated with bath tiles. Showmen and their families favoured the distinctive and expensive polished red granite monuments standing up to two metres high in cross or block form (fig. 5). The gypsies commemorate their dead with large white marble angels which also stand to two metres or more (fig. 6). These groups hold the most expensive funerals in Cambridge with funeral director's fees and monument costs sometimes amounting to over £3000 (expenditure above £500 by anyone in Cambridge is rare). Costs of flowers, food and drink may also be more substantial than other Cambridge funerals. They are some of the few groups in our society where death is regarded as an acceptable area for overt, competitive display between families.

Class differences are also reflected to a certain extent in variation between burial areas. St Giles' cemetery is strongly connected with members of the university while the city cemetery holds the majority of the deceased town dwellers. The surrounding village churchyards and their extensions now contain the remains of many commuters and retired people who have moved into the countryside. This movement by wealthier elements of the urban population has resulted in major changes in the structure of village communities; in the nearby village of Foxton only 25% of the

Fig. 3. The Roman Catholic part of the Cambridge City Cemetery.

community are still residents from birth (Parker 1975, p. 234). The class differences are also apparent in the undertakers' use of different churchyards and cemeteries. The two firms associated with the lower classes carried out thirty-four of the fifty-eight inhumations in the city cemetery as opposed to nine out of thirty-eight inhumations by the upper class establishment.

The majority of the Cambridge population are cremated (64% in the 1977 sample, just higher than the national average of 62% for that year). In 1979 at the Cambridge Crematorium, out of 2943 cremations, 2255 were scattered in the grounds, thirty were interred at the crematorium, four were placed on shelves in the Columbarium, one was placed in a temporary deposit and 655 were taken away for burial or scattering elsewhere. By 1969 one tenth of Catholics in Britain were receiving cremation rites (Ucko 1969, p. 274), six years after the ban was lifted by the Pope in July 1963. The decision to cremate or inhume the deceased is not as arbitrary as has been suggested elsewhere (Clarke 1975, pp. 51–2). The trend in cremation since the Second World War has been one of extremely even growth (see fig. 7) with a rate of increase of 1–2% p.a. Furthermore the cremation movement has spread to a large extent as a class-associated phenomenon through the emulation of upper class preferences in the twentieth century.

There are very few studies of modern western death rituals. Gorer's study of death, grief and mourning (1965) is useful for his attention to religious observance as well as to the treatment of the dead. His questionnaire survey covered the whole of Britain with a sample of 359 cases and was aimed at understanding how people coped in mourning their dead rather than how status and other factors might account for variability in funeral ritual. One study was carried out thirty years ago in America and was specifically concerned with the manifestation of status in funerals (Kephart 1950). Although he had little quantitative data relating to status during life, Kephart noted that in Philadelphia there were class differentials in the relative cost of funerals, frequency of cremation, elapsed time between death and burial, viewing the body, flower arrangements, public expression of grief, mourning customs and placing within the cemeteries (Kephart 1950, pp. 639–43). Despite funeral cost being status-related, he suggested that a reversal was taking place, with display in death becoming more and more a dwindling upper class phenomenon (1950, p. 636). This, and the frequency of cremation and placing within cemeteries, seems to match the Cambridge data for 1977, but cost of funerals in Britain is no longer a clear indication of social position.

Trends in mortuary ritual in the nineteenth and twentieth centuries
Changing material culture forms, and relationships

Fig. 4. The Nonconformist cemetery at Cottenham near Cambridge.

between these forms, are here divided into four categories; the siting of burial areas, the placing and marking of burials within these areas, cremation and subsequent treatment of the ashes, and the material culture associated with the funeral and treatment of the corpse. This is an essentially 'archaeological' description which will be followed by a 'social' explanation of these patterns as relations between living and dead and social relations between the living.

The growing industrial and urban centres of the eighteenth and nineteenth centuries used churchyards of parishes subsumed under urban growth for the burial of the majority of the population. These churchyards had been grossly over-crowded since the seventeenth century (Curl 1972, p. 33). By the nineteenth century, the crowding and filth of living conditions in industrial towns and cities resulted in cholera outbreaks and a high mortality rate (Morley 1971, pp. 7–10 and 34–40). The construction of larger burial grounds in areas of open ground on the out-skirts of cities from the 1820s until the early twentieth century was part of a massive onslaught against the insanitary conditions which existed (Curl 1972, pp. 22, 131 and 139–40; Morley 1971, p. 48; see Chadwick 1843; General Board of Health, 1850). These cemeteries were planned as large parks for the public to use as leisure areas in which the achievements of the dead were glorified and consequently where the moral education of all classes could be improved

(Morley 1971, p. 48; Rawnsley & Reynolds 1977, p. 217). Whereas members of the upper classes had been buried on their estates (Curl 1972, p. 359) or within churches, the Public Health Act of 1848 disallowed intra-mural interment and consequently traditional members of the gentry and aristocracy, as well as new members of the upper classes, shared the new burial areas with the rest of the population. The dead were no longer buried at the centre of society but removed from their immediate association with the church to a location separate from the focus of the community. In the new burial grounds space was allocated according to accessibility and view (Rawnsley & Reynolds 1977, p. 220). Consequently spatial patterning within the cemetery was a visual representation of the emerging hierarchy. This was further enhanced by the types of memorials constructed over the graves.

The most magnificent monuments were mausolea — actual houses of the dead. There was a myriad of changing fashions in smaller monumental forms: urns on pedestals, broken columns, obelisks, crosses, sarcophagi and caskets, and the more common and more traditionally English horizontal or vertical slabs. Interestingly, archaeology was a major factor in the design of funerary architecture (Curl 1972, p. 23) with Classical, Ancient Egyptian and Gothic styles copied for all sizes of monument. This re-interpretation in miniature of the huge monuments of man's past can be

Fig. 5. The Showmen's monuments in the Cambridge City Cemetery.

seen as an association with the dignity and splendour of past civilisations and an implicit legitimation of the current social order in terms of those values.

There appear to be few regional variations in funerary monuments today although styles have changed in several major ways. The amount of individual variation has always been large but reducible to several common themes. The major trend has been one of the simplification and reduction in size — monuments were replaced by headstones with stone kerbs delineating the grave plot (mainly between the 1910s and 1960s) and recently monumentalisation has become restricted (in both cemeteries and churchyards) to small headstones without kerbs. This latest phenomenon, the lawn cemetery, was introduced in Cambridge in 1957 and allows easier maintenance of the cemeteries since bereaved families can no longer be relied upon to maintain their individual plots. Since the First World War styles have been simple, plain and 'modern', without any of the fancifulness of Victorian monuments. There have been a number of associ-

Fig. 6. A Gypsy monument in the Cambridge City Cemetery.

ated changes in gravestone fashions. Traditional English building stone has been replaced by foreign white marble and red, black and grey granites. In the last twenty years the cheaper Portland Stone and white marble have become less popular than the more expensive granites, although the association of taste with simplicity helps to explain the new trend in plain slate or sandstone headstones. It is extremely rare to find the profession of the deceased mentioned on gravestones in the last fifty years but this was quite a common occurrence among the upper and middle classes of Victorian society. Today the epitaph symbolises the role of the nuclear family member although designs on the stone can represent profession, hobby, manner of death or religious affiliation. In the 1977 study there were six religious scenes and eighteen flower designs out of seventy-nine headstones — the former were generally associated with Catholics and the latter with Anglicans. No other design symbolism was apparent on any of the other stones.

The construction of bricked graves and vaults was banned by the Cambridge City Council in 1978. The wealthier company owners abandoned their family vaults after the Second World War and have since opted for cremation (Wilson, pers. comm.). The showmen and gypsies were among the last to keep up the use of vaults or bricked graves. Before 1974 the burial plots in Cambridge could be sold in perpetuity but now the Council plans the recycling of cemetery land within the next hundred years with 99% of the population being cremated by the year 2000, thus making cemeteries redundant. Apart from the religious and ethnic divisions apparent in the cemetery, there is a distinction between privately owned and Council owned grave plots. The latter may not have any markers on the grave and are reused every fifteen years. They were traditionally for the poorest section of the community after the cemetery was opened in 1902 but that distinction has since become blurred. The stigma of a pauper's grave has largely vanished and been replaced by the desire for simplicity and lack of ostentation in death among all classes, although welfare burials are still arranged and financed by the Council for those too poor to pay. The giving of bodies to anatomy schools was legalised in 1832 (Polson & Marshall 1972, p. 61) and has become a growing trend in the last 30 to 40 years. In the 1950s and 1960s this was connected with members of the upper and middle/upper classes but has since spread to all classes (Hindley, pers. comm.). Until the 1970s most anatomy donations, after use, were buried in the 'poorer' area of the cemetery but now most are cremated at no expense to the bereaved. The marking-off of the 'paupers' area' is similar to a tradition found in churchyards of the seventeenth and eighteenth centuries where the south side was generally preferred for burial and the north side reserved for the bodies of murderers, suicides and unbaptised children (Johnson 1912, pp. 335 and 350–1). Today there are no distinctions in death for the mentally ill, criminals, suicides or still-borns, despite the Victorian tradition of burial in the prison or asylum, or outside the burial ground or even in certain parts of the churchyard (where they still remained 'out of sanctuary'; Johnson 1912, p. 359).

Cemeteries have outlived their Victorian function as leisure amenities for the display of the achievements of the dead and have become storage areas for the disposal of dead bodies; graves are tightly packed in well regimented ranks and oriented east—west or north—south to make maximum use of space. This is summed up by Polson and Marshall writing on laws relating to the disposal of the dead in Britain:

> In principle, ground consecrated for burial or uncon-
> secrated ground, set apart for burial, may not be used
> for any other purpose. Considerable modification of
> this principle has become inevitable during the present
> century, owing to the growing demands of an increas-
> ing population for living space. Land in cities and large
> towns is at a high premium. The community cannot
> afford to ignore the potential uses to which disused
> burial grounds can be applied and the needs of the
> living have priority over consideration for the dead.
> (1972, p. 247)

The development of cremation was in direct opposition to the Christian doctrine of the resurrection of the body. The campaign for cremation was started in Britain in the early 1870s primarily to introduce a more sanitary precaution against disease and also to make funerals cheaper, keep the ashes safe from vandalism, have the ceremony completely inside and to prevent premature burial (Cremation Society Pamphlet 1975, p. 1). Early cremations were placed in caskets and buried under small memorial tablets within the crematorium grounds. In the 1920s and 1930s ashes were stored in the Columbrarium and marked by small plaques. After the Second World War the numbers of cremations greatly increased and ashes were strewn in the crematorium's Garden of Remembrance to save space. At first, trees, shrubs, birdbaths and sundials were set up as memorials to the deceased individual. These were followed by small bronze plates but now the only feasible means of memorialisation is considered to be commemoration of the name in the Book of Remembrance kept in each crematorium (Polson & Marshall 1972, pp. 192—4). In 1972 65% of cremations were strewn in the Gardens of Remembrance and 12% were taken away for burial or strewing in a churchyard or cemetery, scattering at sea or in the country. Interestingly, in Cambridge in 1977 many more ashes were scattered or interred in local church-yards rather than in the city cemetery. There are over 200 crematoria in Britain, centralised disposal areas burning over 400,000 corpses each year, pulverising and then scattering the ashes or collecting them in plastic containers. Crematoria have been criticised for their poor design (Curl 1972, p. 186); many look more like suburban houses with outsize chimneys rather than places of religious ritual (fig. 8). The emphasis is

Fig. 7. The gradual increase in cremations in the twentieth century.

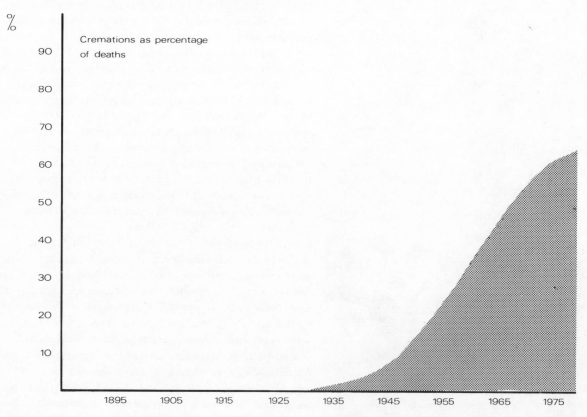

very much on disposal rather than on ceremonies of remembrance and respect to the dead. The whole disposal sequence associated with modern crematoria allows for the saving of space for the living, with the remains of the dead closely concentrated in an area of 1–8 hectares well away from residential areas and with a minimum of memorialisation for the individual or even collective dead.

The pomp and ceremony of the Victorian funeral has recently attracted great interest from historians (e.g. Curl 1972; Morley 1971). Much greater a percentage of personal income was spent on funerals then than today. In 1843 the average cost of a funeral was £15, a considerable sum for many people, with the most lavish costing £1500 and the cheapest £5 (Morley 1971, p. 22). The funeral was a conspicuous display of wealth consumption, and expenditure was closely graded according to one's social position (Morley 1971, pp. 22 and 112–13). Families competed with each other so as not to be outdone in respectability (directly equated with wealth and with salvation; Morley 1971, p. 11). This social competition was manifested by all classes and even the poor would spend comparatively large sums of money on a funeral rather than suffer the shame and loss of dignity connoted by a pauper's burial (Lerner 1975, pp. 99–100; see Bosanquet 1898). The specialist profession of undertaker (along with associated trades of monumental masons, cabinet maker and draper) developed in the early nineteenth century both making possible and encouraging such lavish expense. Formal mourning costume (crepe and black jewellery) and all the paraphernalia of death (black ostrich feathers, large ornate horse-driven hearses, 'mutes' or

attendants accompanying the procession, a solid wood coffin, expensive handles and plates, mourning cards) were part of the huge quantity of material culture produced specifically to honour and remember the dead. In the twentieth century, despite the undertakers and stonemasons having a strong economic interest in maintaining the role of the funeral, there has been a gradual but marked decline in the ceremony of death ritual. Even as early as the 1840s and 1850s funerals were made more simple (Morley 1971, pp. 27–31) and today only royalty and major national heroes and some ethnic minorities receive expensive ceremonies in death. The minorities are the only groups that can still be said to actively compete between themselves in death ritual. Although undertakers have received some criticism for their commercial and exploitative attitude (Mitford 1963, pp. 186–7), it must be remembered that the change in public attitudes towards the celebration of death has made funerals appear as unnecessary expense when previously much more was expected to be spent on them. No longer is the context of death a platform for overt self-advertisement between family groups.

The First World War was a watershed between Victorian and 'modern' funerals (Lerner 1975, p. 91). The massive scale of death, the government decision not to bring bodies home and the large number of unidentified corpses were major factors in bringing this about. Mourning clothes and elaborate processions became more and more unfashionable. Monuments became smaller and more regimented and more simple in decoration, and the coffin and coffin fittings were increasingly of much poorer quality. Although coffins are a major part of the undertaker's bill (on average £100

Fig. 8. A crematorium in Yorkshire. Note the plain and 'functional' style of the architecture.

out of £200) they are mostly chipboard with oak or elm veneer. Traditional styles of handles and plates are retained but these are of thin brass, chrome plastic or plastic, a far cry from the ornate gold, silver and brass decoration of Victorian coffins (Curl 1972, p. 2). Coffins were considered luxury items not available to the poorer classes until the seventeenth century (Cunnington & Lucas 1972, pp. 156–7). By the Victorian period they were universal objects for display as well as containers for preserving their contents as long as possible (Curl 1972, p. 29). Since then they have become temporary receptacles for corpses before final removal from society. One funeral director commented on this change:

> Strangely the public accept the veneered coffins quite happily, the desire for a simple and inexpensive funeral overcoming any traditional thought of a solid oak or elm coffin. It is a personal observation that where traditional thoughts as to the coffin occur, these are frequently found in the less well-off section of the community who will spend more on a funeral than the affluent.

There have been a number of changes in the treatment of the body. Embalming has become more and more common as a temporary means of arresting decay – about 75% of corpses are embalmed in London (W.G. Garstin & Sons, pers. comm.) although under 30% in Cambridge receive this treatment (embalming is a process where a formalin-based red liquid is substituted for the blood and a green solution is pumped into the stomach). The corpse's shroud is very similar to a nightdress – the same basic form since the nineteenth century. Among European immigrants (Poles, Greeks, Ukrainians, Italians), gypsies and showmen there is a tradition for burial in best clothes although this is less strong than it used to be. Until just after the Second World War, toys were sometimes placed in children's coffins and females were dressed in their best clothes with jewellery in northern England (Hindley, pers. comm.). In the rural parts of the British Isles in the nineteenth century, beer mugs, jugs, bottles, candles and coins might be placed in the grave (Johnson 1912, pp. 294–5) but this tradition seems to have long died out.

In conclusion, the funeral can be seen as changing from its role as a celebratory rite of passage into more of a consumer package deal where low expense is a major factor in deciding the nature of the funeral. This is clearly highlighted in the magazine *Which?* for February 1961, pp. 43–5, which gives advice on funerals purely as commercial products where cheapness is a major concern.

Towards an explanation of British mortuary practices

It has been proposed that two interconnected relationships have to be investigated in order to explain the symbolism of mortuary ritual. The first is the categorisation or 'placing' of the dead by the living. The second is the way in which the dead may be used as one of many modes of social advertisement between competing groups. Mortuary prac-

tices should be regarded not as a microcosm of social organisation but as the material expression and objectivation of idealised relationships formulated about the dead by different individuals or groups within society.

All archaeological evidence is made up of relationships or associations within different symbolic systems. These associations, expressed in material form, are social constructions of category classification. In any society symbolic links are expressed as specific associations between material forms. The treatment of the dead can be studied in terms of these relationships. Some of these can be outlined as follows: the spatial and topographical positioning of the dead in relation to the living (what kinds of boundaries exist to separate the places of the living and the dead – not just rivers, fences etc. but also spatial distancing, e.g. burial under the settlement, burial on a hill overlooking the settlement), the relation between the physical abodes of the living and the dead (the place of the dead in the form of a bed, a house, a settlement, a rubbish pit; how much energy is invested in the places of the dead as opposed to those of the living), differentiation among the dead (what groups and roles are expressed and idealised in death ritual and why (e.g. why might all dead have the status of chiefs?)), what artefacts are expressly associated only with the dead, what artefacts from the living are 'hidden' with the dead (e.g. why might weapons be buried but tools inherited?), the relation of disposal contexts to other forms of death-related expression (e.g. ancestor shrines, cenotaphs). All of these factors will affect the way in which death is seen as the context for social advertisement; which social groups compete against each other (families, sodalities, neighbourhoods etc.) and in what ways is that competition acceptable (how does it compare with other expressions of personal wealth or power such as house design, clothing and jewellery, ownership of possessions etc.).

Some of these issues have been explored in the previous section but an explanatory framework is still needed to interpret the changes in the symbolism of mortuary ritual. Our changing relation to the dead can be explained in terms of the replacing of traditional agencies of social control, notably religion, by the new agencies of rationalism, science and medicine within the framework of modern capitalism. The reduction of ceremony and monumentalisation as well as the increase in cremation may be partly explained within this framework. Available studies of patterns of religious belief indicate an increase in secular ideologies of death; no assumptions need to be made about life after death (in 1965 50% of Britons were likely not to believe in or to be uncertain about an afterlife; Gorer 1965, p. 33) and the corpse is seen more and more as a piece of unwanted matter which should be disposed of in as hygienic and efficient a way as possible. Many writers have commented on the effect of this attitude in causing psychological problems among the bereaved who are unable to cope effectively with the death of their loved ones without the aid of imposed ritual sanctions (Curl 1972; Hinton 1972; Kastenbaum & Aisenberg 1972; Parkes 1975; Gorer 1965; Schoenberg *et al.* 1975). The dead are no longer seen to exist in the material world of the living. Cremation in our society solves two supposedly uncontentious problems; the efficient and hygienic disposal of the dead and prevention of any wasting of space in the storage of those disposed remains. However it is just as hygienic to inter a corpse in a cemetery as it is to burn it (see Curl 1972, p. 167). Also the notion of saving the land for the living presupposes a shortage of land yet there is plenty available for leisure activities. In 1951 a mere 0.13% of the land surface was used for burial — hardly a massive use of space (Curl 1972, p. 162).

In the Victorian period public health and hygiene, sanitation and medical services became integral features of everyday life and became incorporated with religion and scientific and technological progress as a means of power legitimation. There was a direct equation of class with hygiene, health, cleanness and neatness of residence (Morley 1971, pp. 7—10); the dirtiest members of society were naturally the lowest. Victorian attitudes to hygiene and health have been well documented elsewhere (see Dubos 1965; Salt & Elliott 1975; Sigerist 1944, 1956). Interestingly, the approval of cremation came at a time when major advances were being made in drainage and water supply, refuse and sewage disposal and production of frozen and tinned foods (see Salt & Elliott 1975, pp. 37—8, 42, 56—7 and 60). There have been numerous studies of the role of medicine as a form of social control (see Ehrenreich 1978; Illich 1975; Navarro 1976, 1978; Zola 1975). Death can be said to have been appropriated by the medical profession since hospitals and nursing homes are the main places of death, with doctors as important as undertakers and clergy. In their attempts to prolong life as long as possible, doctors are involved in a self-frustrating war against death. It has become a medical failure rather than a natural process. Death is invariably associated with old people who are increasingly removed from their family environments. Most deaths occur in hospitals or nursing homes (*c.* 60%) and the likelihood of deaths of children or young people has become far more remote. What was in the Victorian period a natural process of transition is now the end of a living person whose recognition after death is more and more slight.

These changes have reduced the power of the dead as symbols manipulated by the living, and we are losing a language of death celebration (Curl 1972, p. 337). A further factor in this change is the general context of social advertisement in twentieth-century Britain. The Victorian conspicuous consumption and display of wealth was not limited to burial ritual but occurred in other rites of passage, dress, housing, diet and all forms of social interaction. The reason for such ostentation in death has been interpreted as the result of mass urban migrations and the development of a new mode of production with its re-ordered social structure. In this 'world of strangers' the demonstration of

financial power was achieved through conspicuous consumption both at the funeral and in the monument construction (Rawnsley & Reynolds 1977, p. 220). During the twentieth century the expression of social position seems to have become less overt in all spheres. In our post-industrial technocratic society the upper classes define themselves less by property and money ownership and more by education and managerial control (Giddens 1972, p. 346; Tourraine 1974, pp. 41 and 206). The symbols of class allegiance are progressively less clear and less numerous (Tourraine 1974, p. 37) while the managerial classes shy away from conspicuous consumption, controlling by manipulation rather than imperiousness (Tourraine 1974, p. 49). In a society of supposed equality of opportunity there are large differences in inherited and earned personal wealth ownership. In 1960 12% of British adults owned 96% of the personal wealth of Britain (Revell 1966); the identification of the members of this elite is not an easy task, with symbols of class often being ambiguous and confusing. Various attempts have been made to recognise this elite; the monarchy, members of Parliament, directors of large firms, top civil service officials, the heads of the military, TUC council members, bishops and archbishops, directors and large shareholders in mass media, vice-chancellors of universities and judges have all been listed as belonging to this group (Giddens 1972, p. 361). With the exception of the monarchy and some MPs, these individuals do not make themselves socially conspicuous as public figures to the mass of society. Indeed it is only the monarchy and certain individuals of national acclaim who still receive a ceremonial funeral of major proportions. Instead of symbolising the hierarchical differentiation of British society, these state funerals are symbols of national identity to the people of Britain and to the rest of the world. The fact that state funerals are lavish and well-attended does suggest that the relationship between living and dead does not completely account for the decline in death ceremonialism but that changing attitudes of social display are also important.

A major class of memorials commemorating the dead are the war memorials — the Cenotaph in London and cenotaphs scattered all over Britain. They are similar in style and design to other kinds of twentieth-century funerary architecture and yet are not disposal contexts for corpses. They are foci of ceremonies held annually to commemorate the British dead of two world wars. The war dead are commemorated as 'warriors' who died fighting for their country and the ideals of freedom and equality which it enshrines. Nationalism as an ideological means of control is thus legitimated through remembrance of the war dead of Britain (as opposed to the dead of all countries involved in the World Wars). The fact that the soldier buried in Westminster Abbey is named the 'Unknown Warrior' further advances the cause of nationalism since he is related solely to his country, transcending all kinship, regional and class connections.

In summary two main processes can be held to account for the major changes in mortuary practices in nineteenth-

and twentieth-century Britain. The social context of death affects the way in which it is used as a platform for social advertisement — what is considered 'tasteful' is no longer directly related to expenditure of monument size since religious beliefs and medical and hygienic attitudes have changed the status of the dead as a part of our society. Also there is some evidence that social advertisement is no longer accomplished through such conspicuous wealth consumption as was the case in Victorian Britain. In this way class categories as represented and objectified through all forms of material culture may be less pronounced.

Conclusion

This study has been concerned with deriving theories of material culture associated with death ritual from a wider perspective of social theory and an ethnoarchaeological investigation of changing practices and their social correlates. It is hoped that the results can be used in studying societies where only the material culture exists or be re-examined in further ethnoarchaeological analysis.

A number of propositions can be advanced:

(1) The symbolism of ritual communication does not necessarily refer to the actual relations of power but to an idealised expression of those relations.

(2) Relations between living groups must be seen as relations of influence and inequality where deceased individuals may be manipulated for purposes of status aggrandisement between those groups. Ideology as manifested in mortuary practices may mystify or naturalise those relations of inequality between groups or classes through the use of the past to legitimise the present.

(3) The relationship between living and dead should be integrated in studies of mortuary practices; in particular the new role of the deceased individual and the context of death as a platform for social advertisement must be accounted for.

(4) Social advertisement in death ritual may be expressly overt where changing relations of domination result in status re-ordering and consolidation of new social positions.

Proposition (4) is similar to a rule developed by Childe which is worth quoting in full here:

> in a stable society the gravegoods tend to grow relatively and even absolutely fewer and poorer as time goes on. In other words, less and less of the deceased's real wealth, fewer and fewer of the goods that he or she had used, worn, or habitually consumed in life were deposited in the tomb or consumed on the pyre. The stability of a society may be upset by invasion or immigration on a scale that requires a radical reorganization or by contact between barbarian and civilized societies so that, for instance, trade introduces new sorts of wealth, new opportunities for acquiring wealth and new classes (traders) who do not fit in at once into the kinship organization of a tribe.
>
> (Childe 1945, p. 17)

Exceptionally wealthy tombs are cited as support for this argument since Childe notes that they occur at the transitional stage of early state formation in Early Dynastic Egypt, Shang China, Mycenaean Greece, Late Hallstatt Europe and Saxon England.

In conclusion, the ideological dimension of mortuary practices must be considered as a major line of enquiry in studies of all human societies. For the contemporary British material more needs to be done on the relationships between capitalism, nationalism, secular beliefs and attitudes to medicine and hygiene as ideological principles manifested in the material culture associated with death. Secondly, material culture from other contexts (transport, residences, personal possessions, dress, food etc.) should be integrated in a broader study of the degree and direction of social advertisement. Mortuary ritual can no longer be treated as a field of archaeological enquiry which is based on intra-cemetery variability since the treatment of the dead must be evaluated within the wider social context as represented by all forms of material remains. In this way the archaeologist can investigate the social placing (or categorisation) of the dead as constituted through the material evidence of the archaeological record by developing general principles which relate material culture and human society.

Acknowledgements

This work could not have been undertaken without the kindness and help of the manager of the Cambridge crematorium, Mr Wilson, and the following members of the Cambridge funeral establishments, Messrs Fuller, Hindley, Sargent, Stebbings and Warner. The National Association of Funeral Directors and the Cremation Society of Great Britain also provided valuable information. I would like to thank those people in the departments of Archaeology, Anthropology and Social and Political Sciences at Cambridge University who showed interest in these matters. My particular thanks go to Dr John Pickles for his help with Victorian burial customs and to Dr Ian Hodder who was responsible for directing my interests in contemporary mortuary practices.

References

Althusser, L. (1977) *For Marx*, New Left Books, London

Anon. (1975) *The History of Modern Cremation in Great Britain from 1874*, Cremation Society Pamphlet, London

Anon. (1961) 'Funerals', *Which?*: 43–5

Barthes, R. (1973) *Mythologies*, Paladin, London

Binford, L. (1972) 'Mortuary practices: their study and their potential' in L. Binford (ed.) *An Archaeological Perspective*, Seminar Press, New York

Bloch, M. (1971) *Placing the Dead*, Seminar Press, London

Bloch, M. (1974) 'Symbols, song, dance and features of articulation', *Archives of European Sociology* 15: 55–81

Bloch, M. (1977) 'The past and the present in the present', *Man* 12: 278–92

Bosanquet, B. (1898) *Rich and Poor*, Macmillan, London

Brown, J. (1971) 'The dimensions of status in the burials at Spiro' in J. Brown (ed.) *Social Dimensions of Mortuary Practices*, Memoir No. 25 Society for American Archaeology, *American Antiquity* 36: 92–112

Chadwick, E. (1843) *A Special Enquiry into the Practice of Interment in Towns*, HMSO, London

Childe, V.G. (1945) 'Directional changes in funerary practices during 50,000 years', *Man* 4: 13–19

Childe, V.G. (1956) *Society and Knowledge: the Growth of Human Traditions*, Harper, New York

Clarke, G. (1975) 'Popular movements and Late Roman cemeteries', *World Archaeology* 7: 46–56

Cunnington, P. & Lucas, C. (1972) *Costume for Births, Marriages and Death*, Black, London

Curl, J.S. (1972) *The Victorian Celebration of Death*, David & Charles, Newton Abbot

Dubos, R. (1965) *Man Adapting*, Yale University Press, Newhaven

Ehrenreich, J. (ed.) (1978) *The Cultural Crisis of Modern Medicine*, Monthly Review Press, New York

Farthing, D. (1977) 'Conference Report', *The Funeral Director* 57: 339–45

General Board of Health (1850) *Reports on Extramural Sepulture*, HMSO, London

Giddens, A. (1972) 'Elites in the British class structure', *Sociological Review* 20: 345–72

Giddens, A. (1979) *Central Problems in Social Theory*, Macmillan, London

Goldstein, L. (1976) *Spatial Structure and Social Organization: Regional Manifestations of the Mississippian Period*, North-western University Ph.D. Evanston

Goldthorpe, J. & Hope, K. (1974) *The Social Grading of Occupations: A New Approach and Scale*, Oxford University Press, London

Goody, J. (1962) *Death, Property and the Ancestors: A Study of the Mortuary Customs of the Lodagaa of West Africa*, Tavistock, London

Gorer, G. (1965) *Death, Grief and Mourning in Contemporary Britain*, Cresset, London

Hinton, J. (1972) *Dying*, Penguin, Harmondsworth

Hirst, P.Q. (1976) *Problems and Advances in the Theory of Ideology*, Cambridge University Communist Party, Cambridge

Huntingdon, R. & Metcalf, P. (1979) *Celebrations of Death: The Anthropology of Mortuary Ritual*, Cambridge University Press, Cambridge

Illich, I. (1975) *Medical Nemesis: The Expropriation of Health*, Calder and Boyars, London

Johnson, W. (1912) *Byways in British Archaeology*, Cambridge University Press, Cambridge

Kastenbaum, R. & Aisenberg, R. (1972) *The Psychology of Death*, Springer, New York

Keesing, R.M. (1976) *Cultural Anthropology: A Contemporary Perspective*, Holt Rinehart and Winston, New York

Kephart, W.M. (1950) 'Status after death', *American Sociological Review* 15: 635–43

Larrain, J. (1979) *The Concept of Ideology*, Hutchinson, London

Leach, E. (1977) 'A view from the bridge' in M. Spriggs (ed.) *Archaeology and Anthropology: Areas of Mutual Interest*, BAR Supplementary Series 19: 161–76

Lerner, J.C. (1975) 'Changes in attitude toward death: the widow in Great Britain in the early 20th century' in B. Schoenberg, I. Gerber, A. Weiner, A. Kitscher, D. Peretz and A. Carr (eds.) *Bereavement: Its Psychosocial Aspects*, Columbia University Press, New York

Lewis, G. (1980) *Day of Shining Red: An Essay on Understanding Ritual*, Cambridge University Press, Cambridge

Marx, K. (1970) 'The eighteenth brumaire of Louis Bonaparte' in K. Marx & F. Engels *Selected Works*, Lawrence and Wishart, London

Mitford, J. (1963) *The American Way of Death*, Hutchinson, London

Morley, J. (1971) *Death, Heaven and the Victorians*, Studio Vista, London

Navarro, V. (1976) *Medicine under Capitalism*, Prodist, New York

Navarro, V. (1978) *Class Struggle, the State and Medicine: An Historical and Contemporary Analysis of the Medical Sector in Great Britain*, Robertson, London

Nie, N.H., Hull, C.H., Jenkins, J.G., Steinbrenner, K. and Bent, D.H. (1975) *Statistical Package for the Social Sciences*, Second Edition, McGraw–Hill, New York

Okely, J. (1979) 'An anthropological contribution to the history and archaeology of an ethnic group' in B. Burnham & J. Kingsbury (eds.) *Space, Hierarchy and Society*, BAR International Series 59: 81–92

O'Shea, J. (1979) *Mortuary Variability: An Archaeological Investigation with Case Studies from the Nineteenth Century Central Plains of North America and the Early Bronze Age of Southern Hungary*, Cambridge University, PhD Thesis

Parker, R. (1975) *The Common Stream*, Granada, St Albans

Parkes, C.M. (1975) *Bereavement: Studies of Grief in Adult Life*, Penguin, Harmondsworth

Peebles, C. & Kus, S. (1977) 'Some archaeological correlates of ranked societies', *American Antiquity* 42: 421–8

Polson, C.J. & Marshall, T.K. (1972) *The Disposal of the Dead*, Third Edition, English Universities Press, London

Rawnsley, S. & Reynolds, J. (1977) 'Undercliffe Cemetery, Bradford', *History Workshop Journal* 1: 215–21

Revell, J.S. (1966) 'The indefensible status quo', *The Economist*, 15 Jan, pp. 217–19

Salt, J. & Elliott, B.J. (1975) *British Society 1870–1970*, Hulton, Amersham

Saxe, A. (1970) *Social Dimensions of Mortuary Practices*, University of Michigan, PhD Thesis

Schoenberg, B., Gerber, J., Weiner, A., Kitscher, A., Peretz, D. & Carr, A. (eds.) (1975) *Bereavement: its Psychological Aspects*, Columbia University Press, New York

Shennan, S. (1975) 'The social organization at Branc', *Antiquity* 49: 279–87

Sigerist, H.E. (1944) *Civilization and Disease*, Cornell University Press, New York

Sigerist, H.E. (1956) *Landmarks in the History of Hygiene*, Oxford

Sperber, D. (1979) 'Claude Lévi-Strauss' in J. Sturrock (ed.) *Structuralism and Since*, Oxford University Press, Oxford

Tainter, J. (1977) 'Modelling change in prehistoric social systems' in L. Binford (ed.) *For Theory Building in Archaeology*, Academic Press, New York

Tainter, J. (1978) 'Mortuary practices and the study of prehistoric social systems' in M. Schiffer (ed.) *Advances in Archaeological Method and Theory, Vol. 1*, Academic Press, New York

Tourraine, A. (1974) *The Post-Industrial Society*, Wildwood House, London

Toynbee, P. (1980) 'The big funerals come from people living in council houses these days', *The Guardian*, 18 Aug., p. 8

Turner, V.W. (1969) *The Ritual Process*, Routledge and Kegan Paul, London

Ucko, P. (1969) 'Ethnography and archaeological interpretation of funerary remains', *World Archaeology* 1: 262–80

Zola, I.K. (1975) 'Medicine as an institution of social control' in C. Cox & A. Mead (eds.) *A Sociology of Medical Practice*, Collier Macmillan, London

PART THREE

Application: the analysis of archaeological materials

Chapter 11

Boundedness in art and society
Margaret W. Conkey

Conkey examines social boundaries and their relation to the structure of style and design, with particular reference to Palaeolithic art. The style or structure of Palaeolithic art is shown to be characterised by a number of structural features such as non-differentiation of levels, and lack of design-field. Iconic representations of the type found in the Upper Palaeolithic are suggested as having an evolutionary primacy over more complex symbolic organisation, and the development of this ability in the Upper Palaeolithic is linked to the explosion in the richness and variety of material culture at this time. There is evidence for an emphasis on continuity between the background and the picture, between the natural and the cultural worlds, and a lack of directionality in the organisation of the art. Questions are asked concerning how structural congruences and the structural organisation of differences emerged during the Palaeolithic.

This paper is an attempt to weave together some emerging ideas on how to approach prehistoric artforms or a prehistoric art style from a structuralist perspective. It is written with firm conviction that such a perspective is not just useful; we *must* make our inferences about past human life from the structure of archaeological data. I do not intend to consider what has been wrong or off-the-track in archaeology, particularly with regard to the three topics I have chosen to pursue here: social boundaries, style and design analysis. Most archaeologists know well how these three topics tend to coincide in archaeological research. Instead, I will briefly present the notion of social boundaries as just one level and manifestation of discontinuity in human life.

Then I will consider how style in material culture, when viewed from the structuralist perspective, can serve as a potential access to specifying and identifying discontinuities. The structuralist concept of style is exemplified here in a preliminary consideration of certain structural features of Palaeolithic artforms. In particular, we can make some inferences about the structural attributes of image-fields, view these in chronological perspective as is appropriate for the artworks of the first fully *sapiens* populations, and try to support the notion that these structural attributes may have served as fundamental sources of meaning for Palaeolithic users of the art. It is unfortunately beyond the scope of this paper to pursue in any detail the wider social contexts in which the structural features identified may have operated. The level of analysis here is that of images and image-fields. With Palaeolithic art that is so hard to date, to place in time, to place in relation to the many diverse aspects of climate, settlement or social geography, I would argue that it is at this level that there is the most promise of working upward toward how and why such artforms were used.

Central to much anthropological and archaeological research has been the pervasive notion of bounded social entities and 'identity-conscious social groups'. The boundedness of social entities as studied ethnographically, and a focus on boundaries *per se*, have clearly been influenced by our twentieth-century window onto the organisation of human groups. There may be far less boundedness and rigidity of boundaries than we would like to think. Furthermore, much of the literature that has considered boundaries has given priority to the boundary rather than the 'cultural stuff it encloses' (Barth 1969, p. 15), and a concept of boundaries has emerged that lacks recognition of their dynamic attributes. Barth reminds us that 'it is clear that boundaries persist despite a flow of personnel across them . . . categorical distinctions do not depend on an absence of mobility, contact, and information, but do entail social *processes* of exclusion and incorporation whereby discrete categories are maintained despite changing participation and membership' (Barth 1969, p. 9, emphasis added).

It is not the boundaries *per se* that should engage our attention, but the processes of boundary formation; this means that the 'cultural stuff' is relevant. Boundaries are not lacking in dimension; they occupy space, time, action and thought (Leach 1976, p. 33). Just as there are means whereby boundaries may be established, there must also be means to transcend boundaries. The stress on the dynamic attributes of boundaries can be more fruitfully pursued if we conceive of boundary formation – in any domain of human life – as a process that selects, if not sets up, discontinuities. We want to know what the selective forces are that interrupt the continuum, how and why.

Most boundaries realise asymmetry; that is, they separate systems that are different, different in information content. It is the generation and transmission of concepts that is pivotal in the processes of boundary formation, main-

tenance and mediation. Any exchange between two systems of different information content does not result in partitioning or equalising of information, but tends to increase the difference. Boundaries are not static, but open and the sort of interaction going on across boundaries, the forces at work on the 'outlines' of a boundary, are dependent upon the general properties – the 'cultural stuff' – of the respective systems. There is always some boundary regulation going on. Boundaries are thus loci of tension, stress, ambiguity and anxiety. The discontinuities that boundaries embody may, within a cultural context, act to make humans decidedly uneasy, whether it is at the level of life/death, in-group/out-group or of an isolated situation of interpersonal proxemics. Humans mediate or transform these discontinuities, and it is in the analysis of the mediation or transformation that we may gain access to other cultures, past or present.

The asymmetry and discontinuity of information flow inherent in the concept of boundaries is precisely the underlying premise for the archaeological analysis of stylistic discontinuities in material culture as indicators of social boundaries. Until recently, however, archaeological analyses of style did not articulate this premise in this way. In its most simplistic form, the archaeological notion of the relationship between style and boundedness has assumed that what is bounded has one style as distinguished from another. Recently, the concept of style in archaeology has been enhanced by its consideration in terms of information theory (e.g. Wobst 1977). Style has been promoted from being a vague and residual source of variability in human material culture systems to a broad and predominant factor. Given that the processes of artefact manufacture and use are embedded in the cognitive and cultural matrix of the makers and users, this view of the predominance of style is not outrageous. The very activities that produce the artefacts are stylistic (Lechtman 1976, p. 5). Artefact use-wear patterns, for example, must be seen as the result of both style and function (Tringham, pers. comm.). Despite this broad and encompassing role of style that seems almost equivalent to the concept of culture, there are some definitional perspectives that in fact make style not only more operational as a concept, but also one of the specific lines of enquiry into the transformations and mediations of discontinuities that characterise human cultural life.

The phenomenon of style has come to be viewed as dependent on structure (Smith, as cited in Lechtman 1976, p. 4). The basic assumption is that in human behavioural systems there exists a base structure, an underlying semantic structure that is a system of relationships. Although human behaviour and the performance of tasks that produce the material culture studied by archaeologists require a linear, temporal ordering of individual elements, this ordering – and that which it produces – cannot be understood without knowledge of the semantic structure from which it was generated (Greenfield 1978, p. 441). In the manufacturing process, for example, a structure is brought into existence.

Archaeologists have discovered the structured nature of
human material culture, and by, implication, the structured
nature of the broader behavioural systems of which material
culture is a part. At the most practical level, this discovery is
one of the more promising contributions to the need for
more highly specified research questions that characterises
contemporary archaeology. From here, the usefulness of
careful analysis of all structural relationships in archaeology
can be developed; style can now be seen in terms of a general
structuralist perspective.

Structures are systems of relations that can apply to
different content areas, e.g. language or any number of
actions or behaviours. Given that it is the cultural and cognitive *structures* that set the matrix for the elaboration and
enactment of daily life, it is not surprising to discover that
structural resonances, concordances or congruence obtain
among the various domains of cultural behaviour, although
the articulation of these congruences and their particular
manifestations are expectedly variable. Furthermore, disjunctions exist as well; the human tendency to structure
antithetically is widely documented (e.g. Lévi-Strauss 1964).
In general, these disjunctions play just as significant a role in
establishing and maintaining the meaning of cultural life, but
a disjunction, or non-resonant structure, is primarily defined
in relation to, that is, in contrast with the resonant forms.

Structural principles operate in many domains, but it is
not necessary to postulate their origin in any one particular
domain, as has often been done (usually in language). The
framework for a structural analysis is not in terms of structural analogues or structural parallels among domains.
Rather, the task is to identify the common structural
features (Greenfield 1978, p. 441). By definition, the
deviants from these features, the 'anti-structures' or that
which falls outside the structure, are also identifiable. What
we recognise as style is a formal arrangement of interrelationships that realises a structural pattern. 'The particular
patterns of relationships are different at different levels
within the system, thus style is hierarchical, and its manifestation depends upon where we locate to observe the interactions' (Lechtman 1976, p. 5). That is, the patterns of
human behaviour that we can read depend on the level at
which we isolate them, and at which they exhibit style.

Because of the structured and hierarchical nature of
style, since all kinds of manifestations of style may be rooted
in the deep, semantic structure of a cultural system, and
because the structure of style is potentially observable not
just in the artefacts themselves but in the processes of production and use, i.e. human performance, there is a more
substantive basis for the pursuit of style as part of the processes of boundary formation, mediation and maintenance.
Furthermore, archaeologists need not feel limited by the
nature of archaeological data if we can master the general
properties of structure in human behaviour. In fact, the
nature of archaeological data demands that we make inferences from structure. We have not yet fully dealt with such

accessible — to archaeologists — aspects of prehistoric life as
subsistence relationships (cf. Hodder 1978) or technological
styles (cf. Lechtman 1976) in a way that elucidates the
intrinsic cultural patterns of which they are a manifestation.
The challenge is to understand the linkages between media or
styles and the information systems into which they are
keyed, and to identify the variables that structure style at the
surface level (e.g. intent, personnel, context, properties of
the raw material). At present, this has the most potential at
the level of particular contexts. It is paradoxical that archaeologists have been masters of classification — usually broad
classifications to be applied across particular contexts — but
this has been at the expense of enquiring into the classifications and structural systems of relations that brought the
artefacts into existence in the first place.

My own research into Palaeolithic art is, in part, an
attempt to get at the conceptual and/or operational processes
that underlie the manufacture and use of the artforms. I
expect that *if* systems of meaning, or orientational constructs
are realised by the objects or landscapes that humans create,
they should also be observable in the processes that produce
the objects. The very operational stages of production have
the potential to stand as metaphors for the scheduling or
rhythms in other temporally linked domains of everyday life,
as Adams (1971) has shown for the stages of textile work on
Sumba on Indonesia (see also Franquemont & Franquemont
1977). Unfortunately, the aspect of structural concordance
among different behavioural domains that may characterise
aspects of the manufacture and use of material culture (*sensu
latu*) has so far been documented primarily for ethnographically or historically known contexts (e.g. Adams 1971, 1973;
Deetz 1977; Glassie 1975; Nicolas 1966; Wheatley 1971).
There are two obvious questions that follow: (1) how to
identify the structures and structural principles, as well as
the concordances/disjunctions that are expected to exist,
archaeologically, and (2) how do the neat packages of
resonant behaviour that have been described, or the non-
resonant structures that have only infrequently been
described, enhance our ability to interpret human adaptation and, above all, culture change? Furthermore, at a
more pragmatic level, the methodological challenge is the
framing of hypotheses about the message-content or structural roots of an artefact, a technological system, or village
lay-out, as well as how to confirm them.

The following discussion of Palaeolithic art is an
attempt to show how we might put a structuralist perspective
to work in the interpretation of prehistoric life. Palaeolithic
art seems a particularly appropriate data base for several
reasons. First, it has been widely discussed (e.g. Geertz 1964;
D'Aquili 1972; Leach 1976; Munn 1966) that there exists
among humans, at least since the Upper Palaeolithic (i.e.
Homo sapiens sapiens), a cognitive necessity to establish discontinuities in nature and culture in order to segment and
organise experience; there must also be ways to mediate
such discontinuities. Certainly structural principles underlie

the establishment and mediation of such discontinuities, and, furthermore, I believe that there may be some fundamental sources for these structural principles. Second, I believe that in Palaeolithic artforms — the first extensive and systematic systems of visual representation in a permanent archaeologically visible medium — we should find at least these fundamentals, if not also their elaboration. If we can identify the structural features of these artforms, we should be able to hypothesise about their existence and manifestation not only among evolutionary prior human populations but among other domains of Upper Palaeolithic behaviour as well.

Elsewhere (Conkey 1978, 1979, 1980; Fritz 1975, 1976) I have made suggestions about structural features and structural implications of some Palaeolithic artforms. I have suggested (Conkey 1980) that *iconicity* is a guiding principle underlying much Palaeolithic art, and that this is the basis for the embellishment and elaboration of the human material culture systems that literally seem to explode during the Upper Palaeolithic (particularly in relation to the previous tempo of cultural developments; see also Isaac 1972, 1976; Wobst 1977). An icon may be defined as a sign that signifies by virtue of sharing a property with what it represents; iconicity is the quality of a sign or form whereby it shares a property with that which it represents. Sebeok (1976) has discussed the 'international debate over the icon', and it appears that in semiotic circles the definition and qualities of iconic forms are not at all agreed upon. Leach (1976, p. 12) has suggested that iconicity involves a 'planned resemblance', but this leaves us with the problem of recognising intent. My use of 'iconic' tends toward the general and open definitions; it is not confounded by the issues of whether an iconically based form or image is a sign, symbol, index or whatever. Rather, I view iconicity as the process whereby there is some formal property, and hence direct correspondence, of that which is represented *in* the image. Such iconically based forms may serve as signs, symbols or indices; function is not restricted by the representational process.

The iconicity of Palaeolithic art is seen, for example, in the lack of differentiation between the level of the artefact or cave wall surface and the level of the design or decoration. I have referred to this as the non-differentiation of levels (Conkey 1980) (see figs. 1 and 2). Because of the prevailing linkages between shape and design, and because iconic congruence is so widespread, it is tempting to suggest that much of Palaeolithic art is characterised more by what Jakobson has called *effective* relationships among its component parts than by *designated* ones (Jakobson 1960). That is, the attributes of the parts are in the whole, the subject matter is in the media and vice versa, such as in the case of the many animals whose shapes are the natural protruberances of cave wall surfaces. It is not an applied art in which arbitrary designated subjects are created apart from the context of the media.

I have suggested (Conkey 1979) that much of Palaeolithic art may be concerned with constituting the continuities and discontinuities of the human social world; the artforms are means by which continuities and discontinuities are

Fig. 2. Another example of non-differentiation of levels, or iconic congruence. A spatula made from a rib out of which a fish emerges (El Rey, France).

Fig. 1. Two examples of iconic congruence in Palaeolithic art. *A*: the edge of the scapula on which this cervid is engraved 'stands for' the snout of the engraved figure (Altamira, Spain). *B*: the antlers or horns of the cervid(?) depicted here 'take off', as does the barb of the harpoon on which it is engraved, from the body (Rascaño, Spain).

identified and mediated. For example, the iconic use of antler — from cervids who may live on despite the shedding of their racks — has the potential to be a medium through which oppositions of time could be resolved. Or, the symbolic diversity provided by ambiguous 'creatures' (partly human, partly one or more animals) may be informing on contrasts of discontinuities through a message of continuity; in this case, a continuity between the human and animal world. Although difficult to test, such interpretive frameworks for Palaeolithic artforms can be pursued by more systematic analysis of context, of correspondences among animal parts selected and depicted in the 'creatures', for example. Much animal art has been shown to serve very similar roles in ethnographically known contexts; animals are 'good to think', more so than to eat (see Vinnicombe 1976; also Lévi-Strauss 1964).

In an analysis of mobiliary Palaeolithic art materials (Conkey 1978) that were primarily engraved with geometric shapes, I have shown that a wide-ranging set of basic design elements were employed throughout Cantabrian Spain during the Magdalenian, but only some of these are found everywhere, forming a core engraving repertoire. I also found that at least fifteen organisational principles underlie the arrangements of design elements, although not all pieces are characterised by the use of these principles. And, above all, I was struck — as have been previous observers (e.g. deLaguna 1932–3) — by the lack of a design field (see fig. 3). The observations on the non-differentiation of levels and the strong iconic component to Palaeolithic art followed from the recognition that explicit bounding of the space(s) to be

Fig. 3. Examples of lack of design field in portable Palaeolithic art. *A*: a horse 'wrapped around' the bone or antler artefact (La Paloma, Spain). *B*: a geometric design that encircles the antler (El Pendo, Spain). *C*: geometric incisions spill over the sides, around the body of this engraved harpoon (El Pendo, Spain).

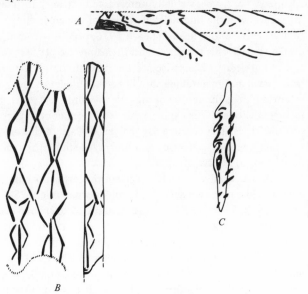

engraved or painted is rare or, if present, is set by the pre-existent wall shapes or artefact morphology. I would like to pursue this aspect of the relative unboundedness of imagery in Palaeolithic art, particularly in the context of the strong iconicity of many artforms.

How will a consideration of design field get us closer to the understanding of structure? First, I take as a starting point the well-known observation made by Lévi-Strauss (in Charbonnier 1969, p. 107) on the fact that art — if not other material culture systems — is an example, *par excellence*, of the take-over or transformation of nature by culture that is at the core of anthropological understanding. The paradox of artistic activity is that although a natural object is often said to be that which is represented, a cultural object is clearly the result. The continuum of nature is interrupted. Just how that continuum is broken and according to what structural or organisational principles is of concern here. The introduction of discontinuity is what is going on in the process of transformation. Second, when one considers the 'sign-space', that is, the properties of the space within which a visual image occurs, it is clear that the use of these properties is not arbitrary. At the most obvious and basic level, the sign-space is built on an intuitive sense of the vital values of space, as experienced in the real world (Schapiro 1970, p. 236). Third, it follows that in the construction of the field in which a visual image is placed, a field that corresponds to a segment of space, we can expect to find models of some aspects of the cognitive and cultural matrix of the makers and intended viewers.

From these premises, the analysis of image-fields in Palaeolithic art becomes fundamental to understanding the structure of Palaeolithic art. Furthermore, given that the segmentation of social time and of social space are central concerns in human life (Leach 1976, p. 34), we should focus on these concerns as fundamental domains in which structural principles are most likely to be played out. Given also the strong iconic component to much Palaeolithic art, it is relevant to first consider the power of iconicity in setting the parameters for segmentation of social time and social space. This can be viewed in considerable evolutionary depth.

Interestingly enough, iconic signs and iconicity have not really been considered to the depth that they deserve (Sebeok 1976, p. 434), despite the fact that they are widespread in animal communication (e.g. Bateson, G. 1972) and in human communication and everyday life. 'Multisensory iconic representations' are not merely present in human communication, but pervasive (Sebeok 1976, p. 1442). The iconic or effective mode must be a foundation mode for the expression and realisation of spatial relations; hence, in a social species, it is also a basis for the expression of social relations as well. Iconicity of spatial ecology is particularly striking among animal populations. Many non-human primates, for example, have an essentially iconic connection between social relations and spatial arrangements: 'territorial tendencies re-emerge in the handling of information'

(Kummer 1971, p. 233). The iconic reciprocity of species to environment is well-exemplified by the ornithologists' claim that 'by examining the alar (wing) structures of a bird, they are able to reconstruct, with amazing accuracy, the physical configuration of the area it habitually overflies, and *vice-versa*' (Sebeok 1976, p. 1444). More succinctly and evocatively stated: 'The form of a horse's hoof is just as much an image of the steppe it treads as the impression it leaves is an image of the hoof' (Lorenz in Wickler 1973, p. xi).

There is a broad evolutionary context for this perspective. Thom (1975, p. 73, as summarised in Sebeok 1976, pp. 1448–9) suggests that the iconic representations of human cognition are the logical extensions of the fundamental workings of the central nervous system of all animals. He assumes that the principal role of this system is 'to map out localized regions to simulate the position of the organism in the environment, as well as to represent objects, such as prey or predator, that are biologically and/or socially necessary for its survival or well-being' (Thom 1975, pp. 72ff. as cited in Sebeok 1976, p. 1448). Given that animals are constantly informed and impelled by meaning-bearing sign-vehicles designed to release appropriate motor reflexes, such as approach or withdrawal (e.g. toward a prey or from a predator), the evolution of behaviours or 'operations which appropriately increase or decrease distance between organisms and stimulus sources must have been crucial for all animal types' (Schneirla 1965, p. 2). By the evolution of the cognitive processes whereby humans not only name concepts and objects but also build internal representations of them and furthermore imbue them with meaning, humans have replaced flight or capture. It is probably not necessary to point out that the human use of symbols, whereby contextual meaning is given in any social instance, is very different from these understandings of animal behaviour. But in reference to the human manipulation of concepts, it can be postulated that the logical interactions among the concepts and their internal representations may be iconic representations of at least the time-space interactions among the objects referred to (Sebeok 1976, p. 1449, in reference to Thom 1975).

Thus, there is reason to believe that there are deep evolutionary roots to the iconic representations of space-time interactions, particularly among social species. Among animals, the manifestations are primarily the result of *action* correspondences, an action in space and/or time that links space and society. For example, there is the approach and counter-approach between two animals, actions that correspond to their socio-spatial positions. In human cultural behaviour that is based on concept formation, the correspondences are more formal ones, in which two or more elements are linked in terms of shared or what are perceived to be similar formal properties. Formal correspondence is the key to the whole notion of representation and the ability of a structure in one medium to stand for another. It is the basis

of the referential act (Greenfield 1978, pp. 417 and 440), and it is the dependence upon and elaboration of referential systems that is characteristically human.

Correspondences are of course, central to the ability to replicate a model. It is the identification of the crucial points as well as the relatively consistent correspondences among points in a pattern that allow for the identification of structure, and, hence, style. The formal correspondence of human iconic representations may be viewed as the root for the growth of not only structural congruence but also its elaboration into antithetical structures that seem to be characteristic of human cultural systems. Thus we can postulate an evolutionary primacy of iconically based space–time relations as a source for systems of visual imagery. Although both iconicity in human communication (verbal or nonverbal) and structural congruence are dependent upon formal correspondence among elements, structural congruence is viewed as hierarchically more complex, a structural transformation of iconicity to a wider behavioural sphere. What is basic to structure at any level of its expression is the construction of relations among constituent elements and the recognition of formal correspondences.

It should not be surprising to elucidate an iconic basis for early human artefacts that may be statements on and enact social space and social time. The multifaceted structure that we can see in Palaeolithic art, in which the parts are seen as related to the whole, shows at least tacit conventions that must have informed the process. Even when based on likeness, the generation of visual forms is culturally conventionalised yet these may be more flexibly coded, and indeed promote more elaboration and embellishment than those based on differences (Eco 1976, p. 191). In assessing the potential sources for image making, it has been pointed out that 'despite the almost limitless number of discontinuous phenomena that can exist, there are only a certain number of images that can actually occur' (Sebeok 1976, pp. 452–3). Although 'we have a virtually unrestricted capacity for playing games with the internalized version of the environment that we carry in our heads' (Leach 1976, p. 36), we never even approach this potential, and the games we play are few and not arbitrary. The processes whereby discontinuities are introduced and maintained should be the subject of our attention, even though, as in the case of iconic representations, the imagery is explicitly derived from continuities or similarities. The baseline for analysis of Palaeolithic art is that these people recognised and portrayed similarities and used them to resolve differences.

A structural approach to Palaeolithic art is nothing new. For the past two decades, Leroi-Gourhan (e.g. 1958, 1965, 1972, 1978) and Laming-Emperaire (1962) have been advocating a structural analysis of cave wall, and, to a certain extent, mobiliary depictions, that emphasises the structural interrelations of the subject matter depicted (kinds of animals, kinds of 'signs'). Leroi-Gourhan, for example, has proposed that the selection of the subjects to be depicted and the locations within a cave where they are drawn (or the type of implement on which they are engraved) is made in accordance with a monolithic, pervasive organisational scheme. Certain animals are almost always found in association with certain others; the associations are between two classes or groups of animals. Furthermore, the scheme is also linked to aspects of context in that certain spatial or topographical associations are also shown. This scheme is at a cosmological level (Leroi-Gourhan 1965); it is an organisation based explicitly on differences, on differentiation between the two classes (perhaps male-associated and female-associated) of depictions, on topographical differentiation within the cave (Leroi-Gourhan 1972). That is, the deliberate associations and structural relationships are drawn from typologies based on differences: in 'signs', in cave locales; in raw materials or types of implements; among animals and humans.

It is not the intent of this paper to evaluate the Leroi-Gourhan hypothesis (see Ucko & Rosenfeld 1967; also Conkey n.d.). It is relevant, however, to note that the structure of Palaeolithic art proposed by Leroi-Gourhan is somewhat disjunctive to the structural features and their implications that I am proposing here. I will be developing here the ideas that, at the level of the image and the use of the image in relation to the raw material, the structure of Palaeolithic art is derived from similarities. Thus there is the non-differentiation of levels and the striking iconicity that has already been noted. Without frames, without boundaries, without specifics or details of context to be found in the image, the image not only merges with but is derived from the raw material: the medium may well be the message. If we can push, as I suggest below, the interpretation of these features of some Palaeolithic art, we could make a case for such artforms to embody notions of continuity, permanence and timelessness.

At the level of the image, the iconic congruence between form and image may well be a similarity with which to deal with differences. To Leroi-Gourhan, however, there is use of differences — at the level of composition and context — to deal with similarities. His interpretation has been that the differentiation of both animal and human worlds into male and female — that is, a continuity between both worlds — is the basis for the structural differentiations among depictions and their placements. Although it is admittedly difficult to confirm either of our propositions on the use of similarities and differences to deal with distinctions and continuities, respectively, it is of structural interest that two seemingly contradictory interpretations are being proposed for two different levels of the conceptual framework behind Palaeolithic art.

Even without the interpretive elaboration offered by both Leroi-Gourhan and myself, it is clear that on the one hand a lack of boundaries or framing does exist at the level of specific images and decorated artefacts and locales, and iconicity is widespread. On the other hand, it is clear from Leroi-Gourhan's quantitative tabulations (1965) that there is a striking tendency for certain subjects to be depicted in association, and that certain classes of animals or signs tend to exist and their members may be used interchangeably according to certain 'rules'. It is important to stress here that certainly not all Palaeolithic art can be shown to exhibit non-differentiation of levels or strong iconicity. I would also not accept many of Leroi-Gourhan's tabulations and assumptions as supportive of his interpretation (see also Ucko & Rosenfeld 1967 or Parkington 1969 for some specific problems in tabulation). Given the spatio-temporal extent and the diversity of media and contexts characteristic of Palaeolithic art, it is unlikely that monolithic approaches are valid. But the tendency for there to be a contradiction in the structural principles that underlie much Palaeolithic art when they are analysed at two different levels of imagery may be the most promising feature of Palaeolithic art to pursue if we are to understand more fully not just the artforms themselves but the context(s) of the makers and users of these Palaeolithic images. In the rest of this paper, however, we need first to develop further the structural views of Palaeolithic art at the level of the image and depiction.

It would not be disputed that in most Palaeolithic art there are no set boundaries or contrasting backgrounds, no explicit groundlines or orientational features, no framing of images, no cropping. Some preparation of some wall surfaces has been inferred, based primarily on grinding or polishing implements rather than on attributes of the walls. The engravings on already formed artefacts (e.g. harpoons, points) certainly imply a prepared medium for the incised forms, but not only is the widespread decoration of artefact forms a relatively late phenomenon in the Upper Palaeolithic, there is also a consistent lack of further definition of the space to be decorated, such as the explicit division of the artefact surface into zones to be engraved as is common with decorated ceramics. Even the natural boundaries suggested by artefact edges are often not respected, and decorations frequently spill over or encircle the artefact.

The common view of these attributes of the image-field is that they are 'noise' and are competitive with the image; that the antler or cave wall—earth surface shows through is somehow perceived as impure (Schapiro 1970, p. 224). Though he admits that this interpretation may be due more to our habit of seeing and a sense of the whole, Schapiro (1970, p. 225) still feels that the unprepared state of the field in Palaeolithic art is, at best, *neutral*. But from a closer analysis of more highly specified properties or components of an image-field, this seems unlikely. We can derive a set of attributes or features of the use of space by those who made Palaeolithic art. Those attributes have the potential to draw out what may be structural features of the operational and, perhaps, conceptual systems underlying the art.

A design-field or image-field may operate as a finding and focusing device; it has the potential to shape the image (Schapiro 1970). The relationship between a design unit and its field may range along a continuum. At one end, there can be an unbounded or 'floating' design. Then there can be an image that is contained in and isomorphic with the medium. Farther along the continuum towards tightly bounded imagery would be an image that is made, then traced, so that the boundary is applied but follows the shape of the image, and then there would be a design that has been set into a predetermined frame or bounded design-field. At the other end of the continuum would be a depiction in which the frame is in the image and vice versa.

In the images at the open end of the continuum, there is a tight connection between the depiction and any bounding of the image. The bounding that there is may be in the attributes of the medium or, at most, a tracing of the image. In these images, the forms of the depictions (signs) are accentuated, rather than there being a field onto which signs are set. It is this end of the continuum that is characteristic of Palaeolithic art; hence its non-differentiation of levels. We find 'floating' depictions of animals and signs (figs. 4 and 5). We find those that take-off from or are congruent with shapes of artefacts, or unmodified bones and antlers, or of cave walls or rock slabs (see fig. 1). We find wall paintings, especially of animals, that are traced or highlighted by engraved lines.

Framing or bounding an image differentiates the field of representation from the surrounding surfaces. There may be none of this in Palaeolithic art. I have elsewhere noted (Conkey n.d.) that this has implications for inhibiting the growth of hierarchical design or referential systems. Without framing, aspects of continuity of the image with its field, with the medium, are more immediate. The disassociation of the image or sign from the design field and from other images is not explicitly made. That superpositioning is widespread in

such an artistic system is not surprising. Repetition and overlap of animal forms are extensive in Palaeolithic art. There is the impression of a flow of animals and signs; there is undifferentiated redundancy in the representational system (fig. 4A). It is not surprising that many serious objections to Leroi-Gourhan's orderly associations are based on how he has 'read' the superpositions, particularly in terms of how many and which animals to count (see Ucko & Rosenfeld 1967). Lack of boundedness reinforces the iconicity of many images that emerge from the raw material. It is tempting to think that it is aspects of *continuity* — between the medium and the message, between attributes of the natural world and of the cultural world — that were the basis for action if not sources of meaning for Upper Palaeolithic peoples.

An undefined, untreated image-field is not devoid of expressive effect (Schapiro 1970, p. 229), and there are more specific properties of the relationship between any imagery and its field to be considered. Even without specific bounding of the design-field, one can pursue further the placement of images in a field. Without a frame, however, many properties are elusive without the perspective of the viewer. Schapiro (1970) has discussed the qualities of upper/lower, horizontally/vertically and right/left in the placement of images within the field; the use of asymmetry in pairing or combining images; reversibility; and relative density of imagery. All of these have fascinating implications for the messages of a visual depiction. None have ever really been considered for Palaeolithic artforms, although most are rather difficult to 'read' in the Palaeolithic art that lacks bounding. (Most of Schapiro's examples and conclusions are drawn from the framed images or artforms that are cropped to fit into frames, especially paintings, of more recent centuries.)

I believe that we could set up a systematic framework for the analysis of these properties of Palaeolithic image fields. Just a few aspects of one property — directionality — may show the way in which such analysis could go. When an animal or human figure is shown in motion, there is a prevailing direction to the depiction, at least an implied direction of movement. But not all animals, and few humans in Palaeolithic art are shown explicitly in motion (figs. 6 and 8; compare with figs. 7 and 9). Certainly the contrasts — such as between the standing bison and the curling bison in the same composition on the Altamira ceiling — are also of interest, but no one has looked systematically at the patterns of animals in motion. With directedness, there is 'an expression of an order of time in an order of space' (Schapiro 1970, p. 231). Without many scenes or what are identifiable as explicit, progressive episodes in Palaeolithic art, it seems that this expression of time in space is not highly elaborated. If, however, notational systems exist — not just cumulative object markings, but sequential ones (cf. Marshack 1972, 1976) — this is one way in which time in space could be expressed, but we have yet to confirm the existence of such systems, much less that they are widespread or systematic.

Fig. 4. 'Floating' images in Palaeolithic wall art, engravings from Teyjat (France). *A*: head of bison. *B*: head of a reindeer. *C*: cows and bull.

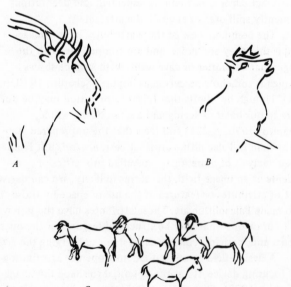

It is probable that there are visual cues that we use to detect motion. Certain signs (e.g. 'arrowed forms') may be read by us as having inherent iconic attributes of directedness, as could the frequent 'meanders' (∿) that involve repetition of an element but in an unspecified direction. The animal movement that is shown is only rarely with groundlines, and is also only an implicit expression — if one at all — of time in space. The very characteristic superpositions of Palaeolithic art are not scenes to our eyes, not the neatly ordered horizontal patterns arranged vertically (or *vice versa*) of explicitly narrative art styles. As noted above, superpositioning is flow, a flow in which repetition and redundancy is emphasised. But the superpositions are not random. Until a systematic study of superpositions is carried out, such as that done by Lewis-Williams (1977) for the rock art of the !Kung San, we cannot rule out the possibility that the superpositions at least hold potential to express time relationships of some sort in space. However, from a structural view, the lack of extensive, explicit temporally linked imagery suggests aspects of timelessness, just as the lack of boundedness enhances the aspects of continuity, at least between image form and medium.

Because there is not always occupation debris associated with many painted caves (or if there is, we are not often sure that it corresponds to the time of the paintings), it has frequently been suggested that certain caves were selected because they were not to be occupied, or were not to be used for the activities that result in hearths, lithic and bone assemblages or faunal accumulations. Further, not only is it suggested that these caves were removed from everyday life, but may not have been very well-known by even the users. It is not clear that many were frequently visited and revisited. Even though we do not often know the access routes taken by prehistoric peoples to reach the many decorated chambers, it has been noted that in some — but by no means all — whatever route was taken, it must have been tortuous and of course, only dimly lit, if at all. Many of the paintings in caves are found in what to us are 'surprising', if not

Fig. 5. 'Floating' animal depictions of the main composition in the round chamber at Santimamiñe (Spain). Black paint: about 2.5 m long. Taken from Leroi-Gourhan 1965 (plate 71).

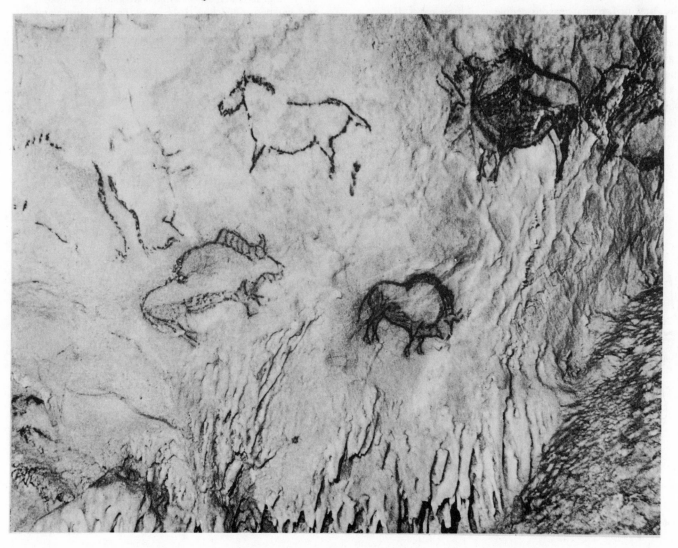

actually hidden, locales. Many paintings can be recognised or identified if viewed from an unnatural positioning of the observer: crouched, upside down, around a corner, through a crevice. All of these features of some caves, of some paintings, have suggested the possibility that these painted caves were liminal or at least transitory places with confusing routes and unpredictable depictions; places where individuals participated in activities that required a context of transition, of liminality, as well as different orientational constructs for viewing and identifying (Pfeiffer 1980, pers. comm.). If plausible, these features of the caves and paintings would add a sense of the 'elsewhere' or 'not-here' to the structural attributes of design that imply continuity, relative timelessness and permanence.

In Pfeiffer's approach, there are attributes of context that can be sought systematically. These attributes, when taken together with attributes of design structure may, in any given instance, add up to a pattern of context, a pattern of use of Palaeolithic art. It has often been pointed out (e.g. Ucko & Rosenfeld 1967) that the contextual analysis of Palaeolithic art has the most potential, particularly given the problems of dating the wall art. We don't yet really know why, how or for what reasons people used these caves. If there are formal aspects of design structure as well as aspects of context that can be considered together, and if there are — as we would expect — correspondences, this is clearly a clue to the interpretation of Upper Palaeolithic life.

It is not a coincidence that the very media of Palaeolithic art that we have to study are media of permanence (stone, antler), and not ephemeral (bark, wood, feathers, skin). I would find it hard to believe that the producers/users

of material culture, of visual arts, did not, at some level, recognise the difference between ephemeral and more permanent media. One could say that the metaphors of ephemeral media are more finite, perhaps more individual, and, hence, 'mortal'. The permanency of stone may make it a more appropriate medium for the expression of metaphors about the social body that goes on despite the death of individuals. The directionality in both time and space of Palaeolithic art-forms is not striking; it is more in the using and wearing of portable art, or the approaching and passing of the wall art by the humans. The active, mobile role is taken by the viewers who must come to most of the wall art. The wearers or users of the portable art — often engraved with images far too minute or encircling to be viewed by anyone at some distance — are the agents, albeit transitory ones. If the re-use of walls and portable pieces is as widespread as claimed (e.g. Marshack 1976), we could consider that it was the stream of individuals through time who punctuated the continuities of space and time, of medium and message. In the properties of image-fields, we may have access to operational principles

Fig. 7. Animals in motion but without groundlines, orientation or elaboration of direction. *A*: Le Portel (France) horse, about 41 cm and painted in black. *B*: The 'Chinese' horse at Lascaux (France). About 150 cm long and done in polychrome paint. Here the 'pacing gait is broken up into separate movements' (Leroi-Gourhan 1965, p. 233).

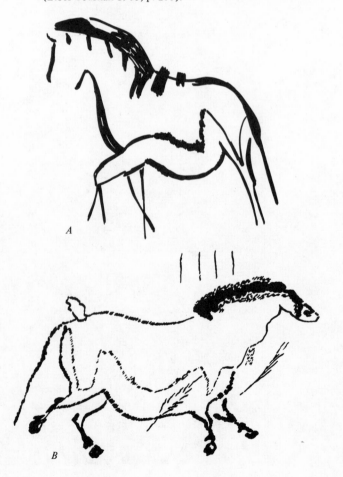

Fig. 6. Static animals in Palaeolithic art. A schematic sketch of two aurochs (wild cows) that were done in low relief on a stone slab (Bourdeilles, France).

Fig. 8. Two aurochs in low relief at Bourdeilles (France), which are conjoined by use of common line – for back of one and belly of the other – but not in motion (see sketch, fig. 6). About 53 cm. Taken from Leroi-Gourhan 1965 (plate 95).

underlying the use of space and expressions of time in space by means of the analysis of directionality and other aspects of composition. It seems that it was the humans as agents who added direction to relatively undirected images of Palaeolithic art; images not bounded by space or by explicit temporal contexts.

In the study of Palaeolithic art, I am interested in the potential sources of meaning which the artforms themselves might have provided. These sources of meaning may be accessible via the analysis of structural features that may be inferred from properties of manufacture or from contexts of use. In advocating a more rigorous and highly specified analysis of the various levels of production and the use of structural attributes in Palaeolithic art, I have two main aims.

First, I want to work towards the identification of the fundamental features of human life that are the source for the establishment of discontinuities in material culture, and

in society as a whole. I believe that it is in a more precise understanding of the iconicity of Palaeolithic artforms that we may find clues to the establishment and mediation of discontinuities via continuities or similarity. What are the correspondences that brought certain Palaeolithic artforms into existence? I am tempted to think that it is from this iconicity that structural congruence emerges.

Thus, second, I am convinced that the interrelated and often common organisation of different behavioural domains was a significant factor in the evolutionary success of human cultural life. Furthermore, we can expect that the organisation of different domains of action and behaviour (and at many levels of action and behaviour) will have discernible behavioural consequences when any two or more modes are coordinated (see Greenfield 1978 for a discussion of how effective the coordination can be in language and action). It may not only be the effective linkages among

Fig. 9. Another polychrome horse depiction from Lascaux (France) that suggests motion but without direction, groundline or orientation. Taken from Leroi-Gourhan 1965 (plate 78).

behavioural domains, but also the coordination and hence multisensory depth of structural features of behaviour that gave certain evolving hominid populations evolutionary advantages.

As prehistoric archaeologists we are trying to bring something that is far away into focus. But the binoculars that we are using, I believe, have been held the wrong way. We are looking in the wrong end, and what is brought into focus is misleading:

> It can be shown that the rigid structures in cells — what you might call the NOUNS of the cells — are very likely secretions of the process. The orthodox view is that there is structure, and it transmits its specificity to process, and yet it's just the other way around . . . Living systems are, in effect, really processes. Unfortunately, the structural 'nouns' which they secrete have attracted our attention because we do not know how to deal with the process.

> (Bateson in Bateson, M.C. 1972)

To turn the binoculars around, we must focus on the secretion of the thing from the process.

Acknowledgements

Although the many new insights I gained from the Conference on Structuralism and Symbolism in Archaeology certainly added to this revision, I am most deeply indebted to Mary LeCron Foster, Ian Hodder and Jim Doran for extensive, provocative and substantive comments. Without Mickie Foster's frank and yet constructive criticism, it is unlikely that this paper would be published; I am particularly grateful for her continued support of my often unreadable ideas. This paper was written while I was a Research Fellow of the National Endowment for the Humanities, and the research and thinking time that that Fellowship provided contributed substantially to my being able to prepare this paper and to my being able to attend this conference.

References

Adams, M.J. (1971) 'Work patterns and symbolic structures in a village culture, East Sumba, Indonesia', *Southeast Asia* 1: 321–34

Adams, M.J. (1973) 'Structural aspects of a village art', *American Anthropologist* 75: 265–79

Barth, F. (1969) *Ethnic Groups and Boundaries*, Little-Brown, Boston

Bateson, G. (1972) 'The logical categories of learning and communication' in *Steps to An Ecology of Mind*, Ballantine Books, New York

Bateson, M.C. (1972) *Our Own Metaphor*, Knopf, New York

Charbonnier, G. (1969) *Conversations with Claude Lévi-Strauss*, Grossman Publishers, Jonathan Cape Editions, London

Conkey, M.W. (n.d.) 'Structural perspectives on Palaeolithic art', manuscript

Conkey, M.W. (1978) 'An analysis of design structure: variability among Magdalenian engraved bones from northcoastal Spain', PhD dissertation, Department of Anthropology, University of Chicago

Conkey, M.W. (1979) 'Structural aspects of Palaeolithic art', paper presented at annual meeting, Kroeber Anthropological Society, Department of Anthropology, University of California, Berkeley, Plenary Session: Structuralism in the Subdisciplines

Conkey, M.W. (1980) 'Context, structure and efficacy in Palaeolithic art and design' in M.L. Foster & S. Brandes (eds.) *Symbol as Sense*, Academic Press, New York

D'Aquili, E. (1972) 'Biopsychological determinants of culture', Addison—Wesley Module in Anthropology, Reading, Mass.

Deetz, J. (1977) *In Small Things Forgotten*, Anchor Books, New York

Eco, U. (1976) *A Theory of Semiotics*, University of Indiana Press, Bloomington

Franquemont, E. & Franquemont, C. (1977) 'Information on spinning and weaving in Chincheros, Peru', manuscript, American Museum of Natural History, New York

Fritz, M.C. (1972) 'Toward an anthropological concept of style', paper presented at annual meeting, American Anthropological Association, New Orleans

Fritz, M.C. (1975) 'The structure of Paleolithic design', paper presented at annual meeting, American Anthropological Association, San Francisco

Fritz, M.C. (1976) 'Design variability among Magdalenian assemblages of engraved bones from Cantabrian Spain', paper presented at meetings of Union International des Sciences Pré et Proto-historiques, Nice

Geertz, C. (1964) 'The transition to humanity' in S. Tax (ed.) *Horizons of Anthropology*, University of Chicago, Chicago

Glassie, H. (1975) *Folk Housing in Middle Virginia: A Structural Analysis of Historic Artifacts*, University of Tennessee Press, Nashville

Greenfield, P.M. (1978) 'Structural parallels between language and action in development' in A. Lock (ed.) *Action, Gesture and Symbol: The Emergence of Language*, Academic Press, New York

Hodder, I.R. (1978) 'The maintenance of group identities in the Baringo district, W. Kenya' in D. Green, C. Haselgrove & M. Spriggs (eds.) *Social Organisation and Settlement*, BAR International Series 47: 47–73

Isaac, G.L. (1972) 'Chronology and the tempo of cultural change during the Pleistocene' in W. Bishop & J. Miller (eds.) *Calibration of Hominoid Evolution*, Scottish Academic Press, New York

Isaac, G.L. (1976) 'Stages of cultural elaboration in the Pleistocene: possible archaeological indicators of the development of language capabilities' in S. Harnard, H. Stekelis & J. Lancaster (eds.) *Origins and Evolution of Language and Speech*, New York Academy of Sciences, New York

Jakobson, R. (1960) 'Why "Mama" and "Papa"?' in R. Jakobson *Perspectives in Psychological Theory*, New York

Kummer, H. (1971) 'Spacing mechanisms in social behaviour' in J. Eisenberg & W.S. Dillon (eds.) *Man and Beast: Comparative Social Behaviour*, Smithsonian Institution Press, Washington, DC

deLaguna, F. (1932–3) 'A comparison of Eskimo and Palaeolithic art', *American Journal of Archaeology* 36: 477–511 (1932) 37: 77–107 (1933) (Non-Representative Art)

Laming-Emperaire, A. (1962) *La Signification de l'Art Rupestre Paléolithique*, Paris

Leach, E. (1976) *Culture and Communication*, Cambridge University Press, Cambridge

Lechtman, H. (1976) 'Style in technology — some early thoughts' in H. Lechtman & R. Merrill (eds.) *Material Culture, Style, Organization and Dynamics of Technology*, Proceedings of the 1975 American Ethnological Society spring meetings, West Publishing

Leroi-Gourhan, A. (1958) 'Repartition et groupement des animaux dans l'art pariétal paléolithique', *Bulletin de la Société Pre-historique Française* 55: 515–27

Leroi-Gourhan, A. (1965) *Treasures of Prehistoric Art*, Abrams, New York

Leroi-Gourhan, A. (1972) 'Considérations sur l'organisation spatiale des figures animales dans l'art pariétal paléolithique' in *Santander Symposium*, Actas del Symposium Internacional de Arte Prehistórico: Santander, Spain

Leroi-Gourhan, A. (1978) 'The mysterious markings in the Palaeolithic art of France and Spain', *CNRS Research* 8: 32–5

Lévi-Strauss, C. (1964) *Le Cru et le Cuit*, Librairie Ploh, Paris

Lewis-Williams, J.D. (1977) 'Superpositioning in a sample of rock-paintings from the Barkly east district', *South African Archaeological Bulletin* 29: 93–103

Marshack, A. (1972) 'Upper Palaeolithic notation and symbol', *Science* 178: 815–28

Marshack, A. (1976) 'Aspects of style versus usage in the analysis and interpretation of Palaeolithic image and symbol', paper presented at IX Congrès, UISPP, Nice

Munn, N.D. (1966) 'Visual categories: an approach to the study of representational systems', *American Anthropologist* 68: 936–50

Nicolas, G. (1966) 'Essai sur les structures fundamentales de l'espace dans la cosmologie Hausa', *Journal of Society of Africanists* 36: 65–107

Parkington, J. (1969) 'Symbolism in Palaeolithic cave art', *South African Archaeological Bulletin* 24: 3–13

Pfeiffer, J. (1980) 'Icons in the shadows', *Science 80* 1(4): 72–9

Schapiro, M. (1970) 'On some problems in the semiotics of visual art: field and vehicle in image signs', *Semiotica*: 223–42

Schneirla, T.C. (1965) 'Aspects of simulation and organization in approach/withdrawal processes underlying vertebrate behavioral development', *Advances in the Study of Behavior* 1: 1–74

Sebeok, T. (1976) 'Iconicity', *Modern Language Notes* 91 (5–6): 1426–56

Thom, R. (1975) 'Les mathématiques et l'intelligible', *Dialectica* 29: 71–80

Ucko, P. & Rosenfeld, A. (1967) *Paleolithic Cave Art*, McGraw-Hill, New York

Vinnicombe, P. (1976) *People of the Eland*, Natal University Press, Pietermaritzburg

Wheatley, P. (1971) *The Pivot of the Four Corners: A Preliminary Inquiry into the Origins and Character of the Chinese City*, Aldine, Chicago

Wickler, W. (1973) *The Sexual Code*, Anchor Press/Doubleday, New York and Garden City, NJ

Wobst, H. (1977) 'Stylistic behavior and information exchange' in C. Cleland (ed.) *Papers for the Director*, University of Michigan Museum of Anthropology Anthropological Paper No. 61: 317–42

Wobst, H. (1978) 'The archaeo-ethnology of hunter–gatherers, or the tyranny of the ethnographic record in archaeology', *American Antiquity* 43: 303–9

Chapter 12

**Ideology, symbolic power
and ritual communication:
a reinterpretation of
Neolithic mortuary practices**
Michael Shanks and
Christopher Tilley

The first part of this chapter attempts to arrive at an adequate notion and definition of ideology. An alternative to the viewpoint of Althusser concerning the nature of ideology is discussed, and the close relationship between ideological and symbolic form emphasised. Material symbols, especially those involved in ritual such as burial of the dead, may play an active part in the misrepresentation or concealment of real social relations. The treatment and arrangement of the human skeleton at burial can be used to provide a number of particularly powerful symbolic contrasts. An analysis of the skeletal remains in Neolithic barrows from Wessex and the Cotswolds in southern England and from southern Sweden is carried out. It is suggested that the preservation biasses can be accounted for in the analyses, and it is shown that non-random selection of bones between and within the tombs can be identified, and that contrasts occur between articulated and disarticulated skeletons, adult and immature remains, left and right parts of the body, male and female. Possible interpretations of the patterning are discussed in relation to ethnographic data, and it is suggested that the burial symbolism was involved ideologically within the context of symmetric kin organisation and asymmetric social control by lineage heads.

Introduction

This paper is an attempt to reinterpret Neolithic mortuary practices in two distinct areas of north western Europe: Wessex and the Cotswolds in southern England and Scania in southern Sweden. The main focus of our attention is the human osteological deposits within earthen and chambered long barrows. First, we present a general theoretical position for the interpretation of mortuary ritual and human skeletal remains. The second section of the paper consists of a detailed empirical study of the human remains from a number of barrows. Finally we proceed to interpret the data in the light of the considerations advanced in the first section. Many of the terms employed in this paper such as 'structuring principle' are defined in chapter 3 of this volume.

The interpretation of mortuary ritual is a particular case of the wider problem of the ideological legitimation of the social order. At the centre of this problem is the relation between a number of dualities, notably activity and consciousness (whether true or false), subject and object (the relation of the individual to 'reality'), and that between the individual and society.

Here we conceive of these dualities as dynamic relational entities within an immanent totality, the social formation. They are aspects of a complex structured whole; aspects from the point of view of participant or analyst. In particular, the context of a social entity or entities (such as mortuary ritual) and its relations to other entities, is an integral part of what that entity is. Change and interaction are necessary rather than contingent, because the structuration of the social formation, resulting in the reproduction or transformation of social form, is a continuing process. The social formation should be conceived as a determinate set of social relations and socially produced conditions of existence for these relations. Interaction is not to be conceived simplistically as reciprocal causality. The individual has part of his existence in his relation to other individuals and nature (both are 'objects' of experience and action) and, conversely, man's objects 'reside in the nature of his being' (Marx 1959, p. 156). The object does not stand opposed to the subject as in empiricism and idealism, but each serves to constitute the other. It would be foolish to deny the separate reality of subject and object but it is equally unsatisfactory to polarise them artificially since every social phenomenon consists of interconnections between structuring principles, praxis, consciousness and action. In this way the subject–object relation is neither a contemplation of an external objective reality nor an ideal creation of that reality (Larrain 1979, p. 40).

Through his practice the individual comes into relation with the object. Practice is activity which appropriates an object – a particular aspect of man's natural and social environment. Through practice, activity and consciousness become unified. Activity presupposes a definite orientation towards the appropriated object. This orientation is achieved, sustained or transformed through the operation and/or transformation of structuring principles which give actions both their coherence and meaning within the overall social formation. They give meaning to the object world. The object world is, therefore, an historical product of man's practice. The objective appearance of objects should be seen as a process by means of which they have a multiplicity of forms and definitions depending on their relation to the entire ensemble of social relations which constitute the totality or social formation:

> All the categories in which human existence is constructed must appear as the determinants of that existence itself (and not merely the description of that existence). Their succession, their coherence and their connections must appear as the historical process itself, as the structural components of the present. The succession and internal order of the categories constitute neither a purely logical sequence nor are they organised merely in accordance with the facts of history. (Lukács 1971, p. 159)

Through practice men reproduce and transform the social formation but at the same time this activity is in accordance with the structuring of that totality. This continual reproduction or structuration operates at both reflective and prereflective levels of consciousness. Consequently, the results and implications of practice go beyond individual intention and choice. As with subject and object, and activity and consciousness, the individual and society, while being analytically distinct, are both preconditions and results of each other's existence.

Mortuary ritual constitutes a particular arena for social activity within the overall totality. It forms an integral part of the structuration of the whole. We wish to argue that ritual activities form an active part of the social construction

of reality within social formations and may be conceived as a particular form of the ideological legitimation of the social order, serving sectional interests of particular groups. In order to defend this position we require a clear definition of what ideology might be, to which we now turn.

Ideology

Ideology may be regarded as practice which operates to secure the reproduction of relations of dominance and to conceal contradictions between the structural principles orientating the actions of individuals and groups within the social formation. It legitimates the sectional interests of hegemonic groups. As Giddens points out, the 'universal interest of dominant groups is that of maintaining the existing order of domination, since such an order *ipso facto* involves an asymmetrical distribution of resources that can be drawn upon to satisfy wants' (Giddens 1979, pp. 189–90). Ideology is not a form of consciousness which distorts objective reality, it is not simply false as opposed to true consciousness, nor is it simply the world view of a particular group (involving either a true or false consciousness depending on social circumstances). Both of these views are based on a categorical distinction between subject and object. The first 'involves a conception of knowledge as being formed through the consciousness or experience of human subjects; ideology is then a distorted perception of reality by these knowing subjects. But this is exactly the classical empiricist conception of knowledge: i.e. knowledge is derived from a subject's experience of an object which is exterior to it' (Hirst 1976, pp. 2–3). The second view examines how the subject's experience is mediated by his social position. The object becomes the origin of ideology. The subject is determined by his social position, his ideas can only reflect reality, the object.

As an alternative, Althusser asserts the materiality of ideology. As elements of concrete social formations, ideologies are both material and ideational constructs whose form is governed by their articulation within the social totality. Ideologies do not consist of ideas as opposed to matter. Insofar as they are conceived as ideas which are embodied in social action, they become 'real' rather than 'ideal'. Ideologies are a part of social relations rather than merely a reflection of those relations. So, 'there is no practice except by and in an ideology' and 'there is no ideology except by the subject and for subjects' (Althusser 1971, p. 159). In *For Marx* Althusser asserts that there can be no end to ideology. It forms an organic part of every social totality and has no history, it is omni-historical. Social totalities can never be realised in experience, there can be no true consciousness of social relations but rather the subject is related to the totality through an 'imaginary relation'. Ideological relations hide and misrepresent real social relations. At the same time they designate a lived, and therefore, a real relation which is both material and necessary rather than being purely illusory. This position represents a clear break with the notion of ideology as false consciousness. Ideology does not represent the real conditions of existence but a representation of an imaginary relationship of individuals to their conditions of existence. If there is an imaginary distortion in ideology it is a direct consequence of the imaginary character of the relationship which is represented in ideology: 'ideology, then, is the expression of the relation between men and their "world", that is, the (overdetermined) unity of the real relation and the imaginary relation between them and their real conditions of existence. In ideology the real relation is inevitably invested in the imaginary relation, a relation that *expresses* a will . . . a hope or a nostalgia, rather than describing a reality' (Althusser 1977, pp. 233–4). As such, there can never be a true consciousness of social relations as this requires either a transcendental correspondence of subject and object, or a perpetuation of the dichotomy subject knows object, object produces subject. For Althusser subjects are constituted by ideology which serves to interpellate the social actor and creates subjects suitable to carry out the required social relations. Only science, theoretical practice, can break with the imaginary – an epistemological break.

There are a number of problems with this approach.

(1) The general concept of ideology has no real specificity. Little consideration is made of conflicts of interests between individuals and groups within social formations which might contribute to the origin of ideology. Only in the postscript to the 1971 essay on 'Ideological state apparatuses' is there any account of ideology in relation to class conflicts. This position is further discussed in his *Essays in Self-Criticism* (Althusser 1976).

(2) Althusser's subjects are passive, reified and helpless. It is only through ideology that subjects are constituted with definite needs and consciousness. This radical anti-humanism leaves little or no room for revolutionary practice. As Larrain puts it: 'the epistemological idealism of the false consciousness has been superceded by the transcendental idealism of the eternal ideology' (Larrain 1979, p. 164). If ideology is the way men live their relations to their real conditions of existence, it is changeable and may be ended altogether, it cannot be omni-historical. This is so if ideology is located in the clashes of interests between definite groups of social actors as in the 'Ideological state apparatuses' essay (Althusser 1971). However, if ideology just relates men to society, their world of being, it can have no end since social actors can never know their social world completely. This position, if accepted, would rob the concept of ideology of any specificity in terms of its locus within a definite set of social relations.

(3) Althusser's conception of ideology is closely related to his epistemology. He is concerned to distinguish between theoretical practice (science) and ideology. Ideological knowledges are an elaboration or reflection of categories given in the imaginary relation in which the subject lives, while science reveals the lived relation as imaginary. As practice, it operates on the forms of the imaginary and transforms them into scientific generalities. The prehistory of any science is a series of theoretical ideologies, and through their transformation science is founded. The notion of the epistemological break is in many respects akin to Kuhn's work on scientific revolutions (Kuhn 1970). The old theoretical ideologies are replaced by the scientific 'problematic' which achieves true knowledge by means of its internal consistency. However, theoretical ideologies continue to co-exist with the problematic which leaves its precise status somewhat dubious. Althusser's epistemology seems internalist, and he wavers between a number of positions: (a) Idealist. Theoretical practice, alone among Althusser's 'instances' of the social formation, appears to be, at times, exempt from the influence of the other instances (Geras 1972). This, in a very obvious way, contradicts Althusser's formulation of the nature of the social formation. (b) Science is opposed categorically to ideology, but the distinction cannot be one of truth as opposed to falsehood since both are formulated out of men's practices, under distinctive conditions of production, and have concrete effects. They are not merely systems of ideas. (c) He is not able to distinguish clearly ideology from science. At one point he merely asserts that 'theoretical practice is indeed its own criteria and contains in itself definite protocols with which to *validate* the quality of the product . . . [It has] no need of verification from *external* practices to declare the knowledges they produce to be "true", i.e. to be *knowledges*' (Althusser & Balibar 1970, p. 59).

The problems we encounter in Althusser's conception might be avoided in the following way. Rather than to define ideology, somewhat negatively, in relation to science, and as a necessary omni-present feature of social formations, we conceive it as a mode(s) of intervention in social relations, carried on through practice, which secures the *reproduction* rather than the *transformation* of the social formation in the presence of contradictions between structural principles at the level of structure, and of clashes of interests between actors and groups at the level of system. This follows from a dualistic conception of societal form. Ideology is not a *form* of practice radically distinct from science. We have already defined practice as a dialectical relation between activity in the social and natural world and consciousness of this world, through the mediation of structuring principles. Concomitantly, ideological analysis involves considering how relations of dominance are sustained at various levels within these relations:

(i) The relation of structuring principles (sources of activity) to the lived experience of activity.

(ii) The relation of structuring principles to the asymmetry of resources: the means to achieve wants.

(iii) The reflexivity of the individual: the individual's practical and discursive consciousness of activity and object.

The main ways in which ideology operates are:

(1) By the denial, or mystification of contradictions between structural principles.

(2) By representing sectional interests as universal.

(3) Through reification, objectification of the present. These are only analytical distinctions, as each of the elements we have separated out reinforces the others. Points 1 and 2 are self-evident; 3 requires further grounding.

Objectification involves the decontextualisation of any factor, its separation or abstraction from its place in the social whole. The world is reified into an already given and immutable form. The totality is atomised into discrete, 'objective' entities which interact according to fixed laws. This naturalised order may be justified internally or externally. Its 'objectivity' may be rationally 'proved', or the objectified social order may be legitimated by reference to the sacred or the traditional, which themselves remain external to ideological practice.

The individual confronts this 'reality' in an ambiguous relation to the 'social' and the 'cultural'. They are, in essence, a product of man, but in immediate appearance the naturalised social order is non-social in character and origin. The category of the natural is correspondingly contradictory. It is, simultaneously, what was not created by man, but in that it is identified with, and sanctifies the social order, it pertains to man.

Objectification, in asserting the immutability of the categories of comprehension and the relations between these objects, results in a fundamental distinction between the synchronic and the diachronic. The specific historical genesis of categories, laws or customary sanctions is either denied or sanctified. Change in these categories becomes contingent to their existence. It becomes something subjective imposed onto objects from outside, an individual's value judgment opposed to the physical reality of the object, an 'ought' opposed to 'is': 'when confronted by the rigidity of the "facts" every movement seems like a movement impinging on them, while every tendency to change them appears to be a merely subjective principle (a wish, a value judgment, an ought' (Lukács 1971, p. 184). 'Facts' become distinct from 'values'. The classification and structuring of the world present in ideological practice is assumed to be value-free, in the sense of not being in pursuit of the interests of a select group. Private interests are depersonalised and universalised.

The power to achieve wants or interests is in a dialectical relation with the individual's discursive and practical consciousness of the social world. Practice involves contextually situated action. Here ideology may separate interests from 'knowledge'. A particular set of structural principles or knowledge of the world becomes divorced from the interests it furthers. This is another aspect of the reified fact-value distinction. It becomes possible to know a 'fact' (something which is knowable or has happened) without expressing approval or disapproval. In the defined and immutable world of ideology, wants and interests are similarly given. Agency is limited, as the individual perceives

only the reality of a limited set of goals which are attainable and objects which may be appropriated. The social world, objectified in ideology, defines the limits of knowledge.

Generally, objectification results in the assumption of the existential reality of polarities such as fact—value, activity—consciousness, body—mind, nature—society. Each half is assumed to be independent of the other, things pertain to one or the other, ambiguities become problematic and the unity of the relations sustained through practice is broken. As such, ideology does not falsify, rather it systematically acts to misinterpret:

> Misinterpretation results from focussing too narrowly on facts which are directly observable and from extracting these appearances from the surrounding conditions which alone give them their correct meaning . . . Cut off from the processes out of which they emerge and their own potential for change and development, the apparent features of events lose their historical specificity and take on the guise of natural phenomena.   (Ollman 1976, p. 228)

So, Marx gives the example of the Cacus who stole oxen by dragging them backwards into his cave so that the footprints would make it appear that they had come from there. Comprehension, through ideology, remains trapped in the immediate world of appearances. Not all objectification is ideological; men classify and construct their reality and this in itself must remain neutral. Objectification becomes ideological when the abstracted forms are regarded as fixed and natural, when they achieve a life of their own and serve the interests of dominant groups.

Ideology and symbolic power

We have seen that ideological representations are those that conceal real social relations, elements of social consciousness. Through man's practical activities they also become embedded within the material products of this practice. As such, they may be conceived as both a creator of practice and a creation of that practice. As social relations involve symbolism, ideological form and symbolic form will be inextricably bound together. To analyse ideological aspects of symbolic orders is to investigate the manner in which signification structures are used to legitimate the position of specific groups. The meaning of a symbol is not arbitrary, it is relational. Symbolic systems exist as structured sets. We deduce the meaning of symbolic forms from their relational positioning rather than considering the constitutive units in isolation. Within the context of a determinate set of social relations the meaning attributable to any symbol or group of symbols will be restricted. This has to be the case, or the power of symbols in relation to the ordering of social life would be negated. The particular relationship between the signifier and that signified will be governed by their structuring within arenas of social action. Symbols can be actively used to mobilise and legitimate sectional interests. Their power as signifiers of the social order may directly bolster systems of domination and legitimate them. They may become instruments for a particular construction and manipulation of the social world. Bourdieu, taking up Marx's notion that the ideas of the ruling class are, in every epoch, the ruling ideas, suggests that the dominant culture produces its specific ideological effect by concealing its social divisiveness under its function as communication. The culture which unites, as a means of communication, at the same time separates and divides and legitimates distinctions by defining all cultures (sub-cultures) in respect to their distance from the dominant culture, identifying the latter with excellence. Symbolic power

> is only exerted insofar as it is misrecognised (i.e. inso-
> far as its arbitrariness is misrecognised). This means
> that symbolic power does not lie in 'symbol systems'
> in the form of an 'illocutionary force' but that it is
> defined in and by a determinate relationship between
> those who exercise power and those who undergo it,
> i.e. in the very structure of the field within which
> belief is produced and reproduced.
>
> (Bourdieu 1979, p. 83)

Material culture can act as a very powerful means of the fostering of this misrecognition; contrasts and relations can be exploited as part of a semiotic code. The perceptual form of material culture can act at either a discursive level, or more powerfully, because less likely to be recognised, at a level of practical consciousness to structure and restructure social practices. Material culture forms part of the phenomenal form of ideology. What is present to the senses in the symbolism in material culture has to be actively produced by agents. Therefore, the conditions, context and form of this production and subsequent use will relate very strongly to the phenomenal form. To this we will return.

The rest of this chapter is only directly relevant to those societies with no self-regulating market for the exchange of goods and services, formalised methods of socialisation (educational systems), political and juridical relations and repressive state apparatus (the latter being an example of the legitimation of ideology by means of direct and indirect physical coercion). All such societies would seem to be characterised by the exercise of power by certain individuals over others. The exercise of this power and the way in which it is exercised depends upon the structural characteristics of any determinate social formation.

Power relations and ritual communication

Control over resources, whether these be defined in terms of knowledge deemed essential to the well-being of the social group, or the actual means of production, form the two primary media through which power is exercised and the domination of individuals and groups is secured. Differences between social formations would seem to be largely attributable to the presence or absence of social control in different contexts. In non-state societies, relations of domination, by specific interest groups, can only be set up and main-

tained at the cost of repeated social actions involving the endless repetition of the same elements. This is because the conditions required for a lasting appropriation of other agents do not exist as they do in contemporary capitalism. In other words, a firm plausibility structure legitimising social hierarchies simply does not exist and must be constantly recreated in the form of a dialectic between social actions and forms of social consciousness. We have already noted that if ideology is to be effective in sustaining the hegemony of groups, the forms and context of its appearance will be of vital importance. Now, the ideological use of symbol systems is likely to be particularly effective in the context of those activities we term 'ritual', hence, we suggest, the frequency of ritual in small-scale societies. Bloch (1975, 1977*a*, 1977*b*) relates ideology to the formalised premises and nature of ritual communication. He stresses two main characteristics, the dissolution of time and the depersonalisation of the individual. Ritual communication is effected by special types of formalised communication involving song, dance and material symbols. Its premises are such that it seems to make the social world appear to be organised in a fixed order which recurs without beginning or end. It serves to project the social into the image and realm of the repetitive processes of nature, thus possessing all the hallmarks of ideology we have outlined above. It is obvious that those who acquire power are likely to institutionalise it in the form of ritual, making it appear to be part of the natural order of things, and as a consequence of this, less vulnerable to attack. Furthermore, the constitutive units of ritual cannot be reformulated at will, but follow from each other as an integral part of the activity. Ritual communication is therefore protected from direct evaluation with regard to empirical realities. A further point is that ritual activities are acted through by agents and as such they are likely to be practically, rather than discursively, available to the individual. It is at this level of practical consciousness that ideological misrepresentation is likely to be most effective.

So, the occasion of mortuary ritual, in common with other life-cycle rituals, may act as a plausibility structure legitimising sectional interests. It does not follow from this, as Bloch suggests (Bloch 1977*a*), that cognition is double, the one form in ritual being distorted, the other, in the day-to-day empirical realities of life, being a true representation. This approach, somewhat simplistically, presupposes that non-ritual activities do not misrepresent social relations. Ritual is only one form, albeit a particularly powerful form, of legitimising social hierarchies.

Ritual, as a form of ideology, can be seen to consist of complexes of symbolic structures. The ritual symbols construct and manipulate the social order and are themselves structured by it. They serve to identify the precarious social construction of reality with the natural order of things. Often these relationships will be exhibited in culturally stereotyped ways and will be represented in culturally stereotyped forms, in what Lévi-Strauss calls 'the logic of the concrete'. It is not only animals which are 'good to think' but a whole range of material symbols. The relationship between that signified and the signifier may relate to a perceived conception of objective differences. Sahlins (1976) suggests that 'the selection of a given material opposition . . . must be true: the penalty of a contradiction between the perceptible object contrasts and the relationships signified is meaninglessness and, ultimately, silence'. In other words, the materiality of symbols, in terms of their similarities and dissimilarities, constrains their patterning and relational use. Turner (1967, pp. 27–8, 1969, pp. 48–9) discusses three properties of ritual symbols. (1) Multivocality or condensation. They may refer to many aspects of the social world and consequently foster deeply emotional responses. Often they achieve this specific quality by a juxtaposition of the grossly physical and the structurally normative, of the organic and the social. (2) Dominant symbols will unify disparate significata. Their meaning will be constant and consistent throughout the total symbolic system. (3) A polarisation of meaning. The significata will be a component of the social and moral orders, principles of social organisation, corporate groupings and norms and values existing in structural relationships.

Non-verbal communication through art, imagery and the metaphorical use of the body is both simpler and more complex than written or spoken language. The syntactic links are likely to be more explicit and fewer in number. Differences between right and wrong are likely to be more clear-cut than in speech acts. At the same time it is more complex in that it is likely to act in multidimensional channels. In relation to ritual activities syntactic links cannot be reformulated at will but follow from each other unquestioned as an integral part of the structural unit. Thus ritual is protected from direct evaluation against empirical data or contradictory statements.

Rey (1979) suggests that class contradiction exists in lineage societies. Whatever one may think of his analysis or the theoretical indeterminancy of the concept of lineage societies, it is apparent that systems of dominance and control do exist. The marriage system becomes the central means by which dominance is exercised by elders over junior members of the lineage, and the relationship between the two is asymmetrical. Meillassoux (1960, 1972) has noted that in agricultural systems land becomes an object of labour. The elders cannot control the means of production as these are so simple that they are readily available to all so control is achieved through kinship regulations and control over procreative women, the producers of the producers of the social product of labour. Control is also exercised over another resource — ritual information, deemed to be essential to the well-being of the group. Ritual action serves to conceal social divisions; in this sense it misrepresents. It is in the nature of ritual action that the individual becomes doubly decentred

from a consciousness of the nature of social reality and as a discrete individual within society.

We can now formulate a number of features which we might expect ritual, as a form of ideological activity, to display in small-scale societies. The first is an emphasis on the identity and solidarity of the local lineage, the collective social group. This will involve a denial of systems of domination maintained by senior members of the community and their appropriation of the collective labour product. Secondly, a consequent emphasis on boundedness serves to express an us/them dichotomy in relation to other social groups.

Thirdly there is an ambiguous relation between nature and culture. The authority of the elders may be projected into the past. Their position may be identified with the ancestors who mediate between them and the gods, if such a concept exists. One might expect a repeated use of the same sacred places. The social order is identified with the sacred order. This sacred order may correspond with nature. But ritual activity, within which the social world is reaffirmed in terms of nature, is social activity. Thus the social order is simultaneously reaffirmed in terms of itself, in terms of its own conditions of existence. This is contradictory, a function of the misrepresentations propagated in ritual. The fourth feature is the use of powerful material symbols in repeated activities and a concordance between different forms of symbolic expression. Over time, as a result of the activity–consciousness dialectic and processes of structuration, the form and content of ritual activities change relationally.

Anatomical classification and body symbolism

Mortuary ritual involves the disposal of the human body. Anthropologists have long realised that the human body provides a potent source of material symbols. However, archaeologists have not realised the potential of this position in relation to one of the most frequently encountered material remains surviving in the archaeological record, the human skeleton. Attention has almost exclusively focussed on attempts to estimate the minimum number of individuals present in relation to collective burial, an exercise fraught with problems, or have variously described individual burials in terms of degree of articulation, whether they are flexed or extended, interred or cremated, and have not gone beyond these rather crude categorisations. Symbolic aspects of burial have almost been overlooked, with the interesting exception of Binford's interpretation of Galley Pond Mound (Binford 1972*a*, pp. 390–420).

Mauss (1973, p. 75) suggested that man's first and most natural instrument was his own body, providing a technical means and a technical object, a framework for classification and a potent source of symbolism. In short the cultural use of the body is part of any society's social construction of reality. It provides a restricted yet rich set of metaphorical possibilities for non-verbal communication. Shared somatic states form part and parcel of the basic conditions for social interaction. Firth (1973, pp. 226–8) outlined four kinds of body symbolism: (i) communication through body action, (ii) treatment of the body as a set of abstract constituents, (iii) treatment of social units in bodily terms, (iv) uses of bodies or their parts actually or iconically.

What symbolic meaning can we attribute to the patterning of human skeletal remains in the archaeological record? To understand a set of symbols it would seem to be necessary to go beyond them and to investigate the classificatory principles on which they are based. Lévi-Strauss (1966, pp. 135–90) suggests that it is only through classificatory schemes that the natural and social world may be grasped as an organised coherent whole. Levels of classification authorise and imply the possibility of recourse to levels formally analagous to the favoured one and differing from it by means of their relative position within the whole. As Ellen (1977) argues, the physical make-up of the body provides a natural set of classificatory possibilities which can be symbolically exploited. It also acts to constrain the total number of possible members of a set. For instance, a beaver remains an animal so long as it fits the possible definitions of an animal which the classifier wishes to express. In other words it will always be, to a certain extent, arbitrary rather than natural whether a beaver is conceived as animal/non-animal. This would not appear to be the case when we are dealing with a physical body rather than a species. Any change in the definition of the body is incapable of severing physically or symbolically the integral association of different parts of the body or the skeleton (skull, ribs, limbs etc.). They form an integral part of an irreducible whole. The total system consists of whole/part relations. Furthermore, limbs or ribs are more likely to be equated in a formal way than different animal species. There are a limited and specific number of contrasts which may be manipulated symbolically. Classification of the body may proceed at two different levels. They form a set which is not arbitrary. At an analytic level the body may be broken down into formally analagous units: limbs/head/neck/trunk/hands and feet. In relation to skeletal anatomy this will take on a slightly different form: skull/ribs/vertebrae/upper and lower limbs/hands/feet. However, joints remain ambiguous areas of transition. The pelvis may be grouped with the vertebrae as part of the trunk or with the lower limbs; similarly the clavicula and the scapula may be grouped either with the ribs or with the upper limbs. We might expect, therefore, that the arrangements of these bones would be variable from context to context. At the synthetic level the bones, once broken down analytically, may be regrouped on another plane. At one level this is likely to be an exploitation of basic body symmetries, between upper and lower body halves, left and right sides of the body or at a less inclusive level between ribs and vertebrae (posterior and anterior of the trunk), hand and

foot bones, upper and lower limbs. As ambiguous transitional areas the pelvis, scapula and clavicula might be grouped together. If, for instance, left/right body symmetries are being exploited, we might expect that the skull and the vertebrae would be grouped together as they are the only parts of the skeletal anatomy which cannot be unambiguously divided into right and left halves.

Archaeological analysis

Skeletal evidence from Neolithic barrows, in which collective burial was practised, was analysed adopting the conception of ritual as a form of ideology, and the skeleton as a non-arbitrary symbolic set. The human osteological deposits were investigated in two distinct regions: Wessex and the Cotswolds, England, and Scania, Sweden. These two regions provide suitable contrasts in mortuary practices for the purposes of this discussion. We assume no necessary isomorphism. The basis of the work is to consider the relationships between parts of the human body and how the discernment of regularities may give us insight into the nature of the structural principles in operation. Are there regular relationships between different classes of bone or is the patterning random? Is it possible to discern regularities in the spatial arrangements of different classes of bone within the tombs? Do such relationships change over time? The number of individuals which the bones represent, even if this could be accurately determined, is irrelevant to the analysis since it is specific classes of bones which are of importance.

The sites and initial quantification

The remains from only five sites (figs. 1 and 2) were described in sufficient detail to allow quantification. These were Fussell's Lodge (Ashbee 1958, 1964, 1966), Luckington (Corcoran 1970), Lanhill (Keiller & Piggott 1938), Ramshög and Carlshögen (Strömberg 1971). The results from the study of the English data were compared with a further fifteen barrows, both earthen and chambered (table 1). Apart from the material presented in Burenhult's study of the dolmen at Hindby Mosse (Burenhult 1973), which is almost entirely composed of skull fragments, the Swedish material has not been published in a form which permits even a qualitative comparison of the mortuary practices at Ramshög and Carlshögen with other sites in Scania. This remains a weakness, somewhat obviated by the excellent temporal control at the two sites and their spatial proximity, a feature lacking in the English data.

Fussell's Lodge is an earthen longbarrow in Ashbee's (1970) and Renfrew's (1973) east Salisbury Plain group. Human remains were found in five piles at the eastern end of a mortuary enclosure (fig. 3: A1–D) and in an overlying cairn, mainly from above pile A (fig. 3: E). Luckington and Lanhill are both laterally chambered barrows, lying at the southern end of the Cotswold group. Both had been extensively disturbed. However, a chamber excavated at Lanhill was untouched, and Corcoran states that for chamber D at Luckington: 'it is possible . . . that this chamber had been opened in Romano-British times, although there is no indisputable evidence that the burial deposit had been disturbed to any extent at that time' (Corcoran 1970, p. 48).

Ramshög and Carlshögen are located in the Hagestad area of south eastern Scania, 1.8 km apart. They form part of a group of eight, and possibly more, tombs associated with contemporary domestic settlement sites. Both are typical Scanian passage graves, differing slightly in the chamber shape and length of the passage. At Ramshög human remains were found as a general fill in the chamber filling (which had

Fig. 1. The distribution of chambered and earthen long barrows in the Wessex–Cotswold region of southern England.

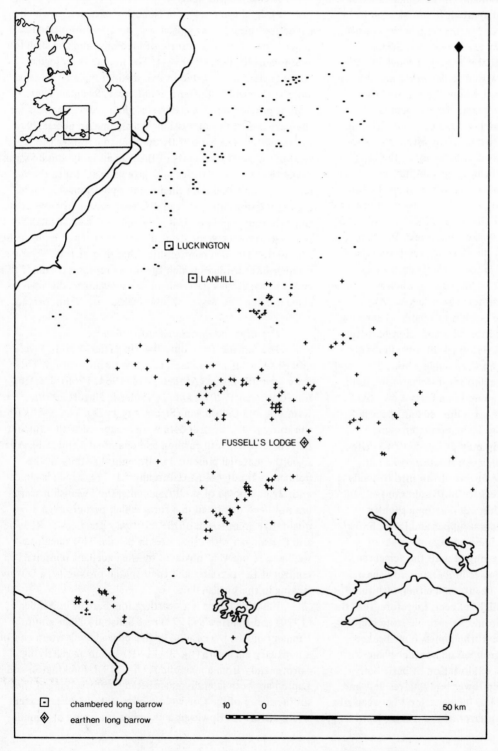

LUCKINGTON

LANHILL

FUSSELL'S LODGE

☐ chambered long barrow

◈ earthen long barrow

10   0   50 km

been somewhat disturbed), in discrete piles adjacent to the chamber walls, in pits in the chamber floor, in the passage and directly outside the tomb to the south and west (fig. 4: 1—9). At Carlshögen the osteological material was confined almost solely to the chamber, apart from a few bone fragments immediately outside to the south and at the entrance to the passage. Within the chamber the remains were discovered in a tripartite pit and in nine discrete piles sub-

divided by laterally placed stone slabs, which were used to divide the chamber into sections (fig. 5: A—I). These deposits were largely undisturbed, as above them was a paved floor on which secondary burial deposits of late Neolithic age were found.

The osteological deposits were first quantified as frequencies of bone types. These frequencies were then grouped into parts of body to bring the number of obser-

Fig. 2. The distribution of dolmens and passage graves in Scania, southern Sweden.

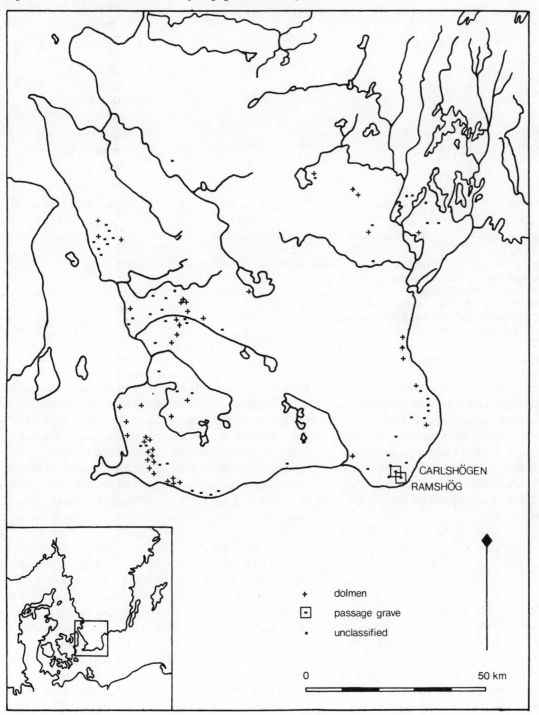

+   dolmen

□   passage grave

·   unclassified

CARLSHÖGEN
RAMSHÖG

0   50 km

Table 1. *Summary of evidence from other long barrows in the Wessex—Cotswold region of southern England*

Name of long barrow (chambered unless stated otherwise)	Selection and/or arrangement of bones	Articulated/ disarticulated contrast	Adult/immature contrast	Male/female contrast	Boundaries of deposits marked	Reference
Ascott-under-Wychwood[a]	X	X		X		Chesterman 1977
Cow Common Long : Swell 1[b]			?	X	X	Rolleston 1876, pp. 139—53
Eyford : Upper Slaughter 1	X					Greenwell 1877, pp. 514—20
Poles Wood East : Swell 5*[c]	X	X		?	X	Rolleston in Greenwell 1877, pp. 524—41
Poles Wood South : Swell 4		X				Greenwell 1877, pp. 521—4
Randwick 1	X					Crawford 1925, p. 129
Hetty Pegler's Tump : Uley 1		X				Thurnam 1854
West Tump : Brimpsfield 1[d]		X				Crawford 1925, p. 138
Lugbury : Nettleton 1				X		Thurnam 1857 Crawford 1925, p. 230
Wayland's Smithy 1 : Ashbury 1		X				Atkinson 1965
West Kennet : Avebury 22[e]	X	X	X			Piggott 1962
Chute 1*[f]	X				X	Passmore 1942
Norton Bavant 13*	X	X				Thurnam 1869, p. 185
Wor Barrow : Handley 1*[g]	X	X				Pitt-Rivers 1898, pp. 58—100
Nutbane*[h]						Morgan 1959

*Earthen long barrows
[a] All seven collections of bones were different. Cist 4 contained bones arranged to look like articulated inhumation.
[b] Skulls and headless skeletons bound mortuary deposits.
[c] Skulls mark boundaries of western half of trench.
[d] The articulation is furthest from the entrance so successive inhumation is unlikely.
[e] All chambers different. Removal of skulls and long bones proposed.
[f] Elaborate circles of skulls surrounded stacked long bones.
[g] Male remains only.
[h] Articulated remains only.

vations per category to an acceptable level, and to permit the discernment of relationships. At this juncture certain differences in the form of analysis of the English and the Swedish data must be made clear. These differences partly arise as a direct result of the form in which the data were published, and also from an attempt to see to what extent alternative groupings of parts of body would effect the analyses. The human skeleton was divided into six parts for the English data and seven for the Swedish:

1 Skull
2 Ribs
3 Vertebrae
4 Upper limbs
5 Lower limbs
6 Hand and foot bones: hand bones
7 Hand and foot bones: foot bones

Claviclae and scapulae were included with the upper limbs, and pelvic bones with the lower limbs. In the English data manubria and sterna were included with the upper limbs; in the Swedish data there were few of these and they were included with the ribs. It was not possible to separate out hand and foot bones in the English data because they were inconsistently recorded in the bone reports. For the analyses the skull was divided into its ten major bones for the English data, while for the Swedish data estimates were made of numbers of complete skulls. Again, this difference arises as a result of different recording methods in the bone reports. Apart from these relatively minor differences in the manner of classifying body parts, the subsequent analyses were identical.

Preservation

A vital question, to be resolved initially, is to establish what effect differential preservation may have had in accounting for any observed differences in relative bone frequencies between parts of body. Information on differential bone fragmentation and disintegration is conspicuously absent from the literature. To our knowledge the only detailed study on this topic is that by Binford and Bertram (1977). Even this study is concerned solely with animal, rather than with human bones, and is, therefore, largely inapplicable to the present study. Binford and Bertram relate the survival probabilities for any given anatomical part to bone density which varies with the age of the animal. Bone density alters, according to them, in relation to the age of the bone at death. This is a non-allometric process so that different bones increase in density through time at different rates. As a consequence of this it is difficult to model the process or to directly infer rates of bone density formation from one species to another. Cornwall (1956, pp. 200–2) noted obvious differences likely to affect differential preservation of bones in the human skeleton. The less solid bones, particularly ribs and vertebrae, are less likely to survive than limb bones and the larger phalanges. In most cases for excavated material, it is almost impossible to estimate numbers of complete ribs present from fragments, since these and some of the smaller phalanges are likely to be lost

in excavation. Rather than attempting to estimate numbers of complete ribs or vertebrae present, we have simply assumed that each recorded fragment represents a complete bone. This goes some way to 'weight' for differential preservation factors in the analyses, but is obviously not sufficient.

The histogram of frequencies of bones according to parts of body for all piles in Fussell's Lodge (fig. 6A) shows a predominance of the more robust upper and lower limbs, but there are also many vertebrae, and few phalanges. However, there are obvious differences in the relative frequencies from pile to pile (see fig. 3). All the remains were interred together and have, presumably, all been subject to the same attritional processes (Ashbee 1966, p. 37). This would seem to preclude the possibility that simple post-interment decay accounts for differences in the frequencies of parts of body in Fussell's

Fig. 3. The total numbers of bones, according to piles and parts of the body, recovered from Fussell's Lodge.

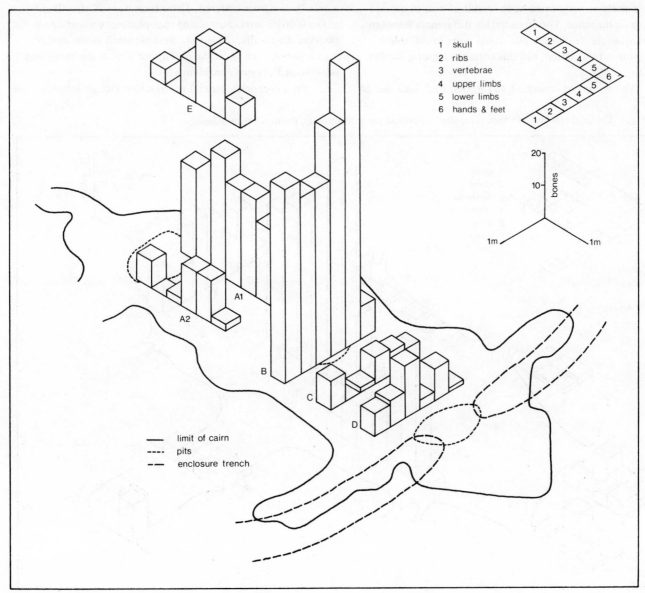

1 skull
2 ribs
3 vertebrae
4 upper limbs
5 lower limbs
6 hands & feet

—— limit of cairn
---- pits
– – enclosure trench

Lodge. Luckington and Lanhill also have a majority of limb bones (fig. 6 B and C). Phalanges are present in some quantity at Luckington, but not at Lanhill where vertebrae are the largest category.

The histogram for all classes of bones at Ramshög shows approximately equal numbers in each class, except for the skull which is under-represented (fig. 6E). The histogram for Carlshögen shows considerably more variation, with ribs and lower limbs predominating (fig. 6D). As at Fussell's Lodge these histograms are slightly misleading due to the considerable variation of bone frequencies between the piles of bones at both Ramshög and Carlshögen (see figs. 4 and 5). Strömberg suggests that since so many different anatomical parts of skeletons were preserved at both tombs, complete skeletons must have been interred (Strömberg 1969, pp. 84 and 90, 1971, p. 248). Preservation conditions at the two tombs appear to be essentially similar, and, on Strömberg's account, any differences between relative frequencies between parts of body must be the result of post-interment decay or disturbance. The considerable differences between bone frequencies from each pile would seem to call this assumption into question, but this criticism requires further grounding.

This account has assumed, so far, that each bone has an equal chance of survival or of selection for inclusion in the burial deposits. Now, we may suppose that since, for example, there are more hand and foot bones in the human body than any other type of bone, they should be relatively frequent, if complete corpses are being interred. Ignoring differential preservation factors between our classes of bones for the present, we could conduct chi-square tests to see whether the observed bone frequencies for each part of body for each pile of bones in the tombs conform to an expected count calculated from relative frequencies of these parts of body in a complete body. A non-significant chi-square value would suggest random selection of bones from one or more complete skeletons. Because of the claims made by Piggott as to the nature of the burial deposit at Lanhill and by Strömberg for Ramshög and Carlshögen — successive inhumation — it was considered that such a test might be suitable for these sites. The results showed that the proportions of parts of body do not conform to what might ideally be expected if whole bodies were interred. These tests were all significant at the 0.001% level. Suspecting that phalanges might be skewing the results, these tests were repeated again, excluding phalanges, but again the null hypothesis of similarity was rejected at the same confidence level.

To incorporate general preservation factors into the

Fig. 4. The total numbers of bones, according to piles and parts of the body, recovered from Ramshög.

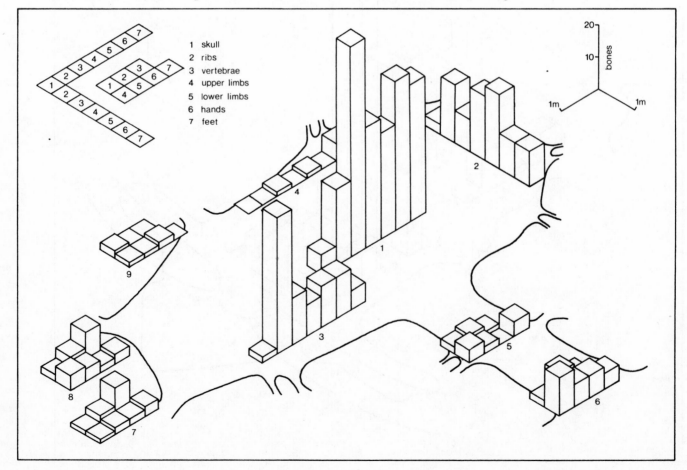

1 skull
2 ribs
3 vertebrae
4 upper limbs
5 lower limbs
6 hands
7 feet

analysis, it was decided to use Spearman's rank coefficient of correlation, as it would be very difficult to specify exactly the effects of preservation on the expected frequencies in a chi-square test. Nevertheless, we may fairly confidently assign a rank, in terms of expected relative frequencies, to each part of the body, taking into account that some bones decay more rapidly than others. Hand and foot bones, although they are small and likely to be lost in excavation, are ranked first as they occur twice as frequently as all other bones put together. Ribs and vertebrae are given higher ranks than the more robust upper and lower limbs as they occur twice as frequently and, as we noted above, numbers of ribs are likely to be overestimated as a result of breakage. The lower limbs are assigned a higher rank than the upper limbs, as they include the larger pelvic bones and are generally more robust. The expected ranking, if a random selection of bones were made, would conform to the ideal normal ranking, even taking preservation factors into account. We are using the test in an attempt to see if (a) complete corpses were interred within the tombs or if (b) a random selection might have been made from the bones of corpses which had decayed elsewhere and interred within the tombs. In the tests there was only one significant correlation, Luckington. The test was significant for the entire burial deposit at Ramshög but was not significant for each discrete pile of bones in which there was a sufficient number of observations to use the test (tables 2–4).

We do not pretend that a rank test, or the manner in which we have employed chi-square, has established in an entirely satisfactory manner that complete corpses were not buried in the tombs or that selection of bones from corpses decaying elsewhere was not made at random, but we do feel that these hypotheses have, at least, not been falsified by the tests and provide a reasonable basis on which to proceed. Indeed Ashbee notes, in relation to Fussell's Lodge, that 'small normally unresistant bones which should have been the first to decay were preserved, at the same time quite massive bones were sometimes far from sound' (Ashbee 1966, p. 37). A similar situation appears to occur in the Swedish tombs. We suggest that a non-random selection of the bone material must have taken place at some point, before or after interment.

Differences in the selection and treatment of parts of body

We have already noted that the histograms of fre-

Fig. 5. The total numbers of bones, according to sections of the tomb and parts of the body, recovered from Carlshögen.

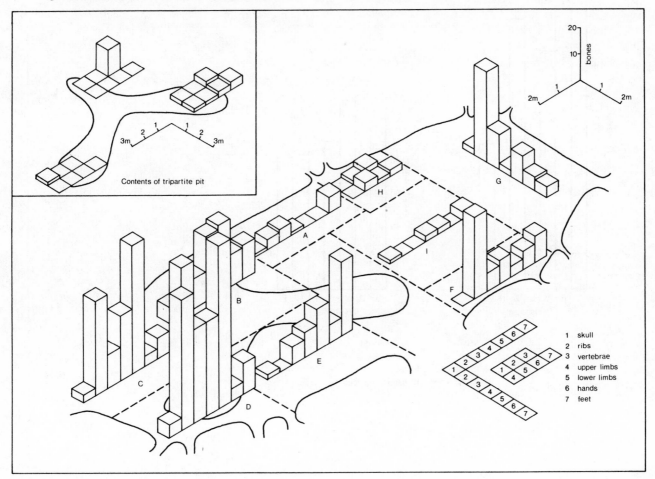

Fig. 6. Total numbers of bones according to parts of the body.

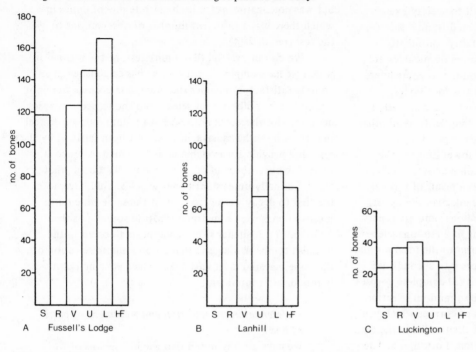

A   Fussell's Lodge

B   Lanhill

C   Luckington

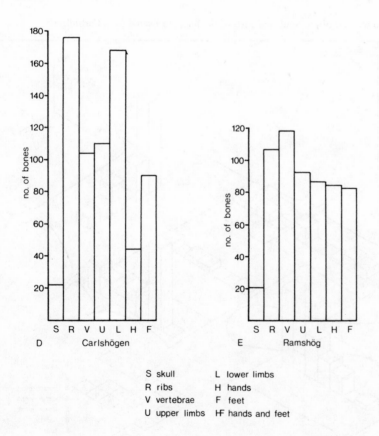

D   Carlshögen

E   Ramshög

S skull   L lower limbs
R ribs   H hands
V vertebrae   F feet
U upper limbs   HF hands and feet

Table 2. *Spearman's rank coefficient of correlation used to test for random selection of classes of bones from complete bodies at Fussell's Lodge (A—E), Lanhill (La) and Luckington (Lu)*

	Observed								Expected
	A1	A2	B	C	D	E	La	Lu	
Skull	4	3	3	1	4	5	6	6	6
Ribs	6	6	3	6	3	6	5	3	3
Vertebrae	1	4	4.5	5	1	3	1	2	2
Upper	2.5	1.5	2	2	5	1	4	4	5
Lower	2.5	1.5	1	3	2	2	3	5	4
Phalanges	5	5	6	4	6	4	2	1	1
$r_s =$	0.1	0.13	0.73	0.77	0.03	0.14	0.6	0.91	

Table 3. *Spearman's rank coefficient of correlation used to test for random selection of classes of bones from complete bodies at Carlshögen and Ramshög*

	Carlshögen		Ramshög	
	Observed	Expected	Observed	Expected
Skull	6	6	6	6
Ribs	2	3	3	3
Vertebrae	5	2	2	2
Upper	4	5	4	5
Lower	1	4	5	4
Phalanges	3	1	1	1
$r_s =$	0.31		0.94	

Table 4. *Spearman's rank coefficient of correlation used to test for random selection of classes of bones from complete bodies in the sections at Carlshögen (A—G) and piles of bones at Ramshög (1—6)*

	Carlshögen							Ramshög					Expected
	A	B	C	D	E	F	G	1	2	3	5	6	
Skull	4	6	6	5	5	6	5	6	6	6	5	5	6
Ribs	2	4	2	2	6	1	1	5	4	1	3	2	3
Vertebrae	1	5	4	3	4	4	2	2	5	3	6	4	2
Upper	5	2	3	3	3	3	5	3	3	5	2	1	5
Lower	3	1	1	1	2	5	3	4	1	4	4	3	4
Phalanges	1	3	5	4	1	2	4	1	2	2	1	1	1
$r_s =$	0.29	0.09	0.03	0.29	0.38	0.60	0.57	0.74	0.32	0.83	0.26	0.34	

quencies of bones according to parts of body for the piles of bones at Fussell's Lodge, Ramshög and Carlshögen show distinct differences within each tomb (figs. 3, 4, 5). The standard deviations and variances, calculated from the percentages, vary considerably, from 7.63 and 48.54 in pile B, to 15.25 and 193.78 in pile A2 at Fussell's Lodge. At Ramshög they ranged between 6.24 and 38.97 in pile 6 to 12.20 and 148.97 in pile 7, with slightly more variance than this at Carlshögen.

Chi-square was calculated for the piles, testing for independence. In other words, the null hypothesis set up was that the proportions of the parts of body do not differ significantly from pile to pile. This was rejected at the 0.001% level at Fussell's Lodge, Ramshög and Carlshögen and indicates a strong association between different piles and different combinations of parts of body, and further confirms that significant differences exist from pile to pile within each tomb (tables 5—7). We may note that the main contributions to deviation from the expected come from vertebrae and lower limbs at Fussell's Lodge, ribs, vertebrae and foot bones at Ramshög, and ribs together with upper and lower limbs at Carlshögen. Goodman and Kruskal's lambda measures are all close to zero — parts of body and piles of

bones are not mutually predictable. Where possible, chi-square was also calculated for pairs of piles. At Fussell's Lodge the null hypothesis of no difference was sustained for piles A and C only, at Ramshög for piles 2 and 6. At Carlshögen the null hypothesis was rejected in all cases at the 0.001% significance level, except between C and D (0.05%). Again, all the lambda measures were close to zero.

As the associations between parts of body and piles of bones were extremely complicated, these were investigated further by principal components analysis (hereafter PCA), carried out on the Cambridge IBM 370/165 computer. The analyses were conducted on standardised frequencies of parts of body according to pile, correlation matrices being calculated both between piles and between parts of body.

The component scores for piles of bones at Fussell's Lodge are plotted on fig. 7A. The main feature is the general spread of piles, and in particular the separation of pile D from the others and from pile C. From the correlation values representing the structure of the respective principal components, it is clear that this separation of D is due to a higher proportion of vertebrae and a lower proportion of upper limbs in D. Both C and D are piles of similar size located towards the entrance of the mortuary enclosure, each com-

Table 5. *Fussell's Lodge: chi-square test for independence between piles of bones, excluding ribs and phalanges* $(X^2 = 37.98)$

	A1	A2	B	C	D	E	Total
Skull	29	8	60	9	7	5	118
Vertebrae	38	2	55	1	16	12	124
Upper	30	13	71	8	3	20	145
Lower	30	13	87	7	10	19	166
Total	127	36	273	25	36	56	553

Table 6. *Ramshög: chi-square test for independence between piles of bones, excluding skull* $(X^2 = 77.55)$

	1	2	3	6	Total
Ribs	24	18	43	8	93
Vertebrae	66	10	15	5	96
Upper	38	20	10	12	80
Lower	33	23	13	7	76
Hands	47	11	13	7	78
Feet	43	11	.6	5	65
Total	251	93	100	44	488

Table 7. *Carlshögen: chi-square test for independence between piles of bones in sections B–C, excluding skull and hand bones* $(X^2 = 152.10)$

	B	C	D	E	F	G	Total
Ribs	18	36	50	0	31	34	169
Vertebrae	11	13	36	7	7	13	87
Upper	24	25	36	10	9	2	106
Lower	26	49	62	16	4	10	167
Feet	13	8	12	28	10	4	75
Total	92	131	196	61	61	63	604

posed of bones from two females. A1, A2 and B, on the other hand have remains from an estimated minimum of 12, 6 and 22 individuals respectively (Grigson in Ashbee 1966). The difference between D and the rest was noted during the excavation, in that it was mistaken for a much contracted articulated burial. A1 and A2, although occurring together furthest from the enclosure entrance, are clearly separated on the second and third principal components (hereafter PC), as are A1 and B.

Component scores for parts of body indicate correlation between upper and lower limbs, high on the first PC, with ribs correspondingly low (fig. 7C). Chi-square was calculated for upper and lower limbs in all piles, to test whether the ratio of upper to lower was the same in each pile. The null hypothesis was sustained. Upper and lower limbs appear to be correlated in all piles and this agrees with the contribution of piles to the first PC. It expresses

variability in all piles, except D. Vertebrae and hand and foot bones are, respectively, high and low on the second PC, reflecting differences between C and D. They are correlated on the third PC, which can be related to differences between A and B.

The general picture to arise from Fussell's Lodge, so far, is one of several overlapping contrasts, that between pile D and the others and between C and D, A1 and A2, A1 and B. The contrasts are predominantly related to the presence/absence of ribs, vertebrae and hand and foot bones to varying degrees and in different combinations. These contrasts are also reflected in other ways. Pile D was mistaken for a much contracted articulation. In fact it consists of remains from two individuals. The limb bones in A1 were mostly complete and stacked along the axis of the barrow with skulls flanking. In B they were much more broken up and laid across the axis. Pile B contained the majority of remains of immature individuals. These differences were also contradicted in other cases. Piles C and D, next to each other consisted of the remains of two female individuals. The long bones in piles A1 and A2 were both arranged along the barrow axis, although the latter were more broken.

The differences both between the chambers in the Luckington and Lanhill barrows, and between them and the piles at Fussell's Lodge, are very clear from the plot of the component scores produced after PCA of piles and chambers according to parts of body (fig. 7B). The high proportion of ribs, vertebrae and hand and foot bones in Luckington and Lanhill separates them from all the piles at Fussell's Lodge, except D. The first PC represents the negative correlation of ribs, vertebrae and hand and foot bones with the skull, upper and lower limbs. This is clear from the plot of PC scores for parts of the body (fig. 7C). Skull, upper and lower limbs are grouped on all PCs, while ribs, vertebrae and hand and foot bones vary. So, Luckington and Lanhill differ from all the piles in Fussell's Lodge, with the exception of D. However, they differ in ways in which the piles in Fussell's Lodge differ among themselves.

The PCA for piles of bones at Ramshög shows a general spread (fig. 7D). A broad distinction may be seen between piles 2, 6 and 3 and piles 4, 8, 1 and 7. This separation can be attributed to higher proportions of ribs and upper and lower limbs in the former, and vertebrae and hand and foot bones in the latter. The separation of 4 and 9 on the second PC is largely the result of very low frequencies of all body parts in relation to the other piles. No clear spatial pattern emerges. The piles of bones within the chamber (1, 2, 3, 4) are clearly separated on the first four PCs. Remains within the chamber appear to be more highly correlated with those outside the tomb or in the passage. Another distinction may be seen between piles 2, 6, 5 and 3 and 1, 4, 7, 8 and 9, in that the former are characterised by a majority of adult remains while the latter have approximately equal numbers of adult and juvenile remains, in terms of minimum numbers of individuals present (Lepikssar in Strömberg 1971). Sex distinctions are not evident. Component scores for parts of body (fig. 7F) indicate a tight correlation between ribs, upper limbs, lower limbs and foot bones.

This picture contrasts, in an interesting manner, with that at Carlshögen. The PCA shows a clear spatial separation between the piles of bones in different areas of the tomb, between the piles in sections A, F, G and H and D, C, B and E and I. Sections A, F, G and H are all adjacent to the chamber walls to the right of the entrance to the chamber from the passage, B, C and D are to the left of the entrance and E and I fall between these two groups of sections (figs. 5 and 7E). The piles of bones in D, C and B contain the most bones with remains of a minimum number of twenty-seven individuals, A, F, G, H of fourteen, and E and I both of twelve. Sex and age distinctions are not apparent in terms of the piles in which the bones were deposited as at Ramshög. The separation of the three groups of sections appears to be based on higher proportions of upper and lower limbs in B, C and D, ribs and vertebrae in A, F, G and H and foot

bones in E and I. As will be apparent from the plot of the component scores for parts of body at Carlshögen (fig. 8A), there is considerably more variability here than at Ramshög.

The overall picture to emerge is a more clear-cut spatial separation of the piles of bones at Carlshögen, which corresponds with greater complexity of the different proportional combinations of parts of body being used to distinguish these piles, cutting across age and sex distinctions. There appears to be clear evidence for the selection and arrangement of body parts both in the English and the Swedish barrows. In the English barrows this seems to involve the arrangement of skulls and long bones and variation in the occurrence of ribs, vertebrae and hand and foot bones. In this connection, it is interesting to note the occurrence of a separate pile of ribs, vertebrae and phalanges in one corner of the chamber at Luckington, while in Lanhill, skulls are set against the chamber walls and long bones are stacked in the middle. Deliberate arrangement of body parts appears to have taken place in other English barrows (see table 1). In the Swedish

Fig. 7. A: piles of bones at Fussell's Lodge. B: piles of bones and chambers at Lanhill and Luckington. C: parts of the body at Fussell's Lodge. D: piles of bones at Ramshög. E: piles of bones in the sections at Carlshögen. F: parts of the body at Ramshög. All plotted in relation to components 1 (horizontal axis) and 2 (vertical axis). Key identifies parts of the body.

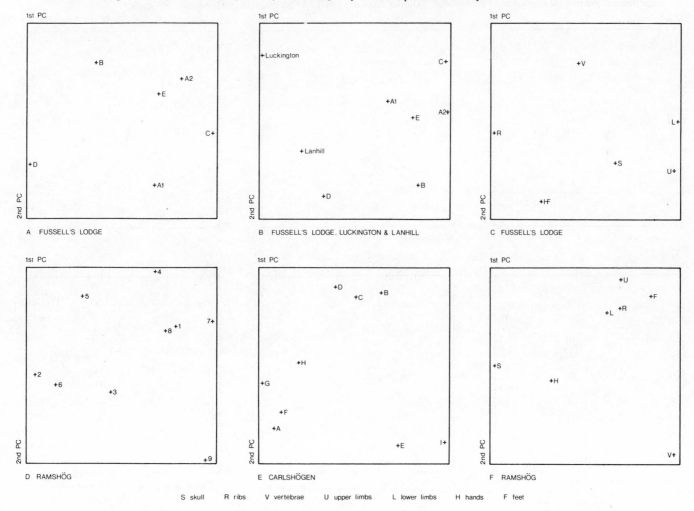

S skull   R ribs   V vertebrae   U upper limbs   L lower limbs   H hands   F feet

megaliths it is harder to summarise the variability in the selection of body parts, the relations are more complex and there are significant differences between Ramshög and Carlshögen. As to arrangement of bones, we may note that in some cases at Carlshögen ribs and vertebrae were discovered arranged on the femora, while in others, skulls appear to have been placed on top of both the upper and lower long bones (Strömberg 1971, p. 247).

Articulated/disarticulated contrasts

One main contrast in Fussell's Lodge is between articulation and disarticulation. Pile D contained selected bones from two females arranged to look like one articulated body. The proportions of parts of body distinguish it from other piles, yet it did not approximate to the ranking we would expect from an articulated inhumation. Piles A1, A2 and B also differed from D in that they contained many individuals. What we have termed a disarticulated/articulated contrast is therefore not simply differential treatment of one individual. At Lanhill there is a single articulated inhumation,

but none at Luckington or in the two Swedish tombs. Information for other English barrows is summarised in table 1.

Differentiation between adult and immature remains

A very convincing picture of differentiation between adult and immature remains emerges from PCA conducted on the data from the three English and the two Swedish sites (fig. 8D, E, F). Adult and immature remains were defined physically. In the English data immature was used to represent pre-puberty remains, but for the Swedish data we included puberty remains in this category, in order to see to what extent this might affect the results.

For the three English sites scores on the first principal component, plotted against the second for all piles and chambers, show a distinct clustering of immature parts of body, compared with the wide spread of the adult ones. The same picture arises from the PCA analyses for Ramshög and Carlshögen. Thus in both the English and the Swedish tombs there would not seem to be any significant variation between piles of bones in terms of relative frequencies of all

Fig. 8. A: parts of the body at Carlshögen. B: left and right body parts at Carlshögen. C: left and right body parts at Ramshög. D: adult and immature body parts at Fussell's Lodge. E: adult and immature body parts at Ramshög. F: adult and immature body parts at Carlshögen. All plotted in relation to components 1 (horizontal axis) and 2 (vertical axis). Key identifies body parts.

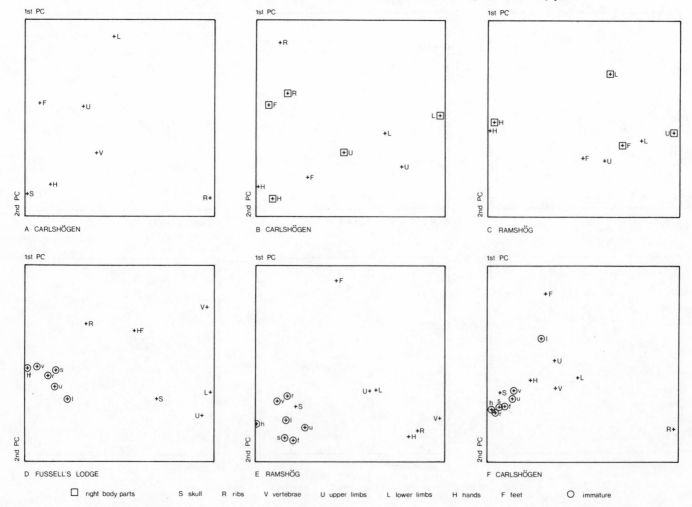

immature remains. Different immature parts of body do not appear to be distinguished. They are being treated as equivalent, and this is in contrast to adult remains.

Chi-square was used to test for general differences in the distribution of adult as opposed to immature remains in Fussell's Lodge, Ramshög and Carlshögen. In all cases the high chi-square values significant at the 0.001% level support the contention that there are significant differences in attitude towards adult and immature remains. It is important to note that at Fussell's Lodge immature ribs are relatively over-represented as compared with adult and this throws doubt on any claim that differential preservation can account solely for the differences. Similarly, the inclusion of the Swedish puberty remains did not affect the results of the analysis and suggests that the important boundary between differential treatment of parts of body was, at least for the Swedish data, between puberty and adulthood.

In the Swedish tombs no clear spatial separation could be discerned between the positioning of immature and adult remains. However, in Fussell's Lodge pile B stood out from the others in that it contained the majority of the immature remains, the others being scattered between it and A1 and A2. It also contained approximately 50% of all the bones from Fussell's Lodge. Immature remains appeared to show no structuring analagous to the adult remains. We can, perhaps, also see the lack of concern with the character of the immature remains in the scattering of some of them between piles B, A1 and A2; they were not collected into piles. B also was distinctive in that it contained all the ribs, the majority of which were immature. This is also the case at the West Kennet long barrow where, in contrast to adult remains, the majority of immature bones, found within the south east chamber, were scattered around indiscriminately (Piggott 1962).

Differentiation between left and right parts of body

So far we have considered treatment of the body in terms of parts of body. A distinction which cuts across these categories is that between right and left parts of body. We assume that any distinctions which arise must be the result of direct selection and cannot be accounted for by any factors of preservation since left and right body parts, in all but the most abnormal circumstances, have an equal chance of preservation and recovery during excavation.

Fig. 9A and fig. 9B are histograms of the relative frequencies of left and right upper and lower limb bones at Fussell's Lodge and Lanhill respectively. A null hypothesis of equal selection of right and left body parts was rejected at the 0.05 significance level for all piles in Fussell's Lodge and Lanhill, using chi-square. Data were unavailable for Luckington. There appears to be a general bias towards left limb bones. Chi-square indicated no significant differences in proportions of right and left limb bones from pile to pile at Fussell's Lodge.

PCA, with upper and lower limb bones divided into

left and right, showed no real differences to the analysis conducted on the piles and the chambers which were not divided in this way. Right and left upper and lower limb bones cluster on both plots. So, although there is a general distinction for left sides of the body, left and right upper and lower limbs do not differ much in their correlation with other parts of the body. However, the clustering is loose and the component scores for upper right and left do differ significantly, especially on the second PC. Perhaps the rather crude classification upper/lower is obscuring some finer distinction in terms of a single bone type, which alone accounts for the significant chi-square value. The sample size prevents testing this further.

Left/right distinctions are more clearly distinguishable in the Swedish tombs. The null hypothesis of equal selection of right and left upper and lower limb bones at Ramshög was rejected at the 0.05 significance level and at 0.01 at Carlshögen. There is an interesting reversal of the relationship, taking the two tombs as a whole. At Ramshög there are more right than left upper limb bones and more left than right lower limb bones, while at Carlshögen there were more left than right upper limb bones and more right than left lower limb bones. Selection for right and left limb bones differs at both tombs in accordance with upper and lower body parts (fig. 9C–D). For instance, at Carlshögen where there are more left than right upper limbs, there are more left than right ribs. The differences between the proportions of upper and lower, left and right limb bones at the two tombs were significant at the 0.05 confidence level for chi-square.

A further question arises as to whether there is any spatial variability between relative proportions of left and right bones between the piles of bones within Ramshög and Carlshögen. At Carlshögen, where possible, chi-square tests were conducted between the piles of bones within the individual sections. The null hypothesis of similarity between proportions of right and left upper limb bones was not rejected except between sections B and D and C and D, at the 0.10 and 0.05 confidence levels respectively. For right and left lower limbs, the only statistically significant differences were between sections B, C and D (fig. 10B). The null hypothesis of similarity was not rejected at Ramshög (fig. 10A). Overall, the same distinctions are apparent within the piles of bones at each tomb, but differ between the tombs. Unfortunately no data were available for left/right distinctions for ribs at Ramshög. Such distinctions are apparent at Carlshögen where left ribs are proportionally more frequent than right. Spatially, there is a difference between sections B and C, with more left than right ribs in the former and vice versa in the latter. Proportions of left/right ribs were too small in the other sections of the tomb to have statistical significance, as were those between hand and foot bones at both tombs. PCAs (fig. 8B–C) support the conclusions drawn above that there are significant differences in the manner in which left and right body parts were treated.

Now, if we consider the tripartite pit at Carlshögen,

Fig. 9. Total numbers of bones according to left and right body parts.

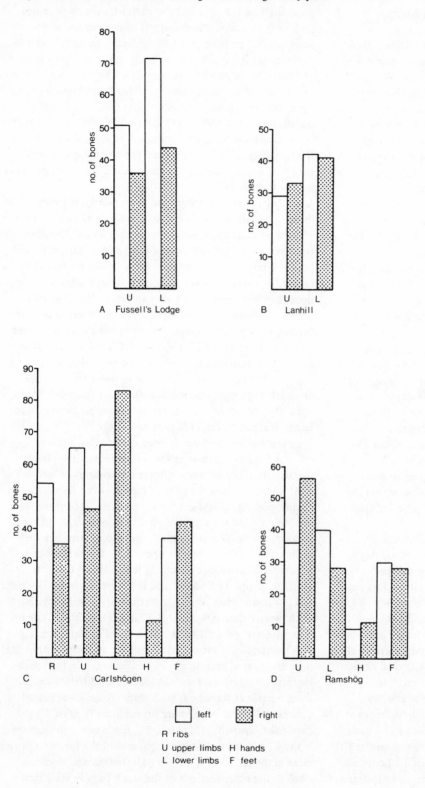

A   Fussell's Lodge
B   Lanhill
C   Carlshögen
D   Ramshög

left   right

R ribs
U upper limbs   H hands
L lower limbs   F feet

Fig. 10. A: total numbers of bones in Ramshög (according to piles). B: total numbers of bones in Carlshögen (according to sections), both divided into left and right body parts.

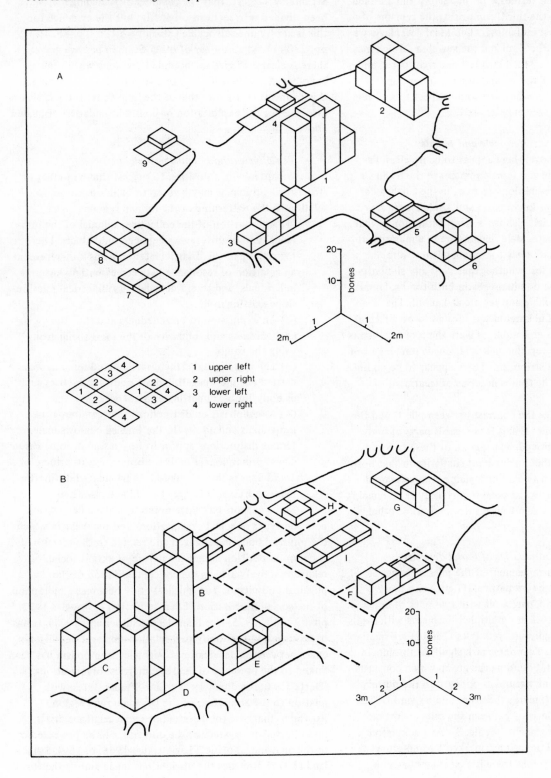

which underlies sections B, C, D and E (fig. 5), a skull is represented in one arm, vertebrae in the second and a mixed collection of bones in the third, comprising the remains of between four and seven individuals (Lepiksaar 1971). As we noted above it is only the skull and the vertebrae which may not be unambiguously divided into left and right parts, and in this pit they are spatially separated from other bone classes which is precisely what we should expect to find if right/left distinctions are being stressed.

Differentiation between male and female

As was noted above, there appear to be no clear distinctions between male and female remains in the Swedish tombs. By contrast, distinctions do exist in the English data. The adult remains from Luckington and Lanhill were sexed and Luckington, especially, shows a clear distinction in that female remains dominate. Male remains are in a majority at Lanhill. Three chi-square tests for independence were performed in order to test whether there was any similarity in the treatment of the dominant sex in both tombs, female in both examples and male and female at Lanhill. The female remains from Luckington were found to be different from the male remains at Lanhill, as were the female remains from both sites. However, the male and female remains from Lanhill had a similar distribution. There appear to be no links between the sexes at the tombs in terms of treatment of body parts.

In Fussell's Lodge the contrast between pile D and the others, and between piles C and D as regards parts of body has already been mentioned. The second of these two contrasts seems to contradict an apparent similarity in that both consist of remains from two adult females. Analysis could not proceed further as, in the bone report, only skull remains are specifically sexed. Table 1 gives information for other English sites.

Marking of the boundaries of burial deposits

We can see the arrangement of the piles of bones at Fussell's Lodge as being symmetrical. Pile B, with most remains, is in the centre, over a pit with two piles of bones on either side. A1 and A2 are multiple interments with skulls and long bones artificially ordered. Piles C and D are smaller collections of remains. Two pots mark significant points in the linear arrangement, bounding the group which contrasts with pile D. An ox skull, natural as opposed to the pottery which is manufactured, marks the other end beyond D. The various overlapping contrasts between the piles are articulated around this arrangement (see fig. 3). At Luckington the limits of the burial deposit are marked by immature skulls. In the Swedish tombs there is a clear emphasis on boundedness and this appears to increase in importance through time. Carlshögen is the later of the two tombs by approximately 250 radiocarbon years (Strömberg 1971, p. 202). Here the remains are all confined to demarcated sec-

tions within the tomb, contrasting with those at Ramshög. Strömberg suggests that the chamber at Ramshög may have been divided into sections originally, but the evidence for this is hardly unequivocable (Strömberg 1969, p. 86, 1971, pp. 250–1). At a number of other Scanian passage graves there is clear evidence for bounded divisions within the chamber (Strömberg 1971, pp. 251–66). It is interesting, in this connection, to note that at the later tomb there is clearer evidence for the exploitation of bodily boundaries, discussed above.

The physical body and the social body

We are now in a position to suggest that a number of structuring principles may be seen to be in operation in relation to the patterning of the human remains:

(1) An assertion of the collective, a denial of the individual and of differences between individuals. The regrouping of the disarticulated remains may represent an assertion of resonance between essentially discrete individuals, and thus a denial of asymmetrical relationships existing in life.

(2) An expression of boundedness and thus the exclusiveness and solidarity of the local social group using the tomb.

(3) The regrouping of the disarticulated remains was carried out incorporating basic body symmetries such as body/limbs, upper/lower, right/left.

(4) An emphasis on distinctions between immature individuals and adults. In the English barrows male/female distinctions appear to be stressed in some cases. These principles are in direct opposition to principles 1 and 2, as is the articulated/disarticulated distinction made at Fussell's Lodge, Lanhill and elsewhere.

Some authors have attempted to make a connection between types of social organisations and the ways in which the physical body is perceived and related to the social body. A common position is that the nature of extant social relations actively affects the conceptualisation of the physical body itself. The physical body becomes a metaphor of the social organisation (Ellen 1972, 1977; Douglas 1973, pp. 93–112, 1975; Needham 1973; Sutherland 1977). It has been suggested that body-part relations may reflect differences between social relations. Right/left symbolism has been linked to the presence of dual symmetrical organisations (Hertz 1960; Needham 1973). Lévi-Strauss states, with relation to the aborigines of the Drysdale river region, Australia, that 'the total system of social relations, itself bound up with a system of the universe, can be projected on to the anatomical plane' (Lévi-Strauss 1966, p. 169). Sutherland (1977) discusses the distinctions made among the Rom gypsies of the United States between upper and lower parts of the body. Lower body parts are deemed to be polluting, the upper pure. This results in a whole series of rules concerning washing, dress, cooking, eating and other practical activities. Such behaviour has obvious practical difficulties, such as the need to wash clothes from the upper and lower parts of the body separately. Sutherland suggests that this reflects, metaphorically, the problems involved in maintaining a moral social boundary between themselves (Rom) and non-gypsies in a situation of economic interdependence (cf. Okely's (1979) work on English gypsies).

Douglas is most explicit about the nature of the relationship between the physical and the social body. To her (1966, 1973) the first logical categories are seen as social products. Social relations provide the prototype for the logical relations between things: 'the organic system provides an analogy of the social system' (1973, p. 12), 'the more value people set on social constraints, the more the value they set on symbols of bodily control' (1973, p. 16), 'the social body constrains the way the physical body is perceived. The physical experience of the body, always modified by the social categories through which it is known, sustains a particular view of society. There is a continual exchange of meanings between the two kinds of bodily experience so that each reinforces the categories of the other' (1973, p. 93), 'the physical body is a microcosm of society' (1973, p. 101).

A major problem with these positions is that they fail to take sufficient account of differences existing between the activity of individuals and groups, and their perception of these activities. There is little consideration of ideology. Bodily symbolism simply reflects social relations and functions to maintain existing social categorisations. A dialectical conception is not apparent, the symbolic use of the body is not conceived in such a way that it could have, in itself, any symbolic power to act back on social relations, mediate and serve to structure them.

Douglas does suggest a more promising line of approach, although this plays only a minor part in her overall theoretical framework, when she states 'any control system since it has to be made reasonable . . . must appeal to ultimate principles about the nature of man and of the cosmos . . . Naked power is decently clothed and made legitimate'. We are concerned with body symbolism in relation to mortuary ritual — a specific moment in the overall social totality, which may be regarded as an autonomous field of social activities which has its conditions of existence in other social relations. Body symbolism may be regarded as possessing multivalent levels of meaning. It can represent, misrepresent and both represent and misrepresent social relations at the same time. Bourdieu (1977, p. 114) suggests that

> understanding ritual practice is not a question of decoding the internal logic of symbolism but of restoring its practical necessity by relating it to the real conditions of its genesis, that is, to the conditions in which it functions, and the means it uses to attain them, are defined. It means . . . reconstituting . . . the

significance and functions that agents in a determinate social formation can (and must) confer on a determinate practice or experience, given the practical taxonomies which organize their perception.

We have already argued in the first section of this paper that differential access to power is likely to be a characteristic of Neolithic societies in southern England and southern Sweden. We suggest that such systems of social control by lineage heads and/or elders is in direct contradiction with another major structuring principle on which such societies operate — socialised production and direct, unmediated reciprocity and exchange relations between kin groups. By their exercise of social control such as denying juniors access to women, ritual information and so on and using procreative women as part of the exchange relationships operating between local lineage groups, the lineage heads or elders are, in effect, transforming kin relations into political relations in order to maintain their authority. In such societies, typically, the direct expression of material interests is heavily censored and political authority relatively uninstitutionalised. The only means of legitimating an essentially arbitrary system of social control, by the few over the many, is 'if the values they pursue or propose are presented in the misrecognisable guise of the values in which the group recognises itself' (Bourdieu 1977, p. 22). The natural and social world must appear to be self-evident. As we have seen, ritual activities by their very nature are one of the most effective means of carrying this out. Such activities serve to lay down a clear dividing line between the thinkable (the present social order) and the unthinkable (some other social order).

We suggest that the principles according to which the human remains were placed within the tombs formed part and parcel of the reproduction of power relations, designed to secure the misrecognition of the arbitrary nature of these relations and secure the reproduction rather than the transformation of the social order, to mystify the contradictions existing between two major structuring principles upon which these societies were ordered, the symmetry of kin relations and the asymmetry of power/political relations. We can clearly see this in relation to principles 1, 2 and 3 (see above). The collective, rather than the individual, is asserted; the regrouping of disarticulated remains incorporates, in the expression of symmetry between body parts, a denial of asymmetrical relationships in life; the stress on boundedness achieves the need for solidarity. That certain of the structuring principles in operation in relation to interment exist in a contradictory relationship should not surprise us in a situation in which major structuring principles in operation in the social totality are in direct contradiction. Ritual activities may very well move out of resonance with the social reality they serve to misrepresent, precipitating under specific circumstances a change of social consciousness among individual actors, which, were it not for new forms of legitimation, would result in a transformation of social relations.

In these mortuary activities we can see an ambiguous relationship between nature and culture, a projection of the cultural (the arbitrary) as if it represents the self-evident natural order of things. An inherent contradiction would seem to reside in the culture/nature dichotomy in relation to the human body. Man is essentially a cultural animal yet the physical body is natural. This naturalism of the body is transformed into a cultural product by bodily posture, gesture and by means of clothing and ornamentation. At death it decays and reverts to a natural state in the form of the human skeleton. The selection and arrangement of classes of bones transforms the natural state of the skeleton into a cultural product (fig. 11). The disarticulated remains may then be reconstituted in a natural or purely artificial way. So, in Fussell's Lodge, disarticulated remains are arranged both purely artificially, and at the same time reconstituted in a semblance of an articulation (natural order). The reconstitution of bones in terms of basic body symmetries is itself ambiguous; it is both a natural ordering (a real material opposition) and a cultural ordering. We noted in the first section of this chapter that this is precisely what ideological objectification seeks to achieve.

Conclusions

The patterning of the human remains in the English and the Swedish barrows appears to be in concordance with the expectations we set out in the earlier part of the paper as to the features we would expect ritual activity, conceived as a form of ideological activity, to display in small-scale societies. We have only considered one element, within an overall complex of activities, the patterning of the human osteological material. However, there is good reason to believe that in the regions we have considered, the human body itself provided the dominant symbolic focus in interaction. It would be difficult to find a more powerful or deeply emotional stimulus than the human body itself. An essential sequel to the work is to consider other aspects of the mortuary practices to assess the extent to which they contradict or support our interpretations. For instance, preliminary analyses of the abundant ceramic material found directly outside the entrance to Ramshög supports our contention that an expression of boundedness was an important structuring principle. Ceramic design elements were classified in terms of boundedness/unboundedness. A bounded design is defined as one delineated on all sides by lines with internal filling (e.g. triangles or horizontal or vertical bands). Unbounded designs are open on one or more sides (simple slashed strokes, wavy or zig-zag lines). The pottery at Ramshög, contrasting with settlement ceramics, has a design structure consisting predominantly of strongly bounded design elements in tightly structured sequences, with a circumscribed use of internal space.

The position worked out in this chapter is at odds with much of the recent discussion in the literature with regard to the relationship between mortuary practices and social organisation (Binford 1972*b*; Brown 1971; Fleming 1972, 1973; Goldstein 1976; Renfrew 1973, 1975; Rothschild 1979; Saxe 1970; Shennan 1975; Tainter 1975, 1977, 1978). In this literature social structure, conceived in an empiricist sense as observable social relations, is considered to be, more or less, directly reflected in mortuary practices, which become a concretion or reification of social structure in an archaeologically visible form. In this perspective the occasion of death becomes just another arena for the expression of social roles and the maintenance of social structure. The thesis that mortuary ritual acts to reaffirm the social order does not in itself explain anything of the specific content or context of that activity. The content is overlooked and is only considered in its supposedly instrumental effect in maintaining the social structure. It fails to explain why certain items should be repeatedly chosen as grave furniture, their specific arrangement, or why other elements of material culture should be considered unsuitable for this purpose. We believe that by a consideration of the structuring principles in operation we have been able to give a plausible account of both the form and the content of the patterning of the human remains in the regions we have considered. Renfrew (1973, 1975) suggested that it was collective identity which was stressed within megaliths. In this we are in agreement, with the important caveat that the expression of collective identity was a direct result of asymmetrical social relations. Mortuary practices do not just reflect, they also invert and misrepresent. In this way they may act as a powerful means to reproduce and legitimate the social order.

Fig. 11. The somatic triangle.

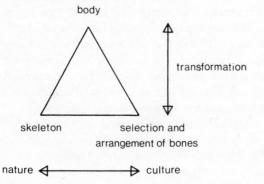

References

Althusser, L. (1971) 'Ideology and ideological state apparatuses' in L. Althusser *Lenin and Philosophy and Other Essays*, New Left Books, London

Althusser, L. (1976) *Essays in Self-Criticism*, New Left Books, London

Althusser, L. (1977) *For Marx*, New Left Books, London

Althusser, L. & Balibar, E. (1970) *Reading Capital*, New Left Books, London

Ashbee, P. (1958) 'The Fussell's Lodge long barrow', *Antiquity* 32: 106–11

Ashbee, P. (1964) 'Radiocarbon dating of the Fussell's Lodge long barrow', *Antiquity* 38: 139–40

Ashbee, P. (1966) 'The Fussell's Lodge long barrow excavations 1957', *Archaeologia* 100: 1–80

Ashbee, P. (1970) *The Earthen Long Barrow in Britain*, Dent, London

Atkinson, R.J.C. (1965) 'Wayland's Smithy', *Antiquity* 39: 126–33

Binford, L. (1972a) 'Galley Pond Mound' in L. Binford *An Archaeological Perspective*, Seminar Press, London

Binford, L. (1972b) 'Mortuary practices: their study and their potential' in L. Binford *An Archaeological Perspective*, Seminar Press, London

Binford, L. & Bertram, J. (1977) 'Bone frequencies and attritional processes' in L. Binford (ed.) *For Theory Building in Archaeology*, Academic Press, London

Bloch, M. (1975) 'Property and the end of affinity' in M. Bloch (ed.) *Marxist Analyses and Social Anthropology*, ASA, London

Bloch, M. (1977a) 'The past and the present in the past', *Man* 12: 278–92

Bloch, M. (1977b) 'The disconnection between rank and power as a process' in J. Friedman & M. Rowlands (ed.) *The Evolution of Social Systems*, Duckworth, London

Bourdieu, P. (1977) *Outline of a Theory of Practice*, Cambridge University Press, Cambridge

Bourdieu, P. (1979) 'Symbolic power', *Critique of Anthropology* 4: 77–86

Brown, J. (1971) 'Introduction' in J. Brown (ed.) 'Approaches to the social dimensions of mortuary practices', *Memoirs of the Society for American Archaeology* 25: 1–6

Burenhult, G. (1973) *En långdös vid Hindby Mosse*, Malmö Museum, Malmö

Chesterman, J.T. (1977) 'Burial sites in a Cotswold long barrow', *Man* 12: 22–32

Corcoran, J. (1970) 'The giant's graves, Luckington', *Wiltshire Archaeological Magazine* 65: 39–63

Cornwall, I. (1956) *Bones for the Archaeologist*, Phoenix, London

Crawford, O.G.S. (1925) *The Long Barrows of the Cotswolds*, Gloucester

Douglas, M. (1966) *Purity and Danger*, Routledge and Kegan Paul, London

Douglas, M. (1973) *Natural Symbols*, Penguin, Harmondsworth

Douglas, M. (1975) 'Do dogs laugh?' in M. Douglas *Implicit Meanings*, Routledge and Kegan Paul, London

Ellen, R. (1972) 'The marsupial in Nuaulu ritual behaviour', *Man* 7: 223–38

Ellen, R. (1977) 'Anatomical classification and the semiotics of the body' in J. Blacking (ed.) *The Anthropology of the Body*, ASA, London

Firth, R. (1973) *Symbols Public and Private*, Allen and Unwin, London

Fleming, A. (1972) 'Vision and design: approaches to ceremonial monument typology', *Man* 7: 57–73

Fleming, A. (1973) 'Tombs for the living', *Man* 8: 177–93

Geras, N. (1972) 'Althusser's Marxism: an assessment and an account', *New Left Review* 71: 57–86

Giddens, A. (1979) *Central Problems in Social Theory*, Macmillan, London

Goldstein, L. (1976) *Spatial Structure and Social Organisation: Regional Manifestations of Mississippian Society*, doctoral dissertation, University Microfilms, Ann Arbor

Greenwell, W. (1877) *British Barrows*, Clarendon, Oxford

Hertz, R. (1960) *Death and the Right Hand*, R. Needham (trans.), Cohen and West

Hirst, P. (1976) 'Problems and advances in the theory of ideology', Opening session of the First Communist University of Cambridge, Cambridge University Communist Party

Keiller, A. & Piggott, S. (1938) 'Excavation of an untouched chamber in the Lanhill long barrow', *Proceedings of the Prehistoric Society* 4: 122–50

Kuhn, T. (1970) *The Structure of Scientific Revolutions*, 2nd edition, University of Chicago Press, Chicago

Larrain, J. (1979) *The Concept of Ideology*, Hutchinson, London

Lepiksaar, J. (1971) 'Das skelettmaterial von Carlshögen und Ramshög' in L.M. Strömberg (ed.). *Die Megalithgräber von Hagestad*, Gleerups, Lund

Lévi-Strauss, C. (1966) *The Savage Mind*, Weidenfeld and Nicolson, London

Lukács, G. (1971) *History and Class Consciousness*, Merlin, London

Marx, K. (1959) *Economic and Philosophic Manuscripts of 1844*, M. Milligan (trans.), Moscow

Mauss, M. (1973) 'Techniques of the body', *Economy and Society* 2(1): 70–88

Meillassoux, C. (1960) 'Éssai d'intérpretation du phénomène économique dans les sociétés traditionelles d'autosubsistence', *Cahiers d'Études Africaines* 4: 38–67

Meillassoux, C. (1972) 'From reproduction to production', *Economy and Society* 1: 93–105

Morgan, F. de M. (1959) 'The excavation of a long barrow at Nutbane, Hants.', *Proceedings of the Prehistoric Society* 25: 15–51

Needham, R. (1973) (ed.) *Right and Left: Essays on Dual Symbolic Classification*, University of Chicago Press, Chicago

Okely, J. (1979) 'An anthropological contribution to the history and archaeology of an ethnic group' in B. Burnham & J. Kingsbury (eds.) *Space, Hierarchy and Society*, BAR, International Series 59: 81–92

Ollman, B. (1976) *Alienation*, Cambridge University Press, Cambridge

Passmore, A.D. (1942) 'Chute Barrow 1', *Wiltshire Archaeological Magazine* 50: 100–1

Piggott, S. (1962) *The West Kennett Long Barrow Excavations 1955–6*, Ministry of Works Archaeological Report No. 4, HM Stationery Office

Pitt-Rivers, A. (1898) *Excavations in Cranbourne Chase IV*

Renfrew, C. (1973) 'Monuments, mobilization and social organisation in neolithic Wessex' in C. Renfrew (ed.) *The Explanation of Culture Change*, Duckworth, London

Renfrew, C. (1975) 'Megaliths, territories and populations' in S.J. de Laet (ed.) *Acculturation and Continuity in Atlantic Europe*, Dissertationes Archaeologicae Gandenses

Rey, P. (1979) 'Class contradiction in lineage societies', *Critique of Anthropology* 4: 41–60

Rolleston, G. (1876) 'On the people of the long barrow period', *Journal of the Royal Anthropological Institute* 5: 120–73

Rothschild, N. (1979) 'Mortuary behaviour and social organisation at Indian Knoll and Dickinson mounds', *American Antiquity* 44(4): 658–75

Sahlins, M. (1976) *Culture and Practical Reason*, University of Chicago Press, Chicago

Saxe, A. (1970) *Social Dimensions of Mortuary Practices*, doctoral dissertation, University Microfilms, Ann Arbor

Shennan, S.E. (1975) 'The social organisation at Branč', *Antiquity* 39: 279–87

Strömberg, M. (1969) 'Die megalithgräber bei Hagestad' in G. Daniel & S. Piggott (eds.) *Megaliths and Ritual*, III Atlantic Colloquium, Moesgård

Strömberg, M. (ed.) (1971) *Die Megalithgräber von Hagestad*, Gleerups, Lund

Sutherland, A. (1977) 'The body as a social symbol among the Rom' in J. Blacking (ed.) *The Anthropology of the Body*, ASA, London

Tainter, J. (1975) 'Social inference and mortuary practices: an experiment in numerical classification', *World Archaeology* 7: 1–15

Tainter, J. (1977) 'Modelling change in prehistoric social systems' in
  L. Binford (ed.) *For Theory Building in Archaeology*,
  Academic Press, London

Tainter, J. (1978) 'Mortuary practices and the study of prehistoric
  social systems' in M. Schiffer (ed.) *Advances in Archaeological
  Method and Theory Vol. 1*, Academic Press, London

Thurnam, J. (1854) 'Description of a chambered tumulus near Uley,
  Gloucestershire', *Archaeological Journal* 11: 315–27

Thurnam, J. (1857) 'On a Cromlech–Tumulus called Lugbury, near
  Littleton Drew', *Wiltshire Archaeological Magazine* 3:
  164–73

Thurnam, J. (1869) 'On ancient British barrows, especially those of
  Wiltshire and the adjoining counties. Part I, long barrows',
  Archaeologia 42: 161–243

Turner, V. (1967) *The Forest of Symbols*, Cornell University Press,
  New York

Turner, V. (1969) *The Ritual Process*, Penguin, Harmondsworth

Chapter 13

**Ideology, change and
the European
Early Bronze Age**
Stephen Shennan

Shennan examines economic, political and ideological change in the development of a bronze industry and in the appearance of particularly rich graves at the end of the Neolithic and beginning of the Bronze Age in Europe. In Wessex, southeast Spain and Brittany there is evidence for the development first of a hierarchy legitimated by communal ritual, and later by the naturalisation of hierarchy in the material symbols associated with individuals, for example at burial. There was thus a change in the representation of social hierarchy. In central Europe, on the other hand, the growth of a hierarchy is associated directly with individual burial differentiation. The adoption of the latter mode of representation in western Europe was associated with the spread of Bell Beakers and the overall structure, which is characterised by continual change and search for material items of prestige, plays a part in the development of the Early Bronze Age metal industry. It is emphasised that both the local and inter-regional contexts need to be examined in the explanation of change.

The end of the Neolithic and the beginning of the Bronze Age (c. 2500–1500 BC) have long been seen as a period of significant change in European prehistory. This inference has been based on the marked changes visible in certain aspects of the archaeological record in many parts of Europe at this time, and also on the assumption implicit in the Three Age system that the transition from one age to another must be of considerable importance. Two aspects of the archaeological record have elicited particular attention, the appearance of bronze artefacts and that of burials containing relatively spectacular grave goods. The most

common interpretation of the evidence is an increase in social differentiation associated with the control of metal resources and their exchange. In the continuing discussion about the factors responsible for the development of this reconstructed state of affairs two main views have been proposed. According to the earlier view, of which Childe was the classical exponent, the changes resulted from diffusion from the east Mediterranean centres of civilisation, as a result of the latter's interest in obtaining central and west European metal resources (e.g. Childe 1958). More recently, Renfrew (e.g. 1973a) has argued that we must seek the explanation for the changes in terms of autonomous locally operating processes. In this paper it will be suggested, first, that the situations reconstructed from the archaeological record need to be critically re-examined, and second, that both frameworks adopted for explanation are inadequate. In these endeavours it is necessary to assign a key role to the notion of ideology.

In this context I wish to adopt the view proposed by Giddens (1979, p. 188) that investigating the ideological is concerned with 'how structures of signification are mobilised to legitimate the sectional interests of hegemonic groups'. This almost invariably involves, as one aspect, 'the naturalisation of the present . . . , inhibiting recognition of the mutable, historical character of human society, . . . in which social relations appear to have the fixed and immutable

character of natural laws' (Giddens 1979, p. 195). Ideologically, the interests of the dominant group in the *status
quo* may be represented as universal, or the existence of
differences may be denied. In such a view it remains possible
to maintain a useful conceptual separation between the economic, the political and the ideological, and to see them as
reacting with one another in different ways, at different
times and on different spatial scales.

While such legitimating ideologies play a key role in
maintaining the position of dominant groups, it should not
be thought that this requires the majority of the social
actors to share in the dominant ideology; this is to regard
people as dupes. Even though many may see through it, they
may still be forced to accept it as one of the conditions of
their own actions, a fact which returns us to the necessity of
relating ideological to political and economic power.

These ideas have a bearing first of all on the situation
which we reconstruct from the archaeological record. Specifically, in the case under consideration here, while the inference of the development of a bronze industry of some kind is
uncontroversial, it is not necessarily the case that the appearance of rich burials stems from an increase in social differentiation. It has been much emphasised recently (e.g. Hodder
1980; Parker Pearson, this volume) that differentiation in
burial is a form of social categorisation. The distribution of
power in society will relate in some way to the categorisation
of individuals but the two will not necessarily be isomorphic
and, indeed, the categorisation may be completely or
partially misleading; this point has been made elegantly by
Bloch (1977) in his discussion of the disconnection between
power and rank among the Merina of Madagascar.

From this viewpoint one could suggest that the contemporaneous appearance of rich individual burials in the
archaeological record of many parts of Europe in the Early
Bronze Age was the result of the rise of an ideology which
sought to legitimate social differentiation, not by hiding it,
but by representing it as natural and immutable through the
use of material culture in the form of prestige items and
ritual symbols which constantly reiterated the message. In
such circumstances material culture as ideology could be said
to be a very direct transformation of social organisation. Of
course, it is not simply a matter of the archaeological appearance changing but of the organisation staying the same. The
position taken here is that ideology is not simply a passive
epiphenomenon of political and economic organisation but
is itself an active force; I will attempt to show how in this
example a new ideology acted back on the organisation and
resulted in a new social dynamic.

In the light of the ideas outlined above, the intention
now is to take some of those areas which have always played
a major part in discussions of the beginning of the European
Bronze Age and to examine those aspects of their archaeological record which have attracted attention, from the
point of view of the reconstructions which have been
suggested and the explanations offered for them.

In Wessex the most notable feature of the late Neolithic and earliest Bronze Age (the Mount Pleasant period of
Burgess (1980)) is the building of the large-scale ceremonial
centres, such as Avebury, Durrington Walls and Marden.
Settlements of this period are very little known in Wessex,
although examples from elsewhere suggest that they were
small, scattered farmsteads or hamlets. Burials present a
problem of dating since the majority seem to have been
unaccompanied by grave goods, and those goods that do
occur tend to be chronologically undiagnostic; it is only in
the later part of the Mount Pleasant period, in the Bell
Beaker phase, that diagnostic grave goods occur in any number and exhibit much inter-burial variation. Nevertheless, the
burials of the Mount Pleasant period in Wessex do show
variation in other respects; both inhumation and cremation
occur, while the spatial and monumental context of the
burials also varies, including the occurrence of cremations at
some of the earlier henge monuments, for example the first
phase of Stonehenge.

In the succeeding developed Early Bronze Age
(Burgess' Overton phase) the construction of large-scale
ceremonial centres ceased. Some sort of activity continued
at the existing centres, although altered in character (Burgess
1980, p. 83); only at Stonehenge was a further phase of construction undertaken, which made it even more impressive.
Burials in this period continued to include both inhumations
and cremations and to vary in their spatial and monumental
context, but the most notable new feature was the appearance of a small number of burials richly provided with grave
goods, the so-called Wessex culture (Piggott 1938); such
burials occur sporadically elsewhere but the concentration
and the richness of those in Wessex is unmatched.

Renfrew (1973*b*, 1974) has argued persuasively that
the scale of organisation involved in the construction of the
major Late Neolithic ceremonial centres of Wessex was such
that they must have depended on a centralised chiefdom
form of organisation, and that a similar inference may be
made from the rich Early Bronze Age burials, as archaeologists and antiquarians have always maintained. Accepting
this as the case, it is clear that they represent different kinds
of hierarchical society, and Renfrew (1974) has labelled the
first as 'group-oriented' and the second as 'individualising'. In
both cases a socially generated surplus is being consumed but
the mode of consumption is very different. It may be
suggested that what we are seeing is the replacement of an
ideology in which the existence of hierarchy was legitimated
by the provision of monuments and ritual 'beneficial' to the
whole community, by one in which inequality was more
openly expressed and presented as natural by means of the
consumption of prestige items and ritual symbols by powerful individuals. The consequences of this will be considered
below but it may be noted here that once such items became
important for elite legitimation, then control of them, and
competition for that control, would have become a significant part of social life.

If we turn to Gilman's (1976) account of southeast Spain during the same period, we find that in the Late Copper Age the megalithic tombs become larger than in previous phases, and that a wide variety of exotic material is found in the tombs, which show considerable variation in this respect. In the Argaric Early Bronze Age the megalithic tombs with their collective burials are replaced by a non-monumental single-grave burial rite, again with great variation between the burials in terms of their grave goods, in which metal objects now play a much greater role.

Gilman (1976) has also proposed some reasons for these changes. He suggests that social differentiation was becoming apparent in the Late Copper Age as a result of subsistence innovations, but that this differentiation was expressed in egalitarian ritual forms which had developed in the Early Neolithic. In the wake of the subsistence changes the distribution of power became increasingly inegalitarian and incompatible with previous collective ritual forms, which were replaced by richly provided individual burials. In effect, Gilman is saying that hierarchies need to be sanctioned by appropriate ideologies, that the ritual of collective burial, despite the deposition of grave goods, was not appropriate to such ideologies, that the contradiction was in some way felt as the degree of hierarchical differentiation increased, and that this led to the rise of an ideology and associated ritual of a similar type to that seen in Wessex, in which hierarchy was legitimated through the consumption of prestige items by individuals. Gilman's account raises a great many questions which need to be answered but I propose to accept the broad outline of his reconstruction. One point, however, is worth noting. Gilman devotes most of his attention to burials when considering the matter of social change. Monuments other than those associated with burials are lacking, but the degree of elaboration of the Copper Age settlement of Los Millares, particularly its defences, and the indications of craft specialisation in this period (Chapman 1982), suggest that social differentiation was already strongly developed in the Copper Age. Rather than postulating an increase in social differentiation with the Early Bronze Age, as Gilman does, it may be that we can see the Early Bronze Age change rather as the 'catching-up' of conservative ritual with previous social changes (see below).

In Brittany, one of the other key areas for the beginning of the European Early Bronze Age, there is a sequence not dissimilar from that of southeast Spain (see L'Helgouach 1976; Briard 1976; Coles & Harding 1979). The Late Neolithic/Copper Age period is characterised by megalithic monuments and tombs, although the latter do not contain anything like the exotic material of those in southeast Spain and are relatively undifferentiated in this respect. They are replaced by single-grave burials, under barrows in Brittany, which show a great deal of differentiation in their contents, including metalwork.

The monumental nature of the Late Neolithic tombs, and the other megalithic phenomena of Brittany, suggest again that here we have a hierarchically differentiated society prior to the Early Bronze Age, and that the Early Bronze Age sees a change in the form of its ritual expression, with a move from collective monumentality to individual consumption of goods.

To summarise, it has been argued that in all three of the areas discussed hierarchical differentiation was present in the Late Neolithic/Copper Age, and that such differentiation continued in these areas into the Early Bronze Age. Nevertheless, the ideologies associated with these successive hierarchies were very different, and as a result they operated in very different ways, as I will argue below.

If one compares this sequence with that in some of those areas of central Europe which achieve prominence in terms of their rich burials in the Early Bronze Age — most notably the Elbe–Saale area of Germany, Bohemia, and, to a lesser extent, Moravia — the contrast is marked. In the Late Neolithic of these areas evidence for monumental structures is completely lacking. What settlement evidence there is suggests scattered, very small-scale settlement, with no indication whatever of a settlement hierarchy. Burials occur in large numbers but they are almost invariably single earth-pit graves with no structure more monumental than a small, low round mound. The only respect in which they show any variation is in their associated grave goods, and analysis of the burials in this regard (Neustupný 1973; Shennan 1977) indicates only limited differentiation beyond that associated with age and sex. All the other evidence indicates that we are not dealing here with hierarchically differentiated societies whose burial ritual was based on an ideology of the concealment of politico-economic distinctions, but rather with a genuinely slight degree of differentiation. That is to say, whereas the areas of western Europe discussed above were characterised by marked social differentiation and an ideology involving the collective consumption of surplus, hierarchy was relatively little developed in central Europe at this time although inter-individual differences were being expressed at burial by means of grave goods. This lack of differentiation continues in these areas until the later Early Bronze Age, at which time burials with rich grave goods, including sophisticated craft items and goods obtained by long distance exchange, appear in both the Elbe–Saale area and Bohemia and Moravia. From this I would infer that a hierarchically differentiated society had arisen in these areas, in which the expression of inter-individual differences at burial continued but had now taken on the role of legitimating the hierarchy through the consumption of prestige items.

As we have seen, Gilman (1976) maintains that the appearance of the new 'individualising' burial rite in southeast Spain was the result of the local incompatibility between increasing stratification and existing ritual practice in a regionally autonomous process. Nevertheless, it should be noted that the convergent developments described are essentially contemporaneous in all the areas discussed; furthermore, all the areas discussed are actually linked immediately prior to their local Bronze Ages by the possession in varying degrees of various parts of the Bell Beaker assemblage (see Lanting & van der Waals 1976). The possibility should therefore be considered that the developments described are not all regionally autonomous but form part of a larger process. Gilman (1981) recognises this possibility and argues that throughout Europe the developments of the Early Bronze Age stem from contemporaneous processes of agricultural intensification, in temperate Europe involving the plough and in southern Europe Mediterranean polyculture and irrigation. Any overall account of the development of the European Bronze Age must take these factors into account, but there are problems with Gilman's argument (see, for example, Shennan 1981) and it is inadequate to specify the type of convergence which actually occurs. In order to understand this it is necessary to take into account the inter-regional connections which are clearly apparent and the nature of the local situations which have been described.

It is suggested here that the essence of Gilman's (1976) argument for southeast Spain is also valid for the other areas of western Europe which have been discussed; that is to say, in the Late Neolithic considerable social differentiation had developed which was increasingly incompatible with existing ritual forms. The reasons for inferring the existence of such differentiation in these areas have already been given. In what sense is it possible to talk about incompatibility? This is in general an extremely problematical issue to which I will certainly not be able to give an adequate answer here. The particular line I wish to adopt is as follows. The theoretical possibility exists that a particular situation of hierarchical dominance may be associated with any one of a number of different ideologies which may to varying degrees, and at various levels, either seek to disguise that hierarchy or present it as 'God-given'. However, from the elite's point of view, the latter may in some contexts be seen as more satisfactory since at times of conflict it removes the possibility of subordinate individuals calling on traditional social values of an egalitarian nature to sanction their disagreements with the elite. Although it does not seem plausible to argue that the ideology associated with the major monumental constructions of the Late Neolithic in the areas discussed was an egalitarian one, I would suggest that the fact that we are dealing with *monuments* which were the product of collective labour is a significant one; that they imply an ideology in which the position of powerful individuals was seen as dependent on the collective activity of the community. The subsequent change in ideology which characterises the Early Bronze Age saw a drastic decline in the scale and importance of collective ritual enterprises of this kind. The rituals involved in this new ideology were based not on the collective labour of the community but on the consumption in burial of prestige items and symbols obtained by means of contact with members of elites elsewhere and/or through the activities of specialist craftsmen. In this way the elite would have become distanced from the community and their power

and rank would appear to be dependent on their own efforts. As a group they would have become ideologically more secure but this was at the expense of the possibilities of intra-elite competition for control of such items which were now presented.

The change to an ideology more favourable to elite control was not the result of a further local increase in ranking in any of these areas, but stemmed from the stimulus of the appearance of the Bell Beaker assemblage and burial rite together with an associated ideology derived from Corded Ware Single-Grave traditions in northern and central Europe, where collective labour had not been mobilised in the same way and where the consumption of items as grave goods in individual graves, marking the existing but limited social distinctions, had long been prevalent. This ritual tradition had the potential for development as part of a more explicit and secure elite ideology which local collective forms did not possess. In a sense it could be said that the relation between power and ideology had become problematical in these parts of western Europe and the adoption of ritual and ideological innovations was a solution to that problem; the fact that these innovations did represent a solution to problems which had arisen independently in different parts of Europe was one of the main factors accounting for their widespread diffusion. Braudel (1972) has drawn the distinction between structure and conjuncture in history; I would regard the local situations I have described as structural in his terms and the diffusion of these innovations as a more specific conjuncture.

It may be considered as a reasonable corollary of the situation described above that in those parts of western Europe where collective monumental traditions existed but where the process of hierarchisation was not so well-developed, the innovatory new ideology would not necessarily have been adopted, since it is not the question of contact but of structural reasons for adoption which is important. Gilman (1976) has noted that in less developed parts of Iberia collective burial traditions continued well into the second millennium. A similar phenomenon may be noticeable in Brittany. At the time of the appearance of the rich, first series Armorican tumuli on the coast, megalithic burial traditions continued in the interior and it is only with the later second series barrows that single grave traditions are found there (Briard 1976).

Before going on to look at the consequences of the new ideology in the Early Bronze Age, it is necessary to consider whether the available evidence concerning the nature, pattern and timing of Bell Beaker contacts at the end of the Late Neolithic support the role which I have proposed to give them. Burgess (1980) in particular has suggested that in Britain many innovations traditionally considered to be of Beaker origin were in fact present long before. This is not the place for an extensive discussion of the Bell Beaker phenomenon (see Lanting & van der Waals 1976; Mercer 1977 for extensive description and discussion), but the main issues must be considered.

First, there can be no argument that the pattern of Bell Beaker contacts in some form or other ranges over most of central and western Europe, including all those areas which have been discussed. With the possible exception of the Urnfields at the end of the second millennium, they are unique in this linking of central and western Europe. There are two main phases of contact; at the end of the first phase, decorated Bell Beakers are introduced into the indigenous assemblages of central Europe, where what has come to be regarded as the 'classic' Bell Beaker grave assemblage (only rare in occurrence) of decorated Bell Beaker, tanged copper dagger and wrist-guard comes together. Analysis of the burials suggests that this represented a new development in the expression of male prestige at burial in this area, replacing the Corded Ware beaker and stone battle axe, but still in the context of only a very limited degree of hierarchical differentiation (Shennan 1977).

Once this new assemblage had formed it spread very widely and quickly. It is found in limited numbers but quite regularly over large parts of central and western Europe; its prestige probably derived at least in part from the innovations which some of the objects represent, particularly the metalwork and its associated technology. In much of central and northwest Europe, where the various Corded Ware assemblages were prevalent in the immediately preceding phase of the Late Neolithic, it represented a change, and elaboration, of the prestige items in the context of a relatively unchanged ideology in which grave goods indicated individual distinctions at burial.

In Britain the innovations of the new Bell Beaker grave assemblages, and the metallurgical skills associated with the production of some of their items, appeared in the later part of the Mount Pleasant phase, when the major monuments of Wessex were still very much in use. Although, as Burgess points out (1980), many individual features of Late Neolithic and Early Bronze Age burials which used to be regarded as of Beaker origin can now be shown to have a longer ancestry, it is maintained here that the particular aspect not present earlier was the consistent use of grave goods, especially exotic or high-quality items, to indicate differentiation, including prestige, in a way which had not previously occurred, and which ultimately presupposed an ideology different from the prevailing one. The monument-based ideology was not superceded immediately; the period before this occurred must have been one of ideological competition.

In Brittany the Beaker associated innovations were similar. This was rather less the case in southeast Spain where, as we have seen, large quantities of exotic goods are to be found in the collective tombs of the local Copper Age. Here too, however, the marked changes already described follow the later central European connected Beaker phase; monuments decline and individual burial with exotic grave goods, which have a much increased metal component, becomes prevalent.

We have, then, in the Bell Beaker phase, at the very beginning of the Bronze Age a highly significant pattern of contact linking virtually the whole of central and western Europe in what is essentially a time of innovation diffusion and adoption in various spheres (not all of which have been discussed here), including ritual and ideology, in a number of very different local situations. As we have seen, to understand the developments of this period it has been necessary to consider both the local sequences and the inter-regional pattern of contact. In a sense this phase can be said to mark the base-line for the Early Bronze Age throughout western and central Europe. After it, inter-regional connections continue but their nature and significance are very different.

On the basis of the argument so far, a widespread ritual form and ideology are being postulated which involve the representation of inter-individual differences at burial by means of grave goods. Despite the widespread distribution of this ritual, at least in central and the northern part of western Europe, it was only in the small number of widely scattered areas already discussed, with the possible addition of one or two others such as Portugal, that its potential for elite legitimation was initially used, since only in these areas was hierarchy strongly developed. This had occurred during the course of the Neolithic in Britain, Spain and Brittany, for different local reasons. In central Europe, on the other hand, the process was different as here chiefdoms appear for the first time, or at least for the first time in the best part of a millennium, in the later Early Bronze Age. Thus, whereas in western Europe rich Early Bronze Age graves appear as a result of the changed ideology of pre-existing hierarchical societies, in central Europe such hierarchies actually develop at this time and the existing burial ritual simply accommodated this by increasing the range of goods deposited both quantitatively and qualitatively, so that the same end result was reached as in western Europe.

The question naturally arises, what factors were involved in the development of hierarchical societies in central Europe at this time? One major problem in answering this question is the lack of information on subsistence and land use, and their organisation in this period, so that the investigation of their role is extremely difficult. It may, however, be noted that the introduction of the plough and the other associated secondary products of domestication (Sherratt 1981) occurred no later than the Middle Neolithic, of the order of a millennium earlier than the later Early Bronze Age on a recalibrated radiocarbon time scale.

On the present evidence it is difficult to avoid relating the increase in social differentiation in some way to the growth of the copper and bronze industry and the opportunities it offered for the generation and control of a surplus. If one looks at the spatial distribution of those parts of central Europe which attract one's attention in terms of their evidence for social differentiation, one is inevitably drawn towards those agricultural areas adjacent to local metal sources. Furthermore, if one compares the dates at which such evidence appears in these areas with the dates when major Bronze Age exploitation of the adjacent metal resources began, a relationship seems to emerge. Thus, at a time when the early Unĕtice graves of Bohemia and the Elbe—Saale area are characterised by largely undifferentiated inventories of ceramic goods, both southwest Slovakia, adjacent to the Slovakian ore sources known to be exploited at an early date, and the Danube valley, close to the Alpine sources which were also exploited early, contain cemeteries which suggest the beginnings of more marked social differentiation (S.E. Shennan 1975; Vladár 1973; Christlein 1964; Schubert 1973). The metal sources of the north Bohemian and central German (Elbe—Saale) areas, which also included tin, only became important in the later Early Bronze Age, with the development of a true tin—bronze industry and of more sophisticated casting procedures. It was only at this time that the rich Unĕtice cemeteries of Bohemia and the *Fürstengräber* of central Germany appeared (Coles & Harding 1979), and document the emergence of hierarchies in this area. Nevertheless, despite this apparent correlation and the likelihood that monopolistic control of the newly important resources would have provided a basis for power, the reasons why metal became important remain unclear.

Going back now to the larger scale and looking again at western as well as central Europe, I would argue that from a variety of different starting points all the areas to which I have given detailed attention had by the later Early Bronze Age (c. 1700—1600 BC) reached a situation where the maintenance of the hierarchies which had arisen was closely bound up with the consumption of prestige valuables. This had two aspects. On the one hand, as we have seen, it stemmed from the prevalent ideology involving legitimating rituals which emphasised the consumption of prestige items obtained through contacts with elite groups elsewhere, so that elites became distanced from their communities and appeared to be more independent of them. On the other hand, although the elite as a group had become ideologically more secure, the fact that prestige and rank were now represented in terms of objects meant that those objects now acquired an intrinsic value. This meant that they could actually be used to create a position (cf. Brush 1980). A medium for competition was thus created which had not previously existed and which greatly extended the possibilities of intra-elite rivalry.

The archaeological evidence for the consumption of such valuables comes, of course, from burials. We do not know if this was the sole type of occasion on which such consumption occurred but the fact that it did occur at burial must be significant. I would suggest that it relates in some way to the problem of the succession to power in such societies. This is the sphere in which competition and stress are at their greatest, either because the rules of succession are not themselves clear and leave open the possibility of competition, or because the jurally defined successor still has to prove himself in the field of elite activities (cf. Helms 1980); the rich burials received by certain individuals may be more

an indication of the connections and resources which could be mobilised by the leaders of the next generation than a reflection of their own position.

The situation described had its own new dynamic since power was now ideologically defined to depend on the ability to obtain supplies of exotic materials and objects, and intra-elite competition led to an emphasis on the active seeking-out of distant contacts. The archaeological record of the later Early Bronze Age and Middle Bronze Age in central and western Europe provides ample evidence for the operation of processes such as those which have been described, not just in the rich graves which were one of the starting points of this study but in the strong similarities between the objects of elite expression in all the areas discussed and the widespread use of specific materials obtained by exchange, such as amber (Shennan 1982). These show that at the level of prestige items, contacts between the upper levels of the local hierarchies were maintained in the later Early Bronze Age, although those connections were of a very different nature from the inter-regional contacts and similarities which characterised the Bell Beaker phase, while the links between southeast Spain and the other areas were less marked. Such connections were a more or less inevitable corollary of the situation which has been postulated, since so long as a number of areas had social systems which depended on the supply and consumption of prestige goods, goods which could only be obtained by contacts with elites elsewhere, a network of reciprocal demand and contact was automatically created which would have a tendency to incorporate areas not initially part of it. This process undoubtedly occurred in, for example, the western part of central Europe during the middle Bronze Age.

To conclude: in the case of the beginnings of the European Bronze Age it can be seen that the ideological change described had a direct effect on the form and operation of the power base in western Europe, while in central Europe the existing ideology and ritual was able to accommodate the process of hierarchisation. In relation to the aims stated at the beginning of this chapter, it follows from the argument which has been presented that the situations generally reconstructed from the archaeological record of the Late Neolithic and Early Bronze Age have been inadequate in certain important respects. It also follows that, despite Renfrew's demolition of the Childean diffusion framework for the beginning of the Bronze Age, his own argument for a series of autonomous local processes is also unsatisfactory. What we see is a convergence of local trajectories and an interaction between them based on the influence of a widespread ideology and subsequent elite interactions. Price (1977) has referred to such processes as 'cluster-interaction', and recently Renfrew (1982) has referred to 'peer polity interaction' as having an important role in the beginnings of the Bronze Age in the Aegean.

More generally, I would suggest that archaeological explanations of social change which fail to take account of ideology are likely to be unsatisfactory. In particular, ranking, competition, the way in which power is exercised and the use of valuables are all ideology-dependent and must be recognised as such. This does not mean that ideology is a *deus ex machina* whose changes are arbitrary and completely independent; I have tried to show that this was not so in the case under study. The archaeological record is not inscrutable but making inferences about the past is even more difficult than we thought.

Acknowledgements

The first draft of this paper was presented at the conference on relations between the Near East, the Mediterranean World and Europe 3rd–1st millennium BC, held at Aarhus in August 1980. I am grateful to the organisers for the invitation to attend the conference, and to them and to the British Academy Overseas Conference Fund for making my attendance financially possible. For comments on the first draft I am very grateful to the participants in the Aarhus conference, the editor of this volume, Colin Renfrew, Lew Binford and to my wife, Susan Shennan. Needless to say, the paper's inadequacies are my own responsibility.

References

Bloch, M. (1977) 'The disconnection between power and rank as a process: an outline of the development of kingdoms in Central Madagascar' in J. Friedman & M.J. Rowlands (ed.) *The Evolution of Social Systems*, Duckworth, London

Braudel, F. (1972) *The Mediterranean and the Mediterranean World in the Age of Philip II*, Collins, London

Briard, J. (1976) 'Les civilisations de l'âge du bronze en Armorique' in J. Guilaine (ed.) *Les Civilisations Néolithiques et Protohistoriques de la France, La Préhistoire Française Vol. II*, Centre Nationale de la Recherche Scientifique, Paris

Brush, N. (1980) *The Cross-cultural Standardisation of Prestige Items: Some Archaeological Implications*, unpublished MA dissertation, Dept of Archaeology, University of Southampton

Burgess, C.B. (1980) *The Age of Stonehenge*, Dent, London

Chapman, R.W. (1982) 'Autonomy, ranking and resources in Iberian prehistory' in A.C. Renfrew & S.J. Shennan (eds.) *Ranking, Resource and Exchange: Aspects of the Archaeology of Early European Society*, Cambridge University Press, Cambridge

Childe, V.G. (1958) *The Prehistory of European Society*, Penguin, Harmondsworth

Christlein, R. (1964) 'Beiträge zur Stufengliederung der frühbronzezeitlichen Flachgräberfelder in Süddeutschland', *Bayerische Vorgeschichtsblätter* 29: 25–63

Coles, J.M. & Harding, A.F. (1979) *The Bronze Age in Europe*, Methuen, London

Giddens, A. (1979) *Central Problems in Social Theory*, Macmillan, London

Gilman, A. (1976) 'Bronze age dynamics in southeast Spain', *Dialectical Anthropology* 1: 307–19

Gilman, A. (1981) 'The development of social stratification in bronze age Europe', *Current Anthropology* 22: 1–8

Helms, M.W. (1980) 'Succession to high office in pre-Columbian circum-Caribbean chiefdoms', *Man* 15: 718–31

Hodder, I.R. (1980) 'Social structure and cemeteries: a critical appraisal' in P. Rahtz, T. Dickinson & L. Watts (eds.) *Anglo-Saxon Cemeteries 1979*, BAR British Series 82, Oxford

Lanting, J.N. & van der Waals, J.D. (eds.) (1976) *Glockenbechersymposion Oberried 1974*, Fibula-van Dishoek, Bussum/ Haarlem

L'Helgouach, J. (1976) 'Les civilisations néolithiques en Armorique' in J. Guilaine (ed.) *Les Civilisations Néolithiques et Protohistoriques de la France, La Préhistoire Française Vol. II*, Centre National de la Recherche Scientifique, Paris

Mercer, R. (ed.) (1977) *Beakers in Britain and Europe*, BAR International Series 26, Oxford

Neustupný, E.F. (1973) 'Factors determining the variability of the Corded Ware culture' in A.C. Renfrew (ed.) *The Explanation of Culture Change*, Duckworth, London

Piggott, S. (1938) 'The early bronze age in Wessex', *Proceedings of the Prehistoric Society* 4: 52–106

Price, B. (1977) 'Shifts in production and organisation: a cluster interaction model', *Current Anthropology* 18: 209–34

Renfrew, A.C. (1973a) *Before Civilisation*, Jonathan Cape, London

Renfrew, A.C. (1973b) 'Monuments, mobilisation and social organisation in neolithic Wessex' in A.C. Renfrew (ed.) *The Explanation of Culture Change*, Duckworth, London

Renfrew, A.C. (1974) 'Beyond a subsistence economy: the evolution of social organisation in prehistoric Europe' in C.B. Moore (ed.) *Reconstructing Complex Societies*, Supplement to the Bulletin of the American Schools of Oriental Research No. 20

Renfrew, A.C. (1982) 'Polity and power: interaction, intensification and exploitation' in A.C. Renfrew & M. Wagstaff (eds.) *An Island Polity: The Archaeology of Exploitation in Melos*, Cambridge University Press, Cambridge

Schubert, E. (1973) 'Studien zur frühen Bronzezeit an der mittleren Donau', *Bericht der römisch-germanischen Kommission* 54: 1–106

Shennan, S.E. (1975) 'The social organisation at Brancˇ', *Antiquity* 49: 279–88

Shennan, S.J. (1977) *Bell Beakers and their Context in Central Europe: A New Approach*, unpublished PhD dissertation, University of Cambridge

Shennan, S.J. (1981) 'Comment on A. Gilman "The development of social stratification in bronze age Europe" ', *Current Anthropology* 22: 14–15

Shennan, S.J. (1982) 'Exchange and ranking: the role of amber in the European earlier bronze age' in A.C. Renfrew & S.J. Shennan (eds.) *Ranking, Resource and Exchange: Aspects of the Archaeology of Early European Society*, Cambridge University Press, Cambridge

Sherratt, A.G. (1981) 'Plough and pastoralism: aspects of the secondary products revolution' in I. Hodder, G. Isaac & N. Hammond (eds.) *Pattern of the Past*, Cambridge University Press, Cambridge

Vladár, J. (1973) *Pohrebiska zo staršej doby bronzovej v Brančˇi*, Slovenská akadémia vied, Bratislava

Chapter 14

**Sequences of structural
change in the
Dutch Neolithic**
Ian Hodder

In this chapter the evidence of pottery decoration and shape, axe decoration, burial, settlement and economy is linked in comparable sequences of change which can be identified on both the North European plain and on the adjacent loess soils. In the first phase, found only on the loess, individual units within social groups can remain in close proximity, the social groups gradually expanding outwards. Pottery, burial and settlement show little concern with contrasts and oppositions. In the second phase, seen in the later LBK and Rössen and early TRB, there is outwards expansion, the spatial coherence of local groups is complicated by shorter term, more dispersed settlement and there is perhaps evidence of new forms of social dominance. There is a concern with oppositions in the pot decoration, a large number of vessel forms and large amounts of decoration, complex burial ritual in the TRB, and nucleated ditched villages in the Rössen. The material culture helps to form and legitimate the social categories in a period of increasing contradictions. In the third phase, the PFB, there is less emphasis on oppositions and categorisation in material culture and the various classes of evidence suggest a transformation of earlier tensions. The historical nature of the enquiry is stressed and the appropriate use of symbols such as shapes of burial mounds is outlined.

The setting
The physical environment of the Netherlands and adjacent areas can be divided into three major zones (fig. 1). The first area is the coastal sedimentation of the Rhine–Maas (Meuse) delta. Up to about 3000 BC the coastline retreated inwards, while after this date it began moving out again. This general movement, and the minor transgressions within it,

may have resulted in much covering and destruction of early sites and it is not until the third millennium BC that numerous sites (e.g. the Vlaardingen culture) occur on these deltaic soils.

A second environmental zone comprises the sands behind the delta which are intersected by wide marshy valleys and brooks. Peat bogs developed in some areas. Newell (1970, 1973) has documented the dense Mesolithic settlement in this area prior to the earliest Neolithic. The loess zone covering part of the area between the 50 m and 200 m contours in fig. 1 along the northern foot of the Ardennes–Eiffel hills makes up the third zone. The minor valleys which broke up this landscape were filled in the PFB culture (see below) and later prehistory as a result of deforestation. In contrast to the second zone, Mesolithic occupation was sparse on the hills.

The pottery sequence of the TRB and beaker cultures
Little is known of the earliest Neolithic on the North European plain (zones 1 and 2) in the Netherlands. The economies of the Swifterbant and Hazendonk settlements (Louwe Kooijmans 1976) involved food production, hunting, gathering and fishing, and there was some extension of Michelsberg sites into the southwest of the area in the late fourth millennium BC. But it was not until the development of the western branch of the TRB (Dutch: Trechterbeker) culture in the

Netherlands around 2700 BC that the sands to the north of the Rhine became densely occupied by inhabitants with a fully Neolithic way of life. The TRB was followed by the PFB (Protruding Foot Beaker) culture covering the North European plain and adjacent areas from about 2400 BC, and then by the BB (Bell Beaker) culture around 2300 BC.

The analysis began with a consideration of changes in pottery form and decoration from the TRB to the PFB. Study of the TRB pottery followed Bakker's (1979) important reappraisal of the chronological phases of the TRB west group. His phases A to G have been built up from the examination of closed associations of finds, and they attend gradual changes in the form of the deeply incised 'tiefstich' decoration, in the frequency of decoration, and in the range of pottery types produced.

The changes in the organisation of the decoration are clearest in the buckets and wide-mouthed bowls (fig. 2). In phase A, the decoration is divided into areas of horizontally and vertically organised incisions (fig. 3), but there is no line drawn between the rim and belly areas of the pot. In this phase all of the pots are frequently decorated although the neck areas of the beakers and jugs are usually plain.

In phase B the same distinction between a horizontally decorated rim area, and a vertically decorated body zone is maintained on the buckets and bowls and large parts of the surfaces of the pots are still adorned (fig. 4). However, the distinction between the horizontally and vertically organised decoration is more marked, with a zig-zag line separating the two areas. Now a second level of decoration can be identified in that within each of the two zones the horizontal/vertical distinction is repeated. There is no correspondence in the spacing of the decoration in the two primary zones, and this lack of cross-referencing is also seen in the placing of the handles (fig. 5).

While the decoration in phase C begins to cover slightly less of the surface of the pot, the organisation of the decor-

Fig. 1. North western Europe: relief map. Source: Louwe Kooijmans 1976.

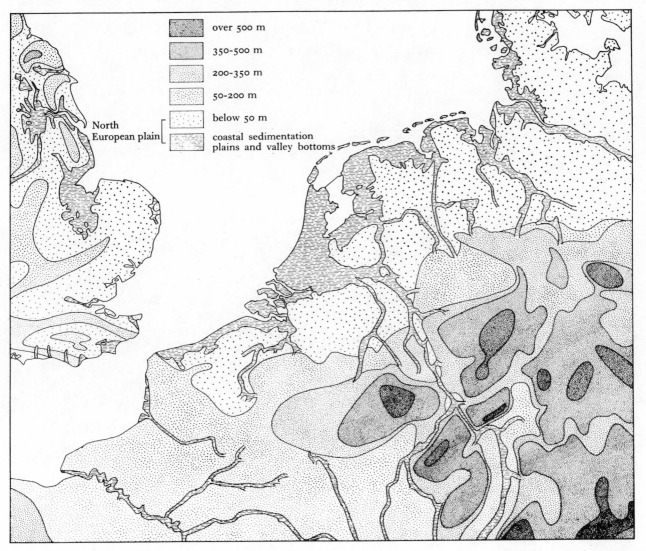

over 500 m

350-500 m

200-350 m

50-200 m

below 50 m

North European plain

coastal sedimentation plains and valley bottoms

Fig. 2. Bakker's pottery phases. Scale 1:9. Source: Bakker 1979.

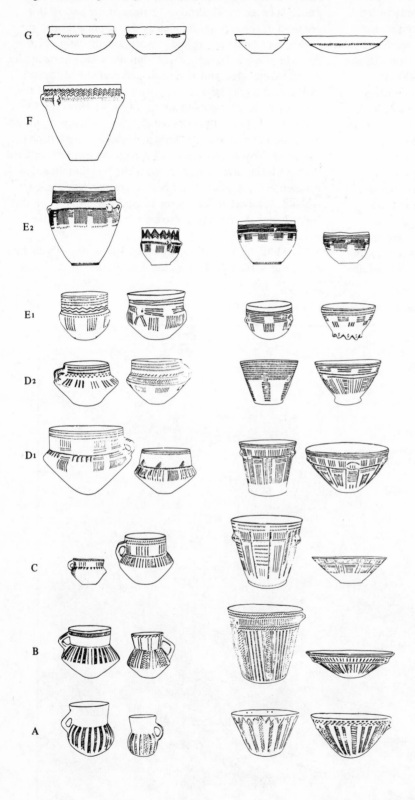

ation reaches its most complex state. Fig. 6 shows that a further subdivision of the pot into h/v (horizontal/vertical) oppositions sometimes takes place. Within the horizontal and vertical bands already achieved, even smaller h/v patterns occur. In the upper part of the pot (the horizontal zone) spaces now occur which break up the continuous horizontal and vertical sequences. These spaces can be seen as providing contrasts to the horizontal or vertical decoration as part of the h/v dichotomy.

Despite the proliferation of the simple h/v scheme, the primary distinction between horizontal decoration near the rim and the vertical decoration lower down is the most marked. The line drawn between the two primary areas is usually the thickest and most distinctive (see fig. 6a). Analysis of the overlap of incised lines showed that it was this line that had often been drawn first. The primary vertical lines moving downwards from the major horizontal line often have a considerable thickness, thus setting up the major primary distinction continued from phase A.

The design structure can be represented as the generation of the h/v dichotomy to form a dendritic pattern (fig. 7). Not all pots have the full dendritic system, but most do use the same generative rules. A distinctive characteristic of this type of design is that the original design structure severely constrains further development and elaboration. The design proceeds by the subdivision of bounded areas, and the placing of the motifs at one stage is limited by the boundaries that have already been created.

The dendritic design organisation of TRB phases A to C is characterised by the drawing of boundaries and contrasts between different areas of the pot surface, and between horizontally and vertically organised decoration, and it pro-

ceeds by subdividing and splitting existing bounded zones. A complex set of contrasts and oppositions is achieved. The importance of the boundaries themselves is indicated by the lack of cross-reference between the different zones. Within each bounded area, the decoration proceeds in its own terms without reference to the decoration in other zones. More specifically, the placing and lay-out of the designs in the different zones are usually unrelated. This lack of cross-referencing is shown in fig. 8 where the spacings between bands in the upper decoration do not correlate and they do not correspond to the h/v features in the lower part of the pot. The handles are, however, linked into the design.

Pots of phases D and E frequently continue to use the same design structure (fig. 9c and d). But D is also in phase in which a series of changes begins to be produced. For example, fig. 9a shows a pot in which the upper and lower zones are equal so that the primary h/v distinction has been lost. Even in fig. 9c the major dividing line between upper and lower zones is less clear. However, on this pot there is still a lack of cross-referencing between the different zones.

By phase E, cross-referencing between the different bands becomes common in that the breaks within one band often correlate with the decoration in other bands (fig. 10b and c). In this way the motifs and bands form a set of contrasts between horizontal, vertical and blank areas, without

Fig. 4. Phase B pot from Bronneger – D21. Source: Bakker 1979.

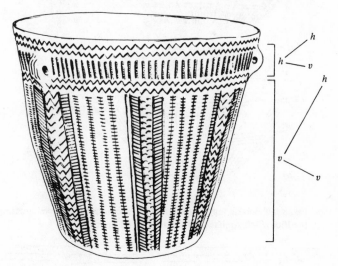

Fig. 3. Phase A pot from Bronneger – D21. Source: Bakker 1979.

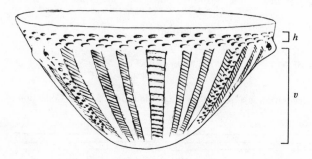

Fig. 5. Schematic representation of the sequence of decoration in the lower part of the pot in fig. 4 in relation to the handles. Source: Collection of the Biologisch-Archaeologisch Instituut, Groningen.

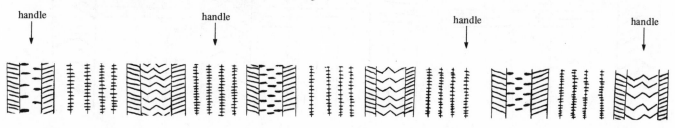

the drawing of boundary lines. Fig. 10*a* shows the decoration on a very small and unique, crudely made bowl. The gradual collapsing of the h/v structure to produce a series of equal zones is here apparent. In E2 the dendritic set of contrasts is transformed more frequently than in earlier phases in order to produce a design structure of a simpler sequence of often continuous zones (fig. 10*d*), similar in some respects to the PFB decoration to be described below. Also in E2 the amount of the pot surface that is decorated begins to decrease and by phases F and G decoration has almost entirely disappeared from the pots.

The above discussion of changes in the organisation of TRB pottery decoration has been based mainly on an analysis of the buckets and wide-mouthed bowls which demonstrate most chronological variation. But the decoration on other classes of pottery is of a similar nature. Tureens and shouldered pots usually exhibit the same h/v contrasts (fig. 2). The funnel beakers and jugs, on the other hand, have vertical decoration on the belly zone but the upper horizontal area is usually replaced by a blank neck zone.

In summary, the TRB pottery decoration can be defined as dendritic, being built up from a basic contrast between horizontal and vertical organisation. Through time this structure is gradually transformed so that clear boundaries are not drawn, but there is cross-referencing and contrasts between the different zones. In the latest phases (but mainly in phase E2) the overall dendritic system becomes lost in favour of a series of horizontal bands of zones and the proportion of the pot surface that is decorated gradually decreases. A number of other changes can be identified. In particular, the overall percentage of pots that have any decoration decreases in the last phases (F and G). Also there is some indication that the variety of pot forms decreases. For example, the funnel beakers occur in phases A to E but not in F and G. In general, the TRB is characterised by a wide range of distinct pottery forms (including collared flasks, baking plates and 'biberons') and pots appear to be made or used for specific functions. For example, Bakker (1979, p. 118) describes the TRB custom of burying poorly shaped, undecorated pots with wobbly bases around the peripheries of megalithic graves. But by the latest TRB and certainly by the time of the PFB pots, the range of distinctive types had decreased.

Fig. 6. Phase C pots from (*a*) Drouwen – D19 and (*b*) Bronneger – D21. Source: Bakker 1979. h¹ or v¹ indicates a horizontal/vertical contrast produced by the use of a blank area.

Fig. 7. The generative structure of Dutch early TRB pottery.

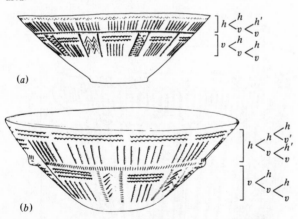

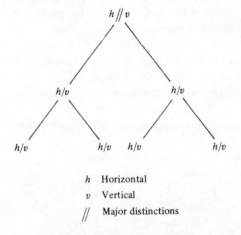

h Horizontal
v Vertical
// Major distinctions

Fig. 8. Schematic representation of the relationship between areas of decoration in a 'rollout' of the pot in fig. 6*b*. Source: Collection of the Biologisch-Archaeologisch Instituut, Groningen.

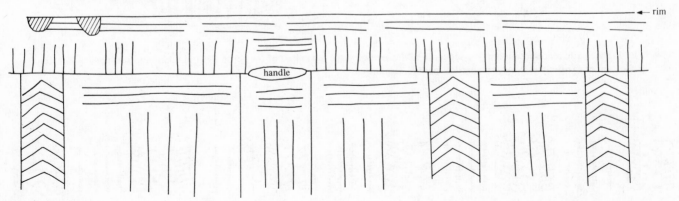

Fig. 9. Phase D1 pots: (*a*) and (*b*) from Drouwen – D19, (*c*) Bronneger – D21, (*d*) Emmen – D43. Source: Bakker 1979.

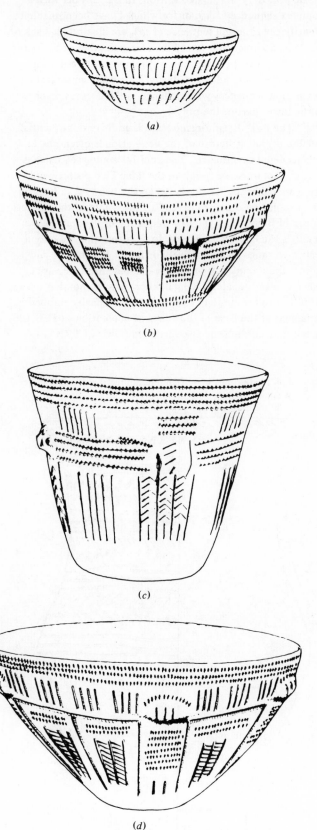

The later part of the TRB sequence is contemporary with early PFB. C[14] dates suggest an overlap since the TRB continues to about 2100 BC. The sherd of a 1*a* corded protruding foot beaker occurred in a grave at Angelslo together with TRB F and G sherds (Bakker & Van der Waals 1973), and it seems probable from the C[14] dates that PFB began by phase E (Bakker 1979; Louwe Kooijmans 1976, p. 283). It is not surprising then that the changes identified in the organisation of the later TRB pottery design have some similarities with the PFB decoration.

The surface of PFB pots is divided into a series of horizontal bands in which there are fewer contrasts and oppositions than in TRB phases A to E (fig. 11 and Van der Waals & Glasbergen 1955). The cord impressions which circle

Fig. 10. (*a*) schematic representation on small, crudely made, TRB bowl. Source: Collection Biologisch-Archaeologisch Institut, Groningen (1918/X 16). (*b*) phase E, pot from Bronneger – D21. Source: Bakker 1979. (*c*) phase E, pot from Darpvenne. Source: Bakker 1979. (*d*) phase E2 pot from Vadelermeer. Source: Bakker 1979.

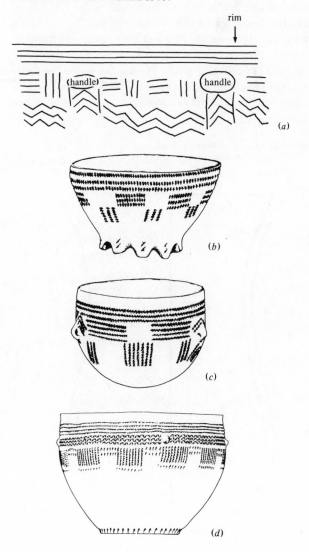

the pot, and which may have had some function in supporting the pot during manufacture (Van der Leeuw 1976), either show simple repetition or alternation of zones (fig. 11). If the zone nearest the rim is labelled A, and the next zone A if it is similar to, and B if it is different from, the first zone, then a series of alternating zones can be described as ABABAB. Sometimes, however, there is reversal within the repetition so that a cross-cutting pattern emerges, as in fig. 12. In the sequence ABA'B, A' represents the reversal of A.

It is important to emphasise that the notation systems used are simply descriptive devices chosen to clarify the two types of decoration in the Dutch Neolithic. The systems are not claimed to represent models in the 'minds of the makers'. It would be possible to use the linear PFB notation system for TRB pots, but the scheme would be less able to capture the complexity of contrasts that is found in the TRB. On the other hand, the PFB decoration is not well described as a hierarchy of subdivided bounded areas. Rather, the PFB design structure is built up as a series of horizontal zones and the structure allows expansion and addition. There is no logical limit to the ABAB . . . sequences. The design structure incorporates fewer contrasts and could be described as additive or sequential rather than dendritic. The other major difference between the PFB and TRB design structures is that the PFB decoration is built up from cross-references between the different zones. The designs within the different areas of the earlier TRB pots were independent of each other, but the PFB pots emphasise relationships between zones (fig. 12).

While sequential notation systems (such as ABAB) are sufficient to capture the structure of PFB decoration, many of the pots defy simple description. In fig. 13 pots with a complex sequence (13*a*), or for which I have been unable to identify the ordering sequence (13*b*), are illustrated. Lack of a balanced sequence is found on a large number of PFB pots in that towards the lower end of the pot, the decoration often comes to a 'full stop'. In fig. 14 are shown several decoration sequences which change as the decoration ceases in the lower part of the pot.

The PFB design organisation is additive or sequential, but the overall structure of the decoration is often unbalanced and asymmetric. The additive zoning sequence is also characteristic of trends in the later TRB pottery and there are other similarities between the two types of pottery. The decoration does not extend to the whole of the surface of the PFB pots, and the low frequency of decoration parallels the late TRB pottery. In addition, there is only a restricted range of distinctively different PFB shapes and forms, and a tendency towards a decrease in shape variety was noted in the later TRB. (Bakker, pers. comm. has drawn attention to the similarity between the vertically stabbed ornament at the base of the zones of decoration of PFB 1*a* pots and decoration on the cordoned bowls of TRB G.)

Fig. 12. Decoration on PFB pot. Source: Lanting & Van der Waals 1976.

Fig. 11. PFB pot from Aalten. Source: Lanting & Van der Waals 1976.

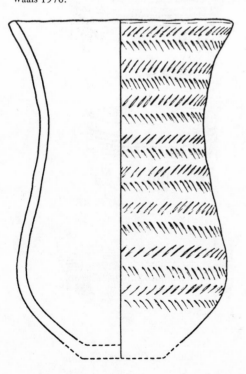

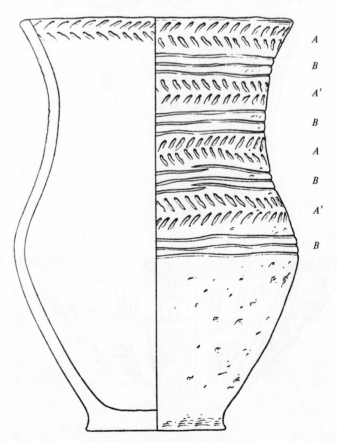

In summary, the TRB–PFB pottery development commences with the dendritic TRB A to E decoration in which the gradually increasing hierarchy of h/v dichotomies produces a proliferation of contrasts and oppositions. Distinctions are formed by the h/v contrasts, by the use of lines of different thicknesses to emphasise the contrasts, and, in phase E2, by the use of cross-referencing between different areas of the pot surface. The highly complex designs of TRB A to E are associated with a pottery assemblage in which there are many distinct pottery types and functions, and almost every shape category is associated with a distinctive version of the overall decoration scheme. On the funnel beakers, for example, a contrast is made between vertical decoration on the body of the pot and lack of decoration on the neck area, in order to emphasise the opposition between the two parts of the pot. But, in general, the amount of decorated pottery is high in these phases.

The additive or sequential PFB design organisation comprises horizontal zones with frequent cross-references between the zones, but there are fewer types and levels of contrast. There is some evidence of a move towards this zoning sequence in the late TRB (from E2 onwards). In the late TRB and in the PFB, all the trends identified in the early TRB are reversed. In addition to the decrease in contrastive designs, decorated pots become less common, and the amount of the pot surface that is decorated decreases. There is less variety in pottery shapes. While it will be important in future work of this nature to provide quantitative evidence of these various trends, many of the developments have been recognised and described in rather different terms in Bakker's (1979) comprehensive study.

Related sequences of change

Stone battle axes of the TRB and PFB show some trends which are similar to the pottery. For example, as the decoration of TRB pottery decreases through time, so does the decoration of battle axes. Of the two major types of TRB battle axe in the Netherlands, the earlier Hanover type is decorated with parallel grooves and the later knob-butted type is undecorated.

Changes occur in the burial evidence in the same chronological sequence. The pottery design of TRB A to E has been described as incorporating increasing numbers of contrasts and oppositions. Complex communal burial and associated ritual are known throughout the early TRB phases. But in phases F and G, and perhaps earlier, megaliths ceased to be constructed. There is little evidence in the individual burial under barrows in the PFB, of the multiple stages of ritual normally associated with megalithic communal burial. It is possible that extensive burial activity which is not identifiable archaeologically became common in the later TRB phases, but the close association between the change in design organisation and the cessation of construction of megaliths in the TRB, and the association between the PFB decoration and a particular burial rite (individual burial under barrows) is considered here to be of interest.

The construction of tombs in the early TRB argues for the presence of corporate groups, and Renfrew (1976) has suggested the use of communal burial mounds and monuments to symbolise local competing groups and lineages in north and west Europe. The particular burial rite of repeated interments over long periods of time in substantial monuments suggests that ties with the ancestors may have been

Fig. 13. PFB pots from Drente, Holland. Source: Van der Waals & Glasbergen 1955.

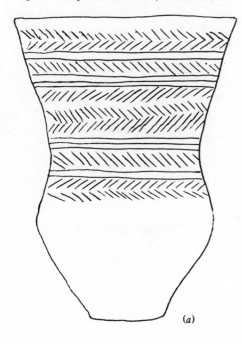

(a)

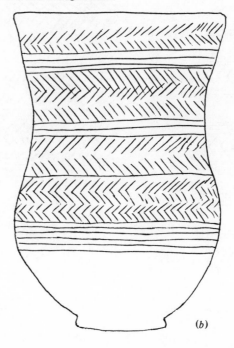

(b)

used to legitimate dominant sub-groups (whether senior men or lineages or lineage heads) within society (Friedman 1975). Shennan (chapter 13) and Shanks and Tilley (chapter 12) indicate the types of links that may have existed between the burial ritual and increasing social hierarchies. But the dead and the tombs may also have functioned in a different way. Although only constructed in phases A to E, the megaliths from the Drente region often show use throughout many or most of Bakker's pottery phases. However, this evidence of long-term use is contradicted by the settlement evidence. The pottery from the settlements seldom spans more than one or two of Bakker's phases. The settlements themselves seem slight and impermanent in that little evidence survives of substantial buildings or dense villages. The method of house construction may have impeded the recognition of long-term sites, but the pottery evidence suggests that the long-term, stable burial mounds were not associated with settlements of a similar nature in the Netherlands. Sherratt (1981) has demonstrated that the expansion of Neolithic occupation onto the sands of the North European plain may have been facilitated by the use of the plough and pastoralism, associated with less long-term, more mobile settlements than are found in the megalith-free Early Neolithic of central Europe.

The tombs, and an ideology related to ancestors, may have functioned not only to legitimate dominant groups, but also to legitimate their traditional rights tied to one place. Control over dispersed and changing settlement was achieved by the dominant lineages through links with tombs and the

ancestors. Bloch (1971, 1975) provides a relevant example from the Merina on the central plateau of Madagascar, where communal burial 'tombs are the symbols of the continuity of the group not only because they are containers of the ancestors but because they are the containers of the ancestors fixed in a particular place . . . The importance of the tombs is that they create the permanent relationship of people to land by placing them there' (ibid., 1975, p. 208).

If the tombs refer to stability and the past, then it might be expected that an appropriate tomb form would have been chosen. The shape of the tomb might be expected to evoke past conditions of stability, and traditional rights. Ashbee (1970) summarises the numerous suggestions made by European prehistorians about the shapes of the long barrows. These barrows, in which stone and wooden burial chambers are frequently enclosed in north and west Europe, are similar to the long houses of the earlier phases of the Neolithic in central and north Europe. The similarities occur in the trapezoidal and long rectangular forms of burial mounds and houses, in the large size of both constructions, and in their general east–west orientations. It has been noted elsewhere (Hodder 1982) that detailed similarities between settlement and burial form occur in Neolithic Orkney. For the north and west European data, I am grateful to Mike Parker Pearson for the suggestion that the form of the megalith burial mounds was appropriate in the context of a changing and relatively mobile settlement pattern because it evoked the past stability of the earlier Neolithic in central

Fig. 14. Dutch PFB decoration sequences: (*a*) Van der Waals & Glasbergen 1955. (*b*) and (*c*) Van der Leeuw 1976.

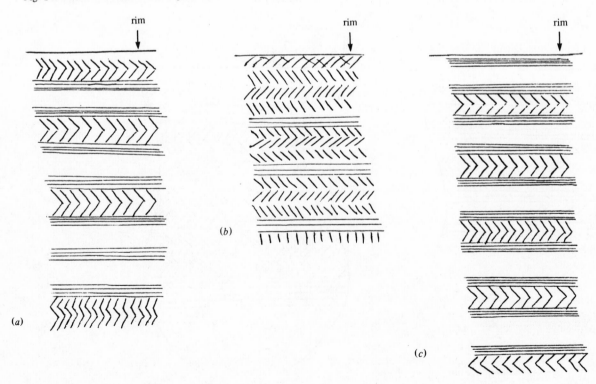

Europe (see below). This historically specific association further legitimated the dominant groups tied to the ancestors.

How does the early TRB pottery form and decoration relate to this model? Within the social and economic system as described, a series of contradictions and contrasts are emerging. There is a concern by dominant and subordinate groups to emphasise traditional, stable ties to ancestors, in the context of shorter term, expanding settlement (Bakker 1979, p. 74). It is at the locus of this tension and contradiction that the burial ritual acts. There may also be tensions between senior and younger men, and between men and women. Regional distinctions in pottery styles (Voss 1980; Bakker 1979, p. 133) and battle axe types emerge by phase D2 in the TRB, indicating a social contrast between spatial groups. The various distinct categories of pottery form and decoration, being involved in daily activities, would serve to separate these activities, and the individuals associated with them, setting up symbolic contrasts and forming the social distinctions in a context in which there was a concern about the contradiction of a traditional social structure. Miller (chapter 9) shows how contrasting pottery categories may be used symbolically to differentiate and sustain social categories. The rich decoration on the pots would itself emphasise the categorical differences between activities and individuals and would draw attention to transfers of pots and their contents between groups within society (see Braithwaite, chapter 8). The pot shapes and decoration are an active component in the interaction between and legitimation of social categories. That the organisation of the decoration itself also shows a concern with oppositions and contrasts suggests that it may have been involved in a similar process. I have shown elsewhere (1982; see also Faris 1972) how in certain societies the motifs and organisation of pottery decoration may be given specific and detailed symbolic meanings. The particular TRB concern with categorical distinctions that has been seen in several spheres of activity may have extended to the organisation of the pottery decoration. The contrasts and oppositions in the decoration would act, perhaps as a mnemonic, perhaps as a comment, to reproduce and to 'naturalise' the social categories.

In the latest TRB there is little decoration on pots and there are fewer classes of pot form. In the PFB also there is less evidence of formal and decorative contrasts. Equally, however, the social and economic contradictions, evident in TRB A to E, are less apparent in the later phase. While it is probable that hierarchies existed, as elsewhere in the Corded Ware (Shennan 1977), and that finer, more complex beakers and battle axes are associated with high status groups, the burial ritual (individual barrows scattered over the landscape) is not contradicted by the settlement pattern, which probably remained relatively short-term and dispersed. There is some evidence that settlement expanded onto a wider range of soils, including those with less nutrients, and there are specialised and localised economic emphases such as the fishing at the PFB Aartswoud settlement. PFB pottery styles are widely distributed despite local manufacture, as evidenced by diatom studies (Jansma, pers. comm.).

These social and economic changes, responding to the contradictions in the earlier phase, may have encouraged and been based on a still more intensive use of secondary animal products (Sherratt 1981), allowing a greater range of environments to be used. While there is insufficient present evidence in Holland for the precise social and economic strategies which may have been followed in the PFB, Bloch (1975) provides a relevant illustration in his contrast between the Merina and Zafimaniry in Madagascar. For the Zafimaniry, and unlike the Merina, land is not ancestral and the investment in the land is only for a short time. Labour, not land, is the important limiting factor, and the question becomes 'do we have enough people for weeding, keeping birds off the crops, etc?' The Zafimaniry, unlike the Merina, may actually welcome the addition of a local group from outside because this will increase the labour force. The world view is structured so that it allows the transformation:

outsiders → neighbours → affines → kinsmen

The system is facilitated if there are some pre-existing links between separated units. If the forest becomes exhausted in a local area, a household may wish to join or depend on another locality. There is thus an emphasis on connections and relationships between groups. The Zafimaniry stress the system of marriage alliances — emphasis is placed on inter-locality marriage links, especially with the parent settlements. There is no territorially based descent group, and the regional unit is extremely weak and vague, with the domestic unit stressed.

The decrease in identifiable contrasts and categorical oppositions in the pottery forms and decoration of the late TRB and PFB could have acted to deny the earlier social distinctions, and to emphasise connections and inter-relationships. By expressing a decreased concern with categorisation and by drawing less attention to the boundaries between these categories, a new pattern of social and economic relationships could be set up. Whatever the precise interpretation of the social and economic processes, the changes in pottery organisation and in the use of decoration do seem to be related to decreases in observed contrasts between settlement and burial and between regional groupings. After the period considered here, the Veluwe beakers in Holland indicate a return to a concern with the drawing of symbolic distinctions.

The above hypothesis for the interpretation of changes in cultural data from the TRB to the PFB could be supported by providing better evidence of settlement duration and economic function, of social organisation within the settlements, of the stages of burial ritual, and of the different functions of the pottery classes. But the hypothesis can also be assessed by examining a different but related sequence on the loess.

The Neolithic sequence on the loess

The areas of rich loess soils to the east and southeast of the region so far considered were first inhabited by groups with a type of material culture, termed Bandkeramik, in the period around 4400 BC. In the first instance the early Linearbandkeramik (LBK), unlike the early TRB, moved into extensive areas of high nutrient soils. Loess soils are extremely fertile and this fertility may have been greater in the Atlantic period (Modderman 1971). The good porosity and aeration of the soil are associated with a regular particle size so that the ground is easily worked. Also in contrast to the TRB, Mesolithic densities appear to have been low. The setting was different and the settlement strategy of the LBK groups also differed from that of the TRB.

It is now generally accepted, following Modderman (1971), that the hypothesis of short-term wandering LBK settlements should be abandoned for the Netherlands and lower Rhine (if not for all the LBK) in favour of long-term stable and gradually expanding occupation. Radiocarbon dates from a number of sites indicate occupation over hundreds of years, there is evidence for gradual shifts of houses within the same settlements (e.g. at Sittard and Elsloo) and long-term use of cemeteries attached to settlements, as at Elsloo (Modderman 1970). But it is the recently collected seed evidence from LBK sites that is the most telling. Willerding (1980) has noted considerable variety in the seed assemblages from LBK sites in different regions of Europe. The economy was regionalised but it was also well-developed in that, for example, most of the plants were probably grown in separate plots or fields. The fields seem to have been small and surrounded by hedges, or by the edges of woodland, and the landscape was not extensively opened (Knörzer 1974; Groenman-van Waateringe 1978; Bakels 1978). Such small-scale clearance could support long-term settlement without soil exhaustion in the neighbourhood of the site. The weed species identified indicate no lack of nitrogen in the soil (Willerding 1980) and the removal of biomass from the fields may have been limited by taking only the spikes during harvesting (ibid.). The small, dispersed nature of many of the early settlements (Aldenhoven Plateau 1971–1975), the rich loess soils, and the farming methods did not lead to a need for frequent moves, and long-term settlement could be supported.

The settlement, burial and economic evidence suggests long-term occupation in preferred locations on the loess (low terrace edges near water). Gradual outwards expansion, in which social groups could expand but remain in distinct clusters of settlement, was possible because of the wide-spread occurrence of preferred loess environments. Outward accretionary expansion of LBK settlements has been amply demonstrated by Sielmann (1971, 1972) and at the Aldenhoven Plateau (Aldenhoven Plateau 1971–1975). Statistical tests on LBK sites of different phases in the Untermaingebiet (Hodder 1977, p. 270) indicated that earlier sites were more clustered than later sites, and that gradual outwards expansion had occurred.

However, the evidence amassed by Sielmann indicates that, by the end of the LBK, sites on the edges of the settled area were already moving into less favourable environments (Louwe Kooijmans 1976, p. 239). At the same time, there is evidence of 'internal stress' (ibid.) in that earthworks of a clearly defensive character can be identified. In addition, the earlier widespread pottery types become regionalised (e.g. Dohrn-Ihmig 1973, 1974; Bakels 1978). Dohrn-Ihmig has shown how the percentages of pottery motifs in the Rhine–Maas, Rhine–Main and Middle Rhine (Plaidt) regions differ although there is considerable overlap. Several LBK cemeteries in Europe show little evidence of incipient hierarchies, but for the late LBK in the Paris Basin, Burkill (pers. comm.) has recognised particularly rich graves which are not limited to one age category. In Holland, the Elsloo cemetery represents the latter half of the LBK sequence. Here, Van de Velde (1979) suggests that some 'richer' graves can be identified within sex categories, on the basis of the diversity of goods in the graves and the presence of widely traded artefacts. However, no data are available from Elsloo concerning the ages of individuals, and the variation noted by Van de Velde may be linked to age. In the Elsloo settlement, differentiation in the size and form of houses increases in the later phase (Moddermann 1975, pp. 272–3).

By the end of the LBK there are some indications of an increasing concern with bounded groups as peripheral fissioning increased, of competition between groups, and perhaps of incipient small-scale ranking. It is of interest to note that the organisation of the pottery design also becomes more differentiated and contrastive through time. As fig. 15 suggests, the earliest pots frequently show little separation of decoration into distinct zones or bounded areas. In Conkey's terms (this volume), there is no design-field and the possibilities for differentiation and categorisation are slight. The designs themselves are often not carefully executed. But through time, oppositions between different parts of the pot become more apparent. In particular, a rim zone can be distinguished from a belly zone, both in terms of shape (the appearance of a concave neck section) and decoration. Van de Velde (1980, p. 15) notes that when there is decoration on the rim or neck there is also decoration on the belly zone. The decoration of the two zones may be entirely independent, and this difference may be accentuated by a line or narrow band separating the two zones. However, in some cases an interruption or accent in the upper zone is related to the decoration below it. In addition, the bands of decoration become more densely filled so that the difference between band and non-band becomes more distinct. In these ways, a series of oppositions, mostly binary, become more marked through time. Van de Velde's structural analysis of LBK design (fig. 16) indicates that much of the decoration incorporates simple bilateral and rotational symmetry. In general, simple oppositions and contrasts characterise much of the LBK pottery design, but the concern with these oppositions and the boundaries between them increases through time in congruence with changes in settlement, economy and society.

 After the LBK, the tendencies already identified continue on the loess. Distinctions between regional styles of pottery (e.g. Gering and Grossgartach) become more distinct (Dohrn-Ihmig 1974), and in the following Rössen culture, clear regionalisation is evident in the varied pottery decoration. By the end of the Rössen (around 3600 BC), settlement has nucleated into large villages. Palisades or earthworks occur. The houses are still substantial long timber buildings, but the agglomeration contrasts with the

Fig. 15. Stylistic changes in LBK pottery from Geleen, Sittard and Elsloo. Lower row: period 1*b*. Upper row: period II*cd*. 2nd and 3rd rows: intermediate styles. Source: Louwe Kooijmans 1976.

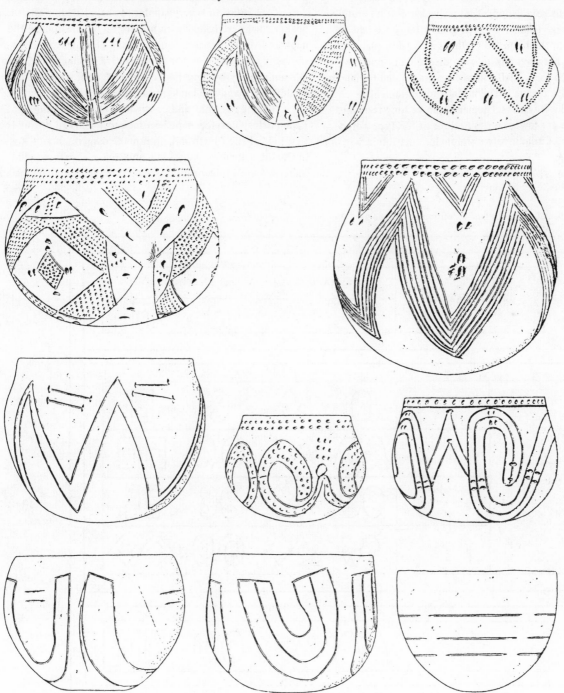

frequently dispersed scatter of LBK houses. There is a gradual and slight spread out of the limited zones preferred by earlier settlement, with moves off the loess and a spread of settlement up the valley sides, onto the interfluves and higher ground (Whittle 1977, p. 146). The Rössen also saw an extension of settlement onto the lower terraces and alluvial plain of the lower Rhine and onto the sands of the North European plain itself.

During the Rössen, population nucleated in settled villages within preferred environments, but there was also expansion onto less favourable soils. The rich and easily worked loess soils could support intensive agriculture and the growth of large villages. In such areas attempts could be made to maintain the bounded group as a physical reality. The differences between groups were displayed in pottery styles. Unlike the early TRB, there is no communal burial. In the TRB, stability occurs in the burial and settlement is short-term. In the Rössen, settlements can be long-term and nucleated, there are fewer contradictions of the type noted for the TRB, and burial involves simple inhumation in cemeteries.

The design organisation of the Grossgartach and Rössen pottery has some similarities with TRB pottery. By Grossgartach there is a wider variety of forms than in the early LBK, including decorated and pedestal vases, decorated and plain shallow bowls with four pointed corners, decorated shallow bowls, oval cups and straight-sided beakers. As in the TRB, the great variety of forms is associated with a great richness of decoration with designs covering most or all of the surface of the pot in both Grossgartach and Rössen. In Grossgartach the decoration is made up of both horizontal bands and arrangements of triangles and other motifs which are separated in distinct sections of the pot. By Rössen, the design organisation is very similar to the TRB. In particular, beaker forms are found with horizontal decoration on the neck and vertical decoration (e.g. long pendant triangles) on the belly (fig. 17). Further contrasts are produced on some Rössen pottery by 'negative' ornamentation, where motifs are left open and the background is hatched.

The oppositions and contrasts emerging during the LBK pottery development become more marked during the first half of the fourth millennium (Grossgartach and Rössen) in the loess areas of the middle and lower Rhineland. The increased use of decoration is associated with a differentiation

Fig. 16. Types of symmetry and repetition in LBK pottery decoration. Adapted from Van de Velde 1980.

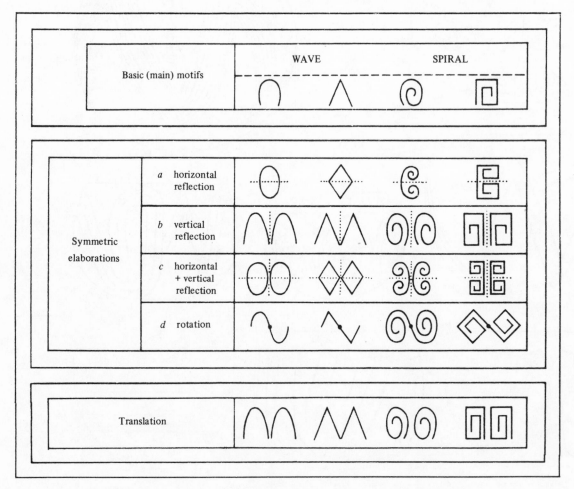

of shape categories and with increasing contrasts in the decoration and shapes of individual pots. These associations and temporal trends are reminiscent of the TRB A to E phases and a similar explanatory model is suggested. An increasing emphasis during the LBK—Rössen sequence on symbolic and functional oppositions in the pottery appears to be linked chronologically to increasing contrasts between regional groups, between defended settlements, between egalitarian and non-egalitarian principles, and between large nucleated villages on the loess and the spread of settlement onto thinner and less productive soils. The distinctions in pottery form and decoration and the increasing use of decoration could have been produced as part of the formation and legitimation of social and economic categories, as has been suggested for the TRB sequence. But there are differences between the two sequences which are informative.

The dendritic structure of the TRB A to E pottery decoration allows a large number of contrasts to be identified at different levels. It can be claimed that the LBK and Rössen pottery involves fewer contrastive dimensions than the TRB pottery, since the main concern in the former cases is with simple neck/body, and single horizontal/vertical oppositions. This hypothesis must be supported by quantitative data, but it is clear that on the rich soils of the loess the stable local groups are less contradicted by settlement dispersal and mobility than on the sands of the North European plain. Communal burial ritual is not used to legitimate traditional rights and social control since the latter can be exercised directly over individuals gathered together in large, semi-permanent social units. There is less concern in the LBK—Rössen pottery with symbolically marking out and forming social categories and the boundaries between them.

Fig. 17. Rössen pot from Heidelberg—Neuenheim. Source: Goller 1972.

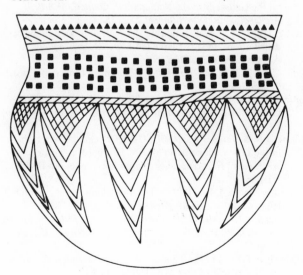

Conclusion

During the phases A to E of the TRB, the dead and burial ritual were used as part of social strategies aimed at legitimating traditional rights. The chronological correspondence between the sequences for the pottery and mortuary data has been suggested as indicating that pottery form and decoration were used to form social categories and to draw attention to interaction between those categories. The material culture marked out and made 'natural' the various social groupings. But no universal nor straightforward 'reflective' relationship is implied between social and material patterning. Material culture variability does not increase simply because social variability increases. The particular relationship occurs because of conflicts between the principles of stable groups and the practice of dispersal and between the traditional principle of equivalent social units divided in terms of age and sex and the strategies aimed at additional forms of ranking and differentiation. The material culture (burial, pots, axes, etc.) is organised into a complex series of categories and oppositions so that the associated activities can play a part in drawing attention to and legitimating traditional rights in a context in which there is increasing potential for the disruption of those rights. The conflicts and strategies involve fissioning, settlement expansion, and new adaptations to the environment, but these economic changes can themselves be used as agents for further social change, working against the traditional stable groupings.

In the early LBK, a similar social structure may have existed to that in the TRB, based on clearly defined descent groups and their joint labour. But here there were few contradictions between the social processes and the productive capacities of society. The rich and relatively 'empty' loess soils allowed long-term and small settlements. These equivalent units came to be contradicted by dominant—subordinate relationships in later phases. In conjunction with the social and economic tensions and competition, fissioning increased, settlement expanded outwards into areas with less productive soils, agglomeration and intensification occurred on the better soils, defensive earthworks were built, and regional distinctions in pottery styles were produced. Pottery shape and decoration became more differentiated as part of the construction of social categories and rights. There are no absolute distinctions between the LBK—Rössen and TRB sequences; only degrees of difference. On the sands of the North European plain, TRB groups could make use of the natural potential of the environment for greater fissioning and settlement dispersal and mobility. Here dominant groups manipulated burial, pottery and the symbols (such as house plans) evoking the earlier, more stable groupings in the loess areas in order to maintain traditional rights.

In the latest phase considered here, the PFB, many of the earlier contradictions are transformed. Settlement dispersal is associated with individual burial rather than with communal burial or with cemeteries located by settlements as in the LBK. The fluidity and flexibility of settlement and individual groups are no longer contradicted by the concern for incorporation in stable, well-defined social units (as had been seen in TRB burial and Rössen agglomerated settlement). In contrast to the TRB, social hierarchy is directly expressed in burial and in a range of distinct artefact styles amongst beaker groups (Shennan 1977). But the new process of legitimation resolved the earlier contradictions and involved a reaction against the earlier proliferation of social and symbolic distinctions in pottery and in the daily activities associated with the use of pottery. There was a concern to break down the earlier emphasis on categorical distinctions and to emphasise access, incorporation, sequence and addition. It was only after the PFB, in for example the Veluwe Beakers, that complex contrastive designs reminiscent of the TRB are again found.

The reconstruction provided above needs to be assessed through the collection of further quantitative data on pottery variation, burial form, social hierarchy, and economic strategy. Yet this study, and the possibility of further assessment, indicate that hypotheses concerned with the use of symbols and symbolic structures as part of social strategies can be tested against archaeological data. In addition, there has been discussion of the specific details of an individual historical context, and particular cultural features, such as the shapes of burial tombs, have been interpreted in terms of that unique context.

Since this study has examined the integration of general social processes in a particular cultural matrix, we cannot expect the same cultural data to be produced in other areas where similar social and economic strategies are acted out. I have not identified any behavioural law predicting the relationship between pottery decoration, burial form and social strategy. In the Dutch context a particular relationship exists. But similar aims and social strategies can be achieved in different ways. While a preliminary review indicates that similar processes to those observed in the Dutch TRB are linked to similar cultural features in other areas in western and northern Europe, in certain cultural groups such as the SOM (Seine—Oise—Marne) in the Paris Basin, megalithic burial is associated with coarse, 'shapeless', undecorated pottery. There are other distinctive characteristics of the SOM. For example, megalithic burial continues later than in other areas, and the group stands out amongst European cultural units in that it resists Beaker influences. It is necessary to carry out a broad comparative study of contexts in western and northern Europe where megaliths occur in order to identify further factors which may be relevant for the explanation of the particular correlations observed in the Netherlands.

Acknowledgements

The work for this article was conducted while the author was a visiting professor at the Van Giffen Institute for Pre- and Protohistory, University of Amsterdam, and it would not have been possible without the patience and aid of the members of that Institute, to whom I am most sincerely grateful. In particular, the work was based on discussion with Jan Albert Bakker whose exhaustive knowledge of TRB and Neolithic pottery is the foundation for any cultural studies in the Netherlands. His careful comments on an earlier draft of this article were of great value. The Directors of the Biologisch-Archaeologisch Instituut, Groningen, and the Rijksmuseum van Oudheden, Leiden, kindly allowed me to study pottery collections. I am also indebted to various colleagues and students, in particular Chris Tilley, Steve Cogbill, Mike Parker Pearson and Paul Halstead, for their criticisms.

References

Aldenhoven Plateau (1971–1975) 'Untersuchungen zur neolithischen Besiedlung der Aldenhovener Platte', *Bonner Jahrbücher* 171: 558–664; 172: 344–94; 173: 226–56; 174: 424–508; 175: 191–229

Ashbee, P. (1970) *The Earthen Long Barrow in Britain*, Dent, London

Bakels, C.C. (1978) *Four Linearbandkermaic Settlements and Their Environments: A Papaeoecological Study of Sittard, Stein, Elsloo and Heinheim*, (Analecta Praehistoria Leidensia II), University of Leiden, Leiden

Bakker, J.A. (1979) *The TRB West Group*, University of Amsterdam, Amsterdam

Bakker, J.S. & Van der Waals, J.D. (1973) 'Danekamp—Angelslo: cremations, collared flasks and a corded ware sherd in Dutch final TRB contexts' in G.E. Daniel & P. Kjaerum (eds.) *Megalithic Graves and Ritual*, Jutland Archaeological Society

Bloch, M. (1971) *Placing the Dead*, Seminar Press, London

Bloch, M. (1975) 'Property and the end of affinity' in M. Bloch (ed.) *Marxist Analyses in Social Anthropology*, ASA, London

Dohrn-Ihmig, M. (1973) 'Gruppen in der jüngeren nordwestichen Linienbandkeramik', *Archäologisches Korrespondenzblatt* 3: 279–87

Dohrn-Ihmig, M. (1974) 'Die Geringer Gruppe der späten Linenbandkeramik im Mittelrheintal', *Archäologisches Korrespondenzblatt* 4: 301–6

Faris, J. (1972) *Nuba Personal Art*, Duckworth, London

Friedman, J. (1975) 'Tribes, states and transformations' in M. Bloch (ed.) *Marxist Analyses in Social Anthropology*, ASA London

Goller, K. (1972) 'Die Rössener Kultur in ihrem Südwestlichen Verbreitungsgebiet' in J. Lüning (ed.) *Die Anfängs des Neolithikums vom Orient bis Nordeuropa*, Böhlau Verlag, Köln

Groenman-van Waateringe, W. (1978) 'The impact of Neolithic man on the landscape in the Netherlands', *Council for British Archaeology Research Report* 21: 135–46

Hodder, I. (1977) 'New directions in the analysis of archaeological distributions' in D.L. Clarke (ed.) *Spatial Archaeology*, Academic Press, London

Hodder, I. (1982) *Symbols in Action*, Cambridge University Press, Cambridge

Knörzer, K. (1974) 'Bandkeramische Pflanzenfunde von Bedburg-Garsdorf, Kr. Bergheim Erft', *Rheinische Ausgrabungen* 15: 173–92

Lanting, J.N. & Van der Waals, J.D. (1976) 'Beaker culture relations in the Lower Rhine Basin' in J.W. Lanting & J.D. van der Waals (eds.) *Glockenbecher Symposion*, Fibula-van Dishoek, Haarlem

Louwe Kooijmans, L.P.L. (1976) 'Local development in a borderland', *Oudheid Kundige Mede Delingen* 57: 227–97

Modderman, P.J.R. (1970) *Linearbandkeramik aus Elsloo und Stein*, (Analecta Praehistorica Leidensia 3), University of Leiden, Leiden

Modderman, P.J.R. (1971) 'Bandkeramiker und Wanderbauerntum', *Archäologisches Korrespondenzblatt* 1: 7–9

Modderman, P.J.R. (1975) 'Elsloo, a Neolithic farming community
    in the Netherlands' in R. Bruce-Mitford (ed.) *Recent Archae-
    ological Excavations in Europe*, Routledge and Kegan Paul,
    London
Newell, R.R. (1970) 'The flint industry of the Dutch Linearband-
    keramik', *Analecta Praehistorica Leidensia* 3: 144–83
Newell, R.R. (1973) 'The post-glacial adaptations of the indigenous
    population of the Northwest European Plain' in S.K. Kozloqski
    (ed.) *The Mesolithic in Europe*, University Press, Warsaw
Renfrew, A.C. (1976) 'Megaliths, territories and populations' in S.J.
    de Laet (ed.) *Acculturation and Continuity in Atlantic Europe*,
    De Tempel, Brugge
Shennan, S.J. (1977) *Bell Beakers and Their Context in Central
    Europe: A New Approach*, unpublished PhD dissertation,
    University of Cambridge
Shennan, S.J. (1978) 'Archaeological "cultures": an empirical investi-
    gation' in I. Hodder (ed.) *Spatial Organisation of Culture*,
    Duckworth, London
Sherratt, A. (1981) 'Plough and pastoralism in prehistoric Europe:
    aspects of the secondary products revolution' in I. Hodder,
    G. Isaac & N. Hammond (eds.) *Pattern of the Past*, Cambridge
    University Press, Cambridge
Sielmann, B. (1971) 'Zum Verhältniss von Ackerbau und Vichzucht
    im Neolithikum Südwestdeutschlands', *Archäologisches
    Korrespondenzblatt* 1: 65–8
Sielmann, B. (1972) 'Die frühneolithische Besiedlung Mitteleuropas'
    in J. Lüning (ed.) *Die Anfänge des Neolithikums vom Orient
    bis Nordeuropa* 5a, Köln
Van de Velde, P. (1979) 'The social anthropology of a Neolithic
    cemetery in the Netherlands', *Current Anthropology* 20:
    37–58
Van de Velde, P. (1980) *Elsloo and Hienheim: Bandkeramik Social
    Structure*, Analecta Praehistorica Leidensia 12, University of
    Leiden, Leiden
Van der Leeuw, S. (1976) 'Neolithic beakers from the Netherlands:
    the potter's point of view' in J.N. Lanting & J.D. van der Waals
    (eds.) *Glockenbecher Symposium*, Fibula-van Dishoek,
    Haarlem
Van der Waals, J.D. & Glasbergen, W. (1955) 'Beaker types and their
    distribution in the Netherlands', *Palaeohistoria* 4: 5–46
Voss, J.A. (1980) 'The measurements and evaluation of change in the
    regional social networks of egalitarian societies: an example
    from the Neolithic of Northwestern Europe', Paper presented
    at 45th Society of American Archaeology Meetings,
    Philadelphia
Whittle, A.W.R. (1977) *The Earlier Neolithic of S. England and its
    Continental Background*, BAR Supplementary Series 35,
    Oxford
Willerding, U. (1980) *Zum Ackerbau der Bandkeramiker*, Beiträge
    zur Archäologie Nordwestdeutschlands und Mitteleuropas,
    Materialhefte zur Ur- und Frühgeschichte Niedersachsens 16

PART FOUR

Commentary

Childe's offspring
Mark Leone

Anyone can use a book against itself, but since I am an interested advocate of the work in these chapters, I want to use some of the apparent discrepancies within the book to show, not its weakness, but its interior strengths. This book began as a conference on structuralism and symbolism in archaeology and appeared to owe its life to Lévi-Strauss and Edmund Leach: to Lévi-Strauss because of structuralism and to Leach (1973, pp. 761–71) because of his prediction that archaeology's next move would be to structuralism. The first discrepancy is that this book is not only not the advent of structuralism in archaeology, it may be the effective antidote needed to prevent that tired method long superceded even among its own practitioners. This book's archaeology superceded, while simultaneously integrating, structuralism and does so at a time of great importance to archaeology. These archaeologists are not concerned with abstract principles of mind, as they would be if literal structuralists. But they are concerned with context, meaning and particular historical circumstances, as well as with the generative principles which unify particular cultures. They are interested in particular structures but within their historical, i.e. material, context.

The second apparent discrepancy occurs when we are invited to understand the archaeology presented here against the New Archaeology, particularly as defined by Lewis Binford. Systems theory, cross-cultural behavioural generalisations and Hempelian positivism, key aspects of the New Archaeology, are seen in the book as methodological errors to be avoided. They are to be avoided because the New Archaeology developed a greater concern with function and adaptation than with change, showed little understanding of the relationship between social action and material form, and no ability to deal with the symbolic and structural aspects of culture, including meaning. Favoured here are theories of social action, ideology, analogy and elaborate consideration of contexts in the past. To achieve these the authors abandon linear notions of cause, the reflective nature of artefacts and vulgar materialism. But even though the reader soon sees that structuralism is considered in context in order to outline generative principles, it could be argued that British material- ism is being contrasted with American materialism. For the British, structuralism does not dominate and in some of the articles here the material, historical and social context does. The move is not from Binford to Lévi-Strauss but from Binford to Marx and his direct descendants. When that becomes apparent, one is no longer enthralled to Leach and a fad going nowhere but to the tradition that links Leslie White and Gordon Childe: historical materialism. The apparent discrepancy is created by the authors' rejection of the New Archaeology. They reject some of it but in certain cases preserve the deeper materialism. Binford and White in America and the authors and Childe in Britain are not devoid of materialism. While the differences professed in this book are very important and occasionally appear discrepant, the deeper tradition creates unity. By using Childe, these authors retrieve an older part of British archaeology and preserve as well the strongest bond they have with theory in American archaeology. We can be very happy these are Childe's off- spring.

There is a simple, accurate but superficial way to resolve this book's rejection of the New Archaeology by pointing out that the types of societies treated by the two schools of thought are different. Binford and his colleagues dealt with hunter—gatherers and early farmers; few dealt with peasants and early states. The New Archaeologists dealt with the deepest past, most primitive technologically, and some eras not fully human. Evolutionary theory, stressing adaptation, environmental effects, systemic change, and subsistence seemed not only more appropriate because of the exigencies of survival but also because among the societies they studied social organisation did not involve stratification, institutions, monuments, separate religious entities, or much beyond kinship. Evolutionary and ecological theory was poorly equipped to handle symbolic elaborations and was safe in the inability since it was felt that the forms these take did not yet exist. However, archae- ologists dealing with fully developed Neolithic societies, with towns, large populations, enormous monuments, metal working and specialisation of all sorts were dealing with societies whose economies were secure enough that their complexity alone could not be fully accounted for by sys-

temic analyses of subsistence, efficiency, population pressure, or the idea that religion is reflective of material reality. More was needed in terms of theory; evolutionary theory was and remains effective in its terms and on societies appropriate to it, but evolution's deeper roots in Marx are needed to deal with societies further from the edge of evolution and survival, and, simultaneously, much closer to ourselves and our condition. Thus, a turn to the Marxist tradition, representing in its course a recovery of Childe, may represent a superficial rejection of the New Archaeology which will turn out to be inappropriate in the long run. The roots, this argument goes, are the same but adapted to differ- ing data. This argument is weak and a different one will take us further.

If one argues that some of Binford's innovations are essential in America, it is because neither Palaeolithic peoples nor American Indians have any direct historical tie to the present, and therefore generalising models of investigation like nomothetic positivism and systems theory are needed to interpret the archaeological record fully and accurately. The argument takes this part of the past and opposes it to the view that Neolithic Europe, the main archaeological data considered in this book, is related more directly to ourselves and so context and history are needed because the tie to the present exists. This argument, one common throughout archaeology, is that some of the past is more accessible than some other parts and the more closely related to us, the more plausible the understanding, which leads to a reduced need for encumbering epistemology. But by focussing on the assumptions making different epistemologies necessary, we can avoid using differing levels of sociocultural integration as a distinction between these British and the American New Archaeologists. The useful distinction to be made between them, which will resolve the discrepancy between the two forms of materialism noted earlier, can be found in their unstated assumptions: for the Americans, the past is unrelated to us; for the British, it is. Both positions are assumptions and by turning them on their heads by using the notion of consciousness to ask how the present is related to the past — not the reverse — the two materialisms, coming from the same source ultimately, can be reconciled.

My argument is that the greatest need is to situate Hodder and his students in terms of the New Archaeology, and both in terms of the materialist tradition to which I believe each is heir. To achieve this, I would like to examine the degree to which both groups take the relationship between past and present to be given, and thus leave it unexamined, how each assumes meaning for the past is achieved, and the position of Gordon Childe on these issues. Childe is important because both groups derive some of their present theory from his work.

Binford, aware that much of archaeology had been guesswork and would continue to be because both simple analogues from the present and sophisticated models all amounted to uncheckable borrowing, turned to hypothetico-

deductive epistemology. When this was connected to nomothetic method, as was more or less inevitable, it became a
search for laws. But before that, the contribution of merit
– one that endures – was one of testing for verification using
independent data. Binford urged sounder arguments and, I
believe, he got them. Laws aside, American archaeologists
did come to know the likelihood of their conclusions with
greater confidence and in that sense knew their knowledge of
the past more accurately.

The hypothetico-deductive approach has only one aim.
That is not to overcome bias, not to formulate laws, and not
to annoy. Its purpose in archaeology is to address the
relationship between past and present. That relationship is
assumed by American archaeologists to have two parts. The
first comes from assuming that the past is dead and knowable only through the present. The second, is that accurate
knowledge of the past is essential to understanding the
present. Binford's epistemological suggestion recognised that
hunches, guesses, even inferences were weak, not because
they were not multiple, but because they all constituted
projections of the present onto the past. Turned into
hypotheses, which could be done only by association with
theory, these projections could be sorted out depending on
how they matched up against evidence argued to represent
their presence in the past. This entire experimentation with
scientific method was important – and remains so – not
because the past is so difficult to know, but rather because of
the many pasts we can and do habitually create. Some
measure of their match with past reality was needed.

Curiously, Gordon Childe, the key link to the past
which this book retrieves, did not seem to care whether or
not he was accurate when interpreting the past. He was not
concerned with many pasts but with one. Childe could have
been concerned with the ladder of inference, which said
that technology and subsistence were safer to draw conclusions about than social life, religion, and so on. It is not
daring to say that Childe is the most important archaeologist
Europe or America has produced. Yet through much of his
life he worked without a word about epistemology, scientific
procedure or nomothetic method. He presented the past,
richly contextualised, full of the reasons for change in
society. And beyond all that Childe was writing about our
past, the European (and thus also, we believe, the Euro-
American) past. No matter how said, whether living out
Marx on prehistory to improve thus on Engels, or to verify
progress by organising the past in a certain way, Childe did
not just travel between past and present. He travelled
between a specific historical past and its conventionally
agreed upon descendants in modern Europe. Such travel
occurs through ethnographic analogy, which, like the following quote, is often vague to the point of being folklore, and
through terms like 'botany', 'geology', and 'chemistry' or
like 'nuisance', 'passionately', 'stupendous', 'sweat and
blood', 'notoriously inimical', and 'useless', all of which are
entirely modern and self-referential.

Thus there grows up to be handed on a great body of
craft lore – snippets of botany, geology, and chemistry,
one might say. If we may judge from the procedure of
modern barbarians [agriculturalists], the legitimate
deductions from experience are inextricably mixed up
with what we should call useless magic. Each operation
of every craft must be accompanied by the proper
spells and the prescribed ritual acts. All this body of
rules, practical and magical, forms part of the craft
tradition. It is handed on from parent to child by
example and precept. The daughter helps her mother
at making pots, watches her closely, imitates her, and
receives from her lips oral directions, warning, and
advice. The applied sciences of neolithic times were
handed on by what today we should call a system of
apprenticeship.   (Childe 1951, p. 81)

Beyond generalised ethnographic analogy, value judgment and projected emotion, Childe's principle thread between
past and present is created by analysing contradictions which
express themselves through the rise of classes and their conflicts.

Progress before the [urban] revolution had consisted in
improvements in productive processes made presumably by the actual producers, and made moreover in
the teeth of superstitions that discouraged all innovations as dangerous. But by the [urban] revolution
the actual producers, formerly so fertile in invention,
were reduced to the position of 'lower classes'. The
ruling classes who now emerged owed their power
largely to the exploitation of just those hampering
superstitions . . . Thus, from the point of view of progress, Egyptian and Babylonian societies were involved
by the urban revolution in a hopeless contradiction.
                                 (Childe 1951, pp. 182–3)

Using analogy, deliberately employing modern bias,
and the materialist dynamic based on contradictions, Childe
created the tie between past and present and, in returning to
analogy and Marxist assumptions, his offspring begin to do
the same here. They may choose to go as far again but may
consider Marx's notion of consciousness to do so and progress further.

It is plausible for Europeans to treat European prehistory as though it were directly tied to the present. Neolithic Europe did after all become the Ancient World and
that is related to the present. That relationship cannot be
said to exist for Neolithic America or for the Palaeolithic
anywhere. These past ages are too different and too separate,
we think. Childe appears on the surface to have written
about prehistory but it is always about Near Eastern and
European prehistory. The difference between that and the
Americans is that the line to the present from the past is
taken to be grounded, not created. It is reasonable to suggest
that Childe is particularist as is proposed in this book, but
only in the Marxist sense that an individual situation is to be
understood and indeed is informed by the historical circumstances, i.e. the material particulars, of its existence. Childe

found the roots of modern situations in the particular events of prehistory and could do so plausibly because he used a theory that brought the particulars of the present out of a past that was assumed to determine them historically. This tie is what made Childe such a success; it was not that he dealt with change in general but with changes that lead directly to the modern present; not just any modern present but our own.

Two things can be said about this way of treating the past. Few have tried to do it until the contributors to this volume attempted to reconnect themselves to Childe by rediscovering Marxist theory. And the congratulations due them are neither small nor beside the point! Second, the assumption Childe made is just that, an assumption; until it is examined, the degree of success he enjoyed is not likely to be duplicated.

To be bold but, I think, plausible, there is no more direct a tie between Neolithic Europe and modern Europe than there is between prehistoric American Indians and modern America. Do we believe in the tie Italian fascists created between ancient Rome and modern Italy? Do Arabs believe in the tie created between ancient Palestine and modern Israel? The questions point to the answer that Glyn Daniel (1963, pp. 128–50) provided years ago. Archaeology creates an image of the past which is not so much a matter of inaccuracy as it is a tie to the present because it is often, maybe always, informed by modern uses. And Gordon Childe understood that. And so, coming from a different position, did Lewis Binford when he emphasised culture process and verification through hypothesis testing as a way of avoiding projection.

In Marxist theory the tie between past and present is neither given nor natural; it is a matter of meanings and a matter of ideology. It is, in other words, created and sustained by those looking back. This is not to take a position of absolute scepticism saying that the past cannot be known; it is to say that, while the facts happened, the meaning or interpretation we give them is culture centred. Given this, and in order to understand the structure of meaning given to the past, Marxist ideas of ideology are useful because so well defined. All this leads us back to Childe by way of the uses of Marx now available through Lukács, Althusser and others.

The notion of consciousness is important to raise here because it helps resolve the discrepancies mentioned earlier. The point of talking about consciousness is to answer the question: Why know history? Since there are two kinds of history within the Marxist tradition of analysis, consciousness helps to identify Childe's tradition. Vulgar history is ideology and includes history as told, written, recited, presented in textbooks, used in classrooms, museums and the modern media. Conventional, colloquial, given history is a modern manufacture, an artefact, if you will, of modern political and economic factors serving not to illuminate how the present came to be but to obscure key relationships

within the present (Althusser 1971, pp. 127–86). Consciousness operates, among other ways, through knowing history's role both in shaping the present and in history's hiding it through vulgarisation (Lukács 1971, pp. 223–55). Consciousness does not occur necessarily through an understanding of history, nor is it acted on through an historical search. Nonetheless, a proper construction of a past which is thought directly determinative of modern conditions may create it. This is especially true among our own societies which believe they draw comprehension of the present and the future from the past.

I am not saying, as did Collingwood (1956, pp. 205–334), that history is what we make it. And I believe Daniel was wrong in saying that just because some political systems abuse archaeology others can keep it more neutral and accurate. Daniel is no real offspring of Childe here. Archaeology and history are so thoroughly modern and so thoroughly political that we have an obligation, in knowing that, to come to terms with the ideological process that is inevitably going to operate in our work. The problem presented by the idea of consciousness solves one question quickly. Since it is not possible to have objective or neutral knowledge of the past apart from theory, drop the effort. There is no point in the severity of an academic stand like Binford's once one realises there can be no separation between what occurred and what it means. A Marxist would say that all knowledge is self-knowledge and all knowledge of history is present knowledge. Furthermore, an effort to create an objective past through use of a scientific method incapable of relating itself to the present masks the vulgarisation which potentially accompanies any deliberate effort to free the researcher from his cultural situation. A more productive effort would be to see that the tie between present and past is what the former does with the latter, not with how the former grew from the latter. In this sense Childe did not write a European prehistory; he composed one. His descendants may choose to do the same.

Childe is important because he knew what he was doing and no one else seems to have. He did what Macaulay did; he wrote a history to be used, not to be emulated. He wrote a political document, not an archaeological one. He did juggle Engels, not to test him but to improve him. He wrote a statement from a political stand, which was of course an ideological and theoretical one as well. That is what provides the consistency in most of the books Childe wrote.

Long before Childe, Macaulay knew that a history was about readers and hearers, not about an objective treatment of subjects dead and removed. By writing his *History of England* Thomas Macaulay wrote in order to affect his readers, listeners, in short, his contemporaries. He wrote a story about the past for the present, having a degree of understanding that a vision of the past communicated effectively could address English identity, national needs, concerns and the moment. It was no ideal academic document and that is why it can be called political. It deliberately presented a view of the past he thought desirable in the present, and it can go without saying that accuracy and objectivity fall into their proper places in view of these as means not ends.

A standard description of Macaulay (Thompson 1942, pp. 294–300) portrays him as a literary artist, of little critical depth, subordinating facts and sources to the principles he was illustrating in history. 'He suggested that history must inevitably be written by advocates rather than judges' (Thompson 1942, p. 297). And he believed in 'the constant comparison of [the past] with the present' (Thompson 1942, p. 298). Critical judgments on Macaulay vary, ranging from 'the greatest historian the world had ever produced', to creator of a method 'altogether destructive of real historical knowledge' (Thompson 1942, pp. 298 and 300). Macaulay wrote before Marx, Darwin or Freud, and was unaware of the problem of dynamics seen by Hegel and handled by the later scholars, and unaware as well of the structure of the impact of historical presentations on the present.

Much of the conventional sketch of Macaulay sounds like Childe and little does not. I use it because Childe requires a context beyond archaeology, beyond scholarship and accuracy to be understood and thus emulated. Obviously, Childe was more careful of facts and sources than Macaulay and, just as obviously, Childe was a good writer and not a great one. He also possessed considerable critical depth. But Childe is unique, an advocate, constantly concerned with how the present came to be, not just or only or even with how the past looked. As Clark put it in the Foreword to *What Happened in History* (1964), 'ever since he went up to Oxford he was fascinated, as perhaps only one could be who came from a different continent, by the unique quality of European civilization: to understand his approach to prehistory we must accept his word, printed after his death, that he took up the subject precisely to find an answer to his question'. Like Macaulay, Childe was concerned with the nature of the present, and like Macaulay, who was a Whig and illustrated Whig principles in history, Childe used Marxism, or at least a materialist dialectic, to compose a European prehistoric past in order to comprehend the present.

I offer this hypothesis to my English colleagues because they are claiming their proper heritage in archaeology and should claim all of it. And because Americans, who assume a break with the prehistoric past, cannot. Gordon Childe was unique because he saw the tie between past and present in the reverse way from the rest of us. He saw, not evolution, process, stages, functional versus structural reconstructions, but politics going from present to past. To communicate his message he, like Thomas Macaulay, chose a grand scale, popular style, accessible medium and a guiding theory that allowed immediate comprehension.

To build upon Childe's contribution I would like to return to the Marxist tradition via Georg Lukács (1971) and

to the matter of consciousness. Childe and Macaulay intended to speak to the present in order to explain its character, uniqueness and identity. Marx and, to some degree, Childe spoke to the present by using historical materialism as a means to achieve 'self-knowledge of capitalist society' (Lukács 1971, p. 229). Such self-knowledge is to be achieved two ways. The first is by studying pre-capitalist societies.

> In precapitalist society the particular aspects of the economic process . . . remain separate from each other in a . . . way which permits neither an immediate interaction [of the aspects or parts of society] nor one that can be raised to the level of social consciousness . . . In capitalism, however, all the elements of the structure of society interact dialectically. Their apparent independence of each other, their way of concentrating themselves into self-regulating systems, the fetishistic semblance of autonomy, all this is – as an essential aspect of capitalism as understood by the bourgeoisie – the necessary transition to a proper and complete understanding of [the parts of capitalism].
> (Lukács 1971, pp. 230–1)

Although a little obscure, the quote says that pre-capitalist, including archaeological, societies can illustrate social life before economics came to dominate society. Such illustration can show that domination carried with it a sense of the interdependence of the parts of society, which creates a false notion of unity. The prior condition made the parts of society appear separate or by themselves because they hid no exploitative, or class relationship. Such a relationship is misrepresented through ideology under the appearance of interdependence. In pre-capitalist

> societies economic life did not yet possess that independence, that cohesion and immanence, nor did it have the sense of setting its own goals and being its own master that we associate with capitalist society. It follows from this that . . . we need much more complex and subtle analyses in order to show, on the one hand, what role was played from among all the forces controlling society by the purely economic . . . and on the other hand to show the impact of these economic forces upon the other institutions of society.
> (Lukács 1971, p. 238)

Before the economy dominated social life and individual identity, societies organised, thought, divided and defined life in a different way. In knowing that things were not always the way they are, consciousness of the way they are now, i.e. determined by economic factors which we hold to be discrete and autonomous, can be achieved more clearly. Childe provided detailed, lucid, and thus powerful visions of pre-capitalist society and the concluding essays in this book pick up the task.

The second way self-knowledge of capitalism is to be achieved is through understanding that the use of history itself 'produces and reproduces the capitalist relation.

[Because] capitalist production [is] a continuous connected process, a process of reproduction, [and] produces not only commodities, not only surplus-value', but history as well, the current 'opposition in capitalist society of past and present [can] be changed structurally' (Lukács 1971, p. 249). Self-knowledge involves understanding that there is a relationship between labour and all its objectified forms, e.g. product, personality, skill, family, day, owner, property and so on, including past. Becoming conscious of labour and the other social categories, which we take to be objectively separate from each other and existing naturally, Lukács argues that we may also renovate the relationship between past and present.

An understanding that the relationship between past and present is conventional or culturally prescribed, but not given or inevitable, is missing from Childe but is nonetheless essential. 'The past only becomes transparent when the present can practice self-criticism . . . Until that time the past must either be naively identified with the structure of the present or else it is held to be wholly alien . . . beyond all understanding' (Lukács 1971, p. 237). Childe saw that through prehistory the present could be illuminated through historical materialism but he did not see that he preserved the conventional relationship between past and present when he took it for granted that the relationship between past and present was governed by natural laws like evolution or progress, for natural laws are incapable of a critique of the present because they are products of it. Childe neglected to see the arbitrariness of his own creation and thus missed a chance to show one view of prehistory versus another, and with that he missed a chance at creating consciousness of the political tie between past and present. Lukács, paraphrasing and then quoting Marx, says that 'thus the succession and internal order of the categories [of history] constitute neither a purely logical sequence, nor are they organized in accordance with the facts of history. "Their sequence is rather determined by the relation which they bear to one another in modern bourgeois society, and which is the exact opposite of what seems to be their natural order or the order of their historical development" ' (Lukács 1971, p. 159). Thus, a Marxist history predicated on consciousness must include all the categories that actually determine human existence within the history and also show that the 'succession, coherence, and connections' are products of the historical process itself (Lukács 1971, p. 159).

My argument has been intended to bring Childe's descendants to an examination of the conventional quality of the tie between present and past and thus to place within their grasp a way it can be acted on. To see this conclusion one may look at America where several moves are made. Since prehistoric America and, basically, most of the Palaeolithic are taken to be unrelated to us, no tie is assumed, making the past hard to know. Knowledge of it is to be achieved through tested analogy in order to ensure accuracy. In practice this set of assumptions and methods produces a

mask, hiding, on the one hand the political quality of the constructed tie between past and present and, on the other, the human imagination's capacity to make the past into any form of the present: Lukács' naive identity.

By contrast, in Europe and Great Britain, a tie is assumed, and substantial work by famous people has built on it to produce a prehistory of merit and popularity. Popularity in such a context virtually means some self-awareness and consciousness. For those who have shown kinship with him here the task is to finish Childe's work by putting prehistory even more completely in the hands of the present. No easy matter, but a worthwhile one.

Acknowledgements

I am grateful to JoAnn Magdoff for making my arguments more precise and for recommending Lukács. Ann Palkovich helped me formulate the difference between the British and American schools and insisted on clarity. I am grateful to both for support and accept full responsibility for flaws in the presentation. The commitment of Ian Hodder and his students to archaeology made this effort worthwhile.

References

Althusser, L. (1971) 'Ideology and ideological state apparatuses' in L. Althusser *Lenin and Philosophy*, Monthly Review Press, New York
Childe, V.G. (1951) *Man Makes Himself*, Mentor Books, New York
Childe, V.G. (1964) *What Happened in History*, Penguin Books, Baltimore
Collingwood, R.G. (1956) *The Idea of History*, Oxford University Press, New York
Daniel, G.E. (1963) *The Idea of Prehistory*, World Publishing Company, Cleveland
Leach, E. (1973) 'Concluding address' in C. Renfrew (ed.) *The Explanation of Culture Change: Models in Prehistory*, University of Pittsburgh Press, Pittsburgh
Lukács, G. (1971) *History and Class Consciousness*, MIT Press, Cambridge
Thompson, J.W. (1942) *A History of Historical Writing*, Macmillan, New York

Index

adaptation, *viii*, 1–7, 9, 12–14, 23, 97, 117, 180
  ecological, 2–3, 7
Althusser, L., 29, 32–3, 35–6, 81, 100, 129–31, 182
analogy, 1–2, 11–12, 14, 19, 21, 33, 39–40, 43, 74–5, 15, 180–1, 184
  ethnographic, 13, 39, 74–6, 181
  linguistic, 19, 21, 40
  organic, 1–2, 12, 151
anthropology, 2, 8, 13, 17, 20–1, 26, 28, 74–5
  structuralist, 20
  use of analogy in, 74–5
archaeology, approaches to
  anthropological, 50–1
  as a cultural science, *viii*, 1, 10, 14
  historical, 4–5, 7, 10–11, 13–14, 162
  normative, 4, 8, 10–12, 49
  Palaeoeconomy, *vii*
  spatial, 5, 6
  use of mathematics in, 5, 6
  use of statistics in, 5, 6; *see also* contextual archaeology, ethnoarchaeology, functionalism, idealism, materialism, New Archae-

ology, processual archaeology, structuralism, systems theory
architecture
  domestic, 54, 63, 65–9
  funerary, 101, 103–4, 106–9, 111–12
  Middle Virginian, 45–6
  public, 54
  Swahili, 63–9
art, 4, 20
  northwest coastal American Indian, 20, 22
  Palaeolithic cave, 7, 20, 23, 115–26 *passim*
  as symbol, 81
asymmetry, 116, 122
  asymmetric social control, 129, 134, 151–2
attribute, 6, 9, 17, 32, 116, 121–2, 124
  of boundaries, 116, 122
  design, 21, 124
  structural, 116, 124
axes, stone battle, 162, 169, 171
  decoration of, 169
  Neolithic, 9
  PFB, 169
  TRB, 169, 171
Azande, 80–7
  chief system, 82, 86–7

location, 81
  marriage patterns, 82
  material culture, 82–7
  pottery, 83–5
  subsistence system, 82–4
  tribal structure, 82

Bandkeramik culture, 172
behaviourism, 5, 30, 41, 97; *see also* functionalism
Bell Beaker culture, 155–60, 163, 176
  in Britain, 159
  in Brittany, 159
  in central Europe, 159
  in Netherlands, 163, 176
  in southeast Spain, 159
Binford, L.R., 1–4, 11, 12, 14, 32, 44, 46 n.1, 99, 134, 138, 179–82
bones, animal, 75
  analysis of, 75
  disposal of, 75
bones, human, 129, 134–41, 143–4, 152
  analysis of, 129, 140–7, 150
  classification of, 134–5, 138
  disposal of, 134, 141, 143
  in Neolithic barrows, 129, 134–52 *passim*
  patterning of, 135, 137,

143–7, 150–2
  preservation of, 138–41
  quantification of, 135, 137–40
boundaries, 54, 65, 81, 84–7, 110, 116–18, 121–2, 171, 175
  between dead and living, 110
  in pot decoration, 115–16, 151
  social, 165–6, 173, 175
boundedness, concept of, 7, 116, 119, 121–2, 124, 134, 150–2, 165, 168
  in pot design, 165, 168
Bronze Age, 155–60
  in Aegean, 160
  in Brittany, 157–9
  in central Europe, 157, 159–60
  in Spain, 157–9
  in Wessex, 156, 159; *see also* Bell Beaker culture, bronze industry
bronze industry, 155–6, 159–60
burial practices, *viii*, 4, 6–7, 9–12, 14, 28, 74, 77, 99–112, 129–52 *passim*, 170, 172
  Bell Beaker, 158–9
  Bronze Age, 156–60

burial practices (cont.)
case study in Cambridge, 101-7
change in, 101-12 passim
differentiation in, 155-7
Dutch Neolithic, 162, 169-70, 172, 174-6
Neolithic, 129, 135-52 passim, 155-8
Neolithic burial mounds, 9-10, 129, 135-8, 162, 169-71
Marakwet, 77-8
social organisation reflected in, 99-102, 110
status in, 99-112 passim
symbolism of, 110-11
treatment of body in, 77, 106
Victorian, 99, 101, 106-11; see also cemeteries, cremation, death, funerary architecture, inhumation, ritual, symbols

capitalism, 27, 35, 133, 183-4
caste system, 89, 91-7
origins, 91, 96
as a social category, 91
association with specific activities, 91-2
categorisation, 7, 14, 17-21, 23, 73, 81, 91, 93, 110, 135, 151, 156, 162, 171-2
cemeteries, 6, 106-8, 111
in Cambridge, 103-5, 107-8
class/status distinctions in, 105, 108
Neolithic, 6
spatial organisation in, 106-8
change, process of, 3, 8, 11, 14, 20, 23, 27, 30, 32-3, 35-6, 53-4, 61, 72, 89, 93, 95, 97, 110, 129, 155
cultural, viii, 72, 89, 91, 97, 101, 117, 155-9, 162-3, 169, 172-5, 180
social, viii, 5-6, 8, 10-12, 14, 26-8, 30-1, 34-7, 50, 86, 101, 151, 160
chi-square test, 140-1, 143-4, 147, 150
chiefdoms, 6, 28, 81-2, 86-7, 100, 156, 159
Azande, 81-2, 86-7
Neolithic, 156; see also state societies
Childe, V.G., 1, 2, 4, 11-13, 48-9, 55, 61 n.3, 100, 112, 155, 160, 180-4
Chomsky, N., 19, 21, 40
Clark, J.G.D., 1, 2, 11-13
Clarke, D.L., 2, 4, 6, 7, 22, 31-2, 36, 54
codes, 7-10, 19
semiotic, 133
complex societies, 47, 50-9, 61, 180

Merina, 47, 55-61
public monuments of, 54, 180
spatial organisation of, 54-60
componential analysis, 17, 21-2
contextual archaeology, 1, 9, 11, 13, 31, 40; see also structuralism
contrast, concept of, 17, 21, 23, 162, 171, 175
in burial of skeleton, 129
categorical, 89
structural, 89, 96
cremation, 99, 101, 103, 105-11, 156
class distinctions in, 103, 105
development of in 20th century, 99, 105, 108, 110-11
culture, viii, 1-7, 9-14, 30, 39, 40, 44, 47-8, 75, 116, 119, 133-4, 152, 180
material culture, 1, 4, 6, 7, 10-14, 17, 26, 32-3, 37, 39-41, 45, 48, 80, 100, 112, 116-17, 119, 124, 133, 156, 162
material culture patterning, 7, 13, 175
curation, 74, 76

death, concept of, viii, 99-100, 105-12, 134; see also burial practices, ritual
decoration
axe, 162, 169
Dutch Neolithic pottery, 9, 162-3, 165-9, 171-4
funerary monuments, 103-4, 106-7
house, 66-9
pottery, 4, 6, 9, 10, 14, 83, 162-3, 165-9, 171-4
stools, 86-7
as symbolic marker, 66-70, 80-1, 83-8, 93, 97
design, 4, 7, 20, 21, 45, 115, 118, 124, 152
artefact, 7
field of, 115, 119, 121-2, 172
pottery, 7
rules of, 7
structure of, 115, 124, 165-9, 171-2, 174
dirt, concept of, viii, 10, 20; see also refuse, purity, women
distribution patterns, 6
Douglas, M., 20, 48-9, 73, 84, 87, 91, 151
Durkheim, E., 1, 2, 4, 18, 27-8, 48

ecology, 2, 12
ecological functionalism, 3
empiricism, 3, 18, 34, 39, 42, 45-6, 48-9, 130
emulation, process of, 89-92, 95-7
Endo, 77-9; see also Marakwet

Engels, F., 31, 34-5, 181-2
epistemology, 14, 18, 28, 39, 41, 46, 48-9, 52, 131, 180-1
equilibrium, 1-3; see also systems theory
ethnoarchaeology, 4, 5, 13, 14, 36, 73-4, 112
studies in, 63-73, 76-9, 80-8, 89-97, 99-112
ethnography, 1, 13, 20, 63, 74
analogy in, 13, 39, 74-6, 181
in East Africa, 63-73
in India, 91-6
in Kenya, 74-9
in Sudan, 80-7
exchange, 6, 133, 151, 155, 157-8, 160
long distance, 157
reciprocal, 6, 160
redistributive, 6

field, 21, 40; see also design, image-field
food consumption, viii, 10, 83-4, 92, 94, 96-7
food preparation, viii, 10, 77-8, 83-5, 92, 94-5, 97
form, 4, 6, 17, 32-3, 36, 50
ideological, 129, 132
material, 180
social, 29, 33, 36-7, 50, 129
symbolic, 129, 132
function, 1-5, 11, 14, 22-3, 28, 180
functionalism, viii, 1-9, 11-13, 18, 23, 26, 28-9
in anthropology, 2, 12
ecological, 2, 3, 12

Giddens, A., 7, 8, 20, 28-9, 32, 36, 75, 81, 84, 111, 130, 155
generative grammers, 17, 21
generative principles, 7, 9, 14, 31-2, 34, 79, 179-80

hierarchy, 17, 21, 23, 90-3, 95-7, 101, 106, 155-60, 168-9
in pot design, 168-9
social, 3, 58, 89-92, 95-7, 133, 155, 170, 176
in style, 117
village, 91-2, 94; see also caste, social relations, status
homeostasis, 2, 3; see also equilibrium
house, 10, 20, 41, 63, 65-8, 70-1, 76
decoration, 63, 66-70
form, 20, 63, 65-7, 69
Marakwet, 76
organisation of space in, 10, 20, 41
place in ritual, 70
Swahili, 63, 65-8

symbolic value, 63-72 passim, 76
hypothetico-deductive method, 3, 5, 39, 44, 180-1

iconicity, 118-23
idealism, viii, 26, 34, 36, 48
ideology, 10, 11, 14, 26, 32-4, 36, 80-1, 86-7, 92, 99, 100, 112, 129-33, 135, 151-2, 155-60, 170, 180, 182
image-field, 116, 119, 121-2, 124
India, 89, 91-2
Iron Age, 96-7; see also caste, pottery
information, 5, 6
flow, viii, 10, 116
system, 4, 117
theory, 99, 116
inhumation, 101, 103-8, 111, 156, 174
class distinction in, 103
Islam, 63, 70
Islamic peoples, 63-70

kingdom, 53, 57
Merina, 55-7
kingship, 53, 57
early Egyptian, 53
Mesopotamian, 53
Merina, 57, 60
kinship, 54, 82, 129, 134, 151
symmetric kin organisation, 129, 150-1

language, 7, 8, 11, 19, 22-3, 29, 33, 40-1
change, 22, 90-1
games, 33
as a set of rules, 7-8, 19
laws, 2-3, 5, 12-13, 30, 32, 34, 74, 176, 179, 181, 184
adaptation, 12-13
behavioural, 13, 176
causal, 30
cross-cultural, 3, 5, 13, 179
culture process, 3
dialectic, 34
natural, 184
predictive, 5
social statics, 2
LBK culture, 162, 172-6; see also Neolithic, PFB and TRB cultures, pottery
Leach, E., 2, 7, 9, 18-20, 28, 41-3, 45, 100, 116, 118, 179-80
legitimation, process of, 9, 10, 32, 36-7, 47, 51-5, 61 n.7, 80-1, 100-1, 112, 129-30, 132-3, 151-2, 155-7, 159-60, 162, 170-1, 175-6
Lévi-Strauss, C., 7-9, 17, 18, 20, 26, 29, 45, 117, 119, 135, 150, 179-80

linguistics, 7, 8, 17–19, 20–2,
  29, 39–42, 90–1
  structural, 8, 11, 19, 20, 29,
  40–1

Madagascar, 47, 55–61, 101,
  156, 170–1; *see also*
  Merina
male/female dichotomy, 7, 22,
  80, 82, 84–5, 87, 129
  in burial, 129, 145, 150
  in tasks, 84
Marakwet, 74, 76–9
  burial, 77–8
  settlements, 77
  social structure, 77
Marx, K., 31–5, 48–9, 51–2,
  101, 130, 132–3, 180–4
Marxist approach, 26, 33–6, 49,
  51, 97, 180–4
materialism, *viii*, 10, 48, 180
  dialectical, 34–5
  historical, 51, 180, 183–4
  reductive, 26, 30, 33–5
megaliths, 11, 155–8, 169–70,
  176
  in Brittany, 157
  in central Europe, 157
  in Netherlands, 169–70
  in Spain, 157
  in Wessex, 159
Merina, 47, 55–61, 101, 156,
  170–1
  agricultural base, 56
  burial, 101
  cosmology, 58–60
  documentary sources, 56–7,
  60
  history, 56–60
  oral tradition, 56–7
  relief, 55, 58
  development of state, 55–60
  sociopolitical organisation,
  55–8, 60
  temporal ordering (*Vintana*),
  58–60; *see also*
  Madagascar
metal vessels, 92–7
  symbol of hierarchy, 92–7
middle-range theory, 5
Middle Virginian folk housing, 39,
  45–6
models, 6–8, 11, 14, 18–19, 29,
  32, 39–40, 42–6, 50, 63,
  76, 80, 89, 180
  behaviourist, 18
  categorisation, 18
  classification, 18
  emulation, 89, 92, 95
  explanatory, 40, 42–6
  formulation of, 44–5, 76
  of the human body, 18
  linguistic, 7, 8, 18–19, 40–2,
  45
  psychological, 18–19
  realist, 39, 42

Neolithic, 9, 11–12, 155–60,
  170–1, 180–1
  barrows, 9–10, 129, 135–40,
  143–7, 150, 152
  Dutch, 162–76 *passim*
  monuments, 9, 156–9, 170–1
  pottery, 9, 162–3, 165–76
Netherlands, 162–76 *passim*; *see
  also* burial practices, LBK,
  PFB, Rössen and TRB cultures, Neolithic, pottery,
  settlements
New Archaeology, *vii*, 1–3, 5–7,
  10–11, 13–14, 74,
  179–80
non-state societies, 133–4, 152

Palaeolithic cave art, *see* art
paradigm, 9, 19, 20–1, 40
PFB culture, 162–3, 166–9, 171,
  175–6; *see also* LBK and
  TRB cultures, Neolithic,
  pottery
Piaget, J., 18, 20, 29
positivism, *viii*, 1, 3, 14, 26, 30,
  34, 36–7, 48, 179–80
pottery, *viii*, 4, 6, 9, 17, 21–3,
  89, 92–7, 152, 162–3,
  165–72, 174–6
  Azande, 83–4
  Belanda, 84–5
  decoration, 4, 6, 9–10, 14,
  83, 162–3, 165–9, 171–4
  Dutch Neolithic, 9, 162–76
  passim
    LBK, 172–5
    PFB, 163, 166–9, 171
    Rössen, 174–5
    TRB, 163, 165–9, 171,
    175
  Indian, 22, 89, 92–7
    NBP, 96–7
    PGW, 96–7
  shape, 10, 22, 93–5, 162–3,
  165–6, 169, 171, 175
  symbolism, 83–6, 93, 96–7
pragmatics, 17, 19, 20–1
praxis, 27, 31–3, 36–7, 41, 48,
  51–3, 57, 80, 82, 87, 130
principal components analysis,
  143–7
processual archaeology, 2–4,
  8–10; *see also* systems
  theory
production, 31, 33–4, 50, 91,
  133–4
  CMP, 35–6
  economic, 31–2
  forces of, 33, 35
  material, 20–1, 23, 31, 35, 50
  means of, 133–5
  mode of, 33, 36
  pottery, 10, 20–1, 85
  relations of, 33–5
  social, 35–6, 51, 134, 151
psychology, 8, 17–19, 20–2
purity, 7, 9, 63, 66–70, 72, 78,

87, 89, 92, 95–7, 150
  Hindu concept of, 89, 92,
  95–7
  of women, 63, 67–8, 72, 78,
  87; *see also* food consumption, food prepar-
  ation, symbols, women

rank coefficient of correlation,
  141, 143
ranked societies, 100
ranking, 10, 97, 101, 161, 172,
  175; *see also* status
refuse, *viii*, 3, 4, 10, 14, 74–9
  in burial rite, 77
  categorisation, 74–8
  distribution, 4
  organisation, 74–9
  studies of, 75–6
relations of dominance, 9, 10,
  101, 104, 106, 110–12,
  130–4, 151–2, 156–8,
  160–1, 169–71, 175–6,
  183
Renfrew, A.C., 2, 3, 5, 152,
  155–6, 160, 169
ritual, 3, 9, 10–12, 20, 57, 70,
  72, 81, 85, 87, 100–12,
  129, 133–5, 151–2,
  155–8, 160, 162, 169,
  170–1
  Azande, 81, 85, 87
  Dutch Neolithic, 162, 169,
  171
  Swahili, 70, 72
role theory, 28–9, 99
Rössen culture, 162, 173–6

Saussure, F. de, 8, 19, 20, 29
semiotics, 19–22, 80
settlements, 7, 9, 10, 63, 65,
  74–6
  Dutch Neolithic, 162, 170–6
  East Africa, 63, 65
  Marakwet, 77
  organisation of space in, 10,
  63
settlement pattern, 6, 7, 47
  regional, 47
  within, 47
sets, 7, 9, 10, 17, 19, 23, 34, 132
  'fuzzy', 22
  material culture, 17, 23
  polythetic, 22
social action, *viii*, 8, 10–13, 23,
  27, 30–2, 34, 36–7, 51,
  58, 60, 77, 79–81, 85,
  130, 132–3, 180
social categories, 5, 10, 18, 81,
  91, 132, 162, 171, 175,
  184
social formation, 26, 29, 30–7,
  50, 81, 129–31, 133
social order, 10, 27, 35–7, 47,
  51–5, 60, 72, 80–1,
  86–7, 107, 129–30,
  132–4, 151–2

  in Azande society, 80–1,
  86–7
  in Merina society, 57
  in Swahili society, 72
social relations, *viii*, 1, 6–11, 14,
  20, 23, 28–9, 33–4, 36,
  47, 51, 54, 63, 78, 82–4,
  99–100, 119, 129–32,
  150–2, 155–6, 175–6,
  180
social theory, 1, 5, 6, 26, 48–50,
  100–1, 112
spatial organisation, 7, 10, 12, 18,
  20, 33, 41, 47, 53–4,
  58–60, 63, 73–4, 76–8,
  88, 106, 119, 124, 152
  in houses, 54
  intra-site, 74, 78–9
  of Merina, 58–61
  of refuse, 74, 76, 78
  in settlements, 7, 9
  social aspects of, 54, 73,
  119–20
  symbolism of, 53–5, 58–61,
  63, 70–3
state societies, 6, 55–6, 100, 180
  development of, 55–6
  in Madagascar, 55–6, 60–1
status, 9, 22–3, 89, 95, 97, 99,
  101–5, 109, 111–12
  Azande, 82, 84, 86
  in burial, 99, 103–5, 109,
  111–12
  Hindu, *see* caste
  social, 22, 90, 101–5, 109,
  111–12
structuralism, *viii*, 1, 7–11, 14,
  17, 19–21, 26, 39, 43,
  45–6, 179–80
  anthropological, 20
  in archaeology, *vii*, *viii*, 1,
  7–9, 11, 14, 39–40, 42,
  44–6, 115, 117, 120,
  179–80
  dialectical, 9, 26
  linguistic, 8, 11, 19, 20, 29,
  40–1
  post-, 20
structural-functionalist theory,
  28–9
structural-Marxist approach, 26
structuration, 1, 10, 29, 31, 34,
  36, 129–30, 134
structure, 6–10, 12–14, 17,
  28–36, 40, 48, 91,
  116–17, 119–20, 124,
  131, 151
  as code, 7, 8
  functionalist view of, 6, 7
  of ideas, 1, 8
  of Palaeolithic art, 115–16,
  118–21, 123–4
  social, 6, 7, 26–31, 33–4,
  36–7, 91, 96, 152
  spatial, 9, 33
  symbolic, 10, 133, 176
  as a system, 6, 7; *see also*

structure (*cont.*)
    generative principles, struc-
      turing principles
structuring principles, 26–7, 29,
    31–4, 36–7, 40–1, 45,
    79, 100, 117–18, 121,
    129–32, 135, 150–2
style, 6, 7, 30, 115–20, 124
  structure of, 115–20, 124
Swahili people
  economy, 64
  houses, 63, 65–9
  marriage, 67–8
  material culture, 63–4
  oral tradition, 72
  people, 63–4
  sites, 63
  trading system, 64
symbols, *viii*, 3, 7, 9, 10, 12–13,
    20, 34, 46, 68, 70, 72–3,
    78, 80–1, 83–5, 86–7,
    93, 110–11, 118, 120,
    129, 132–5, 155–6, 158,
    162, 170, 176
  food, 10, 84–5, 89, 92–3
  hierarchy, 92, 111
  human body, 9, 134–5,
    150–2
  pots, 83–6, 93, 171
  material, 9, 10, 13, 68, 83–7,
    129, 134, 155
  mortuary ritual, 110–11, 129,
    134–5, 155–6
  women, 67, 78
symmetry, 7, 20, 135
  arrangement of bones, 135,
    150
  of body, 135, 150–2
  in pot design, 173
  symmetric kin organisation,
    129, 150–1
syntagm, 9, 20, 40
systems, 1, 2, 5–7, 28–30, 33,
    41, 45, 48, 131
  cultural, 2, 3, 6, 40–1,
    116–17
  ecological, 3, 9, 12
  ideational, 32
  non-verbal, 80
  social, 3–7, 10–11, 26, 48,
    99–100, 151
  sociocultural, 2, 3, 6
  subsystem, 2, 5, 6, 12
  symbolic, 9, 80, 82, 84, 87,
    110, 132
  systems theory, 2–3, 27, 30,
    36, 99, 179–80

taxonomy
  folk, 18, 21
  native, 75
  numerical, 6, 22
trade, 63–5
  goods, 63–6
  Swahili, 64–5; *see also*
    exchange

traders, 63–5
  Indian Ocean, 63–5, 67–8
  Swahili, 63–5
transformation, process of, 7–10,
    20, 29, 32, 34, 37, 88,
    116, 119, 129, 131, 151,
    162, 171
TRB culture, 162–3, 165–9,
    171–2, 174–6; *see also*
    LBK and PFB cultures,
    Neolithic, pottery
tribe, 63–4
  Azande, 80–4
  Belanda, 84–5
  Marakwet, 74, 76–7
  Swahili, 63–73
types, 6, 9
  prototype, 23

variability, 2–5, 10, 19, 22–3,
    40–1, 43, 116, 175
  material culture, 10, 19, 40,
    43, 116, 175
  social, 10, 175

women, 63, 66–8, 70, 72, 78, 80,
    82–7, 95
  control of, 63, 66–8, 72, 78,
    80, 82, 134, 151
  fertility of, 78
  purity of, 63, 67–8, 72, 78,
    87, 95